D1278522

EVALUATING APPAREL QUALITY

Second Edition

EVALUATING APPAREL QUALITY

Second Edition

ANITA A. STAMPER
Associate Professor
The University of Southern Mississippi

SUE HUMPHRIES SHARP
Associate Professor
The University of Southern Mississippi

LINDA B. DONNELL
Business Consultant

FAIRCHILD FASHION GROUP
NEW YORK

Book and Cover Design: Jeff Fitschen

Standard Book Number: 87005-715-4
Library of Congress Catalog Card Number: 90-82756

Printed in the United States of America

PREFACE TO THE SECOND EDITION

The very favorable response to the first edition of this book made obvious the need for a treatment of apparel structure from the perspective of the structure, aesthetics, cost, and expected performance of the finished product. We are grateful for that response and for the feeling of satisfaction we experienced in being able to meet an existing need in the field. Almost immediately, however, we noted some omissions. Among the most troublesome was the lack of sufficient illustrations to convey some of the more complex or unfamiliar structures which we discussed. We have added many new photographs and some drawings to this edition.

In the previous edition, we had omitted a separate section treating neckline plackets. Although referred to in the treatment on sleeve finishes, there is enough difference in function and production technique that a separate section was obviously mandated. We added new information on preparation of the closure location in general, and plackets are treated within that context.

We have also included information related to new technological advances in the textile/apparel industry, the increasing importance of the import situation, and Quick Response, the industry's answer to competition from abroad. These are areas of major impact on the industry today, and they have developed significantly since our original publication.

In addition to the major changes noted above, we also made numerous additions and modifications within the individual chapters. In those chapters or sections where experience in using the text with classes had indicated no changes were needed, we made none. That decision reflects our perspective in working with our classes. Most instructors who use the book as a classroom text will probably find areas they wish to stress more or less, and that is the beauty of teaching; a text is only a starting point for a course. The instructor and the students create the dynamics of the learning experience. We hope this book serves as a good starting point and as a source of guidelines along the way.

We also hope that the book will serve as a reference to students after they graduate and to professionals in the field. As information in any field increases in amount and complexity, the importance of precise and effective communication become even more vital. The foundation of the Quick Response program, for example, is accurate communication among all segments of the apparel industry with the aim of delivering fashion apparel merchandise to the consumer in the shortest possible time. Professionals in the retail setting are in the most advantageous position to relay information about consumer preferences and concepts of quality to back up the manufacturing chain; they can do this only if they are knowledgeable about the product and can communicate that knowledge in clear precise terms that manufacturers can understand. We hope our text helps in providing the terminology and the information to facilitate effective communication.

CONTENTS

1. INTRODUCTION: THE PRODUCTION SETTING 1
History of the Apparel Industry 2
Production Processes 4
Costing 6
Structure 7
Imports 9
Summary 12

2. APPAREL FABRICS 14
Fiber Content 15
Fabric Characteristics 27
Summary 44

3. SHAPING DEVICES 46
Thread and Stitching 46
Darts and Dart Equivalents 50
Seams 55
Seam Types 56
Seam Finishes 76
Summary 85

4. UNDERLYING FABRICS 86
Underlinings 86
Interfacings 89
Interlinings 96
Linings 97
Summary 102

5. POCKETS 103
Inseam Pockets 104
Applied Pockets 112
Slashed Pockets 117
Summary 121

6. NECKLINE TREATMENTS 122
Bindings 122
Neckline Facings 127
Inset Bands 135
Collars 140
Summary 155

7. SLEEVE TREATMENTS 156
Sleeve Types 156
Sleeve Finishes 169
Summary 186

8. WAISTLINE TREATMENTS 187
Edge Treatments 187
Internal Treatments 202
Summary 210

9. CLOSURES 211
Closure Styles 212
Closure Mechanisms 222
Summary 244

10. HEM TREATMENTS 245
Hem Types 246
Hem Finishes 258
Special Hem Treatments 265
Summary 272

11. DECORATIVE DETAIL 273
Soft Trim 274
Hard Trim 281
Fabric and Stitchery Trim 283
Structural Trim 288
Summary 294

12. FIT AND ALTERATION 295
Elements of Fit 297
Ready-to-Wear Sizing 300
Alteration Potential 308
Summary 310

13. CONCLUSION: THE CONCEPT OF QUALITY 312
What Is Quality? 312
Technology/Research 314
Summary 316

Bibliography 317

Index 321

1

INTRODUCTION: THE PRODUCTION SETTING

Any product must be examined within the context of its setting, and in the case of apparel, that setting is the American apparel industry. Now just over a century old, the sewn products industry has grown from small sweatshop operations to highly mechanized, predominately automated, and frequently unionized big business. Billions of dollars worth of apparel are produced by millions of workers in thousands of plants every year in the United States. Many more millions of dollars worth of sewn products are imported into the United States for ultimate consumption. When the ultimate consumer examines these products at the retail level, only a few of the factors which influence ultimate quality can be easily discerned by careful inspection of the garment and its accompanying labels and tags. An understanding of the structure and operation of the industry will not necessarily increase the ability to perceive quality in the finished product. Such an understanding can improve a buyer's understanding of how and why certain decisions concerning quality are made in the industry and how those decisions influence product pricing.

HISTORY OF THE APPAREL INDUSTRY

The apparel industry is relatively new—only approximately 150 years old. During the American Colonial period, all clothing was made in the home by family members. This situation gradually changed as tailors or dressmakers were hired to come into the home and make clothing. Eventually, these dressmakers and tailors began to establish their own shops where custom-made clothing was made and sold. In the last quarter of the eighteenth century, milliners' shops provided the raw materials for dressmaking and accessories as well as the services of milliners and dressmakers. Occasionally, some articles of apparel were also available to women to purchase ready-made. These were most commonly unfitted items such as capes, shawls, and other loose fitting wraps.

It was not until the early 1800s that stores featured both ready-to-wear and custom-made apparel. The quantity of ready-to-wear merchandise was very small and was intended primarily for persons of low socioeconomic status—sailors, slaves, and miners, for example. As some tailor shops began to offer imported ready-mades of superior quality, these goods gradually gained a more widespread acceptance. Then the earlier manufacturers of lower-quality goods began to convert part or all of their production to the new ready-to-wear for men and boys.

The first recorded civilian clothing factory dates from 1825.[1] The early factories were not very different from tailors' operations. The fabric was cut in a factory—usually no more than three layers at a time—and then sent to seamstresses who sewed it by hand at home.

In the middle of the nineteenth century two events occurred which caused major changes in the apparel industry. The first of these was the invention and adoption of the sewing machine. The second was the Civil War. Women went to work in the newly-created factories where they used sewing machines to make uniforms for the soldiers. These factories not only used the sewing machine to introduce mass production sewing, but they also initiated the development of a standardized sizing system. Following the War, these techniques were adapted to the civilian market. By the end of the century, the men's ready-to-wear industry was well established.

The women's ready-to-wear industry did not develop to any great extent until the early 1900s. Even though undergarments, shirtwaist blouses, skirts, and coats were factory produced by the late 1800s,

[1] "The First Hundred Years: 1776–1876," *American Fabrics and Fashions* (Winter, 1976), Vol. 106, p. 64.

women's better dresses continued to be made by the consumers themselves or by their dressmakers. This was due in large part to the complexity of the dress designs and to the very exact fit that was required of fashions at that time.

By the late 1800s Sears catalogue and a number of large department stores such as Bloomingdale's in New York published catalogues containing styles for women's and children's clothing, along with extensive directions for measuring. Women sent these measurements and their fabric selections and received their finished garments by mail. For many women, dressmakers in distant locations provided the same services, and many of the archival collections of nineteenth-century women are filled with references to an active mail-order dressmaking business. Fabric samples, apparel sketches, swatches of trimming, and lengthy written descriptions gave the dressmakers precise directions for executing the desired garments.[2]

Only when styles began to allow more ease of fit and when separates (the blouse and skirt, in particular) were adopted was it feasible to begin trying to mass produce women's clothing. The rise in the production of women's ready-to-wear coincided with changes in fashion and in society—women became significant factors in the nation's work force.

Throughout the early years of the development of the apparel industry, cottage labor—work done by workers in their homes—continued to be the norm. Those factories that did maintain sewing rooms were characterized by deplorable working conditions, thus acquiring the name "sweatshops." Partially in answer to public outrage over these conditions, the International Ladies Garment Workers Union was established in the early 1900s.

In 1914, the Amalgamated Clothing Workers Union was formed to represent men's clothing workers. These unions achieved major reforms and are today respected for their support of educational and social reforms.

By the 1920s, styles in women's clothing had changed from the prewar structured dress to the "flapper" look of the 20s. With this simplification of fashion, mass production began in full swing. By the end of the decade approximately 3,500 dress manufacturers had joined the industry. The majority of the manufacturers were in New York City and established the now-famous "garment district" along Seventh Avenue. In less

[2] *Mississippi Homespun: Nineteenth-Century Textiles and the Women Who Made Them.* Anita Stamper, ed. Jackson, MS: State Historical Museum, Mississippi Department of Archives and History, 1989.

than fifty years, the wearing apparel industry had blossomed from a meager beginning to a multimillion dollar industry.

PRODUCTION PROCESSES

Apparel firms are organized in different ways, depending on the type of operation or product line, but there are certain basic steps involved in the production of any garment. The line, called a *collection* in the better market, may be made from the original designs of a staff designer. This is ordinarily the case for a company producing high-priced, high-fashion apparel, or for designs that are adapted or copied from originals. In either case, the actual production does not begin until the line is decided on, the buyers view the line and place orders, and the fabric is purchased. The selection of fabric may be made before any designing is done or afterwards, depending on the particular designer and firm.

The basic steps involved in the manufacturing of a garment are listed below. Some of these steps may overlap or be performed simultaneously.

1. *Research:* The design staff researches color and fabric trends for the upcoming season. Fabrics must fit the price structure, performance standards, delivery schedules, and fashion demands for the particular market segment to which each manufacturer caters.
2. *Creation:* The designer and the design team develop sketches for the new line based on fabric decisions, recent sales activity of previous designs, and knowledge of the consumer market served.
3. *Model Development:* Sketches for each item in the line are scrutinized by the design staff, and sample patterns are developed. Flat pattern, draping, computer aided design, or a combination of these methods may be employed for development of the initial pattern. Once made, the pattern is cut from sample fabric to test pattern accuracy and trueness to initial design concept. The design may be modified, discarded, or accepted by the design staff.
4. *Style Selection, or "Weeding":* The design, production, sales, and executive staff critique samples for the new line. Each item will be evaluated on marketability and profitability for the consumer market served.
5. *Presenting the Line, or "Opening":* The weeded line is presented at major U.S. markets where the number of orders placed

determine whether line items will go into production.

6. *Fabric and Findings Needs Calculated:* Orders placed for line items determines fabric, findings, and trim needs. Suppliers are contacted and orders placed accordingly. Advanced purchased fabric for "sure thing" basics will be checked for yardage needs.
7. *Pattern Development and Grading:* The production pattern is developed and graded, usually by computer, into the various sizes to be produced. This process is costly and is not done until the line is weeded and shown at major markets.
8. *Costing:* When enough orders have been placed to merit production, the head designer sends collected data, usually in the form of design boards to the production manager for costing. The design boards might include such information as style numbers, sketches, and data collected on fabrics, trims, and findings.

   The production managers prepare the cost sheet. Each manufacturer may have a slightly different method of arriving at actual figures, but the final cost sheet will reflect the following factors: design, fabric, trim, and finding needs and costs; labor costs, including outside contractors if used; transportation and storage costs; and mark-on, which covers overhead expenses and suitable profit margins.
9. *Marker Development:* The marker or master layout is developed via computer to accommodate all sizes ordered for each item which is to go into production. A few small companies still make markers by hand, but most of those who cannot justify the expense of computerized marker-making systems have gone to outside contractors to have this step of the production process completed.
10. *Spreading and Cutting:* The fabric is spread into the required number of thicknesses needed to actuate the marker, based on orders placed. Cutting may be done by vertical saws, circular saws, or laser cutters. Some of the computerized marker-making systems can also drive laser cutters for the most precise cut possible. These systems make reorders of small numbers economically feasible.
11. *Bundling:* The cut pieces are bundled by item, group, or section to allow pieces cut on each fabric ply to come back together during assembly of the garment. Bundles are topped by tickets which are pulled by each operator at the specific garment assembly point and task. Each worker's pay for the day's work will be calculated by the tickets they have pulled.

12. *Garment Production:* Machines are ordered for a particular garment assembly which will meet production schedule deadlines. This is most often done in assembly-line fashion with each operator specializing in one operation or one part of the garment. Quality control stations are established at various stages of construction to catch problems early enough to make corrections, if needed.
13. *Finishing:* Final trims and other finishing details are completed.
14. *Inspection:* Quality control may include trimming threads, checking for construction errors, and tagging.
15. Orders are pulled, packed, and shipped.

COSTING

In evaluating the quality of a garment, it is very important to understand exactly how a garment is costed. Each manufacturer strives to maintain a fairly consistent quality of styling and construction within a set price structure. Within the women's apparel segment of the business, there are three main price categories: *better* (higher priced), *moderate* (for the average consumer), and *budget* (low priced, high volume).

The major costs involved in the manufacture of any garment are for materials, trimmings, and labor. The materials include fashion fabric (what the primary garment pieces are made of) as well as any other fabric used for interfacing, interlining, underlining, and lining. Fees may also be added to cover the costs involved in receiving, inspecting, and storing fabrics. The shipping fee may be rather nominal unless a fabric is imported from Europe or the Orient, thus requiring costly freight charges. Trimmings include such basics as buttons, zippers, and pads in addition to such decorative trims as embroidery, pleating, topstitching, and applied trims. All of these add to garment cost.

Labor is perhaps the most complicated aspect of the cost sheet, and frequently accounts for a major part of the total cost. This includes all labor involved in the manufacture of the garment—designing, producing the pattern, grading the pattern into the desired sizes, producing the marker, spreading the fabric, cutting the fabric, sewing, pressing, and packaging. Many companies have conducted time and motion studies to determine the actual labor necessary for each operation in the production of a garment before setting construction costs. These costs are recorded on a master file to be used when figuring production costs of subsequent garments requiring the same construction techniques. Other firms calculate the average time it takes to complete one garment of each new style. Some companies will subcontract some of the steps involved in the production process. These are easily figured by dividing the costs by the total number of garments. Companies that do everything in-house will include costs for such things as marking, grading, and cutting as overhead expenses. Designing is also sometimes included here. Some of these expenses will not be included again on reorders if they are one-time costs.

Each company's labor costs depend on such variables as the type of equipment used by the company and the degree of automation. For example, many new sewing machines may allow for as much as a 40 percent increase in sewing speed. Labor spread over a larger number of garments means lower labor costs per unit. Of course, new equipment is expensive, and the cost of it must be included until it is depreciated. Each manufacturer must weigh carefully the decision to invest in new equipment. The most attractive equipment is versatile and can be adapted to a wide variety of styling details. Costly equipment cannot be allowed to sit idle for long periods of time.

Even though each manufacturer operates within an established price framework, the various cost components may be manipulated. The manufacturer may select a high-cost fabric, but choose a very simple design in order to keep the garment within the set framework. A production manager will decide which operations may be done less expensively and better in-house and which should be subcontracted. Each garment produced by a manufacturer must look like it is worth the cost figured by the manufacturer. If it does not, then the chances are that it will not sell. consequently, the firm may decide to adjust the final determined cost. In addition, a manufacturer may sometimes attempt to increase sales by decreasing the normal markup, hoping to compensate with volume for loss of per unit markup. This is known as "merchandising the cost."

STRUCTURE

Those basic steps in the production of an apparel item may be distributed differently or exhibit slightly different costing influences according to the type of manufacturing facility in which they are executed. According to the United States Census of Manufactures, the domestic apparel industry is composed of three types of firms: *manufacturers, jobbers,* and *contractors*. The *manufacturers,* known as "inside shops," have responsibility for the product from start to finish. The manufacturer purchases fabric, designs the apparel item, cuts and sews the garment, finishes the item, and sells it to the retail store. Designers and boutiques often fall into the inside shop category, and garments from their shops show more hand construction and detailing than would be typical of mass production in general.

Any of the individual apparel production operations may be done by smaller firms known as "outside shops." *Jobbers* may be used to design the garment, to buy the fabric, or to sell the garment. Their major investment is in people; the major investment for contractors, who cut and sew, is in equipment. In most industries, the jobber is the middleman. In the apparel industry, the firm that conceives a line and sells it is referred to as the manufacturer, even if that firm does not manufacture the goods.

There are advantages and disadvantages associated with both the outside shop and the inside shop. The outside shop provides the business person, who often has a minimum amount of capital, with the opportunity to capitalize on a good idea or the ability to sell or perform limited operations during the production of a garment. Because of the limited investment, the outside shop makes style flexibility much more feasible. It may recognize a new style more quickly and is much more easily able to adapt to change. Almost all manufacturers have to contract some work out during peak seasons. Fashion often necessitates the need for outside contractors. Most manufacturers also use *contractors* for specialized operations such as pleating, embroidery, and quilting, all of which require special machinery.

There are disadvantages to using outside shops or contractors. Quality control is more difficult. Also, there is a greater potential for communication and timing problems as well as the need for many physical movements of goods. The large manufacturer, however, may buy fabric in bulk and receive cost benefits along with more fabric design options.

Because of the nature of the product, large inside-shop operations tend to dominate the men's apparel industry. On the other hand, because of the need for more style flexibility, the women's wear segment of the industry is more often characterized by outside-shop operations. The firms producing high-fashion apparel are generally the smallest and least complicated in organization. As mentioned previously, the trend is toward larger, more comprehensive companies.

In discussing the structure of the domestic apparel industry, it is important to note that contractors may be located beyond U.S. boundaries. They may be located anywhere in the world where labor, machinery, and transportation are available. Several types of foreign production are found in the industry. A manufacturer may purchase a complete production package either through an agent or through a company representative abroad; he or she may purchase fabric in one country and send it to another to be cut and sewn; the manufacturer may purchase fabric and cut it domestically, then send it abroad for sewing.

IMPORTS

As more of the value added to the product is added outside the boundaries of continental United States, the line of demarcation between domestic and foreign production becomes blurred. Amendments to the Wool Products Labeling Act and the Textile Fiber Products Identification Act, effective on and after May 17, 1985, identified three categories for indicating country of origin on textile products:

1. Products made entirely in the United States can be labeled with the words "Made in the USA" or some other clear and equivalent term such as "Product of USA," "Crafted with Pride in USA," "Tailored in USA," "Manufactured in USA," or "Made in New York, USA," for example.
2. Products made in the United States using foreign materials can be labeled with words such as "Made in USA of Imported Fabric" or equivalent terms.
3. Items partially manufactured in the United States and partially manufactured in a foreign country should be labeled in a manner consistent with indicating the origin of the components or manufacturing operations. For example, a label including a statement such as "Sewn in USA of Imported Components" would satisfy the disclosure requirement.[3]

In addition to the provisions of this labeling, a media blitz by the Crafted with Pride in the U.S.A. Council, Inc., formed in 1984, has helped focus public attention on the source of the textile products they buy. The Council's regular tracking reports on the effectiveness of their advertising has been verified by other sources, and most research studies report consumers' perceptions of textile products made in the United States as superior to imported products.[4] Some retailers are also supporting the move to promote American made goods.[5]

The increasing concern on the part of the American textile industry

[3] *Federal Register,* (Wednesday, April 17, 1985), Vol. 50, No. 74, pp. 15100–15107.

[4] Robert E. Swift, "Sales Power of 'Made in U.S.A.' " *The FIT Review* (Spring 1989), Vol. 5, No. 2, pp. 14–17.

[5] Michael Barrier, "Walton's Mountain." *Nation's Business Reprint,* April 1988.

and related organizations, including many retailers, to stem the flow of imports and the degree to which apparel is partially constructed outside the continental United States results from the degree to which domestic employment in the sewn products industry has been adversely affected by increasing numbers of imported apparel items and increasing dollars in value of those items.

Prior to the 1960s, imports did not appear particularly threatening to the apparel and textile industry. Prior to this time, the small quantity of imports were either of poor quality, intended for the low end of the market, or high-priced fashions considered status symbols for the relatively few who could afford them. The dollar amount of imported apparel tripled during the 1960s and 1970s, and the increase seems destined to continue.[6] For the first half of 1989, textile and apparel imports reached the highest level in history, totaling 5.9 billion square meters, a 10.9 percent over the same time period of the preceding year.[7]

The phenomenal growth of imports has resulted primarily from the intense competition that characterizes the fashion industry. Producers and retailers continue to seek means to compete for lower prices and better values, for exclusive rights to merchandise, and for new and different fashions. Many foreign countries can compete favorably with domestic producers because of lower standards of workplace environment and lower wage rates.

Domestic manufacturers have responded to the threat posed to jobs by imports by looking for ways to combat the real and expected price advantages promised by imports. Media campaigns such as those organized and financed by the Crafted with Pride in U.S.A. Council, mentioned earlier, have tried to focus consumer and retailer attention on the advantages of domestic purchasing policies. Product quality, patriotism, and issues of social conscience have all been raised regarding the extent to which imported textile products have eroded markets for domestic products. In addition to the real and perceived advantages to "buying American," there are certain problems inherent to importing, and these problems are causing some manufacturers and retailers to back away from previous levels of investment.

One of the chief problems in foreign manufacture is quality control. In countries where body build, sizing, and standards differ from those in the United States, it is not always easy to realize the desired quality in materials and/or manufacturing procedures. For foreign manufac-

[6] *Statistical Abstracts of U.S.* (Washington, D.C.: U.S. Department of Commerce, 1984), p. 785.

[7] *Textile Hi-Lights* (Washington, D.C.: ATMI Economic Information Division, September 1989), p. iii.

turing, the problem is compounded by difficulties in communication created by language and cultural differences. In order to produce abroad, the manufacturer must send clear, exact specifications along with patterns and samples. Firms may work through an agent—which is costly—or send a company representative abroad. For retailers buying from foreign manufacturers, the importance of precise communications is no less crucial, and the retailer must also work with the extended lead times required for reordering hot merchandise and with the problems of returns when quality proves unsatisfactory.

Some larger manufacturers such as Arrow Company and Seminole Manufacturing have switched production back to the United States. Retailers such as J. C. Penny and Walmarts and marketing cooperatives such as Frederick Atkins have increased the percentages of domestically produced textile products which they purchase.[8]

Domestic apparel manufacturers have worked to provide incentives other than price advantage to combat the rising tide of imports. "Quick Response" is a campaign promising timely delivery of desired goods and is based on two premises: automation throughout every stage of the production to point-of-sale pipeline and cooperation among all segments of the industry. From the textile manufacturer through the apparel design and manufacturing process, distribution points, stocking in the retail stores, and purchase by the ultimate consumer, in the ideal Quick Response scenario, each component of the product is identified by a bar code or other machine readable code. The code allows tracking of the product at all points, and information about style, fiber content, color, size, manufacturer, and distribution is available on a nearly instantaneous basis which facilitates the speed of restocking what the customer wants. Where such systems have been put in place, results in such basics as hosiery, men's wear, and domestics have shown sales hikes of up to 40 percent over traditional restocking methods.[9]

In pure Quick Response, fabric purchases are made electronically, come in to the apparel manufacturing facility with bar code labels, and are read into inventory lists. Designers and pattern makers use computer aided design and manufacturing to develop the apparel designs, produce hard copy of design variations for use in presentations to potential buyers, make and grade the patterns by computer, then gen-

---

[8] Ralph King, "Made in the U.S.A." *Forbes* (May 16, 1988), pp. 108, 110, 112.
Michael Barrier, "Walton's Mountain." *Nation's Business Reprint* (April 1988).

[9] *Connections: Textiles, Apparel, Merchandising*. Supplement to the March 1989 issues of America's Textiles International, Apparel Industry Magazine, and Apparel Merchandising. (Atlanta, Georgia, Billian Publishing Company, 1989).

erate markers via computer-driven plotters. Spreading and cutting is also computer controlled, as is tracking of the bundles during construction. Many steps of the construction process are automated, and the finished garments are packaged, labeled with bar codes, and shipped to the retailer. Retail inventories are handled by scanners, and bar code readers at point-of-sale transmit the sales information directly to the buyer for use in reorders on at least a weekly basis. At this point the data itself is able to initiate a reorder, which is handled electronically. Restocking of sold units can be done within about two weeks as opposed to twelve or more using traditional methods.

Quick Response has amassed a number of industry members, including Leslie Fay, Counterparts, Levi, Haggar, Health-tex, Warnaco, Maidenform, Warren Featherbone, Greif Companies, Milliken, Donnkenny, and retail stores such as Mercantile, Dillards, Toys "R" Us, Macy's South/ Bullock's to support the concepts and technology which promises to give domestic producers a definite competitive edge over foreign producers.[10] There is general agreement in all segments of the textiles and apparel industry that Quick Response offers enormous potential for effectively competing with imports based on how quickly the industry and retail stores can respond to customer demand as well as the promise of increased quality control. There are still difficulties to be worked through before Quick Response is in place in the majority of the necessary manufacturing, distribution, and retail points in the United States. Compatibility of all the electronic systems which must interface must be assured; training and retraining of employees who must use the new technology is necessary; and considerable expense is required to install the computerized systems which are necessary to drive Quick Response at any level. Companies who have made the decision have been able to document positive change. Those that have not, especially smaller businesses, are for the most part favorable to the idea, but still investigating the most cost effective method of implementation.

SUMMARY

Many factors interact to affect the final price and value of an apparel item. Although the concept of quality or value as a direct correlate of durability may appear foremost in the minds of many consumers during a casual discussion of the term, in fact aesthetic concerns actually dom-

[10] Ibid.

inate most traditional treatments of apparel quality. Standard books on apparel construction, magazines like *Consumer Reports* and *GQ*, and research studies of measured quality or consumers' concepts of quality often focus on construction details which are much more closely related to the appearance of the garment in question than its expected durable life. A hem that is uneven in length is just as durable in most cases as one that is perfectly aligned, but the perception is that the uneven garment is of poorer quality.

Quality, then, is a broad term, and one which encompasses many different aspects of a garment. Cost, because it relates to the factors of production just discussed, does not always reflect aesthetic or durability benefits but manufacturing solutions to certain production problems.

Most of the remainder of the text will provide an in-depth look at construction components that affect, to varying degrees, the appearance, function, and cost of apparel items. None of these components, however, can be evaluated in complete isolation. Some generalizations can be made as to comparative cost or quality of similar construction components, but all the specifics that resulted in the garment's final cost cannot be ordered with precision except in terms of the particular garment and its manufacturer. For example, slash pockets may be a more expensive sewing technique than constructing patch pockets. But it does not automatically follow that a garment with slash pockets will be more expensive than the same garment with patch pockets. All of the other techniques used on that particular garment, the fabric and trimmings used, the machinery used, and all other overhead expenses involved must be considered as well. Hopefully the text will provide a better understanding of comparable apparel structures as well as a more precise vocabulary for communicating about those structures.

2

APPAREL FABRICS

Although a complete evaluation of textiles is beyond the scope of this book, understanding the importance of apparel fabrics in determining the quality of the finished product is critical. Each step of the textile manufacturing process—fiber preparation or production, yarn production, fabrication, and finishing—will affect, to some extent, the characteristics and properties of the finished fabric. Frequently, however, much of the information about what was done to the textile at any particular step is not available to the apparel manufacturer, to the merchandise buyer, or to the ultimate consumer. This chapter will deal primarily with those aspects of textile quality that are discernible by careful inspection or by analysis of the label and/or hang-tag information. Readers wishing to pursue the more detailed or technical particulars concerning textile quality can refer to some of the books listed in the bibliography found at the back of this text. Some basic textile background is assumed.

One additional note which should help to avoid future misunderstanding is that fabric cost and fabric quality, as measured by performance and durability, are not necessarily interrelated. In many instances, the factors that increase fabric cost do so because the production process is lengthened or made more complicated. For example, a fabric with an integral design (a design formed as a unit with the fabric structure) is produced more slowly, and hence is more costly, than a fabric with a similar pattern that is printed on; however, the costlier fabric may not be any more durable. One of the difficulties in adequately evaluating textile products is that so many factors are involved in creating the final product.

FIBER CONTENT

Only those fibers typically used in apparel are discussed here. For each fiber, both advantages and disadvantages are presented, but the reader should note that these terms are relative, and their appropriateness depends upon intended end use. Fiber absorbency, for example, is a definite advantage in a towel but would represent a disadvantage for a windbreaker jacket.

WOOL AND SPECIALTY HAIR FIBERS

All of the fibers in this group (wool, mohair, cashmere, alpaca, angora, camel hair, llama, guanaco, vicuna, and qiviut) are noted for their warmth and are used primarily in winter clothing. The hair fibers are also very absorbent, contributing to their comfort characteristics in cold, damp weather. Most wool fabrics are easily cut and sewn. They press well and are preferred for tailored garments and apparel that requires some molding during construction. In the men's wear field, for example, tailor-made sports and suit coats are steam-and-stitch molded to fit the male contour without excessive use of seams and darts; wool is an ideal fiber for this type of construction. Some of wool's ability to be molded is lost, however, when finishes are applied to the fabric to make it washable. Washable wools frequently are better suited for use in skirts, slacks, untailored jackets, sweaters, socks, and similar items.

Many wool fabrics are tightly woven or finished, or are napped, and these fabrics rarely ravel. Wool flannel, for example, needs no seam finish unless one is desired for aesthetic reasons. Both the natural cohesion of the wool fiber and its felting property help retard raveling.

The felting property which is responsible for wool's excellent tailoring qualities may cause some problems during wear. Heat, moisture, and agitation cause the wool fibers to shrink and mat together. These three conditions occur in the underarm area, for example, and may cause unsightly felted spots. Persons who perspire heavily should protect wool garments worn close to the body by using waterproof shields. An alter-

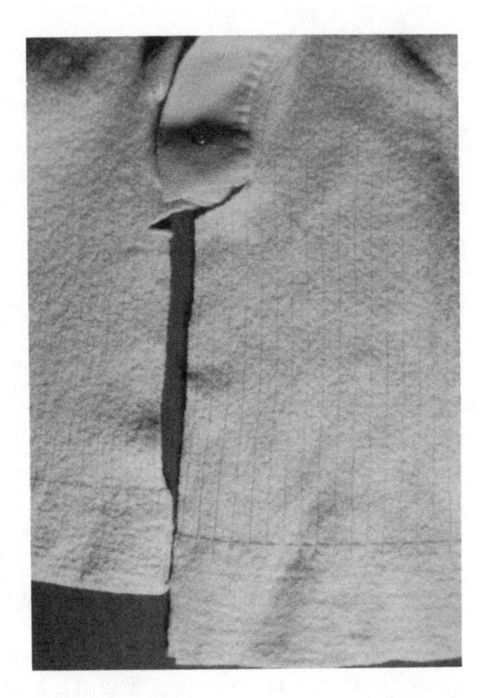

***2-1. Wool sweater halves: Machine washed and dried twice** (LEFT). **Machine washed and dried only once** (RIGHT).*

native would be to avoid wool in garments that fit closely to the body and are neither lined nor meant to be worn over other items of apparel.

Since wool shrinks under the above-mentioned conditions, dry cleaning is usually the recommended care procedure. If laundering is attempted, it should be done only in cold water with neutral detergent and a minimum of agitation. Figure 2-1 shows a man's size medium wool sweater which was machine washed and dried once, then cut in half and the right half machine washed and dried a second time, demonstrating the two types of shrinkage from which untreated wool suffers—relaxation and progressive.

Washable wool fabrics or apparel items that have been specially finished to permit laundering with no damage to the wool fiber are now available to the consumer. Care-label instructions should be followed exactly, and excellent results can be expected despite the reluctance of consumers to deviate from traditional care methods for wool.

Some relaxation shrinkage usually occurs during the first cleaning or laundering of wool products. This will be more pronounced in loosely fabricated textiles. Home sewers should pre-shrink wool fabrics if end-of-the-bolt information does not indicate that the fabric has been pre-shrunk. Wool garments should not be purchased in sizes that allow very little ease.

Wool fabrics can be straightened if they have been finished off-grain. this is an advantage in home sewing, but can be a disadvantage in ready-to-wear if the fabric was off-grain before cutting and construction. Such fabrics will straighten during cleaning, distorting the shape of the garment.

All of the hair fibers are expensive. Finer, softer qualities of wool are more expensive, but often less durable, than coarser, cheaper types. The specialty hair fibers are also more expensive than wool. Cashmere, angora, and soft types of camel hair are considered luxury fibers. They are very soft and comfortable, but subject to felting and abrasion damage. They are usually better adapted to soft styles than to tailored garments intended to retain crisp lines.

All hair fibers, even in blends, are attractive to moths. Even blended fabrics are susceptible and should be given the same precautions as all wool fabrics. Some dry cleaners can apply moth resistant chemicals; moth balls or crystals are also effective is discouraging attack by moths but have their own disadvantages of odor and toxicity. Garments stored clean and inspected frequently in bright light will be less likely to suffer damage.

SILK

Silk is also considered a luxury fiber, and it is used primarily in designer fashions and in more expensive ready-to-wear. In the United States, silk constitutes less than one percent of the total fiber used in apparel. Its main appeal is aesthetic. Silk has a uniquely dry, supple feel which is not duplicated by any synthetic on the market today.

In filament form, silk requires careful handling. Sheers may slip and shift during cutting and may require extra precautions and shorter stacking to hold the fabric grain true during cutting. Tightly woven or knitted fabrics may show needle and pinholes if alteration is required or if sewing errors must be corrected. Spun and noil silk are easier to handle during cutting and construction and have a hand similar to cotton.

Silk can be straightened if the fabric has been finished off-grain, but the home sewer should check the colorfastness of the dyes used in the fabric if dampness is to be used in the straightening process. Silk should always be pressed with steam, and should usually be dry cleaned rather than laundered. This requirement relates as much to the dyes and chemical finishes used on the silk fabric as on a lack of dimensional stability in silk.

COTTON

Although the price of cotton has increased during the last decade, it still remains fairly competitive with most synthetics. The absorbency and comfort of cotton make it a continuing favorite for baby clothes, men's briefs and undershirts, and all types of summer and winter apparel for all people of all ages. In most, however, cotton is still found more frequently as a blend with polyester than as the single fiber present.

Most all-cotton and cotton-blended fabrics are easily cut and sewn. Those combining small yarns and very high count may resist easing and may pucker slightly at seams. Gathers in such fabrics will pouf out rather than drape.

Unless all-cotton fabrics have been given a permanent finish, they will straighten if off-grain. If they contain significant amounts of polyester and/or if the label indicates that the fabric is wrinkle-resistant (or permanent press, wash-and-wear, etc.), straightening potential is very limited. Although most cottons and blends have such a finish, labels and fabric bolt ends should be carefully checked. A growing percentage of imported garments for children, many available at very low prices in discount stores, are all-cotton and lack a finish to improve resilience. Consumers expecting such a finish are likely to be very dissatisfied with fabrics and garments that require ironing.

Cotton fabrics, especially knits, tend to shrink during laundering unless treated to prevent this. Over-the-counter fabrics should be shrunk before the garment is cut. In the ready-to-wear field, apparel and fabric manufacturers are jointly responsible for determining the amount of expected shrinkage from a fabric and then making the appropriate sizing, finishing, or labeling decisions before the garments are constructed. Fabric testing by the fabric manufacturer, the apparel manufacturer, or an independent testing agency is one means of determining expected fabric behavior and the appropriate labeling information. There are few clues for the ultimate consumer of the product when such steps have been taken, however. Certainly garments that are labeled with such terms as "pre-shrunk," "Sanforized," "pre-washed", or even "stone washed" will not be expected to shrink noticeably during laundering. But the garment simply labeled with fiber content of all cotton and laundering information may or may not shrink enough to be no longer serviceable after use. Most reputable manufacturers are concerned enough about their reputations in delivering satisfactory goods that they take the necessary steps to insure controlled cotton fabric shrinkage, but not all do. Retail store buyers have a critical role to play here in learning which manufacturers typically deliver goods that perform as expected, in dealing with reputable manufacturers, and in reporting to manufacturers any problems with performance.

Laundering is the recommended care procedure for most cottons and cotton blends, but care labels should always be checked. Some fading usually occurs in laundered fabrics in which cotton is the only or the predominant fiber. This fading usually occurs gradually, but becomes quite noticeable if two matching articles of clothing are not laundered the same number of times. Fading is much more noticeable in solid color, piece-dyed fabrics than in patterned and/or yarn-dyed fabrics where design variations help to obscure some of the fading.

LINEN

Like silk, linen is a luxury fiber, found in designer clothing and expensive ready-to-wear lines. Linen's share of the apparel market is very small, slightly less than silk's. Fabrics made from flax range from very sheer handkerchief linens to heavy suiting fabrics. Linen is one of the most comfortable apparel fibers. It is more absorbent than cotton and dries more quickly. It is a strong fiber, but abrades easily when

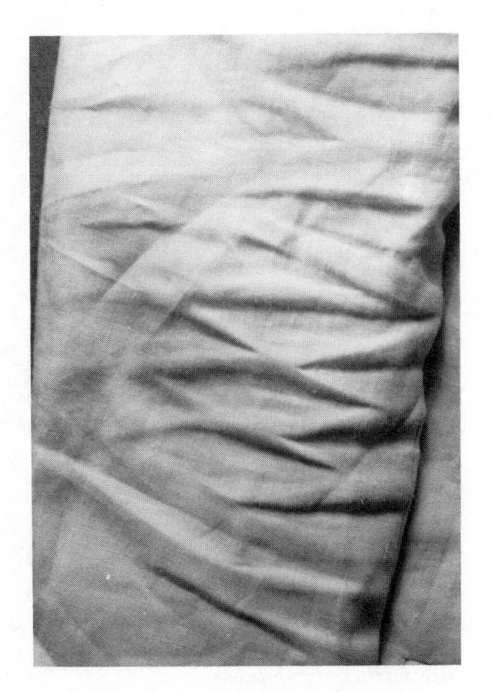

2-2. Linen suit sleeve after two hours wear.

creased repeatedly in the same place or when fabric folds are subjected to wear. It handles very much like cotton during cutting and construction.

One of the major disadvantages of linen, aside from its cost, is its very poor resiliency. Linen fabrics wrinkle very easily and need to be damp ironed at high temperatures to remove laundering wrinkles. For this reason, dry cleaning is often the recommended care procedure. Tailored styles present fewer problems in this respect, for they can be pressed in the flat, even if laundered. Gathers, especially in restricted areas such as sleeves and bloused bodices, can be very difficult to iron so that the garment appears as neat as it was originally.

ACETATE

During the last two decades, acetate's share of the apparel market has been reduced significantly by synthetics such as polyester and nylon. Today, acetate is found primarily in formal and bridal wear, in lining fabrics, in lingerie, and in some sleepwear. Acetate's low strength, poor abrasion resistance, and low resiliency make it unattractive for apparel that is to be worn frequently and where durability is an important consideration. Dry cleaning is usually recommended, another negative factor for clothing that is worn often. Some acetate fabrics are colored with

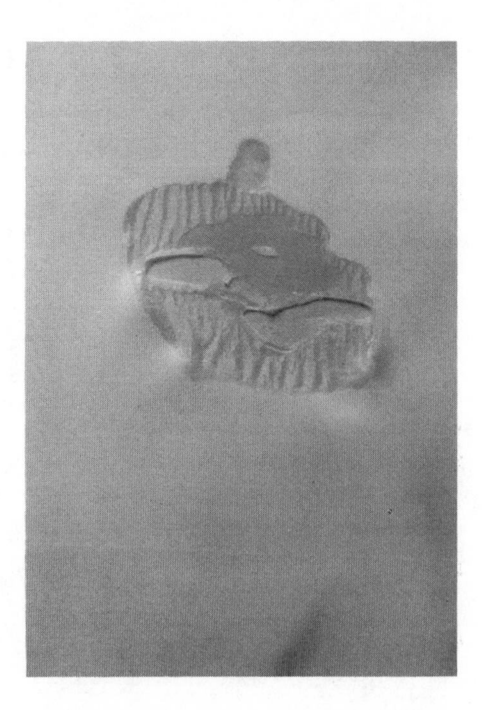

2-3. Acetone-based fingernail polish remover spill on acetate taffeta after one minute time lapse.

unstable dyes which change color by reacting with atmospheric contaminants or with the chemicals in deodorants and perspiration. Acetate dissolves in acetone-based fingernail polish remover.

All apparel acetate is produced in filament form. Fabrics usually ravel easily and require seam finishing. Stitching holes show in many acetate fabrics, and this limits alteration and correction of construction errors. Stitching must be done carefully to avoid puckered seams. Lengthwise seams in acetate tricot are particularly likely to pucker if not handled very carefully. Pressing must be done at low temperatures to avoid melting and glazing the acetate. Straightening potential for off-grain fabrics is very limited.

TRIACETATE

Similar in many respects to acetate, triacetate has better resiliency and dimensional stability because of its higher heat-setting temperature. In apparel, triacetate is used primarily in knitted suede cloth, in plush fabrics for robes, and in brushed tricots for winter sleepwear. It can rarely be straightened if off-grain.

RAYON

Rayon is enjoying increasing popularity after a period of decline in the 1960s and 1970s. The unique draping quality of rayon makes it ideal for revivals of period styles and for contemporary soft looks. Many of the rayon fabrics marketed today are of high-wet-modulus or high-performance rayon fibers which have improved strength, resiliency, and dimensional stability over regular, or viscose type, rayon.

Care labels, as always, should be checked carefully, but most viscose rayon requires dry cleaning. Viscose rayon exhibits both relaxation shrinkage, when fabric finishing tensions are relaxed during laundering or cleaning, and progressive shrinkage, which is related to fiber characteristics as opposed to fabric finishing techniques. Because of its poor dimensional stability as well as its weakness, laundering is not recommended for viscose type rayons.

High performance rayon types, on the other hand, are most frequently washable. They are most frequently used in staple length in spun yarns that resemble cotton somewhat in hand and appearance. Rayon and polyester blends have replaced cotton and polyester blends in many end uses such as chino, gabardine, crash, and challis apparel fabrics. Even if the blends appear similar to poly/cotton blends on the rack, the poly/rayon blends soften much more during wear and cleaning and drape more closely to the body. In larger sizes, this characteristic can be used to advantage in selecting fabrics which do not add to apparent body size through stiffness.

All rayon is absorbent. Blended with polyester, rayon provides more absorbence than a comparable cotton component. In apparel lines emphasizing comfort characteristics, rayon might be the preferable fiber for a blend with polyester for this reason.

Rayon fabrics wrinkle easily. Filament rayon may slip during cutting and sewing, and it tends to ravel badly. Staple rayon handles more like cotton, but may still shift somewhat during cutting because of the fiber's drape. Most washable rayon and rayon blends have a permanent finish for improved resiliency. Fabrics finished for improved resiliency have been heat-set at some point to crosslink the surface finish molecules, and they do not straighten appreciably if finished off-grain.

POLYESTER

Since its introduction in the 1950s, polyester has revolutionized most consumer expectations of apparel performance. The combined properties of strength, dimensional stability, and resiliency have enabled apparel manufacturers to produce clothing that is fashionable, durable, and easily maintained. Most fabrics that contain polyester have been permanently finished for a smooth appearance and stable size. Garments that have been heat set or cured after construction cannot be altered for a larger size. Not only are the smoothness and size permanently set, all construction details are also set, and seams or hems that are let out retain the original crease lines. Grain positions are also permanent, so off-grain fabrics are not problematic unless there is a directional pattern combined with noticeable grain distortion.

With polyester fabrics, such a diversity of textures, weights, and patterns exists that generalizations about cost, cutting, and sewing requirements is not possible. Most sheer, filament yarn fabrics tend to slip and shift during cutting and sewing. Raveling is also a common problem. When filament yarns are shiny and untextured, these problems become acute, and resulting fabrics quickly become unsightly during wear and use unless handled with extreme care. Seams of tight-fitting garments pull apart; brushes with rough or sharp objects loosen yarns streamers from the fabric and pull printed patterns out of alignment. Figure 2-4 shows a fabric with the latter problem. The printed jacquard weave has slick polyester warp yarns which exhibit the print. (The weft yarns of rayon staple did not react with the printing dyes and remained a solid color.) During wear, the slick warp yarns snagged and pulled partially out of the fabric, resulting in the misaligned print. The misaligned print

2-4. Filament polyester yarn snags distort printed motifs.

shows up as light stripes against the darker ground and as dark stripes in the light areas of the motifs.

Staple yarn fabrics handle more like cotton or rayon, but many polyester staple fabrics have a tendency to pill during use and laundering. This is a problem which is virtually impossible to predict at the final product level, although reduction in pilling can be accomplished by the fiber/fabric manufacturers in a variety of ways by lowering fiber tenacity so pills can break away, by twisting the yarns more turns per inch, by increasing the yarn count in the fabric, by singeing the fabric during the finishing, and by applying certain chemical finishes to the fabric. All of these factors cannot be determined even by the apparel manufacturer without extensive communications among all stages of the production process from fiber manufacturer to apparel designer/ fabric buyer. The problems of making those determinations at the retail level are extensive.

Polyester is heat sensitive, so pressing must be done carefully to avoid melting and glazing the fabric. Flat seams and smooth creases are difficult to achieve if the fabric has been heat set prior to garment construction. In such cases edge-stitching can help to flatten construction details.

NYLON

Nylon is also a high-strength synthetic fiber with good dimensional stability, but it is used primarily in blends or in warp-knit lingerie fabrics. With the exception of "windbreaker" jacket shells, nylon is rarely used as the single fiber in woven fabrics. Its resilience is good, but it recovers more slowly than polyester, which therefore is preferred for woven apparel fabrics. Nylon does figure in the apparel market as an important component of knitted suede cloth and plush sleepwear fabrics. Brushed nylon tricot is a popular fabric in the sleepwear market. Nylon is also very important as a component of many blends, especially with wool, acetate, and triacetate; it adds strength to those fibers even when used in very small percentages. Nylon is the major fiber used in stretch apparel such as foundation garments, dance and exercise wear, and hosiery.

Laundering is the usual care procedure for nylon. Pressing is done with a warm iron only to prevent melting and glazing the fabric. Dark or brightly colored nylons often bleed during the first few launderings, and for this reason should be laundered separately or with similar colors.

Nylon is heat sensitive and will melt and glaze if ironed with too much heat. Most nylon fabrics have been heat set, so off-grain fabrics do not straighten during laundering.

ACRYLIC/MODACRYLIC

The major apparel use for acrylic is in knitwear, especially in sweaters and sweater-like garments. It is also used in sweatshirt knits, jerseys, and fake furs for the cut-and-sewn knit apparel market. Acrylic rarely straightens if off-grain, and knitted yard goods are easily distorted from grain trueness during processing. In a horizontal pattern, grain distortion may be very obvious, possibly resulting in poor sales. Woven acrylic fabrics present no particular problems in cutting and handling, but acrylic knits may stretch considerably during layout, cutting, and handling. Such knits then shrink back to their original size and shape when first laundered by the consumer. Laundering is usually the recommended care procedure, as many types of acrylics stiffen and become distorted if dry cleaned.

Modacrylic is most commonly found in fur-like fabrics. Its inherent flame-retardant qualities make it ideal for fabrics with a long pile or nap, either of which provides ideal conditions for combustion if the fiber itself is flammable.

LESS COMMON FIBERS

Several other fibers deserve mention here, even though their share of the apparel fiber market is quite small. In some cases, these fibers are special-function fibers which need to be present in very small amounts to effect the desired function. In other cases, the fiber's presence in the apparel market is relatively recent and may increase substantially in the future.

SPANDEX/RUBBER

Spandex and rubber are examples of special-function fibers. They are elastomers—fibers used to impart both extension and recovery to stretch apparel. Elastomeric fibers are found in slacks, dance and exercise wear, support hosiery, foundation garments, and elastic fabric. Only a small percentage of the total fiber weight need be an elastomer in order to make a stretch fabric. Of the two elastomers, spandex, a synthetic, is more expensive than rubber, a naturally occurring fiber, but the former offers many advantages. Spandex has greater flex life, higher strength, better dyeability, and better resistance to chlorine, dry-cleaning solvents, perspiration, cosmetics, and oils. Spandex also has much better resistance to heat and can be given a heat set. Heat setting allows the consumer ease in maintaining the appearance of apparel items such as active sportswear and evening or party clothing.

RAMIE

A very old natural fiber which is currently making apparel news is ramie. Ramie is a natural cellulosic fiber very similar to flax in its characteristics. Ramie is used most often in knitted sweaters which are imported into the United States from a number of countries, but some is also used in woven fabrics and apparel items. The fiber itself comes from the stems of the ramie plant, which grows in China and the Philippines, among other places. Recent developments in chemical retting or decortication of the fiber decreased the amount of time formerly required for processing and have, in turn, made the fiber much more commercially attractive. Most ramie is blended with cotton, but polyester, rayon, and flax are other fibers which may be found blended with ramie.

In terms of properties and performance, ramie can be most easily classified with flax. The ramie is slightly coarser in diameter, but other characteristics are very similar, with the exception that ramie is the less costly of the two fibers.

OLEFIN

Olefin, also known as polypropylene and polyethylene depending upon production technique, is a synthetic thermoplastic fiber used more commonly in the industrial and home furnishings fields than in apparel. One type of olefin is utilized in panties and briefs, where the fiber's high wicking property is utilized to facilitate the evaporation of moisture. Wicking, the ability to move moisture along the surface of the fiber, is also the property which has prompted the use of olefin as one of the major fiber components in double-knit thermal undergarments. There, the fiber transports perspiration rapidly to the outer layer of the double knit where it can be evaporated off without cooling the skin surface. Winter clothing for active sports such as skating, cross-country skiing, hunting, hiking, and for outdoor work performs a critical function in helping the body maintain its critical internal temperature in hostile environments. The wicking action of the fiber worn next to the skin is a part of a sophisticated, interactive system which must function accurately not just for comfort but to protect the wearer from hypothermia and even death. When the body is active, heat is generated and perspiration results, even in below-zero temperatures. When that same body becomes still for rest or at the culmination of the activity, any wetness next to the skin would cause rapid cooling of the body.

2-5. Olefin briefs dried in a commercial dryer, contrary to care labelling instructions on the garment.

Olefin is very heat sensitive. Most apparel items containing olefin will bear care labels that warn against dry cleaning or drying in a dryer. Figure 2-5 shows a pair of women's briefs that have been dried in a commercial laundry dryer. The care label specified line drying. Olefin reacts with many chlorinated hydrocarbons, including dry cleaning solvents, and thus cannot be dry cleaned (unless the cleaners uses alternative solvents), or spot cleaned with many solvent-based spot cleaners.

In addition to the limited apparel uses in undergarments, olefin is also used occasionally as a blend in fake fur fabrics and as a fiber web in windbreaker jackets and pants. It has limited dyeability, and for this reason, as well as its extreme heat sensitivity, is rarely found in fashion apparel.

FABRIC CHARACTERISTICS

Certain characteristics of an apparel item are established once the fiber content is selected, but many of the fiber's original characteristics can be altered to some extent by subsequent steps in processing. Yarn manufacture, fabrication methods, and finishing procedures are all capable of altering or enhancing some of the basic fiber characteristics. The following section will cover several of the factors that affect the appropriateness of a fabric for a particular apparel item.

YARN STRUCTURE

All yarns can be divided into two major types, based on the length of the fiber used in their manufacture. *Spun yarns* are made from staple fibers that are from one-half to eighteen inches (1.27 to 45.72 cm) in length. Spun yarns have a more natural appearance and hand than filament yarns. They seem more absorbent, porous, and comfortable. They ravel and shift less, have less tendency to pucker when stitched, press flat more easily, and show construction errors less. Wrinkles are usually less apparent in spun yarn fabrics.

Filament yarns can be subdivided into two types: smooth and textured. The characteristics of smooth filament yarns are basically the reverse of those for spun yarns. They are often selected for their shiny, smooth appearance and/or their ability to be packed tightly together for air or water resistance. In Figure 2-4, very smooth and very low twist polyester filament yarns were used in the warp direction to give maximum light reflectance to the jacquard patterned warp float design and to afford the piece dyed fabric tone-on-tone contrast with the duller, texturized,

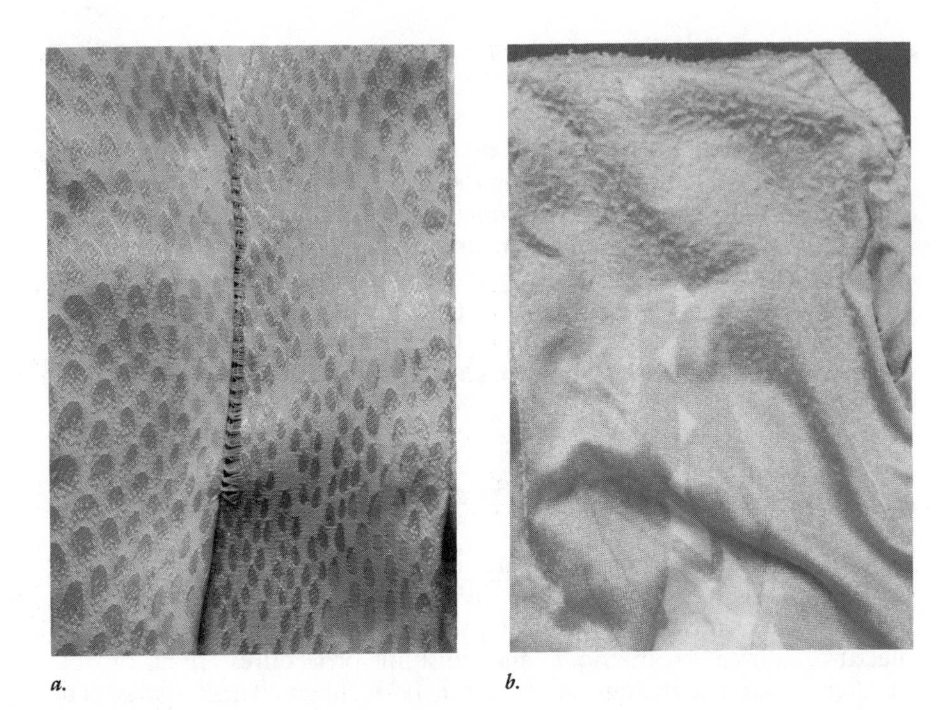

a. b.

2-6. Filament yarn problems: (a) yarn slippage at waistline dart of blouse made from smooth filament warp yarns; (b) abraded filament yarns pill on fabric surface.

and tightly twisted weft yarns. Two other filament yarn problems are shown in Figure 2-6. The darts and side seams of the blouse (a), which is designed to fit the body closely, have slipped during the stress of wear. Although filament yarns usually resist pilling because of the lack of fiber ends on the fabric surface, once the filaments are broken by abrasion, pills may form. The bathing suit shown in Figure 2-6b has extensive pilling in the seat area, which was abraded during use.

Texturizing filament yarns provides some of the characteristics more like those of spun yarns, but requires a shorter production time than that required for spinning yarn from staple fibers. Garment cutters usually prefer working with spun-yarn fabrics, which can be stacked higher without shifting during cutting. These fabrics also resist raveling and fraying while being handled along the production line.

FABRICATION METHOD

During the next stage of the fabric construction process, the selected yarns are combined to produce a fabric. The manner in which this combination takes place is known as the *fabrication* method. As a rule, fabrics in each fabrication method category have certain similarities that dictate acceptable styles and construction techniques.

WOVEN FABRICS

Woven fabrics are made with two sets of yarns interlaced at right angles to each other. Unless manufactured with stretch-textured or elastomeric yarns, they have very little stretch. Most woven fabrics ravel from cut edges and require seam finishes. Woven fabrics make up the largest single share of the apparel fabric market. A tremendous variety is available within this category, from thin, drapeable chiffon to thick, stiff melton cloth for winter coats. Grainline position is more important in woven fabrics than in any other type.

KNITTED FABRICS

Knitted fabrics are composed of a loop structure that resists raveling when cut. Some single knits, such as hosiery, may run or "ladder," however, when a loop breaks and releases the connecting column of loops. This is more of a problem with knits made of filament yarns. Most knits stretch, especially crosswise, and thus can be used in close-fitting garments without as much concern for fitting ease as would be required in a more rigid woven fabric. As knits do not ravel, they do not require seam finishes unless they roll. Rolled seam allowances create a thick, lumpy appearance on the exterior of the garment, but suitable seam finishing can give a flatter seamline. Velour, jersey, panne velvet, and stretch terry are examples of fabrics that have a great deal of stretch and roll badly when cut.

KNIT VARIANTS

Knit variants, which have been used in the home furnishings field for some time, are beginning to be seen in apparel as well, especially in bulky, novelty yarn constructions. These fabrics consist of laid-in yarns held in place by a series of connected or unconnected loop stitches. The laid yarns usually predominate in the fabric and form the design. They may be deposited in any desired pattern, and thus are not directionally restricted as is the case with the design yarns of woven or knitted fab-

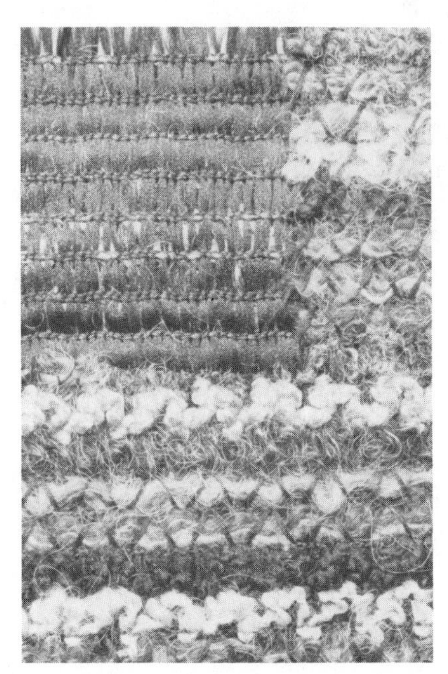

a.

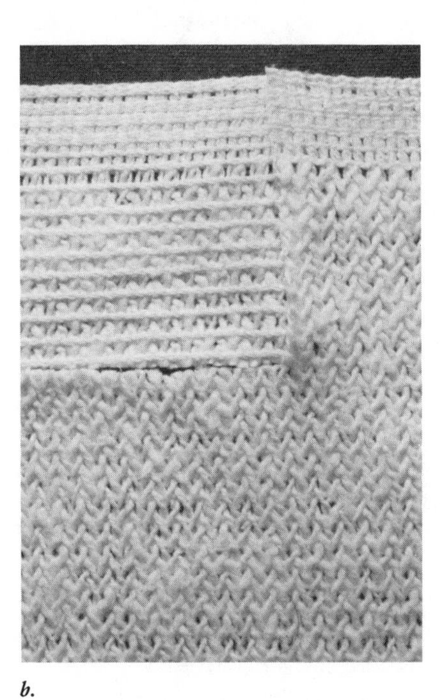

b.

2-7. Knit variant fabrics: (a) wool-blend, bulky novelty yarn fabric; (b) all cotton fabric with less textured surface.

rics. Also, it is not necessary that they be strong or consistent, as the fabrication process places no stress on them. Weaker but more decorative yarn structures than those required of more traditional fabrication methods are thus possible. Figure 2-7 shows two examples of apparel fabrics made by the knit variant method. In the upper corner of each, a small section has been cut out and reversed to show the technical reverse of the fabric, with its distinguishing chainstitch. In both of these examples, the chainstitching which forms the ground portion is in disconnected rows. In some examples, the lines veer from right to left and overlap.

Computer-aided design and production are very prominent in this fabrication method, and consequently, the fabric is rapidly produced. It does not ravel like woven fabrics, and it has some stretch potential. Most of the apparel fabrics made this way are coat and jacket fabrics which are bulky and thick, but light in weight. Their loose structure increases their resilience.

NONWOVEN FABRICS

Nonwovens, such as fiber webs and films, are also used to some extent in the apparel industry. Fiber webs are used as supporting fabrics—primarily as interfacings—rather than as fashion fabrics except for disposables and costumes. Films play a more prominent role in outerwear. Expanded films are used for shoes, purses, gloves, and some coats, and plain films are used for waterproof garments. The garment sleeve shown in Figure 2-8 is of an olefin nonwoven, Tyvek, which is used here in a windbreaker jacket. The garment pictured shows the effects of many months hard wear, with the resulting tears in the outer fabric skin. The fabric itself is extremely soft, water resistant, and comfortable, a functional fabric choice for the end use.

LEATHER, SUEDE, AND THEIR SUBSTITUTES

Fur, leather, suede, and polyurethane suede substitutes are important in expensive apparel lines. They have a high initial cost, and all present special cutting and/or sewing requirements for the manufacturer. Real

2-8. Olefin nonwoven fabric in garment sleeve after extended wear.

skins must be handled individually so that any flaws or scars can be avoided or at least placed inconspicuously in the garment. The suede substitutes do not have that kind of limitation during the cutting process.

Seaming leaves puncture holes which show in case of repairs or alterations; seams must be glued or stitched open to keep them flat. Easing is virtually impossible. In the construction of apparel using all of these materials, bulk must be avoided.

MULTICOMPONENTS

Multicomponent fabrics—double weaves, bonded fabrics, or quilted structures—tend to be thick, stiff, and bulky. They are best restricted to simple styles with a minimum of crossed seams.

True double cloth consists of two distinct fabric layers held together by an additional, very sparse set of yarns which are not visible on either side of the completed fabric. True double cloth can be separated into two layers at the cut edges of the garment and the raw edges turned in toward each other to provide a very neat and effective edge finish. This will result in a completely reversible garment with no facings, linings, or seam finishes required. Such fabrics are quite expensive, however, and are most commonly used in designer lines. Partial double cloth and double-faced cloth are also more expensive than simpler woven fabrics, but they do not offer the finishing advantages of true double cloths. They may also present problems of bulk at seams.

Bonded fabrics require no lining and usually no seam finishes. Bonded fabrics tend to have a stiff, rather unnatural appearance and, in many cases, reflect an attempt to salvage a fabric not durable enough to be used alone in apparel. Exceptions to this are found in coats and jackets. In such applications, bonding a thin layer of foam to the coating fabric increases the insulating properties as effectively as using an interlining, but with much less construction expense. Topstitching is usually required to keep seams and edges flat.

Quilted fabrics are commonly used for winter robes as well as for fashion jackets and coats. Three-layer constructions are more durable than those with no backing fabric, and quilting stitches made with filament thread present a real problem of slipping out when cut at garment edges. Even seam finishing may not be sufficient to control this problem. Tricot used as a backing is very inexpensive, but tends to snag and pull very easily. Foam is used occasionally as the middle layer, or padding, for quilted fabrics. It results in a much stiffer silhouette than down or fiberfill. Garments made from foam-lined quilted fabric stand away from the body and add considerably to the impression of body size.

Regardless of fabrication method, the complexity of the fabric relates directly to its cost, and thus to the cost of the garment. Plain fabrics with color or design added after manufacture are less expensive than fabrics with in-loom styling. The latter is a slower process, and it must be done earlier in the production process. The earlier a styling decision must be made, the more risk is involved because of the time lapse between styling and point of sale and the rapidity with which the fashion market changes.

FABRIC WEIGHT

Fabric weights range from very light chiffon and tulle to heavy blanket and coating fabrics. The lighter fabrics are more suitable for elaborate detailing, soft styles, narrow straps, gathers, patterns cut very full, and sharp construction points, such as in faced scallops or pointed collars. More fabric weight is required for tailored styles, close fitting garments, or bold detailing, such as bound buttonholes, welt pockets, and contoured seams.

Piped seams, bound edges, buttons, zippers, and applied trims require careful coordination to fabric weight in order to avoid distortion of the basic structural lines of the garment which can be caused by sagging or protrusion. Supporting fabrics such as interfacings, underlinings, and linings require the same careful coordination with garment weight in order to achieve the desired effect. In addition, the climate of different geographical areas affects the range of fabric weights that will find ready markets.

FABRIC BODY

While there is a correlation between fabric weight and fabric body, the latter refers to the tendency of the fabric to hang flat or close to the body. A fabric with considerable drape adds little to the appearance of body size, even when used in a full garment. A style with less actual yardage may, when made of a stiff fabric, add several inches to the appearance of size.

Fabric body is also one of the most important considerations in selecting a fabric to achieve the desired aesthetic effect in a design. A case in point is the importance of fabric drape in costumes for the dance. The rhythm and movement of the dancer's body can be enhanced by the selection of a floating, draping fabric such as chiffon. A more formal, stylized effect is achieved by the stiff tulle and net of the ballerina's tutu.

OPACITY

Fabric weight, color, and fiber content will affect the amount of light that passes through a fabric. Very sheer fabrics in pale colors can be virtually transparent, allowing undergarments and the garment's inner construction details to be visible on the outside. In Figure 2-9, a section of selvage has been turned back under the fashion fabric of sheer polyester chiffon to show the degree to which construction details in such a fabric would be visible in the finished garment. Even the pin holes from the tenter frame can be seen with close inspection.

Sheer fabrics require special seam finishes which are unobtrusive when viewed from the garment's exterior. Facings that do not end at a design line of the garment (at a pleat, tuck, seam, or dart, for example) mar the intended effect of the garment. Tab fronts are preferable to extended front facings; bound rather than faced necklines also avoid this problem. Inseam or slash pockets and bound buttonholes are inappropriate unless the garment is to be underlined for increased opacity. Men's white summer slacks and shorts often present such problems of transparency

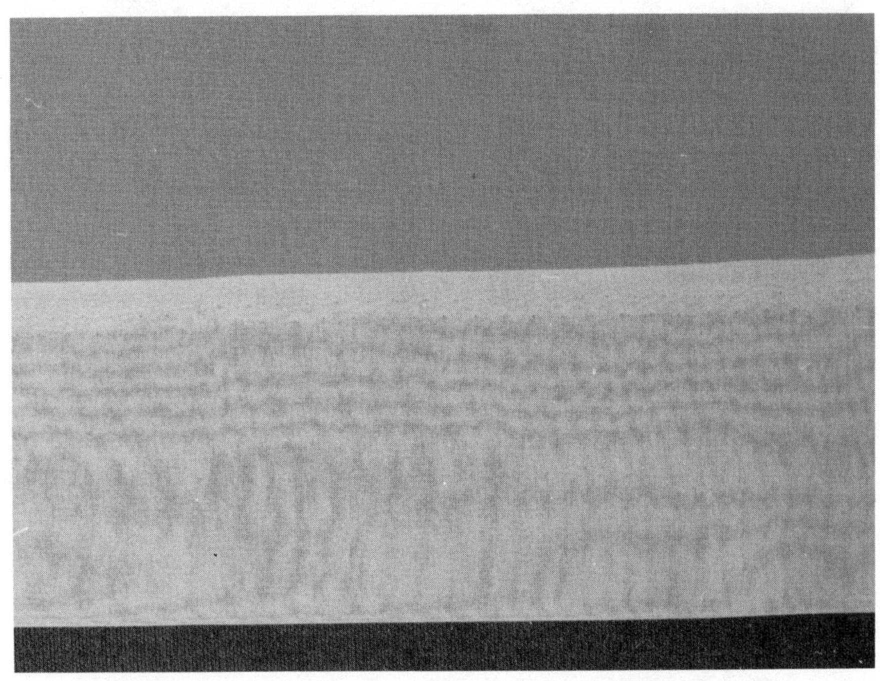

2-9. Sheer fabric with section folded under to create double thickness.

when pockets, shirt tails, and undershorts are visible through the slack fabric.

Apparel designers, manufacturers, and fabric purchasers share the responsibility for selecting fabrics which are appropriate for their intended designs and functions. To some degree, buyers and retail sales personnel can compensate for miscalculations at that stage by developing creative display and marketing strategies for difficult garments. For example, the serviceability of some transparent or translucent garments can be extended with attractive undergarments, such as camisoles, which are meant to be seen and are thus part of the intended fashion look. If a blouse or shirt is translucent, then flesh-colored undergarments will not show through as will fabrics which are several tints lighter or shades darker than the skin of the wearer. Slack liners or slips may help counteract the effects of bottom-weight fabrics which are still light enough in tint to be translucent. Other options include partial cover-ups, such as vests, sweater vests, or jumpers for blouses. Tunics or long overblouses serve the same purpose for slacks made from translucent fabrics.

COUNT OR GAUGE

Count refers to the number of yarns in one square inch of woven fabric, and gauge refers to the number of stitches per inch in a knitted fabric. Both terms can be interpreted in much the same way. High-count fabrics are more durable, but they resist easing, have a stiffer look, and show a greater tendency to pucker and wrinkle. Very low-count fabrics, on the other hand, are spongy and difficult to keep from stretching during construction. They slip and shift during cutting and sewing. They ravel badly and soak up stitches, making it difficult to remove stitching from the fabric. They never look crisp and flat and should be avoided for very tailored garments. Underlinings can be used to give more body to low-count fabrics.

FABRIC STABILITY

Dimensional stability refers to the maintenance of original size during use and care. Many factors affect dimensional stability, but the property itself cannot be visually evaluated in new fabrics or garments. Labeling information is the best source of advice on properly caring for a garment in order to minimize size changes. Stability also refers to the tendency of yarns to maintain their original placement in the fabric as well as to the tendency of the fabric to return to its original size after being stressed or extended.

The first characteristic, yarn shift, can be determined by holding the

2-10. Yarn shift in silk fabric woven with filament warp yarns and low twist, staple weft.

fabric between the thumbs and forefingers of both hands and firmly pulling on the fabric. Any distortion of yarn placement as a result of this mild stress indicates potential durability problems with the fabric. If the same test reveals no yarn shift, but does leave the stressed fabric puckered, this indicates the potential for fabric growth. Fabrics that exhibit growth from mild stress can be expected to show severe deformation in areas of high garment stress, such as at knees, elbows, and the seat. Both shift and growth can be serious problems.

FABRIC FLAWS

Even first-quality fabrics contain flaws that, if positioned in an obvious location, will detract from the appearance of a garment. Such flaws include irregularities of size or color in the yarn, impurities in the yarn, broken or knotted yarns, soiled spots, weaving or knitting errors, holes, runs, color variations in solid color fabrics, misregistered prints, smudged prints, and unintentional color variations in prints. Fabrics are classified as "firsts" or "seconds" according to the average number of flaws per yard.

FABRIC FINISHES

Brushing, glazing, embossing, and pleating are examples of finishes used primarily for aesthetic rather than for functional reasons. Brushing or napping a fabric increases its insulation potential, but it also increases the likelihood that the surface fibers will ball up, or pill, during wear. The brushed surface of the lightweight cotton/polyester blend fabric shown in Figure 2-11a has never been worn or washed. However, during storage, light pilling has occurred. The fleece jacket fabric in Figure 2-11b has been worn and laundered several times, and the pills are much more pronounced. Glazed fabrics have reduced absorbency and will show wrinkles and abrasion more easily than similar fabrics that are unglazed. Both embossing and pleating can result in a stiff, paper-like quality if the fabric itself was originally somewhat stiff.

The majority of the finishes used on fabrics are functional and are rarely visible. Their presence can be detected only if noted on labels or

a. *b.*

2-11. Pilling of napped fabrics: (a) new, unwashed fabric; (b) worn and laundered fabric.

hang tags. Flame retardant, bacteriostatic, water resistant, antistatic, durable or permanent press, and wrinkle resistant finishes are applied to fabrics to improve their performance for particular end uses. As the application of a finish entails additional processing steps as well as the use of additional raw materials, fabric costs will be affected. Most manufacturers note the presence of such finishes on labels and hang-tags because the finishing treatment can represent a competitive advantage in the marketplace.

GRAINLINE

One of the most critical elements in apparel construction is the grainline position of the fabric relative to its placement in each piece of the completed garment. The three grainline positions are lengthwise, crosswise, and bias direction

The lengthwise grainline in most fabrics is strongest and has the least amount of stretch and shrinkage potential. In the majority of garment pattern pieces, the lengthwise grainline will be placed perpendicular to the floor. In apparel manufacturing, the degree to which a pattern piece can be adjusted to maximize marker efficiency is referred to as "tilt." In better quality apparel, the degree of tilt is kept very small if used at all, for even slight deviation can change the way the garment hangs in relation to the body. In minor garment sections manipulation of grainline can frequently be used to advantage in certain designs. Vertical stripes, for example, can be cut so that garment collars, cuffs, yokes, and/or pockets have horizontal stripes. Even in major pattern pieces, controlled manipulation can be used to effect desired design features. Flared skirts give a slimmer appearance if the lengthwise grainline is placed closer to the sides than to the center front and back. This type of grainline manipulation must be handled very carefully, however, to achieve exactly the desired results. Only someone thoroughly knowledgeable of fabric behavior and apparel design should attempt grainline manipulation.

The crosswise grainline has more stretch and more shrinkage potential than the lengthwise grainline. It is usually placed parallel to the floor, going around the body, in major apparel pieces—skirt or dress panels, slack panels, sleeves, jacket fronts and backs and side panels if any are present. When fabrics have border designs such as border prints or scalloped edges in Schiffli embroidered eyelets, then the crosswise grainline can be used perpendicular to the body if the garment pieces are cut relatively straight so that there is no curve at the hem edge. This type of cut should not be used in a tightly fitted garment unless an underlying fabric such as a lining or underlining is also used to take the stress of body expansion during wear. Otherwise, the crosswise stretch of the fabric will distort the shape of the garment.

The bias direction is directly between the lengthwise and crosswise grainlines and has the most stretch potential of all. The bias direction of a fabric is never cut perpendicular to the floor except to achieve a particular design effect, or if the pattern piece is too wide to fit on the fabric any other way.

The bias direction tends to drape and hang more closely to the body and to roll more evenly than the other two grain positions. Because of its capacity for smooth shaping, the bias direction is particularly utilized for certain garment details or types, such as cowl necklines, rolled collars, men's ties, bows, and bindings. Before the popularity of stretch-textured woven fabrics made of synthetic fabrics and the use of elastomers such as spandex, comfortable but close-fitting garments and undergarments were made by using the bias cut of the fabric. That cut gave comfort stretch to the apparel. Additionally, stripes and plaids may be cut with garment seams on the bias so that chevron effects can be obtained with the fabric design, an effect shown in Figure 2-12.

As a piece of fabric is manufactured, all three grainline positions are fixed relative to each other. The lengthwise and crosswise grains are at

2-12. Bias cut used at seamline to create chevron of fabric stripes.

right angles to each other, and the bias is directly between the two. During subsequent stages of production, however, distortion can occur. The crosswise grainline can slope from one selvage to the other *(skew)*, or it may curve in the center of the fabric *(bow)*. In some fabrics, both deformations may be seen. Such fabrics are described by the term *off-grain*.

There are two instances in which off-grain fabrics can cause serious problems when used in apparel. In the first instance, the fabric has not been given a permanent finish and, therefore, can relax and return to its original grainline formation when laundered. When a pair of cotton jeans is laundered, for example, and the side seam swings to the front of the leg, this is an indication that the fabric was off-grain when the garment was cut, then righted itself during laundering.

The reverse of this same problem can occur in knitted garments which are knitted off-grain, straightened during finishing, then return to their original formation after laundering or dry cleaning. Figure 2-13 shows a skewed wool/angora knit fabric which straightened during the first dry cleaning, pulling the pocket at an angle. The pocket's vertical edges are perfectly aligned with the vertical wales of the garment; the horizontal edge of the pocket bottom is also carefully aligned to the ribbing which finishes off the sweater hem. It is the fabric skew, not faulty construction, which has created the very visible lack of alignment in the decorative pocket and the true vertical and horizontal lines of the garment as a whole.

2-13. Skewed wool/angora blend knit after cleaning.

Knitted fabrics are less stable than woven and are more easily pulled out of alignment during finishing; also, multiple yarn feeds in a circular knit garment automatically insures that the fabric will be off-grain as it is knitted. With a single yarn feed, as in hand knitting, the fabric will be only one row of stitches out of alignment. As the number of yarn feeds into the same basic pattern increases, then the greater the problem.

If the original deformation was severe, the garment may become unserviceable after laundering. Garments that are suspected of not having permanent finish should be analyzed very carefully in order to determine grain trueness. Sometimes, the wrong side of the fabric will show the grain position more clearly than the right side, so both should be examined.

The second instance in which off-grain fabrics can present problems occurs when an obvious directional pattern combines with severe grain distortion in fabrics that are permanently finished. The pattern may be striped, plaid, or created just by the use of large or novelty yarns. In such cases, the lengthwise grainline cannot be placed perpendicular to the floor without having the horizontal elements in the pattern at an undesirable angle on the body. This type of grainline problem is much easier to detect, as the effect is present on the garment at the point of sale, rather than appearing after use and laundering. Figure 2-14 shows a fabric which was skewed prior to printing. The plaid design was printed on, then the fabric straightened after laundering. The resulting pattern is badly skewed, making the fabric virtually unusable.

2-14. New, unwashed cotton flannelette fabric printed off-grain.

SPECIALTY FABRICS

Beyond the considerations covered in the preceding sections, some fabrics may require special handling in order to achieve the desired effect in the garment design. Such specialized handling frequently leads to increases in garment cost. The specialized handling may include design considerations, increased yardage requirements, increased difficulty in developing an efficient marker, a special spread, or increased construction time.

DIRECTIONAL FABRICS

Pile fabrics, napped fabrics, and some knits have variation in the amount of light reflectance that occurs, even within the same grainline direction, depending on the fabric position. A pile fabric, for example, will appear lighter in value when viewed with the pile running downward. If the same piece of fabric is turned so that the lower end of the piece is held uppermost, then the pile will be angled upward and will appear darker in value. In such fabrics, all pattern pieces for the same garment must be placed in the same direction so that the finished garment will

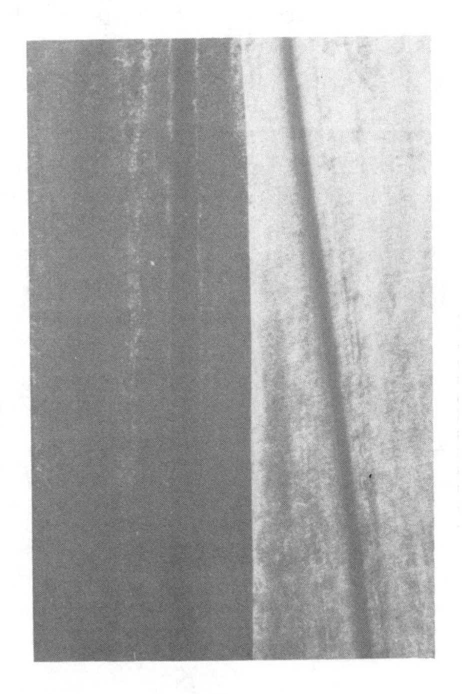

2-15. Napped rayon panne velvet fabric seamed with nap running in opposite directions on the two sections.

2-16. Directional fabric; small-scale print with vertical orientation.

have a consistent color value. This requires more careful planning in developing the layout and may require more fabric yardage than would be needed for the same design made in nondirectional fabric.

One-way designs require the same consideration in layout and are more costly to manufacture because the fabric must be spread face up rather than face-to-face. If the directional pattern is not symmetrical vertically or horizontally, then matching the pattern at garment seamlines will be even more difficult. In lower cost apparel lines, manufacturers do not always attempt to match directional patterns. Even if the cut yields a vertical match at a center back seam, for example, the production time allotted for constructing that seam may not be sufficient to encourage the operator to ensure that the lines do, in fact, match. In Figure 2-16, the directional pattern is small and runs only in the vertical direction; there is horizontal repetition. As the size of motifs increases, or if a second direction of non-repetition is added, then the difficulty of handling the fabric is complicated. One aspect of increasing levels of cost and aesthetic quality in apparel is the manner in which directional patterns are handled. In the most expensive lines, a match should be expected at every seamline in which the two edges being joined are the same size and corresponding grainline position.

LARGE DESIGNS

Very large stripes, plaids, or other motifs require careful placement of the design elements on each pattern piece to avoid a discordant effect. Such designs should be matched at garment seamlines, pockets, lapels, etc. This matching requires much more time in fabric spreading, pattern placement, and sewing than if the fabric pieces were left unmatched or if the garment were made of a plain fabric. There is also the strong likelihood of fabric waste, as pattern pieces must be placed for design matching rather than for yardage conservation.

BULKY FABRICS

Quilted and bonded fabrics, fake fur, and other thick fabrics require relatively simple designs and a minimum number of crossed seams. Complicated designs with numerous seams tend to result in rigid garments and tedious construction. Machines may have to be adjusted to accept several layers of bulky fabrics.

SUMMARY

Fabric selection is one of the most important considerations in the way an apparel design is interpreted by a manufacturer. It is the fabric that the consumer sees first. A closer inspection of a garment is made only when the fabric is visually appealing. Once the initial appeal has been made, however, the fabric has much more to deliver in effecting a final, positive buying decision on the part of the consumer. Fiber content and fabric finishes govern the garment's cost, performance, and care requirements. Other fabric characteristics, such as yarn structure, weight, body, opacity, count, fabrication methods, stability, flaws, finishes, and grainline affect the fabric suitability to a particular garment design, its cost, and its quality. Specialty fabrics with directional designs, large and/or symmetrical motifs, and bulky fabrics complicate the manufacturing process and thus increase apparel costs.

Although fabric is a very important component of total garment cost, making generalizations about any single aspect of fabric is extremely difficult. Some fibers are more expensive than others, but that cost can be offset by simple fabrication and finishing methods. On the other hand, inexpensive fibers can be processed in expensive ways. In looking at the final product, there are many factors that have an impact on the total cost and on the aesthetic, durability, comfort, and ease-of-care aspects of apparel quality.

In addition to all of the functional qualities that affect fabric suitability and cost, the scene is further complicated by the fashion element. Even high-quality fabric may be rejected if the consumer perceives it as dated. A case in point is filament polyester gabardine and double knit. They may be very functional, high-performance fabrics, well suited for slacks and tailored garments, but they are usually relegated to lower priced lines and to consumer groups that tend to be less fashion-conscious because they are viewed by many as being out of fashion. A thorough knowledge of the complex fabric component is essential for professional evaluation of garment quality and for being able to communicate aspects of quality to consumers and colleagues alike.

3

SHAPING DEVICES

Once the fabric has been selected and cut for a particular apparel item, the next step is to shape the flat fabric pieces to the desired three-dimensional form. Darts, dart equivalents, and seams are the means used to create that third dimension. Thread stitching is still the method used almost exclusively to secure shaping devices; therefore, the appearance and durability of any dart, tuck, or seam depends upon the type of thread and type of stitching used in securing the shaping device.

THREAD AND STITCHING

Thread selection is a very important aspect of seam formation and can affect durability, appearance, and even comfort. Selection of the proper thread for the apparel item is a complex task requiring knowledge of and decisions about the following:

1. fiber content
2. yarn structure (spun, monofilament, smooth or texturized multifilament, or core)

3. degree and direction of twist
4. number of elements (single, ply, cord)
5. chemical or mechanical finishes (glazing, polishing, mercerizing)
6. size
7. strength
8. color (available color range and colorfastness)
9. put up (how the thread is packaged for sale, including size of put up)
10. sewability (how the thread performs with the machine/fabric/seam combinations in which it will be used)
11. seam performance (appearance of seam including potential skipped stitches, puckering, and abrasion resistance)

All of these matters are considered critical to the apparel manufacturing process both in determining the ultimate price of the garment and in establishing the desired level of quality. By the time an apparel item reaches the retail level, however, many of these factors are unknown or are difficult to ascertain via casual inspection. There are, however, several aspects of thread which can be determined by the apparel buyer or by the consumer making a decision about an apparel purchase. The use of contrasting thread, for example, calls attention to the stitching itself and must be executed almost without error to avoid detracting from the garment it is meant to enhance. Forming seams with colorless, monofilament thread can lead to substantial savings for the garment manufacturer over a period of time. No inventory of thread colors is required, nor is there downtime to rethread machines between style lots. Seams formed with this thread can cause irritation to the wearer, however, for the cut thread ends are very sharp. If cut ends are numerous and/or if they come in contact with the skin during wear, they can lead to consumer dissatisfaction.

Multifilament threads are generally stronger than spun threads, but when a stitch does break, many adjacent stitches are lost because the filament thread is so slick. Thus, overall durability of the stitching is best when spun thread is used. One very important aspect of thread/fabric coordination is that the thread should be weaker than the fabric it joins. Broken stitches can be repaired, but if the thread is too strong, excessive stress will cause the fabric to split at the seamline. There is no way to repair this type of damage and still maintain the garment's original size.

Stitches used to secure the garment parts are classified by method of application. The Federal Government, in Federal Standard 751A, has established seven categories of stitches. Those most often found in industry are shown in Figure 3-1.

DIRECTION OF SUCCESSIVE STITCH FORMATION

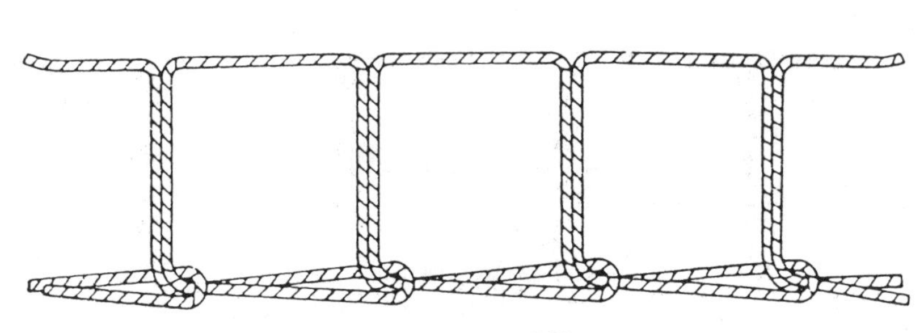

a. Stitch type 101

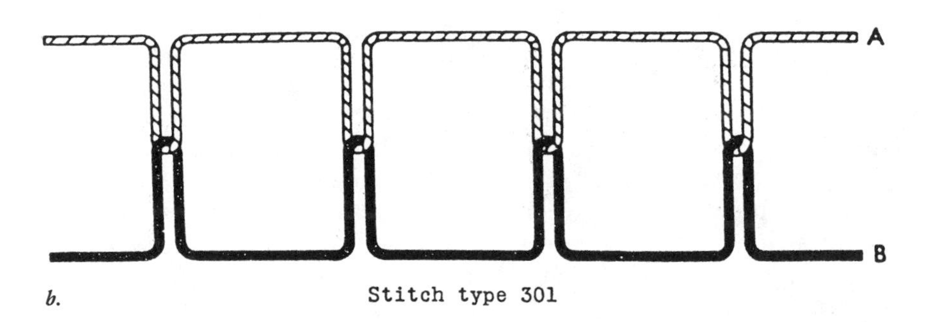

b. Stitch type 301

DIRECTION OF SUCCESSIVE STITCH FORMATION

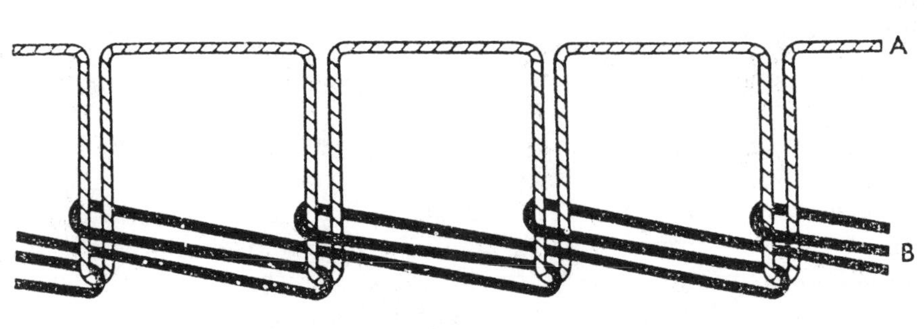

c. Stitch type 401

3-1. Classes of stitches according to Federal Standard 751A: (a) 100 series: single thread chainstitch; (b) 300 series: lockstitch (hook and bobbin-type similar to that produced by most home sewing machines); (c) 400 series: multi-thread chainstitch; (d) 500 series: overedge and safety stitch;

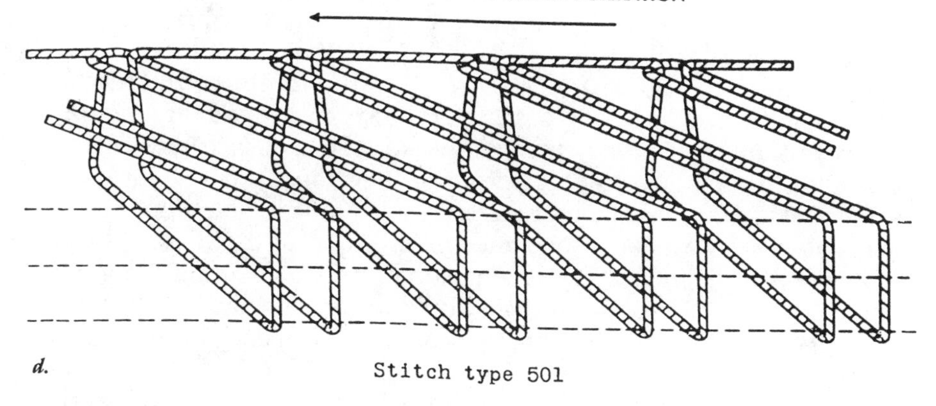

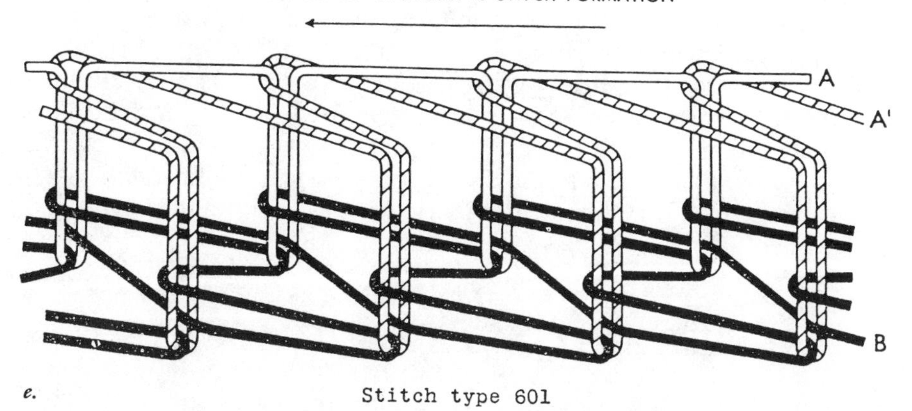

3-1 (cont.). (e) 600 series: coverstitch on flat seam stitch (200 series, hand stitches not illustrated). Drawings taken from Federal Standard 751A, United States Government Printing Office, Washington, D.C.

Within each of these categories will be many variations, all designated with the same numerical division (i.e., 501 or 503 are variations within the same category). Selection of the actual stitch within each category or between categories is usually made by the apparel production staff according to structural criteria, cost limitations, and the equipment which is available. Not every apparel manufacturer has every machine, so some choices are made on the basis of what is possible rather than ideal.

In addition to stitch category and type, the length of the machine stitches influences garment cost, appearance, and durability. Shaping devices secured with long stitches (five to eight per inch) are faster to sew and thus less expensive to produce than those secured with short stitches. Although usually more attractive for topstitching, long stitches may allow the garment to gap and pull away from the stitching, especially in areas of stress. When a long stitch breaks, the result is a greater opening in the affected seam than would occur with shorter stitches.

In general, the stitch length should be regulated to correspond to fabric type and to the amount of stress the stitching will bear. High-count, thin, lightweight, soft fabrics usually require about twelve stitches per inch in order to be sewn securely. Heavy, coarse, low-count fabrics, on the other hand, look better and are more durable when sewn with longer stitches. Stitches that are too short might split the yarns of these fabrics and actually weaken the seamline. Eight to ten stitches per inch, or possibly even less in some cases, would be more appropriate for heavy fabrics. With tightly woven fabrics, too, there is an additional problem of structural jamming when each stitch forces an additional yarn into a fabric which has extremely small yarn interstices in which to fit the added yarn. The result is puckering, particularly in seams which occur on the true grainline of the fabric such as at the center front and center back.

DARTS AND DART EQUIVALENTS

A dart or a dart equivalent adds three-dimensional shape to a single section of cut fabric. Although a seam—the joining of two separate sections—may be used to secure one edge of the dart or dart equivalent, the shaping potential is independent of that seam. Darts and their equivalents are used more frequently at locations of major body contours—bust, shoulders, waist/hips, for example—and in apparel fitted to the body. In very loose-fitting garments, the excess fullness of the fabric folds into wrinkles which radiate to the fullest parts of the body, and the wrinkles serve the function of darts.

DARTS

A true dart has a point at one end, at least, and possibly at both ends. In a *single-pointed dart,* the stitching lines resemble a large triangle. The dart is formed by bringing the right sides of the fabric together so that the upper and lower stitching lines of the dart are aligned, then stitching from the wide end (the cut edge) to the point. The point of the dart is intended to stop just short of the fullest part of the body at that location. Single-pointed darts usually occur at the back shoulder or back neck of jackets; at the front and/or back waistline of slacks, shorts, culottes, and skirts; at the side bust of fitted garment fronts in women's apparel; and at the front and back of bodice waistlines of fitted dresses with waistline seams.

A *French dart* is a type of single-pointed dart. It is a diagonal bust dart that originates at least two inches (5.08 cm) below the bust point at the garment side and ends just short of the fullest part of the bust. It is used primarily in one-piece, semi-fitted dresses where it combines the fitting functions of the bust and the waistline darts. Single-pointed darts that are very wide at the point of origin or that occur in thick, bulky fabrics should be trimmed to a width of five-eighths inch

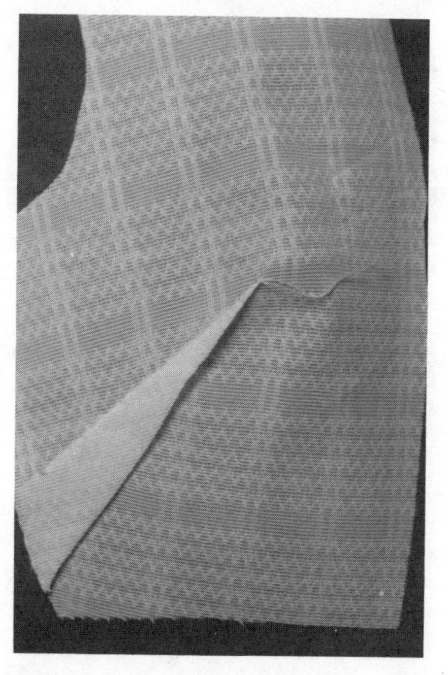

a.

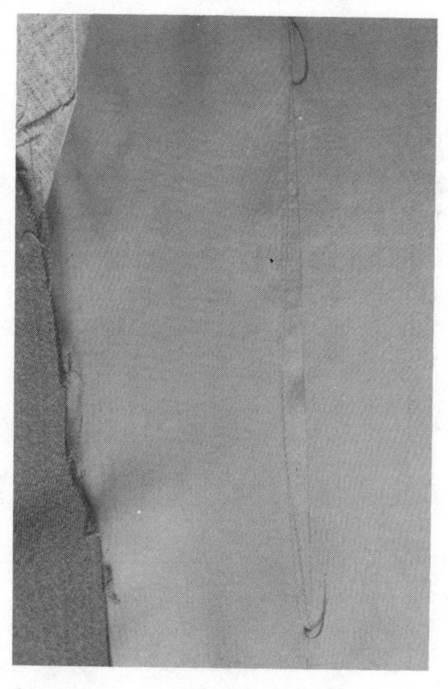

b.

3-2. Two types of darts: (a) single-pointed French dart; (b) double-pointed dart.

(1.59 cm) and as close to the point as possible while still maintaining the specified trimmed width. The remainder of the fold, to within one-half inch (1.27 cm) of the point, should be clipped open. The trimmed edges should then be pressed open and finished like the seams in the garment. This treatment reduces bulk and makes the seam that will cross the dart end much neater.

Double-pointed darts occur in fitted or semi-fitted garments that have no waistline seams and in which the garment fabric does not have enough stretch to accomplish the desired degree of fit. Men's suit coats and blazers usually have such darts in the jacket front. The fullest part of the dart coincides with the waistline, and this fullness tapers to nothing at the full part of the chest and hip. If the dart is very wide in the middle, it may require clipping from the fold almost to the stitching line in order to allow the dart to spread flat when the garment is pressed.

All darts must have points carefully stitched so that the stitching line very gradually tapers virtually to nothing; otherwise, a bubble or dimple

a.

b.

3-3. Comparison of two dart points: (a) correctly stitched; (b) incorrectly stitched.

will appear at the end of the dart. Figure 3-3 shows one dart with the point stitched correctly and another with the stitching toward the point not tapered sufficiently.

Also, the thread ends at the point must be secured to keep the first few stitches from coming loose. Continuing to sew for an inch (2.54 cm) or so after the needle leaves the fabric causes the threads to twist around each other. If left one to two inches (2.54 to 5.08 cm) long, the twisted or chained off threads will hold the stitches of the dart point securely. If the threads must be clipped very close, as in a sheer fabric, then they must be knotted first. Darts should be pressed toward the center of the body. When the dart is folded and pressed properly, no creases or "wells" should be seen on the right side of the garment, and the raw edges of the dart should be aligned exactly with the raw edge of the garment.

DART EQUIVALENTS

The shaping and fitting functions of the dart can be assumed by other devices which offer a very different appearance. The fullness which would be controlled by the dart can be controlled by easing, gathers, tucks, pleats, or released darts. With the exception of easing, all of the other

a.

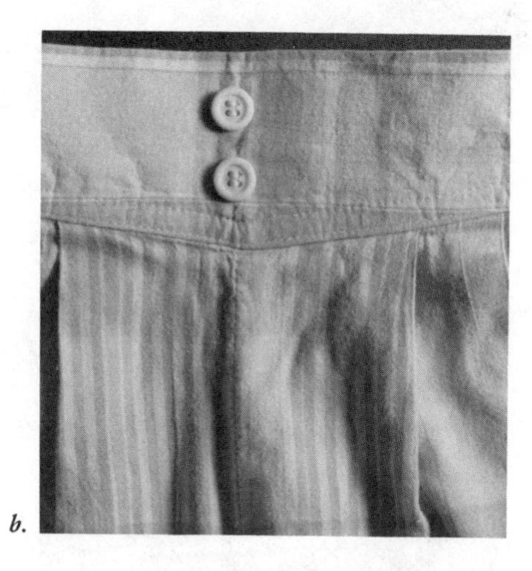

b.

3-4. Released darts or tucks functioning as dart equivalents: (a) in slacks; (b) in skirts.

dart equivalents usually require more fabric than needed for darts. They offer the advantage, however, of being more adaptable to a wider variation of shapes than the stitched dart. An excellent example of where this is true is in fitted slacks. If only darts are used to fit the slacks to the body, then there will be very few bodies which match exactly not only the two dimensions of hip and waist, but the graduation between the two. Most dart equivalents, on the other hand, provide for the body to extend the fabric as much as is needed below the secured end. Easing the larger edge of one garment section so that it will be the same length as the section to which it will be seamed is an effective dart substitute only when the fullness to be handled is slight or when the change in body contour is not very abrupt. (See Figure 3-20.) Shoulder darts in coats and jackets are frequently converted to ease, especially in men's apparel.

a.

b.

3-5. Gathered seams: (a) gathers evenly distributed; (b) gathers unevenly distributed.

Gathers can be used for a soft look and when the amount of fullness is too great to be handled by easing. Bathing suits with bust gathers caught in the center front seamline or perhaps twisted around a ring at the center front are examples of the creative use of dart equivalents. Whether used as a shaping device, a design feature, or both, the effectiveness of gathers depends upon their even distribution along the shorter garment section. Figure 3-5a shows gathers which have been evenly distributed along the seamline and smoothly joined to the shorter fabric section. Figure 3-5b shows lower quality construction, with uneven distribution of gathers.

If a more controlled look is desired, then tucks, pleats, or released darts can be used. All of these terms are used to describe what is basically the same technique; that is, lapping the fullness out of the garment. The lap may be on the outside or inside; it may be stitched on the inside or outside or both; it may be in the form of one large lap or several smaller ones. The basic characteristic is that the seam, or cut, edge is smooth and flat, and fullness is released at some point from the actual seamline to what would be the dart point if a regular dart were being used. In many garments that have this styling detail, additional tucks or pleats are used beyond what would be necessary just to accommodate the fullness of the dart.

STANDARDS FOR EVALUATING DARTS AND DART EQUIVALENTS

1. Stitch length is appropriate to the fabric and to the expected stress at the stitched location.
2. The thread matches the apparel fabric.
3. No creases or wells are present on the right side of the dart.
4. No dimples or bubbles can be seen at the dart point.
5. Matching darts are identical in size and angle.
6. Fullness is evenly distributed in dart equivalents.
7. Sufficient fabric is allowed to achieve the desired design effect in dart equivalents.

SEAMS

When garment shaping and fitting require that two or more pieces of fabric must be joined, then a seam is used to effect that join. The seam may be straight, flared, or shaped. Various types of fabrics and designs require different seams and seam techniques. The placement, size, and type of seam determine whether alteration is possible in the garment, and if so, what type and amount. The seam provides for the fit and the silhouette of the garment.

As with thread selection and stitching, many aspects of the seam selection process are made based on equipment which is available to the specific manufacturer. If one type of seam is specified by the designer or by the production staff sending a job out for contract requires a sewing machine which the production facility does not have, then an alternative must be selected. Small contractors are less likely to have specialty equipment, and using available equipment may result in increased cost to do the equivalent by alternative methods. This is an example of the sometimes unpredictable relationship between cost and quality or durability factors. The alternative may be of comparable durability and very similar appearance, but may cost considerably more to produce because specialized equipment was not available.

The Federal Standard 751a, mentioned previously in regard to stitch types, also lists and describes exact specifications for seam types. Many apparel manufacturers use this to specify how an apparel item is to be constructed. Unfortunately, not all do, so there is considerable variation and resulting difficulty in precise communication regarding what is expected when construction specifications are written using common names for seam types.

Almost all of the subsequent major categories of apparel structures relate in some way to seams for their determining characteristics. Pockets, sleeves, waistbands, and neckline treatments, for example, cannot be successful if the seams that are used to create them are of the wrong type, finished incorrectly, and/or made unskillfully. The importance of seams as the basic structural components in other techniques, the large number of seam treatments to be discussed, and their resistance to analysis as levels of classification led to the following alphabetical arrangement of terms describing both seam types and seam finishes.

SEAM TYPES

The only subdivisions used in discussing the variety of seam types are based on whether or not the seam requires any additional treatment in order to be considered finished. Seam treatments within each of these categories (i.e., finished seams and unfinished seams) appear in alphabetical order.

FINISHED SEAMS

Some seam types, by the very nature of their structure, either do not require or cannot be given any additional treatment. This does not mean that finished seams are less expensive than seams requiring additional treatment, for some of them require several exacting steps to complete. This classification means that seams constructed according to the definitions given in the text are finished, that is, seam finishes are not applicable.

ABUTTED SEAM

The abutted seam joins two plies of fabric, edge-to-edge, without a seam allowance or overlap. The seam may be made by joining the two plies over an underlay strip or by covering the edges with a flat lock stitch. The latter reduces bulk, but is less stable.

The abutted seam is used for the endwise joining of piece goods as they are rolled on a bolt or roll for shipping, as a method of joining interfacing without introducing any bulk at the seam, on garments such as slickers that are then coated with waterproofing, in foundation garments where bulk would be irritating to the body, and to join suede, leather, vinyl, and felt.

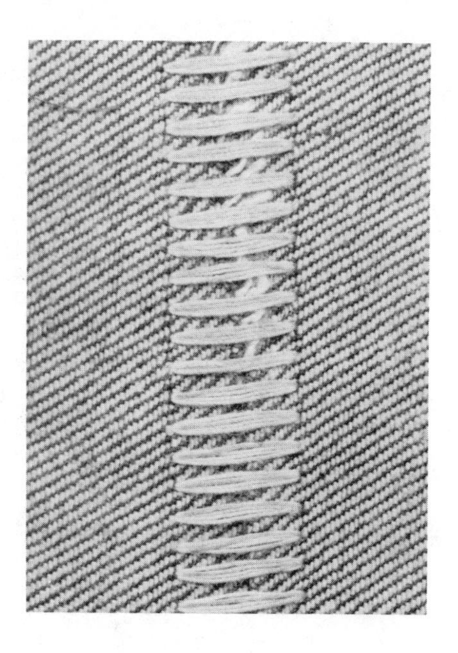

3-6. Abutted seam.

ENCLOSED SEAM

The enclosed seam results when two garment plies of identical or nearly identical cut are joined right sides together, then turned so that the seam allowances are sandwiched between the two plies. Enclosed seams are found on reversible garments, lined garments, collars, cuffs, facings, lapels, and waistbands, for example. Such seams require some additional steps to ensure a successfully finished product. The seam allowances must be trimmed to no more than one-fourth inch (.64 cm), less in heavier fabrics; graded if the fabric is thick; clipped at all concave curves, and notched or trimmed very narrowly around convex curves; and understitched if possible.

EXPOSED SEAM

In an exposed seam, a small seam allowance is overedged flat to the garment and exposed on the outside. It is found most often in sporty knit garments, adding decorative detail at very low cost. It can also be found on suede or leather where it is used to eliminate bulk, but it is much less common in those fabrics, which tend to receive more expensive treatments, than it is in active sportswear, very casual garments, and undergarments.

3-7. Enclosed seam.

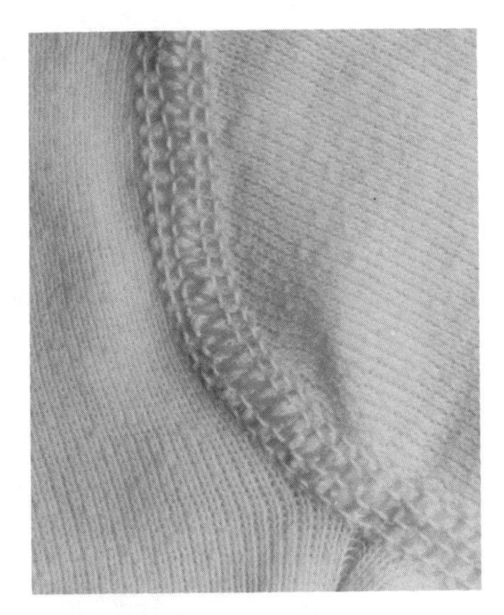

3-8. Exposed seam.

FALSE FRENCH SEAM

This is a plain seam made to resemble the French seam (see French Seam below) by the face-to-face enclosing of the folded seam allowance edges. It is a strong finish, but very time-consuming to execute. It is used instead of a French seam on transparent fabrics that ravel easily and on curves where a French seam would be more difficult to construct.

FLAT-FELLED SEAM

The flat-felled seam results from enclosing both seam allowances by interlocking opposing folded edges beneath two parallel rows of stitching which penetrate all plies. It can be produced in a single operation with a felling foot attachment on an industrial machine. Several steps are involved in nonindustrial production. The seam is usually made on the right side of the garment. Fabrics that are very bulky or spongy are not suitable for this treatment, nor are sheer or dressy fabrics.

The flat-felled seam is found most frequently on light to medium weight, staple yarn woven fabrics in casual styles. Play clothes, work clothes, pajamas, jeans and jean-styled garments, and men's shirts are some examples of apparel items that frequently contain flat-felled seams. The flat-felled seam is strong and durable and presents a very neat

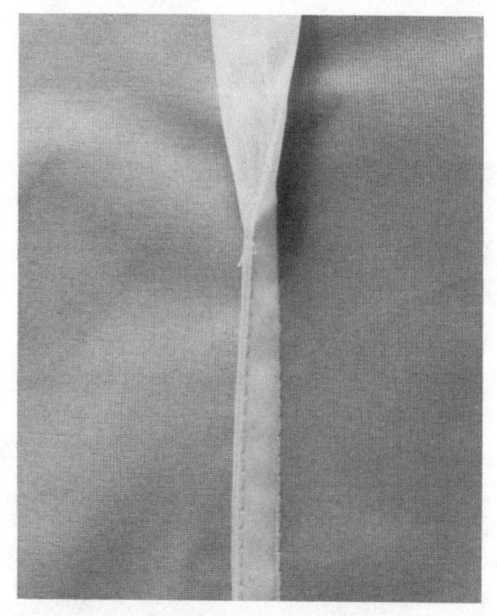

3-9. False French seam.

3-10. Flat-felled seam.

appearance as well, but often puckers after laundering, particularly if stitches were short and the apparel fabric tightly woven.

FRENCH SEAM

The French seam is constructed so that a narrow seam is contained within a larger one, producing a very neat interior and exterior for sheer fabrics. It is done only on straight seams or on those with very slight curves. It is constructed in two separate operations: the first operation joins together the wrong sides of the fabric; the second seam joins together the right sides so that the second stitching encapsulates the first seam. It is the most attractive type of seam for fabric that is truly transparent. The French seam can be found on children's and infant's wear, underwear, and outerwear of transparent fabric; a variation of it finishes inside pockets on men's better slacks.

FUSED SEAM

The fused seam is formed by a melting process which joins the seam lines of thermoplastic fabrics. Either a heated press or an ultrasonic sewing machine (which uses sound waves to generate the required heat via molecular activity and friction) can be used. The advantages of not using thread are obvious. The maintenance costs of equipment used to fuse seams are usually much lower than those of regular sewing machines. Thus, the fused seam is very inexpensive to produce, provided, of course,

3-11. French seam.

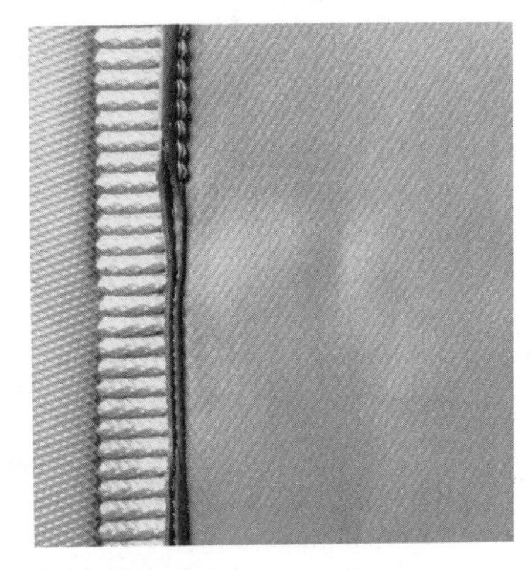

3-12. Fused seam.

3-13. Glued seam.

that the producer has the necessary equipment. Its appearance is usually so different from a regular stitched seam that many consumers associate it with low-quality/low-style apparel, but it can be very durable.

The fused seam can be found on plastic rain clothing, thermoplastic work clothing and/or disposable garments, interfacing, and as a substitute for regular quilting on quilted fabrics. It is considered to be an important seaming technique for the future.

GLUED SEAM

This is a lapped, single-ply seam joined by adhesive. It is used on disposable garments, on suede, leather, and vinyl until the seams are stitched, or in areas where there is no strain during wear. It is also used as an aid in sewing and, in a few instances, as a replacement for sewing—for example in patch pocket and belt loop applications.

The durability of the glued seam is related directly to the durability of the adhesive, and most of those in use for this application are very durable. Repositioning of the glued seam is not possible, and bleeding of the glue onto the garment proper can be unsightly. This, too, is a seam predicted to grow in popularity as the industry grows in sophistication.

HAIRLINE SEAM

The hairline seam is closely stitched with a zigzag or overedge stitch completely covering the very narrow seam allowances. If the seam is constructed using a 500 series machine, then the excess seam allowances are trimmed away as the seam is stitched. If a zigzag stitch (or 300 series machine) is used to make the seam itself, which resembles a line of satin stitch embroidery, then the stitching is done on the regular seam allowance, and the excess fabric is trimmed away after stitching. The hairline seam is used for collars and other areas where there is no strain and where the finished seam is enclosed, to eliminate the raw edges that show through on sheer fabrics and on fine fabrics such as silk organza, organdy, and lawn which fray and ravel easily.

LAPPED SEAM WITH RAW EDGES

This seam is formed by overlaying two plies face-to-back along the seamline, then joining them with a centered row or rows of stitching. A raw edge is thus exposed on each side of the garment. This treatment is used to eliminate bulk on interfacing and interlining. It can lead to considerable savings in fabric if the size of the seam allowances can be reduced on the marker. The full amount of overlap would be too great if the seam allowances were left a full five-eighths inch (1.59 cm). Leather, vinyl, felt, and suede/leather substitutes are often treated this way.

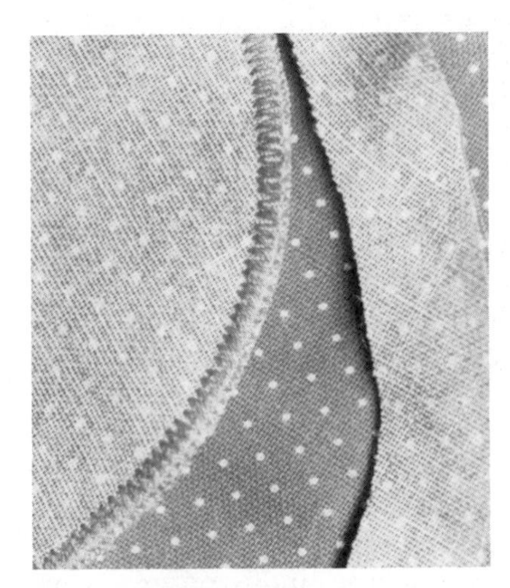

3-14. Hairline seam.

3-15. Lapped seam with raw edges.

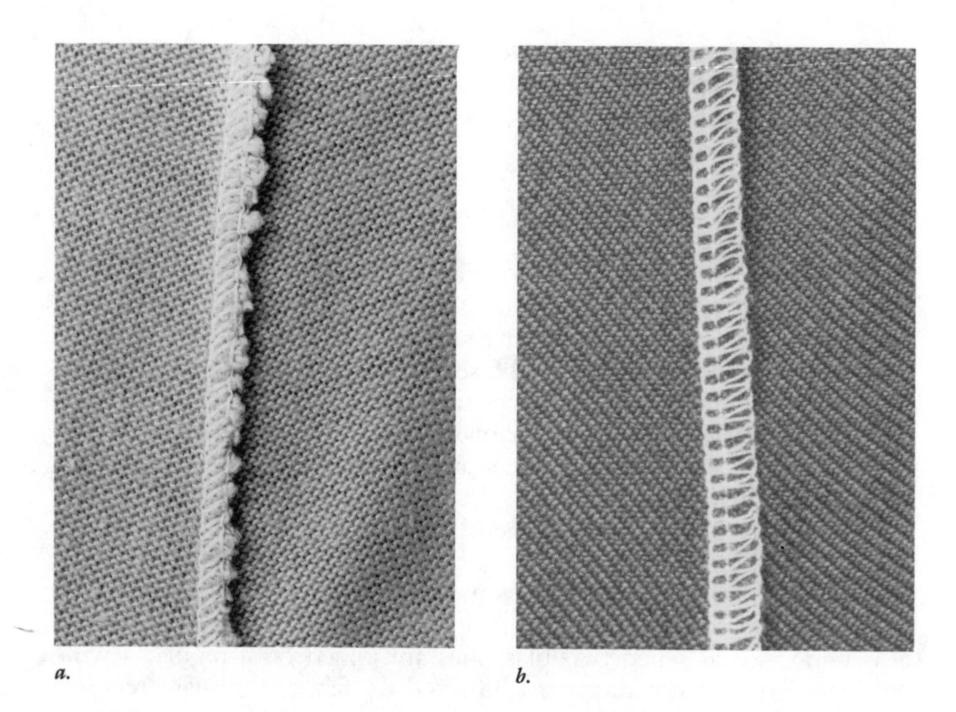

3-16. Overedged seam: (a) three thread; (b) four thread.

OVEREDGED SEAM (MERROWED OR SERGED)

This is a narrow seam in which the raw edges are overcast and the seam itself stitched simultaneously. A special machine is used industrially to create this type of seam. The 500 series machines trim as well as overedge the seam allowance. Machines in this series commonly apply from three to five threads to the overedged seam. These additional threads increase cost and durability. The overedged seam is found on knit garments, especially undergarments, lingerie, and play-clothes; on sportswear and children's clothing; and to form both enclosed and decorative exposed seams. It is a very efficient method of creating and finishing a seam and is also very economical. It is not appropriate to very thick, stiff, or bulky fabrics or to tailored garments.

UNFINISHED SEAMS

In this category are those seams that may require additional treatment in order to prevent the raw edges of the seam allowances from raveling, rolling, or stretching. Depending upon the type of fabric used in the garment, a seam finish may not be required, but in most cases additional treatment is applied once the techniques described in the seam definitions are completed.

BIAS SEAM

The bias direction of all woven fabrics and some knits is very stretchy. For this reason, all-bias seams require special handling to avoid stretching, but to allow enough ease so that the seam can extend as much as the garment fabric on each side of the seam. Either extreme results in ripples at the seamline. The former, a stretched bias seam, has horizontal ripples in the actual seamline. A bias seam with insufficient ease produces diagonal wrinkles from the seamline into the garment body. If a bias ply is joined to a straight ply, the problems are somewhat different, and the greatest danger is that the bias ply will stretch, then pleat over on itself, and the pleat will be caught in by the seamline stitching.

Most industrial sewing machines used for applying bias stripping have been designed to minimize distortion to the bias, but operator skill is also important as when two bias plies are joined on a regular sewing machine. Experience with the machine and the fabric are usually required to achieve the correct amount of ease without producing a stretched seam.

3-17. Bias seam.

All-bias seams are found most frequently in skirts. Some dresses are also cut with the bias grain perpendicular to the floor, in which case all lengthwise seams will be on the bias. Garments with dolman or kimono sleeves will have portions of the shoulder and underarm seams that may be on partial or true bias. The bias/straight seam is found more commonly in the application of bindings and similar finishes, on men's curtain waistbands, and in decorative areas of some garments, such as western yoke shirts where the pattern of the fabric bias contributes to the overall design.

CORDED/PIPED SEAM

The corded and piped seams are primarily decorative, but the additional material included in the seam also contributes some measure of body and stability. The corded seam differs from the piped in that it contains a piece of round cord to fill out the bias strip which protrudes into the seamline area. The seam itself is stitched with a folded and/or corded bias strip of either self fabric or a contrasting fabric included in the seamline so that when the seam is completed, a narrow portion of the fold or rounded edge is visible on the right side. Cording is much more common than piping, because the former is more three-dimensional and yields much more decorative emphasis than the flat fold of piping.

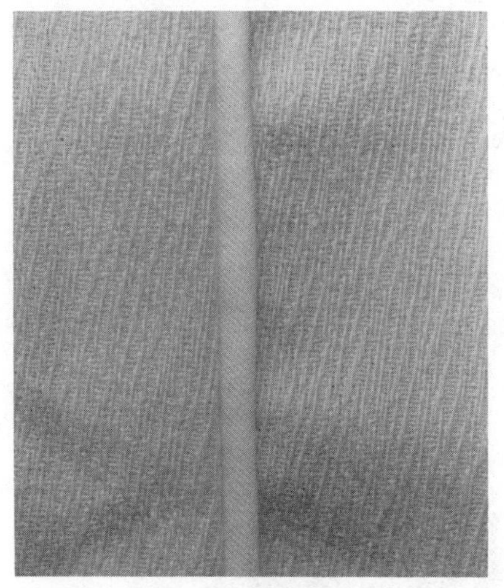

a.

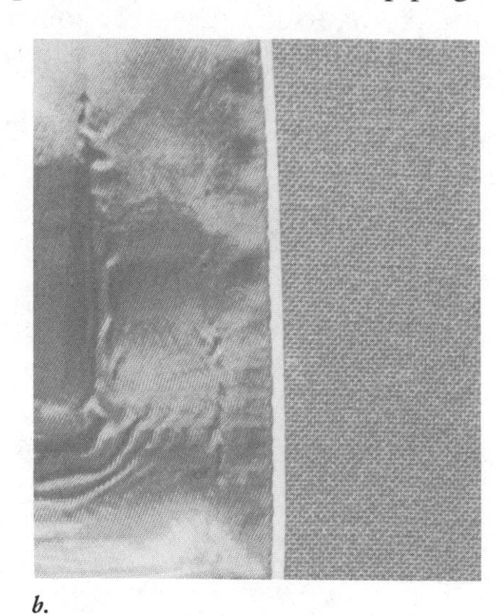

b.

3-18. (a) Corded seam; (b) piped seam in man's lined sport coat.

Either cording or piping can be used as a decorative edge on collars, cuffs, and pockets, to accentuate seams, to outline openings, and to add body to seamlines. Each can be included on flat as well as enclosed seams with equal ease, but it is difficult to apply them effectively to sharp curves or points. In such locations, they tend to draw the seam in, creating a tight, puckered look. Neither piping nor cording is particularly attractive on translucent or sheer fabrics, and they may add too much body on drapable fabrics. The application of corded or piped seams adds to the cost of the garment.

CROSSED SEAM

A crossed seam occurs when two straight seams are subsequently joined in a second stitching operation. Such crossing occurs at waistlines, shoulders, underarm/sleeve areas, and in facing applications. In thick, bulky fabrics, there should be a minimum of crossed seams. The original seams require finishing before the second stitching, and some trimming helps to reduce bulk. The seamlines should be perfectly aligned.

EASED SEAM

The eased seam is found when one garment ply is slightly longer than the ply to which it will be joined. In production, the eased seam is accomplished by restraining the fabric ply underneath while allowing the uppermost ply to feed freely into the machine. Easing is a simple process unless a great difference in length exists between the two plies being joined. Tightly woven or knitted fabrics are much more difficult

3-19. Crossed seams.

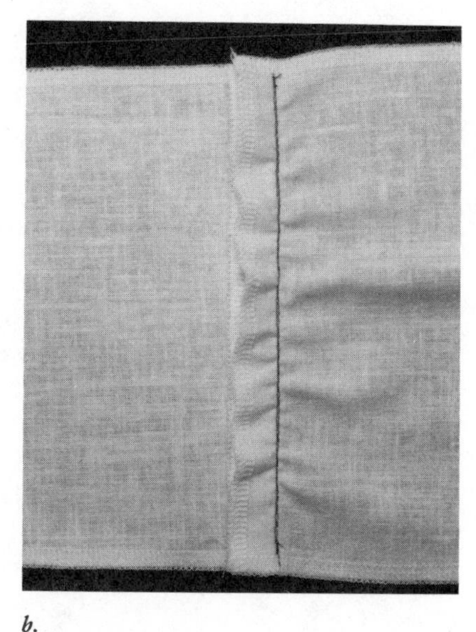

a. *b.*

3-20. Eased seam: (a) sections to be joined; (b) sections joined with easing.

to ease than are lower count fabrics. There are machines on the market to achieve programmable fullness and thus eliminate the need for manually inserting fullness.

Eased seams are found at the sleeve cap of set-in sleeves, at the waist of slacks or skirts where they join the waistband, and at the shoulder seams of jackets or bodices, for example. The fullness should be evenly distributed without pleats or gathers. Machines are more likely to accomplish this quality than manual labor.

LAPPED SEAM

The lapped seam joins three thicknesses from the face of the garment. The uppermost ply is folded under at the seamline, then lapped so that the fold is abutted to the seamline on the flat underply. The seam is then stitched very close to the fold. A second line of stitching may be placed parallel to the first to give a more finished appearance to the seam. Since it is done on the face of the garment, it is a fast construction technique. In designs involving points and corners, the lapped application can be very economical when compared to a square-set seam which would be the other alternative. The lapped seam is found on yokes, gussets, and godets, in particular, but may be used in any location where the seam is not enclosed and does not need to be pressed open or where several fabric layers would occur in the lapped portion; for example, a gathered or pleated garment section would not be used as the lapped portion of a lapped seam.

PLAIN SEAM

This is perhaps the most common type of seam made and is simply the face-to-face joining of two plies of fabric. The seam allowances may then be treated in a number of ways. The plain seam is often the first step in much more elaborate seam treatments. If used in garments that will be lined or in fabrics that do not ravel or roll, the plain seam can be left as it is sewn. Otherwise, it will require some type of seam finish to ensure durability and prevent raveling.

PRINCESS SEAM

This term is used to describe a seam in which an outward curve is joined to an inward curve. It most commonly occurs in the vertical seams of dresses, jackets, coats, and some blouses and shirts. In these garment applications, it may originate at the shoulder seam, where it produces a slight curve, or at the armscye, producing a much sharper curve. From the point of origin, it curves into a vertical line that usually continues to the garment hem. Exactly the same technique is used for applying inset bands or curved yokes. If the curve is very deep, the two plies must be handled very carefully to keep the raw edges aligned. Any fullness to be eased must be correctly located. The princess seam may replace darts and result in a shaped, three-dimensional garment section once it is sewn, or it may produce a flat garment section, in which the seam's purpose is essentially decorative. In either instance, the princess seam is more painstaking to construct than a straight seam. The deeper the curve, the more difficult the construction is. For this reason, the presence of a princess seam will increase total garment cost somewhat.

SLOT SEAM

The slot seam is a decorative seam in which two garment plies, with the seam allowances on each folded inward as for a lapped seam, are either abutted or placed slightly apart on an underlay to which they are then topstitched. The topstitching lines are parallel to the seamline and may be up to three-eighths inch (.96 cm) from the fold on each side. The underlay may be of matching or contrasting fabric. If the seam is

3-21. Lapped seam.

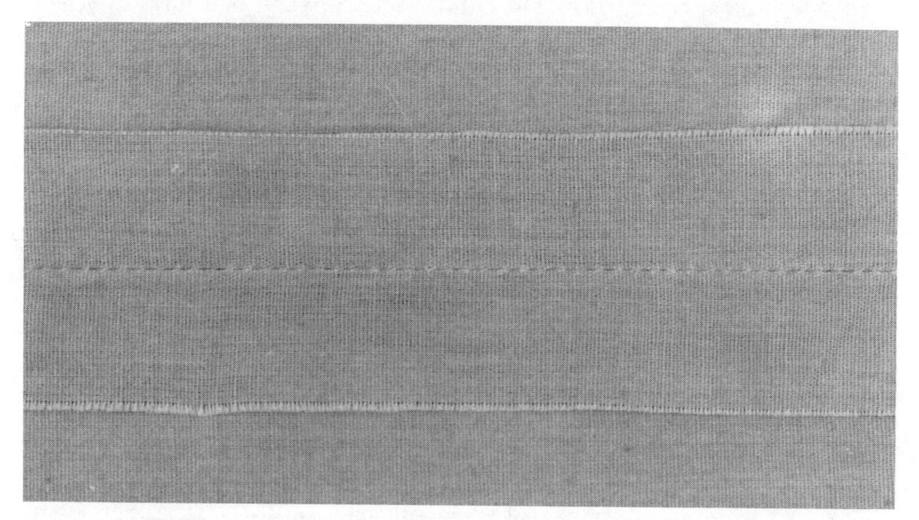

3-22. Plain seam.

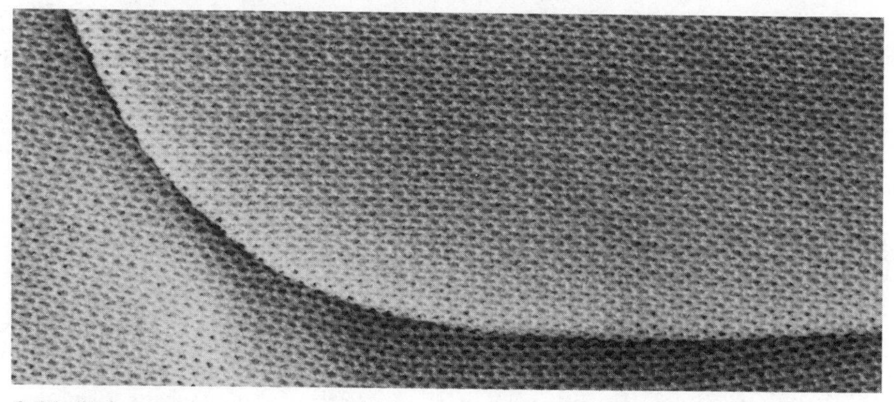

3-23. Princess seam.

curved, then the underlay must be cut with matching shape as the garment seam. It is found most commonly in the vertical seams of tailored skirts and in some yokes. It can add significantly to garment cost in both cutting and construction time.

SQUARE-SET SEAM

An inward and an outward corner are joined to produce the square-set seam. In a plain-seam type of join, the square-set seam requires very careful construction in order to keep the corner sharp and to avoid leaving a hole at the corner. The square-set seam can be found in yokes, placket ends, some sleeve-to-bodice joins, and even waist-to-bodice joins. The square-set seam can be used in styles or fabrics in which having the topstitching visible from a lapped application would be unacceptable. This is a costly seam most often found in higher priced garments.

STAYED SEAM

With the stayed seam, the seam allowances are pressed open, then spanned with a reinforcing strip of fabric (self-fabric or tape, ribbon, or similar products). Each seam allowance is then stitched to the reinforcing strip. The stitching does not penetrate the garment ply. The stayed seam adds support, strength, resistance to stretching, and protection to the skin if a scratchy fabric is used in the garment shell, in which case it may be found in any location of the garment. For the other purposes listed, it will be found more frequently in such areas as the curved underarm seams of bat-wing, dolman, or kimono sleeves, or at the shoulder seams of garments made from stretchy fabric.

STRAPPED SEAM

This is a seam in which the seam allowance on the face or inside of the garment is covered with a stitched-down reinforcing strip. The stitching penetrates both the strip and the garment, so its application is visible on the face of the garment even if the strip itself is applied to the wrong side. Straight strips of single knit fabric are most commonly used to strap seams on either the garment inside or outside. The inside strapped seam is frequently used for reinforcement on yoke, shoulder, and some side seams of light weight knit sports clothes and T-shirts. If the stitching is done in a contrast thread, it must be very carefully done or it will detract from the appearance of the garment. This is because it is done from the garment reverse, and in that location the machine operator has difficulty in aligning the two rows of stitching exactly over the

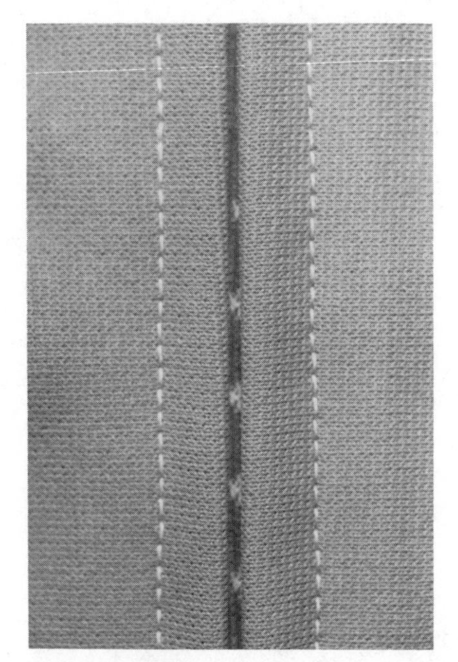

3-24. Slot seam.

3-25. Square-set seam.

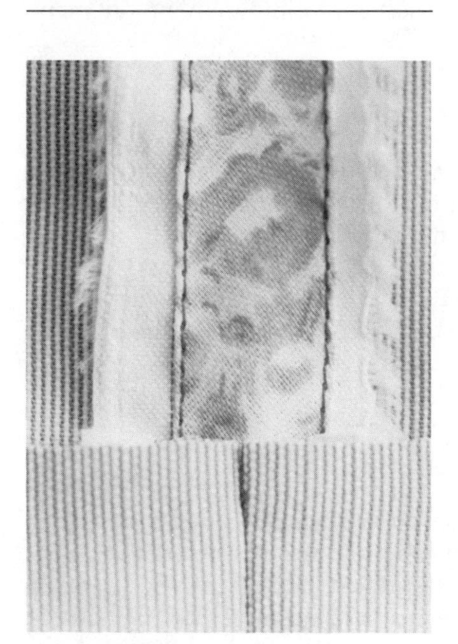

3-26. Stayed seam.

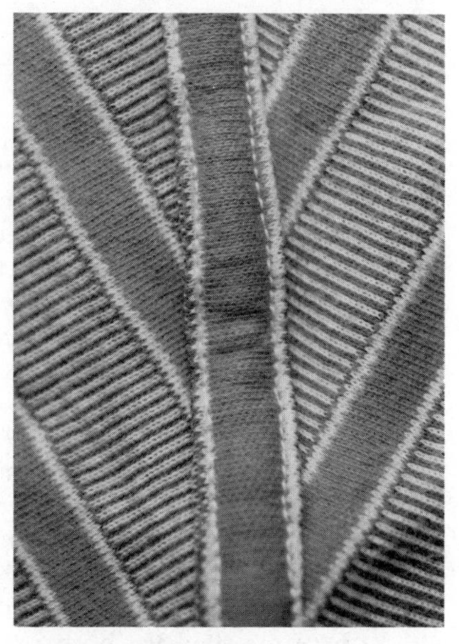

3-27. Strapped seam.

3-28. Taped seam at shoulder of knit garment.

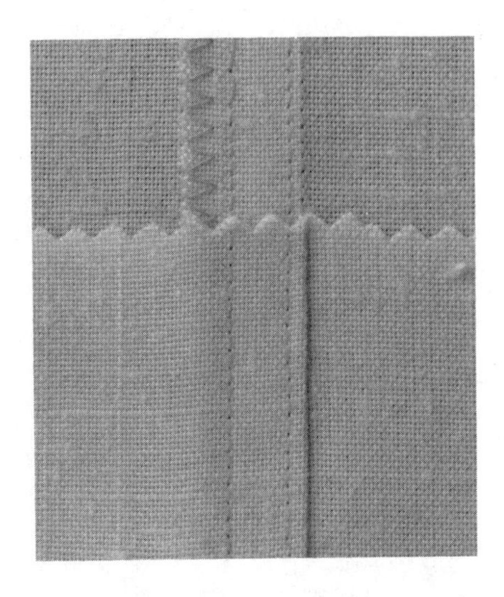

3-29. Topstitched seam.

seamline of the garment. The outside strapped seam is often used for decorative advantage on some garments such as jogging pants, athletic shorts, and sweat jackets. It is also used for reinforcement on men's briefs.

TAPED SEAM

This is also a reinforced seam requiring the use of a fabric strip or twill or ribbon tape, but in this case no additional stitching is required. The reinforcing strip is placed over the seamline and included in the stitching that forms the seam. Its main function is to strengthen and prevent stretching. It is most commonly found at shoulder seams, waistlines of fitted garments, some neckline seams, the crotch seam of men's slacks, and the armscyes of men's tailored jackets.

TOPSTITCHED SEAM

Although topstitching is essentially a decorative touch added to a regular seam, it may also serve the function of flattening seams in fabrics that do not press well. It is also used to emphasize seam and style lines. The seam may be pressed open and stitched parallel to the seam on both sides, catching both seam allowance and garment. It may also be used on seams that are both pressed to the same side, but not if the fabric is very thick and/or spongy.

TUCKED SEAM

This is a seam in which the edge of the uppermost ply is folded along the seamline, then placed exactly along the seamline on the underply. It is then topstiched one-fourth to one-half inch (.64 to 1.27 cm) from the folded edge. The procedure is exactly the same as for a lapped seam, but the stitching is placed further back from the fold. If two rows of stitching were used, one very close to the fold, then it would be referred to as a lapped seam. The tucked seam can be found on yokes, short sleeves with fake cuffs, front closures of shirts and blouses, and in other locations where it is used for decorative advantage. It may be used to disguise a seam in a garment with many vertical tucks.

WELT SEAM

The welt seam begins as a plain seam. One side of the seam allowance is trimmed, then both seam allowances are pressed to one side so that the narrower seam allowance is covered by the wider one. Topstitching is then done so that it penetrates the garment ply and the wider seam allowance. The trimmed inside seam allowance functions as a padding which gives a three dimensional effect to the finished seam, a design feature typical of heavy coats and jackets. If a second row of machine stitching is added very close to the original seamline, and on the right

3-30. Tucked seam.

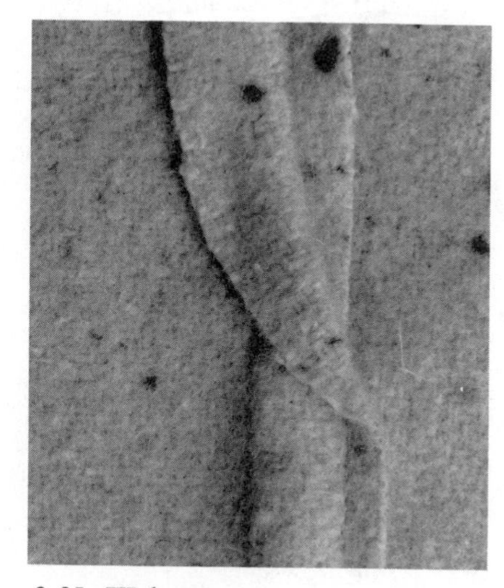

3-31. Welt seam.

side of the garment, it is called a double welt seam. It is used on sportswear made of heavy fabrics and as an accent for seam or style lines.

SEAMS IN SPECIAL FABRICS

Certain fabrics require special seaming techniques. Some of the specialty fabrics include knits, lace, leather, and pile fabrics. Each will be discussed individually, in alphabetical order.

KNITS

The choice of a seam type for a particular knit depends on the amount of stress on the seam and on the type of knit fabric involved. In most cases, these fabrics should be constructed to have some seam extendibility so that they will not break when the fabric is stretched. On the other hand, they must not be stretched so much during joining that the seamline ripples in the completed garment. Knits do not ravel and, therefore, do not require finishes to prevent raveling. Single knits do roll, however, and will need to be treated to prevent this from happening.

LACE

Although lace can be joined with a plain seam, expensive types of lace are more often seamed so that the individual motifs are not disrupted. This is done with a flat, lapped seam stitched by a machine zigzag or by a hand stitch (felling, whip, slip, or overhand) following the design

3-32. Seam in lace.

outline. This is a much more time-consuming method than a regular plain seam, and is reserved for expensive laces and garments, especially bridal wear.

In Figure 3-32, the lace has not been cut along design motifs, but the motifs have been carefully matched. If the motifs are not joined in a continuous pattern or are very large, cutting along motif outlines may not be feasible. In that case, a matched straight seam is acceptable.

LEATHER

Leather, suede, vinyl, and similar materials comprise a group of fabrics that show puncture marks from needles, resist easing or gathering, are somewhat stiff and bulky, and do not press well. Special wedge-shaped needles help in stitching many of these fabrics. Plain seams may be glued open to hold the seam allowances flat, or either lapped or abutted seams may be used instead. Other methods frequently used, depending on garment style, are lapped seams with lacing through punched holes, lapped seams with lacing through eyelets, lapped seams with cross-stitched lacing, or lapped seams with parallel lacing. Thin strips of leather or a similar material commonly are used to do the lacing.

PILE FABRICS

These fabrics may be short or long pile lengths, with sparse to dense coverage. They may have either a woven or a knitted structure. In most

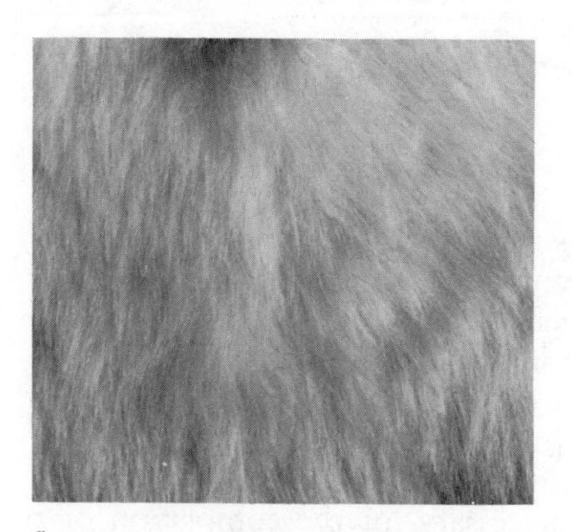

a.

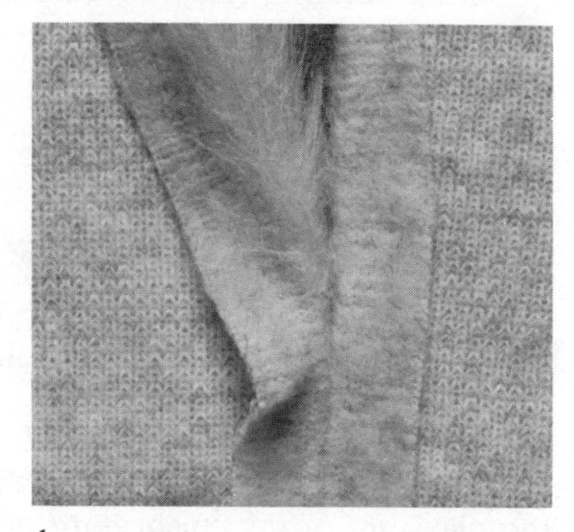

b.

3-33. Seam in pile: (a) right side; (b) wrong side.

cases, it is the pile and not the backing that requires special attention. In order not to distort the pile, seams in these fabrics should be stitched in the direction of the pile. If the pile is long and dense, it must be reduced to avoid bulk. The seam allowances can be shaved or clipped, or the seam can be trimmed very narrow and overedged. The pile should be pulled from the stitching prior to clipping or shaving so that none of the pile, which should be on the garment face, is trimmed away.

STANDARDS FOR EVALUATING SEAM TYPES

1. Seams should be perfectly even; that is, the stitching should be exactly the same distance from the seam edge for the entire length of the seam.
2. Seams should be stitched with the correct stitch length.
3. Seams should be smooth, with no puckers or pulls, and should lie flat.
4. The type of seam should be in accord with the type of fabric, the position of the seam, and the projected care of the garment.
5. The seam width should be in accord with the type of seam, seam finish, and garment design. Wider seam allowances require more fabric, which leads to greater cost.
6. Seams should be finished according to the dictates of the seam type, fabric, and projected garment care.

SEAM FINISHES

A seam finish is any technique that is used to make a seam look neater, to add strength to the seam, to prevent the seam allowance edges from raveling and/or fraying, and to prevent seam allowances from rolling, and to prevent stretching and rippling in some allowances. Exactly which, if any, of these reasons dictates the selection of a seam finish will depend primarily on the fabric used in the garment, with garment style, expected price line, and durability requirements also having a major impact on the decision. Seam finishes are not necessary for the completion of a garment, but they can add measurably to the appearance and to the life of a garment. Since some finishes do require extra labor, they frequently may increase the cost of the garment.

THREADLESS FINISHES

In this category are finishes that rely heavily on the cut edge of the garment itself to provide the best finish, but with the possibility of some other element, such as adhesive, added to achieve a flat look or to prevent raveling.

FUSED FINISH

The fused finish involves applying a heat-sensitive material to the seam allowance edges, then heat-setting the garment until the finishing material melts and forms a coating which will hold the cut edges of the seam allowance stable. The heat-sensitive material can be applied by spraying, or it can be rolled on. The seam allowances are not fused to the garment, but rather the yarns in the seam allowance are fused to each other. This is a very rapid means of achieving a non-raveling seam, but the fused area does change in hand, usually becoming stiffer, which may cause it to be noticeable in garments of soft, drapable fabrics. Its use has been restricted primarily to work clothes and jeans, but even in these applications, the fused edge may be stiff enough to be objectionable to many persons, especially in the upper inseam area.

GLUED SEAM FINISH

The glued seam finish requires that an adhesive be applied between the seam allowance and garment. The seam allowance is then adhered to the garment. This finish is used in many non-raveling fabrics, such as felt, pile, leather, suede, and vinyl. Its primary function is to hold the seam allowances flat, as the fabrics mentioned do not press well, if at all.

PINKED FINISH

The pinked finish is produced by a power machine equipped with a special disc to give a saw-toothed edge, or with pinking shears. This finish will not prevent raveling, although it will impede it somewhat. It should be used only on fabrics that do not fray easily.

PLAIN FINISH

This occurs when a plain seam is left untreated. It is frequently found on inexpensive garments, where the application of a regular finish would have increased construction costs beyond what was acceptable to the manufacturer. The plain finish may even occur on fabrics that ravel easily and that are used in expensive garments if the recommended care is dry cleaning. It is particularly effective on bonded fabrics and on other fabrics that do not ravel easily and on garments that will be fully lined.

THREAD-FINISHED SEAMS

Finishes that require the use of stitching to create the desired effect are included in this section. Thread may be used to cover the edge entirely, to stabilize a portion of it, or to secure a folded or rolled seam allowance in place. This section includes some of the quickest and most effective seam finishes, which are also some of the most commonly found in ready-to-wear apparel.

BOOK FINISH

With the book finish, the raw edge of each seam allowance is folded under and secured to the seam allowance ply by a concealed blind stitch. The blind stitch may be made with thermoplastic thread which will then bond the seam allowances to the garment when heat treated. The book finish is used on garments that will take hard wear. It may be found on the seams of trousers and on unlined jackets and coats.

BOUND FINISH

The single-ply bound finish is constructed by covering the raw edges of each seam ply with a folded ribbon tape or bias binding. Binding is especially good for finishing seams of unlined jackets or coats. It may

3-34. Book finish.

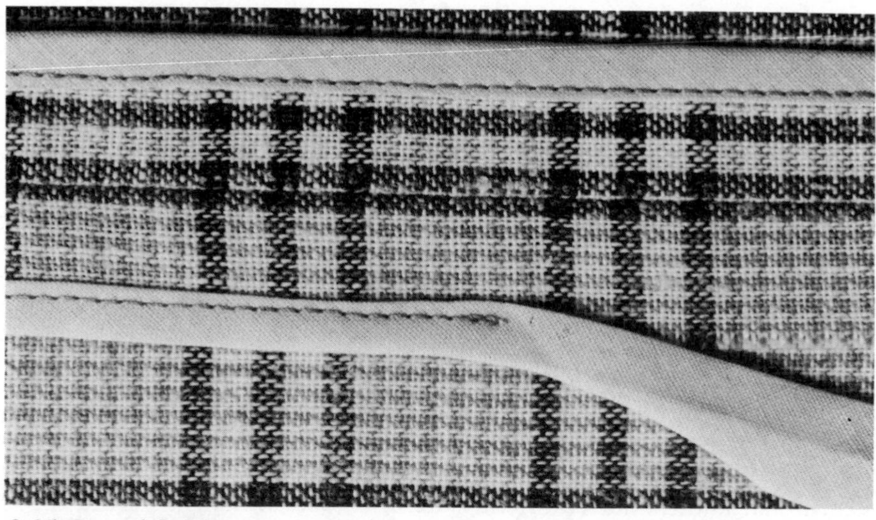

3-35. Bound finish.

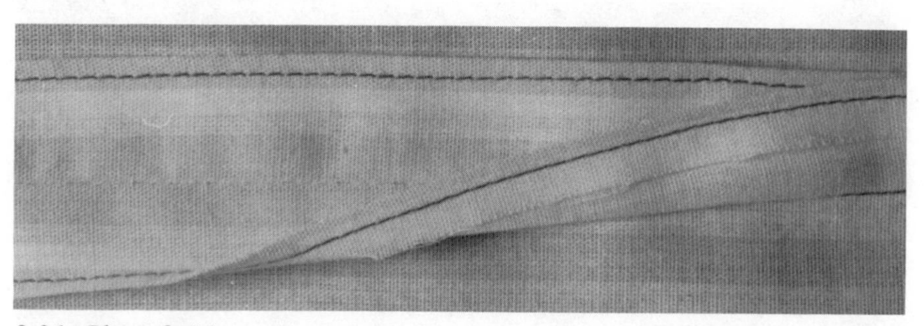

3-36. Clean finish.

be used on fabrics that will irritate the skin or on fabrics that are too thick to be turned under and edge stitched. It adds one ply additional bulk beyond what would occur with the Hong Kong finish.

CLEAN FINISH

Each edge of the seam allowance is turned under and stitched for this type of finish, using a folder attachment to the sewing machine in industrial applications. In home sewing, it is known as a clean finish. It is a neat finish for medium and light weight fabrics, but it is not very effective against raveling. In smooth-finished fabrics the ridges which result from pressing the turned-under edges of the seam allowances against the garment may be unsightly. Straight-edged seams are more easily finished by this method than are curved ones, but they will also continue to ravel up to the stitching line if the fabric tends to ravel badly. This method has little advantage over other, less costly, finishes.

DOUBLE-STITCHED FINISH

The double-stitched finish is made on a plain seam by placing a second row of stitching one-fourth inch (.64 cm) from the first and through both plies of the seam allowance. It is used to reinforce a plain seam when additional finishes are not needed. It may be found on sheer and transparent fabrics and laces. Knits, jerseys, and tricot fabrics are finished in this manner in order to prevent the seam edges from curling. Usually an additional treatment, such as those shown in Figure 3-37,

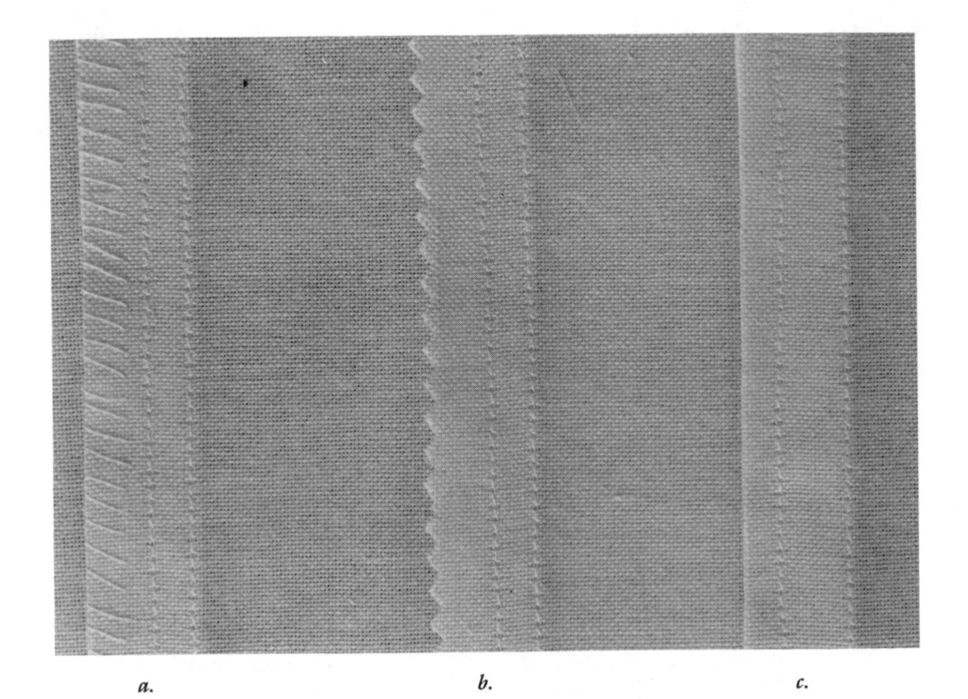

a. *b.* *c.*

3-37. Double-stitched finish: (a) overcast; (b) pinked; (c) trimmed.

a.

b.

3-38. Hong Kong finish: (a) right side of seam allowances; (b) close-up of seam allowance underside.

will be used. These treatments may include overcasting, pinking, or trimming.

HONG KONG FINISH

In this treatment, each seam allowance ply is covered with a bias strip of fabric, only one edge of which is folded under. This finish has slightly less bulk than a regular bias bound application where both raw edges of the binding are turned under. It is constructed in two steps, and thus consumes more work time.

The Hong Kong finish is used frequently in men's jackets where a full lining is not present. For a partially lined jacket, the lining fabric will be cut to make the strips that will be used to finish the seams and also the hem edge and front facing edge. This is a very decorative finish for a seam and adds considerable value when the garment is one which will be worn open or taken off frequently so that the inside construction will be exposed.

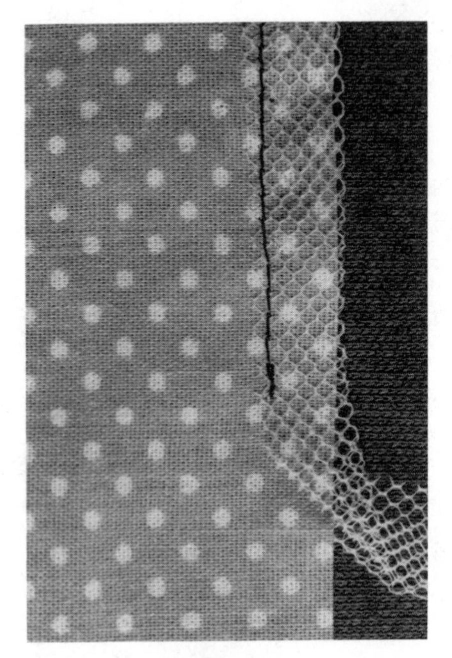

3-39. Net-bound finish.

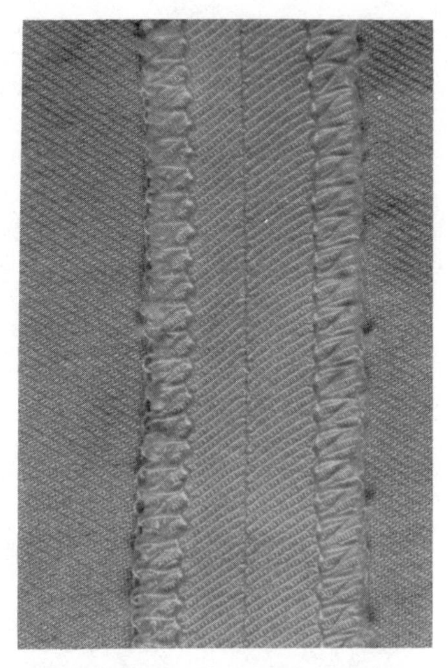

3-40. Overedge finish (single ply).

NET-BOUND FINISH

This finish is made by encasing the raw edge of each seam allowance within a folded net strip. It is an inconspicuous finish that is appropriate for delicate and sheer fabrics such as velvet, chiffon, or lace. It is used on the raw edges of metallic fabrics which can irritate the skin and for edges where other bindings would add bulk. It is used often in lingerie.

OVERCAST FINISH

The overcast finish is made with a series of loose, slanting hand stitches placed to encircle the raw edge of each seam allowance. Hand overcasting may be used in conjunction with a plain seam, a double-stitched seam, a pinked seam, or a stitched and pinked seam. It is used on medium-weight fabrics where a soft, pliable treatment is desired. The overcast can be worked on single plies of the seam allowance or on both plies together. In the double-ply version, both edges of the seam allowance are joined together and covered with a series of loose, slanting hand stitches. The double-ply overcast finish is sometimes found in home sewing and in designer and boutique garments. As with all double-ply finishes, it is not appropriate for very thick or bulky fabrics.

OVEREDGE FINISH

Similar in uses to the overcast finish, this is the machine-sewn alternative. It is the most common single-ply finish used in ready-to-wear. Special sewing machines apply the finish, which is essentialy an edge covering.

SELF-BOUND FINISH (ROLLED)

The self-bound finish is made by folding or rolling one seam allowance ply over and, thereby,enclosing the other, trimmed, ply with a hand or machine stitch. It is used on sheer or transparent fabrics or when a strong, sturdy seam is needed. A folder may be attached to commercial sewing machines to aid in making this finish faster and more accurate than it would be otherwise.

SERGED OR MERROWED FINISH

This is a machine finish that covers both flat, raw seam edges with a series of interlocking loop stitches. It is one of the most common seam finishes and is found on almost all styles and price ranges of apparel.

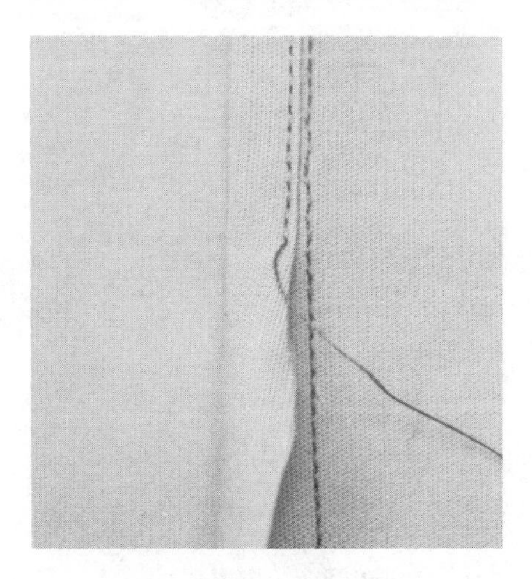

3-41. Self-bound finish.

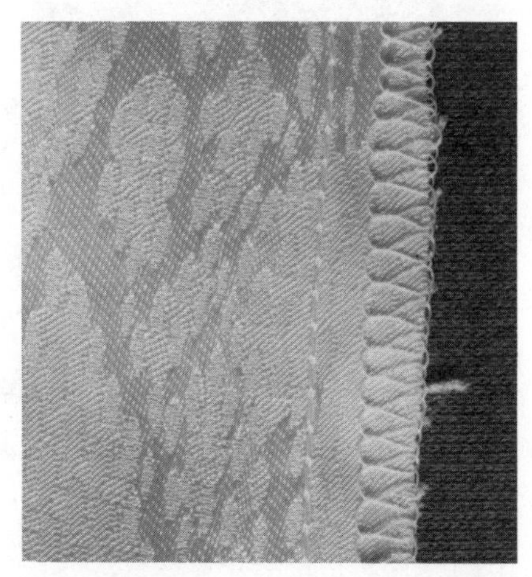

3-42. Serged or Merrowed finish (double ply).

Serging machines automatically trim the seam allowances and apply the stitched edging, using three to five threads. This leads to very little expense compared to some of the other finishes.

STITCHED AND PINKED FINISH

The stitched and pinked finish is made by sewing a line of machine stitching one-fourth inch (.64 cm) from the cut edge of the seam allowance, and then trimming the edge with pinking shears. The finish is useful on fabrics that ravel slightly and on fabric seams that tend to curl.

ZIGZAGGED FINISH

This is a common finish in home sewing utilizing a 300 series machine. It may be worked on single or double plies of seam allowance. This finish is identical in uses and characteristics to the single-ply overedge finish, but the stitch formation is somewhat different. Home sewing machines can form a zigzag stitch, not an overedge stitch, so this is the most common seam finish used in home sewing. It is a very fast, simple, and effective means of securing a cut edge from raveling. If this finish

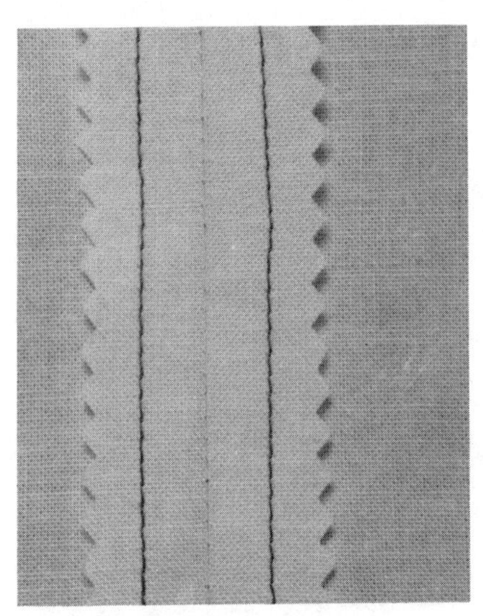

3-43. Stitched and pinked finish.

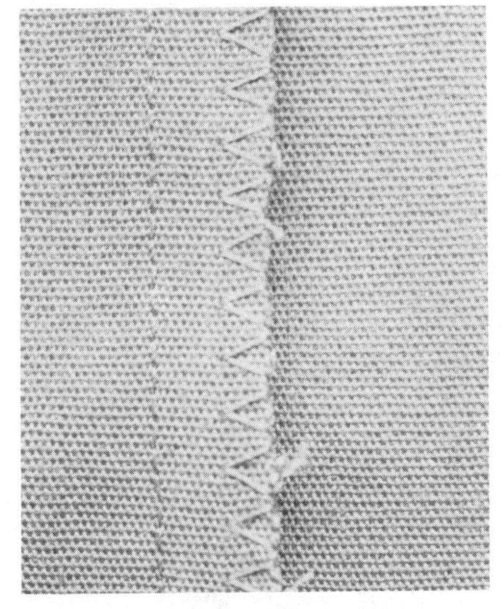

3-44. Zigzagged finish.

is used in a light or medium weight fabric, both plies of the seam allowance may be treated together (double-ply zigzagged finish). In the latter case, both raw edges of the seam allowances are brought together and covered with a series of alternately angled machine stitches. The double-ply zigzagged finish is an alternative to overedging when an overedge machine is not available.

STANDARDS FOR EVALUATING SEAM FINISHES

1. The finish selected should prevent the fabric from raveling, rolling, or stretching and should contribute to the overall neatness of the garment.
2. The finish should not add bulk to the seam.
3. The finish should be applied securely so that it remains in place during normal wear and care.
4. The seam finish should be appropriate to the garment fabric, to the garment design, and to the intended use of the garment.

SUMMARY

Shaping devices form the foundation for the entire garment. If they are poorly selected or shoddily constructed, the entire garment will suffer. None of the subsequent techniques used to structure the garment can be judged independently of the type of seams used to form them. The initial appearance of a garment, its durability, its comfort, its potential for alteration, and its silhouette all depend on the seam types and seam finishes selected for structuring the garment.

4

UNDERLYING FABRICS

Although hidden from view, the underlying fabrics used in a garment play an important role in its finished appearance. They contribute to the garment's longevity, its hand, and its production costs. These underlying shapers include *underlining, interfacing, interlining,* and *lining*. Each of these has a specific function influencing the quality of the completed apparel item.

Linings and interlinings are usually considered "extras" added to more expensive or special-function clothing. Interfacings and underlinings play a more vital role in the shape and look of the garment. This is not to imply that interfacings and underlinings are always necessary to a quality garment, but they do perform shaping and body tasks necessary to maintain adequately some design lines. Within the industry, this whole category of materials is commonly referred to as interlinings.

UNDERLININGS

An underlining is a lightweight fabric cut to duplicate a garment section, applied to the wrong side of the garment fabric and handled as one ply during the construction of the garment. If all four underlying fabrics were present in the same item of apparel, the underlining would be first in order of application. Since it is handled as one with the garment section, underlining adds to the cost of the finished garment mainly because of the additional fabric used, which is usually less expensive than the garment fabric itself.

The primary purpose of underlining is to give additional strength, support and durability to the outer fabric. Underlining can also be used to provide an invisible attachment for hems, support fabrics, and facing edges, a use more typical of home sewing, couture and boutique construction methods than of ready to wear. Underlinings may be used to change the draping quality of the garment fabric or to lend opacity to sheer or lightweight fabrics. Loosely woven outer fabrics may be underlined to prevent stretching or sagging. Since underlining serves to reinforce seams and other construction details, it may be used in any clothing that requires rough wear.

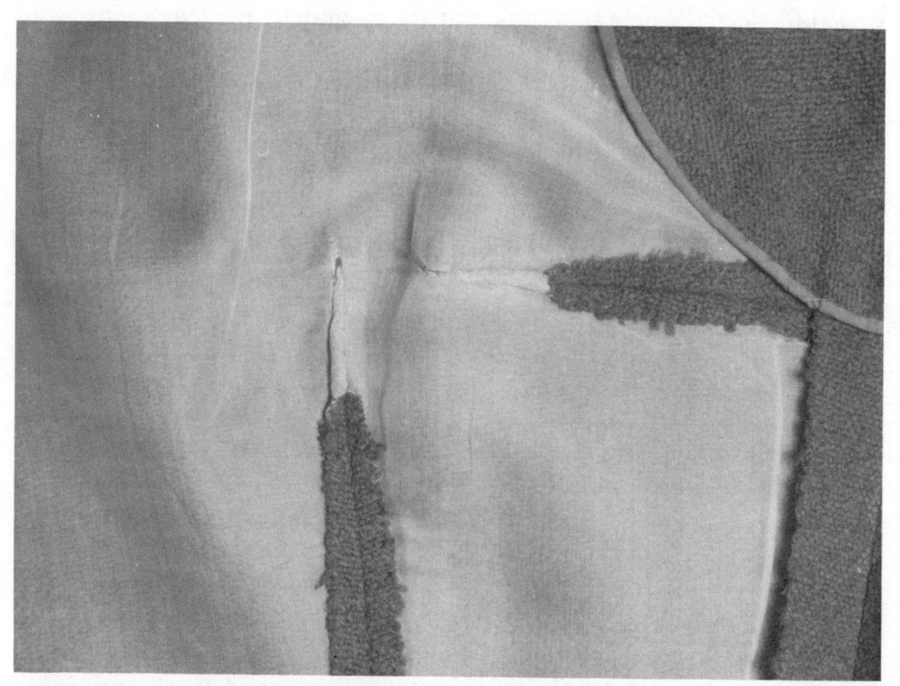

4-1. From wrong side, underlined garment showing trimmed darts and facing with Hong Kong finish (upper right corner).

A wide variety of fabric types may be used for underlining. It may be crisper than, softer than, or comparable to the garment fabric, depending on the purpose it is to serve and the fashion silhouette desired. More than one type of underlining may sometimes be desired. An example is a dress that requires support or crispness in the bodice and more softness in the skirt. Another major requirement in the selection of underlining is that the color and care requirements be compatible with that of the garment fabric. Commercial products manufactured as underlinings are most often used in the industry, although other fabrics such as organdy, batiste, organza, China silk, muslin and lightweight tricot may be used as well. The commercial underlinings come in a variety of colors, fiber blends, and degrees of crispness.

The procedure for underlining a garment is quite simple. As stated earlier, the increased cost of an underlined garment is attributed primarily to the extra fabric required. The underlining is cut from the same pattern as the fabric. In most cases, the two layers of fabric are then treated as though they were one layer throughout the construction phases of the garment. The underlining layer serves to reinforce all construction details, such as seams and darts, and to prevent them from showing through to the outside of the garment.

Another method of underlining is somewhat more expensive, but may be necessary when a bulky fabric is used. With this method, the garment and underlining fabrics are handled separately from the beginning of production through the construction of darts (or tucks for pleats). Then, from this point on, the two fabrics are handled as one. The underlining serves to reinforce the seams and to prevent them from showing from the outside.

STANDARDS FOR EVALUATING UNDERLININGS

1. Fashion fabric and underlining fabric relate well—the garment is neither over-supported nor under-supported for the desired design effect.
2. Garment fabric and underlining fabric are compatible as to color, care requirements, and longevity.
3. The two layers of fabric should fit smoothly and evenly with no pulls or tucks.

INTERFACING

An interfacing is a special type of fabric applied between the facing and outer fabric of a garment to give it body and shape. In an underlined garment, the interfacing is applied after the underlining. Interfacing usually is applied only in those areas where extra body and support are needed. It is used in necklines, sleeveless armholes, and lapped closures to maintain shape and prevent stretching. Interfacing is usually needed to give support in collars, lapels, cuffs, and pocket flaps. It may also be used to reinforce button and buttonhole areas, to add body to hemlines, to prevent seam impressions, and to add firmness to waistbands and belts. Because maintenance of shape is so important in tailored suits and coats, the amount and variety of interfacing used is greater than that found in other types of apparel.

Many varieties and weights of interfacing are available on the market today. This number will continue to expand to meet the demands of new fabrics as they are marketed and the technological advances which will speed production, and improve quality and performance of fabrics. Although neutral-colored (white, gray, black) interfacings are most often used, some companies offer a range of color choices. There is also variety in fiber content, weight, fabrication method, and coating. If optimal results are to be achieved in the garment, it is imperative that the correct interfacing be selected according to the end use.

The selection of the appropriate interfacing to be used in a garment depends on the fiber content of the garment fabric, the weight of the garment fabric, the area in which it is to be used, and the amount of support or stiffness desired in the selected style. Within the same garment, several different types of interfacings may be used. For example, the body of a garment may be supported by a lightweight interfacing while the front opening requires a medium-weight selection. One style may demand a crisp, sharp collar and another may require a soft, rolled collar.

Even though the fabrication of an interfacing may differ from that of the garment fabric, the weight of the interfacing should be compatible with that of the garment fabric and yet not overpower it. The interfacing should not be heavier than the garment fabric, although it may be crisper.

As with many aspects of thread selection, the selection of interfacing is critical to the performance of the finished apparel item but often eludes inspection or analysis by the apparel buyer or shopper. The manufacturer must rely upon accurate information from the interfacing supplier, upon skilled matching of that information with the dictates of the garment style and fabric, and upon testing of sample composites prior to final selection and manufacturing. Those apparel manufacturers with in-house testing facilities may wash or dry clean several possible combinations of shell and interfacing fabrics through a number of cycles to predict ultimate performance accurately.

METHODS OF FABRICATION

As the fabrication method of the interfacing varies, so do its properties. There are three major fabrication methods: *woven, fiberweb,* and *knitted.*

WOVEN

Woven interfacings offer several advantages: strength, stability, and good drape and hand. Because wovens do shape better than nonwovens, in most cases, they are especially effective in tailored clothing. In addition to fabrics made specifically for interfacing purposes, self fabric can be used as can organdy and organza. Wigan and hair canvas are considered excellent choices for wool and wool-like fabrics. Wigan is used when less body is needed such as in sleeve hems and back shoulder areas. Hair canvas is used in the collar, lapel, front area, and other places where more body is usually required to hold the garment shape.

Woven interfacings are usually cut on the straight grain of the fabric; consequently, they require more yardage and perhaps more layout time—particularly if done manually. Woven interfacings will require finishing to prevent raveling or fraying unless all raw edges are completely secured within the finished garment. Occasionally, wovens may be cut on the bias in order to conform to subtle curves, for example in hems. Once the woven interfacing is attached to the garment, there is little give regardless of type.

FIBERWEB

Fiberweb is a nonwoven interfacing made by fusing fibers together with heat. Because it has not been formed by interlacing yarns, it usually has no grain and does not ravel, and may be cut in any direction. There is a small cost-saving advantage to the apparel manufacturer.

Even though there is no construction grain, the fiberweb may have orientation. The way in which the fibers are deposited can introduce directional elements—random deposits for all bias, lengthwise and/or crosswise orientation to give the characteristics of grain. When orientation is present, interfacings should be cut as if they had a grain. Interfacings with crosswise orientation are important for use in knitted fabrics since crosswise stretch is an important characteristics of those fabrics. Crosswise give may be a disadvantage in buttonhole area, however, where maximum stability is needed to prevent stretching during use.

This category of interfacing offers stability with softness and serves well as fusibles. Fiberweb does not drape very well, however, and is not as effective as bias-cut wovens for garment areas that must roll or fold smoothly (in rolled collars, for example).

In Figure 4-2, two strips of interfacing were cut on the diagonal of the full width of fabric, creating a true bias cut in the woven fabric (uppermost) and the equivalent in the fiber web (lower). Both strips were folded in the middle and pinned together at the raw edges. The strips were then placed in a curve roughly approximating the neckline area of a blouse or shirt. The difference in smoothness of roll is apparent.

Weights of fiber web vary from the transparent shears to polyester fleece which can provide a quilted effect with minimal cost to the manufacturer. Thin, soft fiberweb often pills so badly that it disentegrates over time when used in loose facings where laundering can expose it to abrasion.

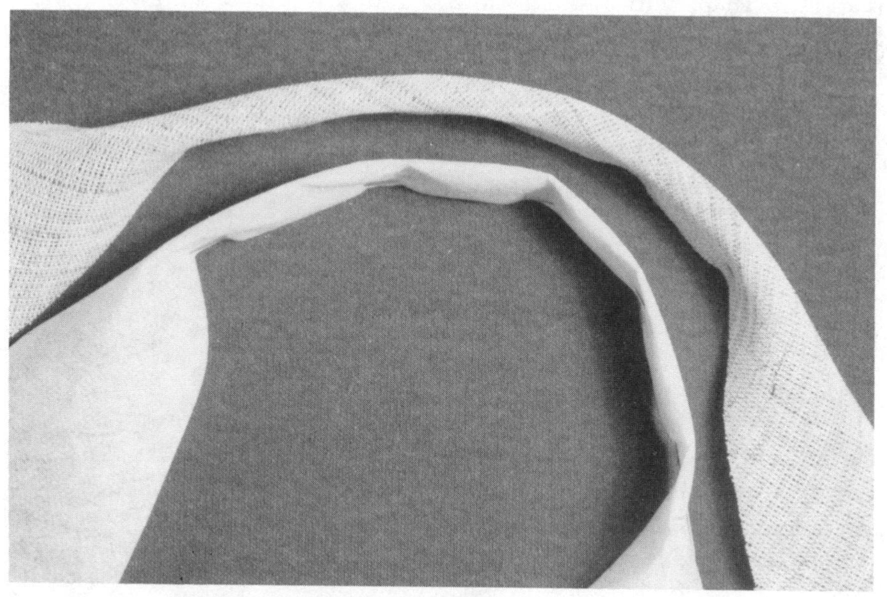

4-2. Rolling characteristics of woven (uppermost) and fiberweb interfacings.

KNITTED

The third category of interfacing, knitted, is much less common than the types already discussed but has made significant inroads in, bodywear/intimate apparel lines. Warp knit tricot and weft insertion, a variation of the warp knit structure with weft yarns inserted to provide cross-directional stability, are the two most common fabric types within this category. The knitted interfacing is usually light in weight and adds stability without eliminating stretchability. It offers a soft hand with drape and roll. Edges must be serged to the facing to prevent curling. Press-on varieties are available, but the addition of the adhesive does stiffen the fabric hand. Some areas of application are in knitted swimsuits, foundation garments, and lingerie.

METHODS OF ATTACHMENT

There are several methods of applying interfacing to a garment: *fused, in-seam application, hand application,* and *strip-sewn*. The one selected is dependent on the price range, the type of garment, and the type and weight of interfacing to be applied.

Although much of the following discussion relates to the application of interfacing to garment pieces, some of the same methods of application, perhaps with modification, are used to create composite structures of interfacing which are subsequently applied to the garment. Fusing

4-3. Chest piece of man's suit showing taped lapel roll line (center top) and taped lapel/facing seamline (left vertical).

and hand or machine pad-stitching are the two methods of application which are most frequently used to secure layers of interfacing materials prior to their application to the garment. The chest pieces in men's suits and sport coats are examples of these composite structures.

FUSED

One of the most popular interfacings on the market today is the fusible. It has an adhesive backing, is available in both woven and nonwoven fabrications, and is adhered to the fashion fabric under the heat and pressure of an iron or press rather than by stitching. Because of its effectiveness and the speed with which it can be applied, it has become a popular choice in all categories of garment manufacturing. The major drawback to fused interfacings is the lack of identical reaction to laundering and dry cleaning which the apparel fabric and the fused interfacing have.

If either shrinks only slightly more than the other, blistering of the larger fabric surface results and is unsightly. If the interfacing shrinks substantially more than the apparel fabric, then the interfaced garment area takes on a blistered or "balloon" effect.

Fusible interfacing should be applied to the facing rather than to the garment in order to prevent the fixative from showing through to the outside. In some fabrics, application of the interfacing to the facing does not provide enough body to the upper garment (collar, cuff, front facing), and it totally eliminates the function of interfacing to prevent seam impressions. Because the adhesive adds extra body, it is important

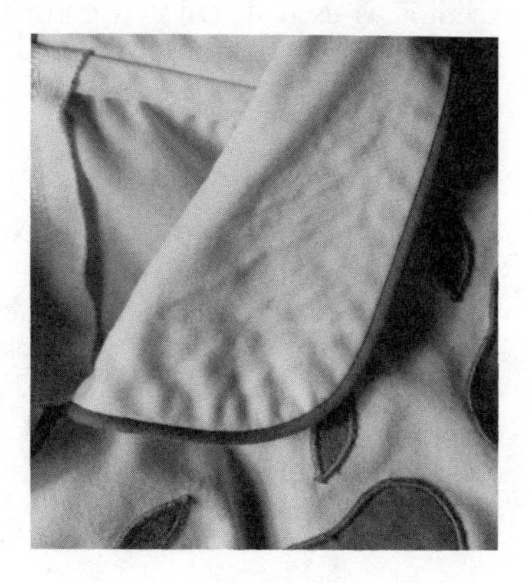

4-4. Fused interfacing in collar showing blisters after unequal shrinkage in laundering.

that the interfacing not be too rigid for the shell fabric. Emphasis on research in developing new interlining products and applications—particularly interfacings—has introduced a broad range of fusible fabrics for use by apparel manufacturers.

IN-SEAM APPLICATION

Light- to medium-weight, nonfusible interfacing is applied by the in-seam method on fashion fabrics of similar weight. The interfacing pieces are joined by a lapped or abutted seam, placed on the wrong side of the garment, and stitched into the garment seam during garment construction. Even though the unit application is easier, the parts of the garment may be interfaced separately, then joined as interfaced garment pieces. In couture and home sewing, the interfacing is trimmed from the seam allowance to avoid excess bulk. In commercial apparel production, the interfacing is trimmed only as the seam is trimmed; therefore, the weight of the interfacing is an extremely important selection factor. Heavy interfacing left untrimmed can add undesirable bulk.

HAND APPLICATION

The heavier and more rigid interfacing fabrics, which are most often used in coats and jackets, may require more work than those of light- or medium-weight which can be stitched into the garment seams. One method of avoiding bulk is accomplished by trimming away the interfacing seam allowance and applying the raw edges to the garment seam allowance with a hand catch stitch, a process shown in Figure 4-5. This method is used in tailored garments produced at home or in couture and in a very few lines of tailored, and expensive, men's suits.

STRIP-SEWN

The strip-sewn method, like the hand-sewn application, is seldom used in commercial apparel production, but is practiced in couture and in apparel constructed at home. As shown in Figure 4-6 this application method requires that the seam allowance of the interfacing be trimmed away and then replaced with strips of lightweight fabric which, in turn, are sewn into the garment seams. The strips may be of any lightweight stable fabric such as organza or lawn. This method eliminates hand work and is used for those interfacings that may ravel during handling or laundering and that are too heavy to be sewn into the seams.

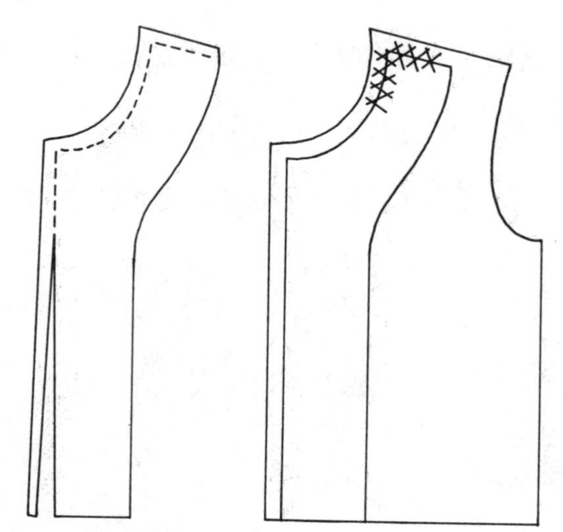

4-5. Hand application of interfacing.

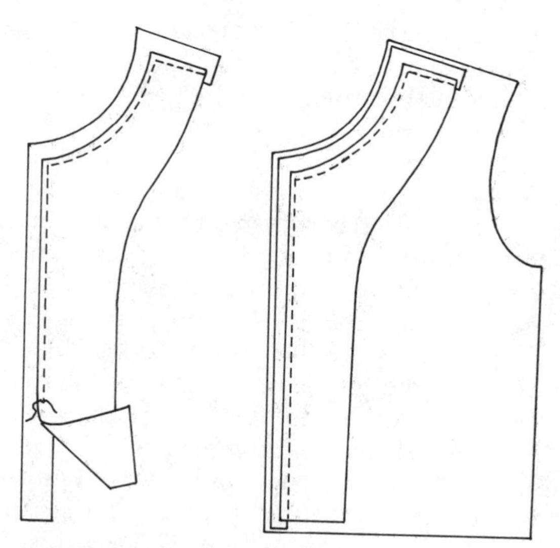

4-6. Strip-sewn application of interfacing.

STANDARDS FOR EVALUATING INTERFACINGS

1. The interfacing complements and reinforces the garment fabric without overpowering it.
2. Care requirements of the interfacing are compatible with those of the garment fabric.
3. Heavy interfacings are not caught in seams.
4. The interfacing does not show through to the right side of the garment.
5. Woven interfacings and nonwoven oriented interfacings are cut on the same grain as the garment areas to be interfaced.
6. Interfacing is used in any areas requiring shape, body, support, and reinforcement, and where seam impressions may be a problem.

INTERLININGS

An interlining is an underlying fabric placed between the outer fabric and the lining of the garment in order to enhance the warmth of the garment. This function requires that the interlining be made of a fabric with insulating qualities. Some common examples are lamb's wool, nonwoven polyester fleece, felt, flannel, and thin blanket fabrics. The fabric must be lightweight and not add undue bulk to the garment. Even though interlined garments are usually dry-cleaned, the care requirements of the interlining should match those of the garment.

The interlining may be applied to the garment in one of two ways: either to the lining in a way similar to the underlining method discussed earlier, or constructed and basted to the garment inside the armhole seams and catch-stitched to the facing edges around the neck and front. The former is more common in the apparel industry, and the latter in couture or in garments constructed at home.

Because the interlining serves no purpose other than that of offering additional warmth to the garment, it is usually found only in more expensive clothing and clothing to be worn in very cold climates. There are less expensive alternatives to interlining which will serve the same function, and many of these are commonly in use. Quilted or pile fabric linings provide the same insulating qualities as a separate interlining, but with fewer cutting and construction requirements. Quilted fabrics in the shell, often filled with down or fiberfill, provide another alternative to interlining for insulation.

STANDARDS FOR EVALUATING INTERLININGS

1. Interlinings are of lightweight fabric with insulating properties.
2. Interlinings do not add excessive dimensions to the garment.
3. The interlining's care requirements match those of the rest of the garment.
4. The interlined garment has adequate wearing ease to accommodate the added thickness.

LININGS

A lining is a unit assembled in the same or similar silhouette as the garment or a portion of the garment. It is applied to the inside of the garment to finish it and to hide the inner construction of the garment. Whether used in a dress, coat, jacket, or pants, the lining serves to give the garment a comfortable, luxurious feeling as well as a functional finishing touch. A lining prolongs the life of a garment by covering the inner construction details and by protecting the fashion fabric from abrasion during wear. In addition, the lining prevents stretching, which can be particularly important in pants and skirts made of loosely woven fabrics; helps to preserve the shape of the garment; reduces wrinkling; and lends ease in slipping the garment on and off.

SELECTION OF LINING FABRIC

Linings may be made of any number of different fabrics. But several considerations should be kept in mind. First of all, the care requirements should be similar to that of the remainder of the garment. And the qualities of the lining should be appropriate to the type of garment in which it is used. For example, a coat lining should add warmth to the garment. A jacket lining must stand up under much more strain and abrasion than that of a loosely fitted dress. A closely fitted skirt might require a stronger lining (more likely woven) than that of a fuller style.

A lining fabric must also be sufficiently opaque to hide the inner construction of the garment. Generally, the lining is lighter in weight than the garment fabric; but it must be heavy enough to conceal ridges formed by the inner construction. It should be smooth enough to enable the wearer to easily slide the garment on and off, and it must be static free so that it does not cling to the garment fabric or to undergarments.

The lining in a garment may match or contrast in color with the fashion fabric and may even be a printed fabric as long as it does not show through to the outer sides.

TYPES OF LINING

Whether or not the lining is partial or full further heightens the cost differential of different lining fabrics. A garment may be partially lined, as in the seat of a skirt or trousers, knees of slacks or trousers, or the shoulder area of a jacket, or it may be fully lined. The amount of lining fabric and the extent of additional labor required for the two types usually mean a substantial cost differential.

PARTIAL LININGS

Lining may be used only in selected garment areas to prevent stretching and sagging. Slacks may have a partial lining in the back only, extending down to slightly below the crotch line. Such a lining would protect the seat area from stretching during wear. Pleated skirts may have a partial lining that comes below the seat area and serves to keep the pleats from being distorted during wear. In jackets, partial linings usually extend over the shoulder area for stability, cover the underarm area to protect the garment fabric from perspiration, and completely cover the inside front panels to give the appearance of a fully lined garment and to cover interfacing shells used in tailored jackets. These partially lined garments still have the functional benefit of a lining, but without the added cost a fully lined garment would require.

FULL LININGS

Full linings can be further subdivided according to whether they extend entirely to the edge of the garment on all sides or whether they are seamed to a facing and/or hem. The garment which is *lined to the edge* will have only one set of pattern pieces, as both lining and garment will be identical or almost identical. Identical cuts cause the lining to roll outward at the garment edges or else wrinkle inside when pressed. This happens because as all seams are pressed toward the inside of the garment, the outermost side loses some of its original dimension in turning the curves. The phenomenon is the same as what occurs when you fold a thick magazine; the outermost pages no longer end at the same place as those on the other side. In couture and home sewing, slight adjustments when cutting or stitching can effectively counter this problem, but in ready-to-wear, no such adjustment is likely. The garment section is constructed into a complete unit; the linings are constructed into a complete, separate unit. Then the two are placed right sides together and the edges stitched with the exception of an opening for turning. This method is usually restricted to such items as vests, pockets, jumper and sundress tops, playsuit tops, short jackets such as boleros (sleeve edges would have to be attached later), swimsuit tops, and some lingerie tops. Sleeveless items such as vests and jumper bodices which will have the armscyes closed must have the shoulder or underarm seams left open until the garment has been turned. Otherwise it is impossible to turn the units right side out. Apparel manufacturers usually topstitch the edges as a final step to keep the lining invisible at the garment edges.

The other main type of lining is the one which is *applied to the garment facing*. Such linings are not cut by the same pattern as the garment itself. Less lining fabric is needed for this type than for the lined-to-the-edge type, but more apparel fabric is used in cutting the facings and deep hems.

When the lining is applied to a facing and hem of a jacket or coat, an opening is left in the upper underarm seam of the lining sleeve or else the bottom edge is usually left open for turning. In jackets the

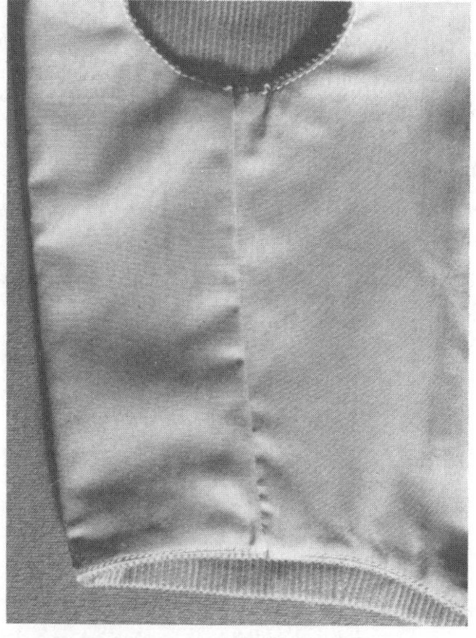

4-7. Garment lined to the edge shown from the inside of the garment.

4-8. Lining band stitched to garment facing and hem band.

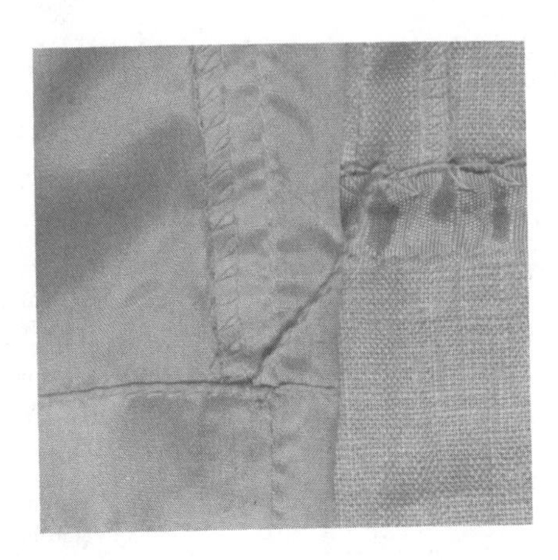

4-9. Swing-tack securing full lining to skirt at hemline.

lining is usually attached at all free edges, with an ease pleat allowed at the hem and sleeve hems. In Figure 4-8, the lining has been applied to the garment facing and bias band hemline by hand blind stitching, a technique rarely seen outside of designer garments (as is the case here) and home sewing. Coat linings, especially when an interlining is present, are often free-hanging. That is, the hem of the coat is stitched, then the hem of the lining is stitched, and the two hems are then attached at seamlines by use of swing-tacks. Swing-tacks are pictured in Figure 4-9 at the hemline of a fully lined linen skirt. They may be made of thread stitching or small lengths of twill tape of similar material. They keep the lining in place during wear but have some leeway for shifting when the lining and garment are not exactly the same size.

One variation of the free-hanging lining is found in all-weather coats. In many of these the lining is attached to a zipper which runs from the hem edge on one side of the garment front up the front edge, around the neckline, and down the other front edge to the hem. In application, one side of the zipper tape is applied to the garment facing; the other side of the tape is applied to the lining edge. The cost of the zipper is additional, but the application method itself is inexpensive and simple. Swing tacks will not be used on this type of free-hanging lining. The zip-out lining is much more versatile for the consumer than a garment with insulation built in.

The lining for a tailored jacket or coat usually contains a vertical pleat down the back, in addition to the horizontal ease folds at the bottom of the sleeve and at the hem of the garment. Pleats or released darts at the shoulders, bust, chest, and elbows provide additional ease at body bulges in better quality garments. This ease allows for body movement without excessive strain and also allows for slight irregularities in the sizes of the lining and apparel units. The depth of the ease pleats varies from virtually nonexistent to very deep. Obviously the amount of fabric consumed by this ease will add to garment cost, so there is a corresponding increase in cost according to how much additional fabric is required. A vertical ease pleat which has parallel pleat lines from neck to hem will require more fabric than one which is tapered from the pleat at the neckline to almost nothing at the waist or hem.

Free-hanging linings are also applied to pants and skirts. The lining may be cut from the garment pattern or may have a separate pattern, as is often the case with pleated, gathered, or darted skirts. Darted skirts, for example, may have a lining with small pleats or ease at the waistline rather than darts; pleated skirts also may have eased or slightly gathered linings with much smaller circumference than the skirt. This reduces construction costs as well as lining fabric costs.

METHODS OF ATTACHMENT

To apply the lining to pants or skirts, the garment sections are seamed together and the zipper or closure area completed; then the lining pieces are seamed together. The lining is then usually placed inside the garment with wrong sides together and the waistline finish completed. In skirts the lining is usually left free-hanging, but in slacks the hems may be attached. In the figure below (4-10), the lining was stitched into the waistline seam when the waistband was applied. The open seamline at the zipper application was folded under and stitched to the zipper tape by hand. This is an expensive treatment; more common to lower price lines would be a simple open seamline at the zipper.

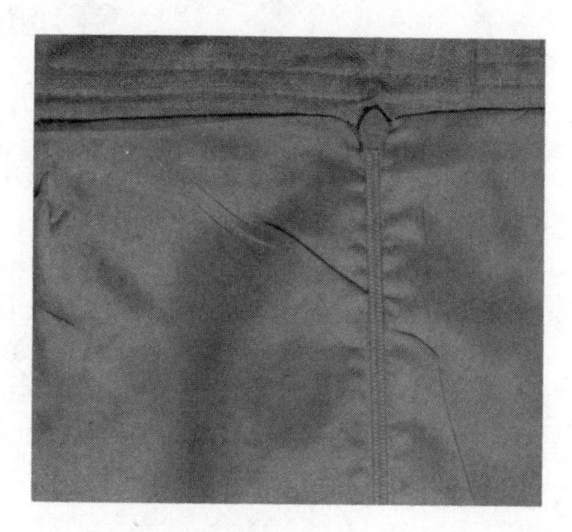

4-10. Lining treatment at zipper and waistline of skirt.

Linings can be applied by hand. A separate pattern is used for the lining, as with most free-hanging linings. The major sections, excluding the sleeves, are joined together and then hand-stitched to the facing edge of the garment. The sleeve lining is then slip-stitched over the garment armscye, leaving a smooth inside finish. There are some real advantages to this method of application. Costs, however, often outweigh those advantages in all areas except custom construction. Hand attachment allows for more accuracy in fitting the lining to the garment. Also, when the lining is applied by hand, the producer usually attaches a portion of the lengthwise seams in the garment proper and in the sleeves during application. These additional attachment points prevent the lining from shifting in the garment during wear.

STANDARDS FOR EVALUATING LININGS

1. The lining fits smoothly inside the garment.
2. The lining provides a neat, clean inside finish.
3. The lining is constructed from a smooth, static-free fabric that complements the outer fabric.
4. The lined garment allows sufficient ease in the lining for body movement without straining the fabric.
5. A partial lining used to maintain the shape of a garment extends at least far enough to accomplish this purpose.
6. On garments lined to the edge, the lining does not peek out to the front.

SUMMARY

The underlying fabrics in a garment—underlining, interfacing, interlining, and lining—are being given increasing notice in the apparel industry today. Even though these fabrics have always been regarded as essential components in construction, a greater awareness of quality in our society is generating more emphasis on them as the basic foundation of the garment. Research efforts are directed toward producing new and innovative products geared to the high-tech demands of the apparel industry. Even though the consumer may never realize it, the inside story is of prime importance to the longevity, comfort, and style statement of the garment.

5

POCKETS

Pockets are fashion elements that can serve a decorative as well as a functional purpose in apparel design. Either or both purposes can be accomplished in a subtle or in a conspicuous manner because of the great variety that is possible by adapting pocket location, size, shape, decoration, and number. Pockets can add a professional touch or elegance to a design, or they can reflect poor construction and unsuitable technique.

Pockets intended to be functional should be positioned at a convenient location to allow the hand to slip easily into them. When the garment is made at home, improper pocket placement can be adjusted easily before the pattern is cut. In ready-to-wear, however, the problem is not always correctable. Furthermore, the purchaser may not have the sewing skills to correct the problem if alteration is possible.

Well-placed pockets can serve the wearer as illusionary devices to enhance body features. Care should be taken in selecting ready-to-wear or in constructing apparel items to assure pocket placement that flatters the figure of the wearer and provides the best possible illusionary results.

The presence of pockets on an item of apparel raises to some degree the cost of producing the item. The extent of cost increase depends on the difficulty of technique used, the increase in number of employee hours required for assembly, the need for specialized labor, and the increase in amount of fabric needed. The variety of names given to pocket types is often confusing, but most can be classified under one of the following types: *inseam, applied,* and *slashed.*

INSEAM POCKETS

Inseam pockets occur at some structural seam on the garment, most commonly at a side seam of skirts and slacks, but possibly in the yoke seam of a jacket or shirt as well. Inseam pockets can be categorized according to whether the two garment seams involved in the pocket application are abutted *(closed application)* or positioned at some distance from each other *(open application)*. Figure 5-1 shows both styles of inseam pockets. In either instance, the inseam pocket provides an excellent means of furnishing a quick and effective garment closure if the pocket is at a waistline position. The pocket bag (inside portion of the pocket) simply can be left open for a few inches. The opening is hidden when the waistband is lapped in position and fastened with a regular closure. This eliminates the need to provide a zipper or buttons/buttonholes at the garment side.

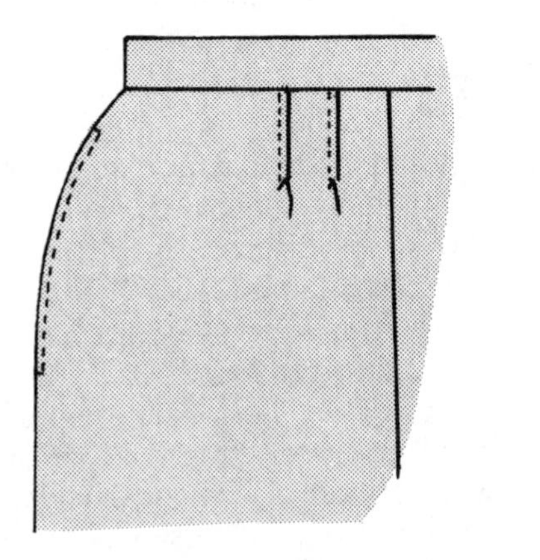

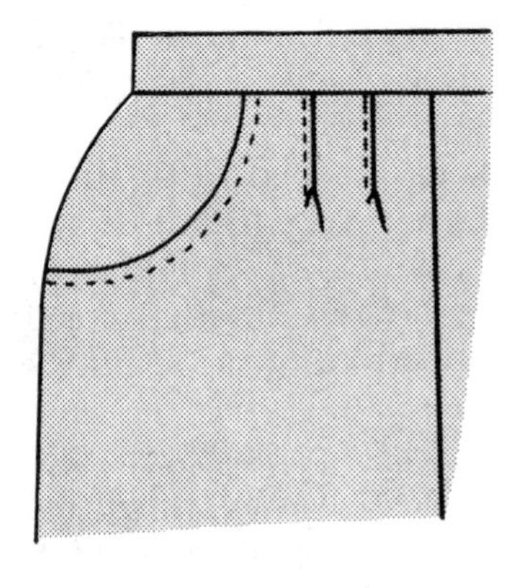

5-1. Closed and open inseam pockets.

5-2. Inseam pocket functioning to conceal waistline closure.

CLOSED APPLICATION

The simplest method of forming a closed application is to extend the fashion fabric outward from the two connecting sections of the garment (Figure 5-3a). Thus, the pocket is cut on with the garment, requiring no separate pattern pieces, and is formed of the fashion fabric. The latter fact may add expense to the garment, for adding a large pocket bag onto the major pattern pieces may cause the fabric layout to be much too expensive in terms of fabric utilization. For that reason, they are rarely seen in ready-to-wear. The advantages are ease of construction (only a single seam is needed to close the garment and to construct the pocket) and appearance, as only fashion fabric will show when the pocket is used.

A more common method of constructing the simple closed inseam pocket is by attaching the pockets to the seam allowance at the proper location (Figure 5-3b), or by attaching the pockets to an extension cut onto the seam at the pocket location (Figure 5-3c). Cutting the pocket bag separately and attaching it to the garment seam allowance or to an extension cut onto that seam allowance is much more common. It does involve extra sewing steps, however, especially if the fabric ravels badly

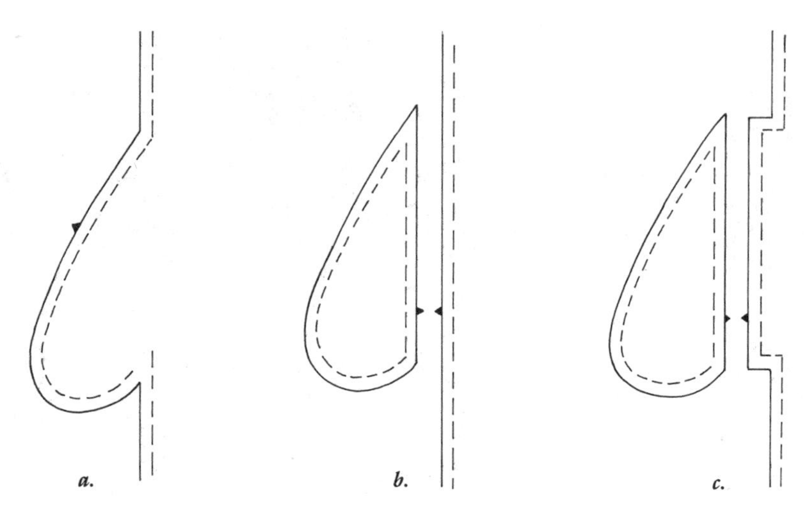

5-3. Inseam pocket: (a) cut on with garment; (b) attached to garment seam allowance; (c) attached to garment extension.

and requires finishing even on pocket attachment seams, but the savings in fabric more than compensate for the construction time. Both forms of the closed application inseam pocket are completed by sewing the raw edges of the pocket together when the garment is assembled.

One variation of this basic method occurs in slacks, especially men's slacks. In this type of pocket, a facing is attached to both portions of the pocket bag so that when the pocket opening gapes during wear, the bag, which is made of a thinner pocketing material, does not show and cause visual distraction from the garment appearance. The use of a thinner, but usually very durable, pocketing material saves on fashion fabric costs and is usually less bulky and more durable than if the garment fabric were used for the bag. This type of closed inseam pocket is invariably topstitched to help keep the bag in place and the opening smooth. This is the most difficult type of inseam pocket to construct.

Closed application inseam pockets are the perfect choices for individuals who have larger figures, since they do not draw attention to the hips. They are also appropriate when unbroken lines are needed to achieve a certain design line in the garment. They are not attractive in sheer fabrics because they show through to the right side of the garment. Figure 5-5 illustrates the degree to which such fashion details as a pocket bag or a facing can show through to the right side of a garment.

Occasionally, inseam pockets on some dresses, skirts, and jackets are held in place by topstitching which outlines the entire pocket bag. This

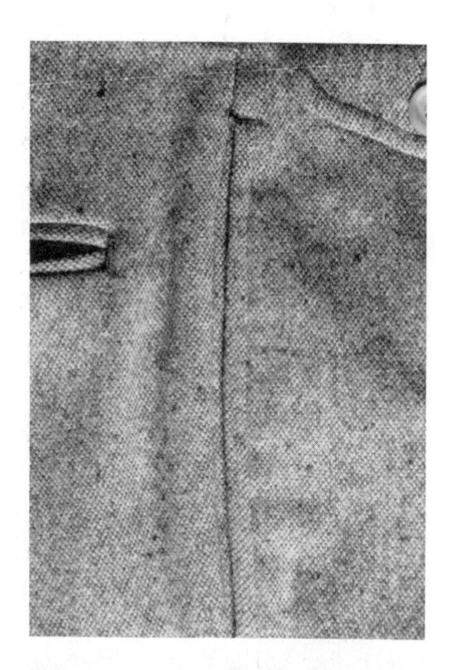

5-4. Faced closed inseam pocket in man's slacks.

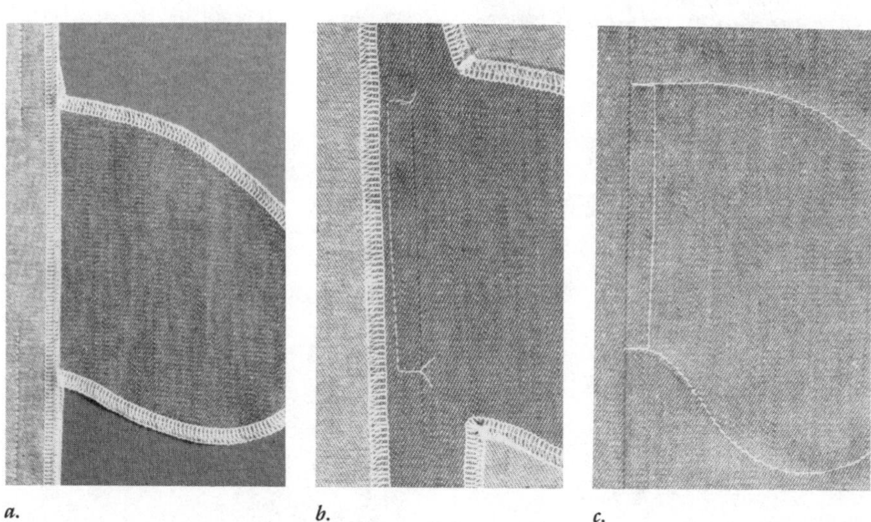

a. b. c.

5-5. Single-ply inseam pocket topstitched to garment: (a) garment seam stitched, leaving opening for pocket; (b) pocket "facing" topstitched in place; (c) completed pocket showing topstitching to secure facing in place and to secure pocket bag to garment.

would be a design feature of the garment. Some garments with visible pocket bag stitching have only one fabric ply in the pocket area. The garment itself serves as the other half of the pocket bag. Such applications require that the garment front pocket opening be hemmed or faced before the topstitching is done. Such an application reduces fabric requirements and eliminates bulk in the pocket areas. All operations on inseam pockets must be done precisely in order to keep the finished pocket sides the same size.

OPEN APPLICATION

If, instead of being abutted, the two seams involved in the inseam pocket application are at some distance from each other when the application is completed, then different techniques are required for its completion. One of the most obvious differences is that an underlay must be provided for the space left open by the pocket design. This type of pocket is usually found at the front hip location on pants, shorts, culottes, and skirts. The open portion can vary in both size and shape. Men's slacks most commonly have a triangular opening that may be only about two inches (5.12 cm) wide at the top. More complicated shapes require correspondingly more construction time. Since it is visible, the underlay

5-6. Selected styles of open inseam pockets.

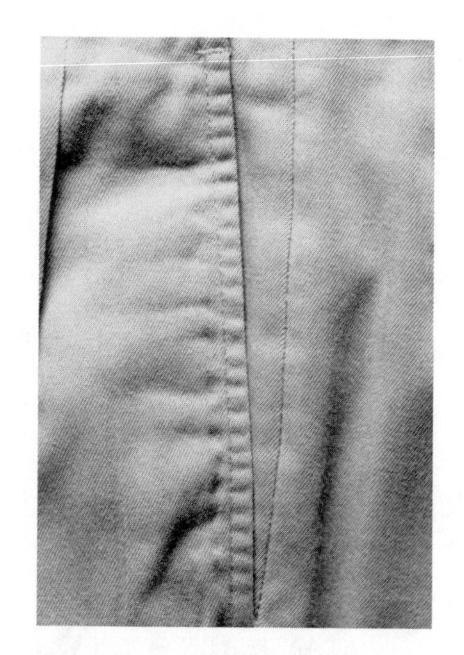

portion of the pocket must be made, at least partially, with garment fabric. If plaids or other designs must be matched, this requires additional cutting and construction time.

In those cases where the bag of the pocket is to be of a lining fabric, a patch of garment fabric slightly larger than the finished pocket opening is stitched onto the pocket bag at the proper location. The top portion of the pocket, where the opening is cut, must be faced. Garment fabric must be used for the facing. If it is not too expensive or thick, it may also be used for the remainder of that side of the pocket bag. Otherwise the facing, like the underlay, is positioned on top of that side of the pocket bag before the opening is faced. The faced opening is then positioned on the underlay with all construction points matched, and the bag of the pocket is stitched together. In men's pants and some women's slacks which are hand-tailored, the bag may be joined with a French seam. This gives a very durable finish, but also increases cost and the possibility or ridges showing on the right side of the garment.

STANDARDS FOR EVALUATING INSEAM POCKETS

1. Functional pockets are positioned at a location convenient for use.
2. Openings on functional pockets are large enough for the hand to be inserted.
3. The pocket depth is correct for the location. (Linings do not extend past hem or facing of the garment.)
4. Openings that are angular or on the garment bias have been reinforced to prevent stretching. Twill or seam tape is often used for this purpose.
5. Pocket openings are reinforced at the beginning and end with backstitching or with bartacks.
6. Seams lie flat without pulling or puckering, and the raw edges have been finished as the fabric and location demand.
7. Lining fabric, if used for the pocket bag, is durable, appropriate, and has the same care requirements as the garment fabric.
8. The body of the pocket has been anchored when possible to maintain position and to prevent sagging.
9. The edges of the pocket opening are the same size, with no puckering or pulling of either side.
10. The pocket lining is recessed enough so it does not show during movement and while sitting.

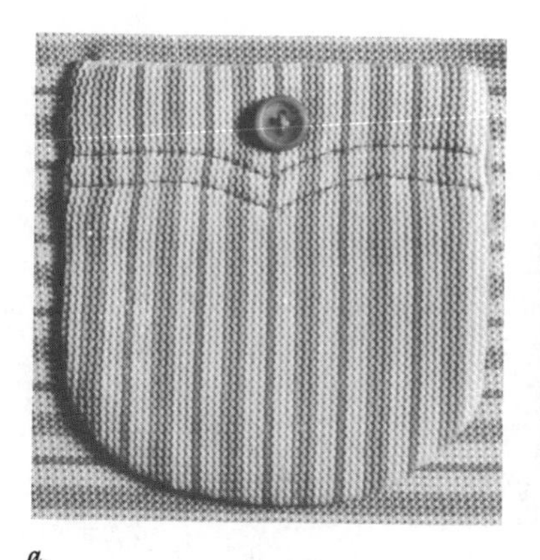

a.

b.

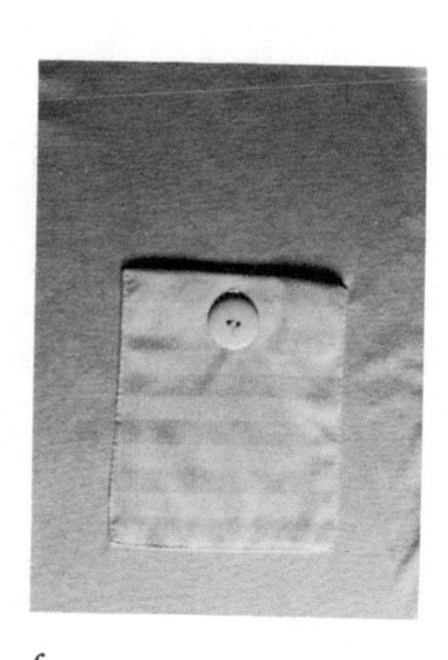

c.

d.

e.

5-7. Selected styles of applied pockets: (a) applied with hand blind stitch; (b) double-stitched application with shaped, separate flap and double-inverted pleats; (c) square patch pocket with an upper folded facing and buttoned closure; (d) bellows pocket (side gussets allow expansion); (e) square, topstitched pocket with decorative flap formed by folding back a faced pocket extension.

APPLIED POCKETS

Applied pockets, often referred to as *patch pockets,* are usually made from the fashion fabric, cut in any desired shape or size. Figure 5-7 shows a variety of applied pockets. They can be faced, lined, and/or interfaced before they are applied to the right side of the garment. Careful consideration is required in determining the placement and size of applied pockets since they play an important role in creating desirable illusions which can flatter the figure of the wearer. Large applied pockets should be reserved for the slim figure, especially when used at the hip level.

The skill required for constructing applied pockets varies according to the difficulty of the shape selected, whether or not a lining is to be used, the type of decoration (if any) used, and the method of application.

SHAPE/LINING

The square applied pocket is one of the easiest shapes to construct and apply, but care must be taken to keep all raw edges concealed and the corners trued. If lining is used, it must be concealed under the applied edges also. Round shapes require more careful handling to keep the raw edges turned under evenly all around during application, unless they are lined, then turned right-side-out for application. Elaborate or highly decorative shapes will usually require a lining or at least a partial facing in order to keep the raw edges turned in evenly all around.

Separate linings are ordinarily used only on medium to heavyweight fabrics in order to eliminate bulk. The separate lining may come to the pocket edge all around or, more commonly, be attached to a pocket hem, really just an extension of the pocket which is turned back. When the lining is joined to a hem, a hole is usually left open in the seam so that the pocket and lining/hem unit can be stitched right sides together, then turned through the lining hole, as shown in Figure 5-8.

Lighter weight fabrics can be used for self-lined pockets. In these, the pocket is cut twice the length of the desired finished size, then folded right sides together for the joining seam. A small slit is cut in the side to be used as the lining, and this provides the opening through which the pocket can be turned (Figure 5-9). In better garments, the slit will be closed before the pocket is applied. In most moderate and budget lines, it is frequently left open.

Many applied pockets have flaps. The flap may be an extension of the pocket which is faced, then pressed back onto itself. Because so much bulk occurs at the pocket edges at the flap fold, such pockets usually have the flap secured either by topstitching at the corners or by a button at the flap center. Flaps are more commonly made and attached

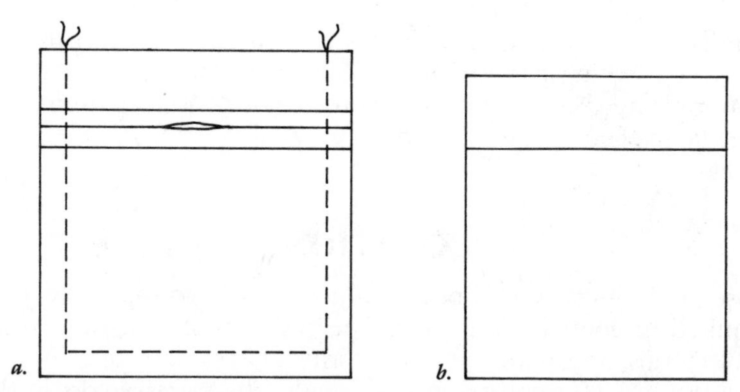

5-8. Lined applied pocket turned through opening in lining/hem seam. (a) Before turning; (b) after turning, wrong side of pocket.

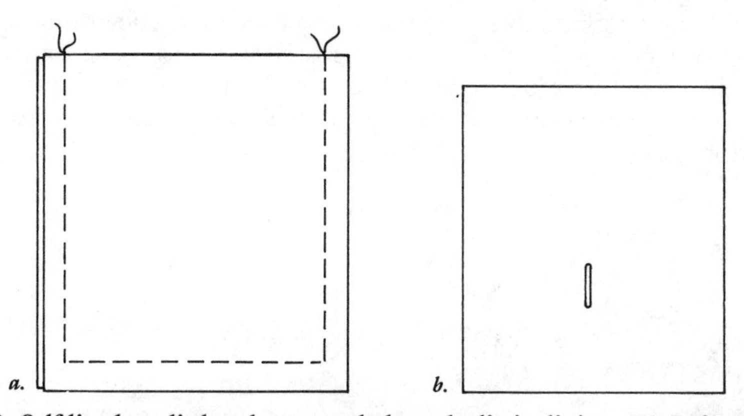

5-9. Self-lined applied pocket turned through slit in lining. (a) Before turning; (b) after turning, wrong side of pocket.

separately from the pocket, and in this way, have a flatter, neater appearance than the self-flapped pocket. Flap shape is also more versatile when the flap is made separately.

A specialized piece of machinery is often used in the apparel industry to simplify the pocket-making process. The pocket press forms, shapes, and presses applied pockets accurately before they are sewn to the garment. Some producers use a piece of metal that is in the shape of the pocket. This is called a die, and die-cut pockets are usually very even, creating fewer application problems. Most applied pockets used on shirts, pajamas, and jeans are now applied automatically by pocket-setting machinery. Most such machinery edge-folds and feeds the precut pockets to either flat or tubular garment sections, then stitches them in place with a preset stitching pattern which includes tacking at the start and finish. Multiple needles can produce more elaborate stitch patterns than single-needle machines, and with absolute consistency from one pocket to another.

DECORATION

The use of bindings around pocket edges can add considerably to the time required to construct a pocket. The addition of lace, ties, ruffles, buttonholes, flaps, appliqués, and other forms of decoration also increases the difficulty of pocket construction. Usually, the primary cost in decorated pockets is in the amount and expense of the trim itself, but the time required to apply the trim may also introduce considerable cost. This is especially true if the decoration consists of pleats, tucks, slot seams with contrasting fabric underlays, inset sections, chevron designs requiring bias cuts and seaming, or expansions such as those found in bellows pockets. Just the extra handling involved in the addition of a trim to a seam slows down the sewing process somewhat and increases production costs.

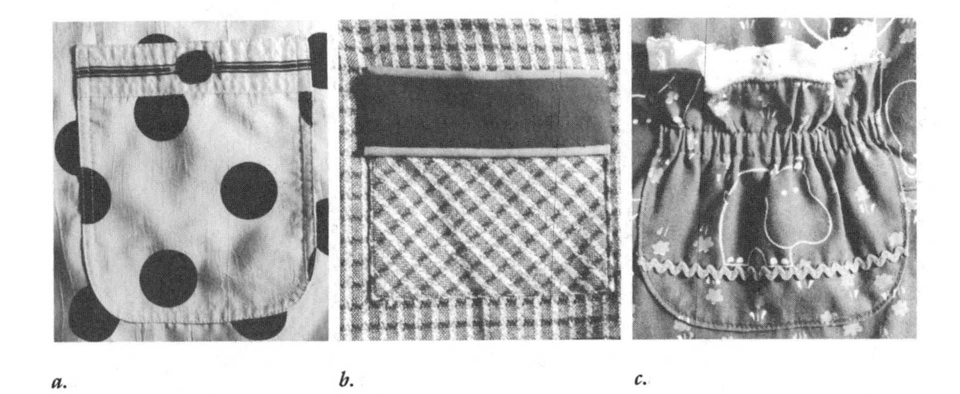

a. *b.* *c.*

5-10. Applied pockets with varied trimming: (a) double-stitched round patch pocket banded at the top with buttoned closure; (b) square, bias-cut pocket corded and banded at upper edge; (c) curved patch pocket with decorative eyelet trim and elasticized fullness.

APPLICATION

Application methods vary, but topstitching along the pocket edge is the easiest as well as one of the most durable methods in use. Topstitching does require some degree of skill in order to maintain an equal spacing from the pocket edge if using a regular sewing machine. The more rows of stitching used, the more difficult equal spacing becomes. In industry, automatic equipment is used to topstitch the pocket in place. This equipment may be single or multiple needle, depending on the desired stitch pattern. Tacking at the beginning and end of the topstitching is done automatically to reinforce the pocket application. Backstitching, triangular stitching, rectangular stitching, rivets, and bartacks are the most common patterns of pocket reinforcement. These reinforcement patterns are shown in Figure 5-11.

Hand application is not particularly difficult, but this method lacks durability and is practical only in home sewing or in very expensive lines of ready-to-wear. A blind stitch is used with stitches placed about one-fourth inch (.64 cm) apart. Stitches that are pulled tightly will cause the pocket to pucker.

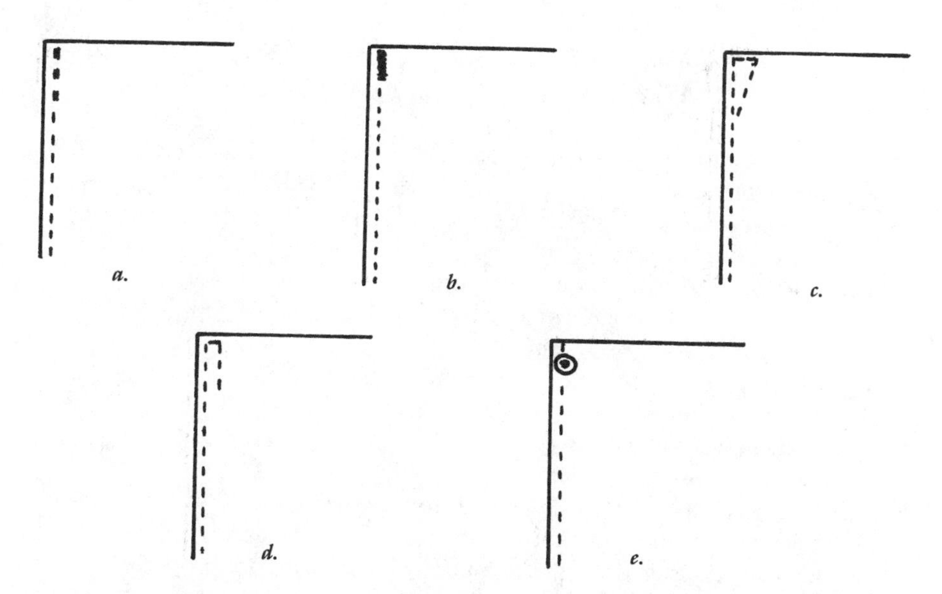

5-11. Reinforcement styles for applied pockets: (a) backstitched; (b) bar-tacked; (c) triangular-stitched; (d) rectangular-stitched; (e) riveted.

Machine stitching that is not visible on the surface of the pocket is the most difficult method used to apply patch pockets to a garment. Even a skilled seamstress must be careful in order to obtain professional results. In industry, specialized machinery and operators are usually needed for this type of pocket application. These additional needs make

STANDARDS FOR EVALUATING APPLIED POCKETS

1. Functional applied pockets are positioned at a location convenient for use.
2. Openings on functional pockets are large enough for the hand to be inserted.
3. The pocket depth is correct for the location.
4. Interfacing has been used when needed to hold the pocket shape.
5. Pockets were cut on grain, and any fabric designs matched. If a bias cut was used, pockets were not stretched and have been properly stabilized with a lining.
6. If corners are present, they are true, with no raw edges or lining fabric visible.
7. Enclosed seams have been trimmed to one-fourth inch (.64 cm) or less.
8. Curves, if present, are smooth and sides are symmetrical.
9. Paired pockets are the same height, the same size, and the same shape.
10. The location of the turning point on lined pockets is not visible on the right side.
11. Linings do not roll to the right side at the edges of the pocket, but remain out of sight.
12. If used, topstitching is an equal distance from the edge at all points, an appropriate stitch length has been used, and all loose thread ends have been removed.
13. Trims or decorations are neatly applied and appropriate for the design and location where they are used.
14. Pocket ends are reinforced properly according to type, location, method of application, and fabric used.
15. Facings or hems are deep enough to stay in position; raw edges have been properly handled as required for fabric and location; understitching is present when needed, and seams are properly trimmed.
16. Pockets and/or flaps lie flat without pulling, twisting, sagging, or rolling.

production costs higher than with the other types of application. This method is used more often on expensive sportswear, men's jackets, and tailored items when a durable yet invisible method of application is desired to maintain garment style.

SLASHED POCKETS

Slashed pockets, or *welt pockets* as they are sometimes called, have one or two strips of fashion fabric applied to the right side of the garment to conceal the raw edges of the pocket opening. Flaps may accompany the welts, and a lining must be applied and turned to the wrong side to complete the body or bag of the pocket and to conceal the small welt seams.

Slashed pockets are used on more expensive tailored suits for men and women and almost always on the back of men's slacks. They are by far the most difficult type of pocket to apply at home and one of the most costly to mass produce unless special equipment is used to construct the welts. This is more frequently the case in today's apparel industry. Automatic pocket welting machines can construct pockets in a variety of welt lengths and styles, can match plaids and stripes, can insert flaps or tabs, and then sew and cut the actual pocket welt. Obviously, such equipment greatly simplifies the construction process and also leads to a more consistent product each time.

Slashed pockets require extra garment fabric for flaps, lining for the pocket bag, interfacing for limp or soft fabrics, and sometimes even a garment lining, which serves to support and to hide the pocket construction. The addition of construction steps and production materials adds to the cost of the finished apparel item, yet pockets remain a very popular means of adding unique design features to apparel. Figure 5-12 shows four of the more typical styles of slashed pockets.

APPLICATION

A variety of methods can be employed to apply slashed pockets, but each technique requires accuracy in sewing and slashing to produce acceptable results. Specialized machinery often used in the apparel industry can perform the various tasks of making slashed pockets with a high degree of precision and speed. The use of this equipment allows production of pockets that exceed the quality obtainable by individuals utilizing standard sewing machines, whether at home or in an industrial setting.

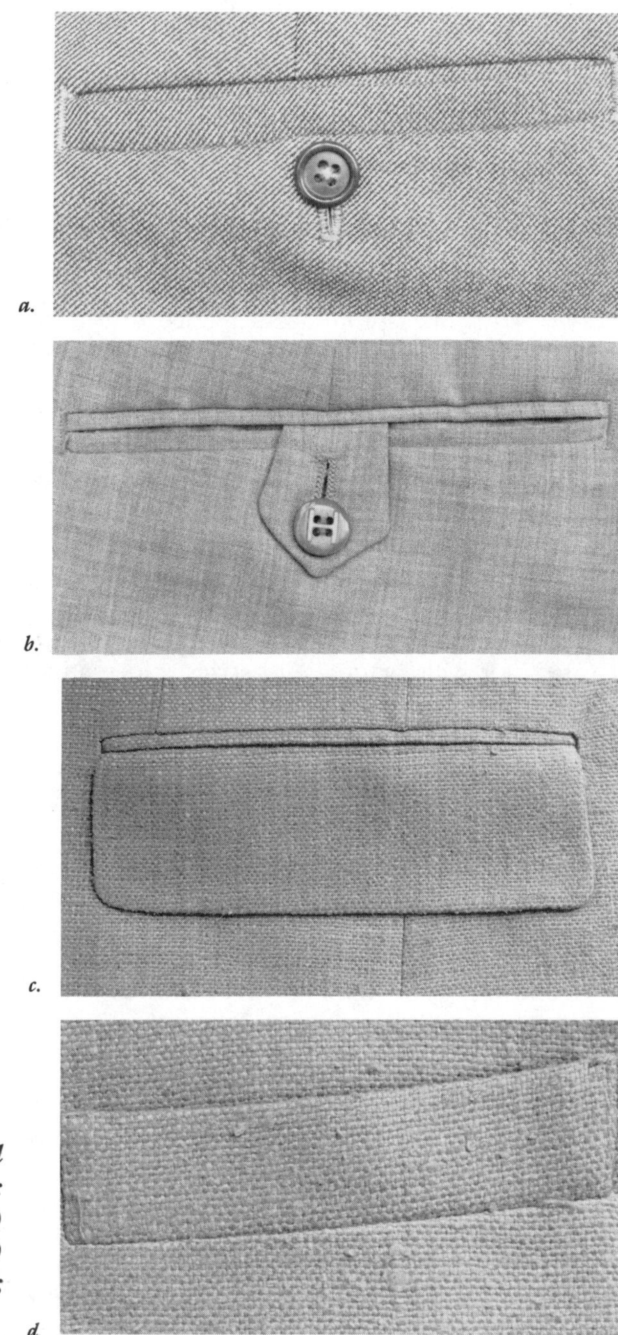

5-12. Some typical styles of slashed pockets: (a) single lip; (b) double lip (besom); (c) double lip with flap; (d) upturned flap.

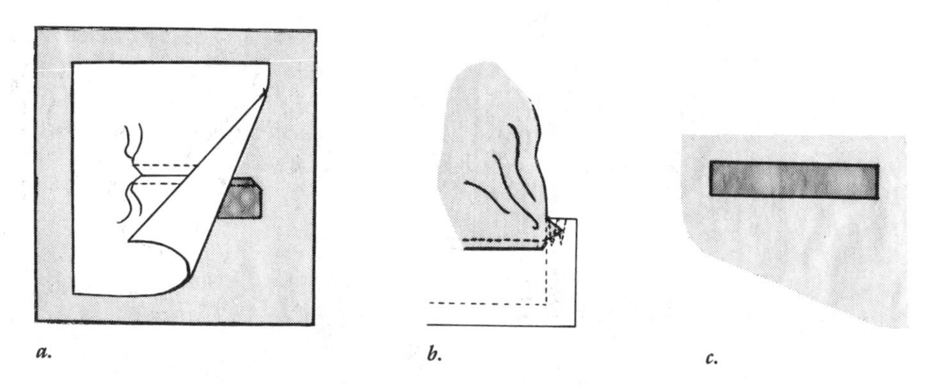

5-13. Traditional method for applying slashed pocket. (a) Steps 1 to 3 completed; (b) step 4; (c) completed pocket.

The traditional method for applying a slashed pocket with no lips and with an upturned flap requires the following steps, as shown in Figure 5-13: (1) the flap is constructed and applied to the right side of the garment along equally spaced, marked lines; (2) the lining section or sections are then placed over the flap and sewn permanently into place exactly on the previous row of stitching and on the remaining marked line; (3) a slash is made halfway between the two rows of stitching and angled to the exact last stitch at the ends of the two rows of stitching to allow the pocket bag and the raw edges to turn through the opening to the wrong side; (4) the triangles formed by angular clipping are secured to the lining of the pocket bag when the side seams are sewn; (5) in the case of the upturned flap, the ends of the flap are secured in position with blind stitching or with top-stitching.

When garments are knitted to shape (full fashioned), details such as

5-14. Equivalent of slashed pocket in full-fashioned knitted garment.

slashed pockets can be included in the fabrication. The slash is one that results from leaving an opening in the fabric as it is being knitted, then knitting on a facing or band and a pocket bag. Figure 5-14 shows such a pocket. This is a more expensive type of pocket than one which is made by cutting into the fabric, but it produces a much smoother and flatter pocket in a bulky knitted fabric.

STANDARDS FOR EVALUATING SLASHED POCKETS

1. Functional pockets are positioned at a location convenient for use.
2. Openings on functional pockets are large enough for the hand to be inserted.
3. The pocket depth is correct for the location. Linings do not extend below the hem fold in jackets.
4. Openings, flaps, and welts have been interfaced when necessary for body and shape maintenance.
5. Pockets were cut on grain with any fabric pattern matched. Bias pockets were properly stabilized and not stretched during application.
6. Enclosed seams were trimmed to one-fourth inch (.64 cm) or less.
7. There are no holes, pleats, or puckers at the ends of the slashed openings. The ends are angled the same at both sides as indicated by the design.
8. Flaps, when present, are the same length as the welts, and lie flat.
9. Fashion fabrics were applied to the pocket lining directly beneath the pocket opening when buttonhole or narrow single welts were used, to prevent the lining from showing when the pocket is being used.
10. Fabric triangles formed at the ends of the slashed openings were secured with several rows of small stitches or with bartacks to prevent holes from developing as the pocket is used.
11. Pocket lining fabric covers the welt seam adequately with no pleating or puckering.
12. Lining fabrics used are appropriate for the location and for the fashion fabric weight and care requirements.
13. Raw edges of the lining are enclosed on men's wear and finished neatly to prevent raveling on women's wear.
14. Paired pockets are identical in length, width at openings, and distance from the garment edge.
15. Pockets lie flat without pulling, twisting, or rolling.

SUMMARY

The addition of a pocket to a garment will increase the cost of that garment, regardless of the type selected. The selection can, however, result in either slight or considerable cost, depending on the equipment available to the manufacturer and the type of construction selected. Although functional, in that they provide a space for carrying items, pockets are frequently included more for their decorative appeal. So important is this decorative aspect that pockets are sometimes "faked" on garments. This is particularly true of the more complicated slashed pockets. They can be imitated by sewing a small strip of fabric on the garment in a typical pocket position. Regardless of the designer's motive for including a real pocket, however, the quality of the construction must be evaluated on functional terms, for if the pocket is there, it must be assumed that the consumer will use it. Therefore, pockets should be usable.

6

NECKLINE TREATMENTS

More diversity of neckline treatments exists in twentieth-century fashion than at any previous time. This diversity is apparent in both style and structure. As the names of necklines styles often change and overlap, even when two very similar designs are being described, structural divisions dictate the ordering of the various neckline treatments. To some extent, the major categories of bindings, facings, inset bands, and collars discussed below have been arranged to reflect increasing cost and/or complexity. However, the variations within each division make an exact ordering very difficult.

BINDINGS

A binding is a narrow strip of fabric used to enclose the raw edges of a neckline. As it is visible on the right side of the garment as well as on the wrong side, it can be decorative as well as functional. The same treatment can be used at armscyes or at any other free edge of a garment and, in fact, frequently is used in order to make the garment design coherent. Most bindings are applied in a similar manner, but the structure of the binding itself dictates the fabric and style on which it is most appropriately used.

BIAS BINDINGS

As the name implies, the bias binding is cut on the bias direction of the fabric (usually a woven fabric). Only rarely is self-fabric used for this binding. More commonly, prepared binding is purchased from a notions/trim supplier. Bias stripping to be used for facings and bindings is available to garment manufacturers in a variety of colors and fabrics. The strips are automatically cut and folded according to intended use, pressed, and wound on cones or rolls for delivery to the apparel manufacturer. Alternatively, they may be cut only and wound on cones for loading into machines that will fold the stripping to the desired width and feed it automatically to the binding machine which will apply it to the garment section. The pattern making, layout, and cutting of the garment are thus simplified.

Bias-bound edges are used primarily on casual women's and children's garments made from woven fabric. The bias cut allows the binding to be molded to fit simple shapes and shallow curves. If the binding is

6-1. Bias binding, hand finished on wrong side of garment.

to be applied to angles such as those found in pointed and square necklines, it must be seamed to remove excess fullness at the small edge, a process called *mitering*. As mitering slows down the application process considerably and requires more exact matching of binding to neckline, it is found in more expensive garments in which the binding is an important part of the total design statement.

A bias binding is usually applied after one shoulder seam has been made in the garment. The binding is folded over the raw neckline edge and topstitched in place. The second shoulder seam is then made through both garment and binding. If the binding and garment are both closed prior to application, the two must be matched exactly in size. The application seam, since it is made within a closed circle, is much slower and more difficult to make. The resulting neck edge does, however, have a neater finish, as no seam edges are visible at the join. Because the increased application costs tend to exceed the price line of the garments on which bias bindings are found, seaming before application is rarely found in ready-to-wear.

KNITTED BINDINGS

Since knitted fabric has inherent crosswise stretch, the bindings cut from it do not require a bias cut. Instead, they are cut straight across the width of the fabric. Occasionally, they are cut lengthwise. The lengthwise cut has less stretch than does the cross cut. Folding, pressing, and packaging may be done in a manner similar to that used for bias bindings in cases where a thin knit is used. More frequently, the underside of the knitted fabric is not folded under but is finished with a machine cover stitch during the application process. This latter method reduces bulk in the finished garment. As with bias bindings, treatments at points can vary from the rare true miter to a seamed or pinched simulation.

Knitted bindings are suitable for use on apparel made from knitted fabric. A wide variety of casual apparel is available today showing this technique as a finish for both neckline and armscye. The tank top is a classic example, whether it is sized for a newborn child or for a member of the older generation. (See Figure 6-2.) In most cases, application follows the same process described for bias bindings. There are some knitted bindings available with finished edges. These are produced on special knitting machines which yield the finished product. Uses and application methods are more similar to those used to apply braids, however. The pre-finished knitted bindings are frequently found on sweaters.

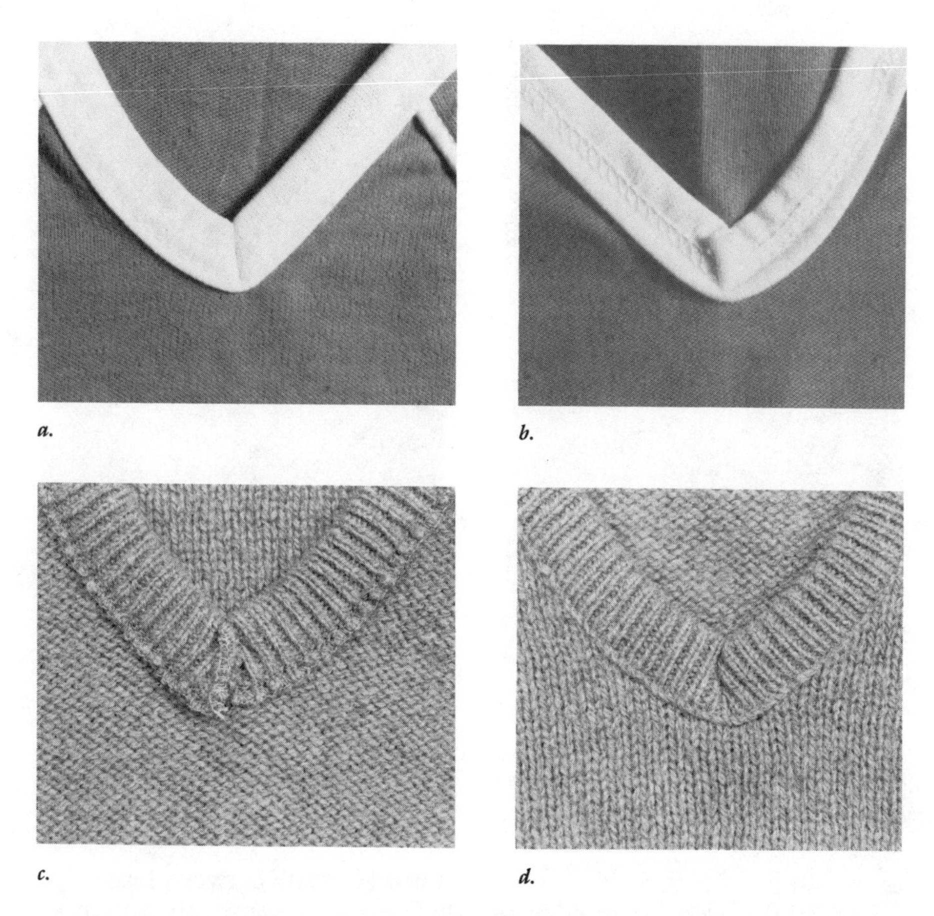

a. b. c. d.

6-2. Knitted bindings at garment points: (a) right side of pinch miter; (b) wrong side of pinch miter; (c) wrong side of seamed miter; (d) right side of seamed miter.

BRAIDED BINDINGS

Braided bindings are more expensive in terms of initial cost. They are made on special braiding machines which operate more slowly than conventional looms or knitting machines. They are usually found only on medium to heavyweight garments. Chanel-type suits for women often have the neckline, front opening, and hem edge completely covered with braid. Braided bindings are almost never applied and then seamed though, as this technique is not appropriate for the more tailored styles

a.

b.

6-3. Braided binding at jacket lapel: (a) right side; (b) wrong side.

on which braid is used. A distinction must be made between braid that is applied flat, close to an edge already finished by some other method, and braid that is used as a finish. The former will be considered in the chapter on Decorative Detail.

Regardless of whether the binding is bias cut woven fabric, knitted fabric, or braided fabric, a critical point of quality is the compatibility of the binding fabric to the garment fabric in terms of care. Colorfastness is of particular concern when contrasting bindings are used and may fade or bleed during laundering.

Another factor in quality is dimensional stability. Unequal shrinkage can also cause the bound edge to pucker or ripple, depending upon which fabric has the greatest amount of shrinkage. Especially if the binding has been stretched during application, laundering may release tensions which cause the binding to shrink and pull up the bound edge. This creates a balloon-like effect in the garment. This effect can be seen in knitted as well as bias bindings, as shown in Figure 6-4.

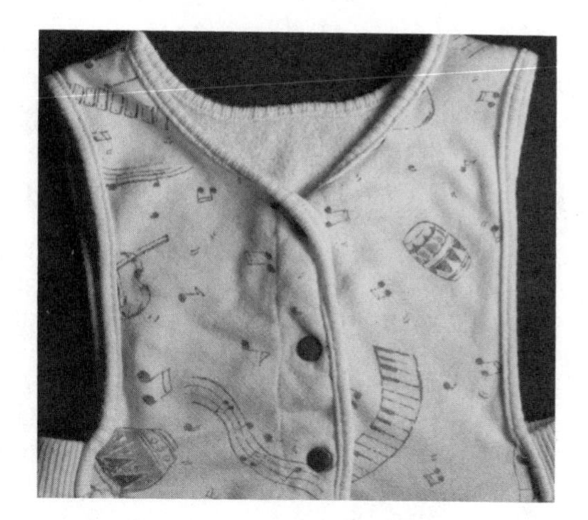

6-4. Knitted binding exhibiting more shrinkage than apparel fabric following laundering.

STANDARDS FOR EVALUATING BINDINGS
1. The width of the binding is even. 2. The binding is securely applied with appropriate stitch length. 3. The binding is suitable in weight, fiber content, care method, and style to the garment on which it is to be used. 4. All raw edges of the binding are concealed. 5. The binding fits the edge to which it is applied without stretching or drawing the neckline. 6. The binding is stitched in place far enough into the binding to hold it securely during wear and laundering.

NECKLINE FACINGS

A facing can provide a smooth, inconspicuous finish for necklines and front openings. Faced necklines are somewhat more expensive to produce than bound ones. This is because of the required additional pattern pieces, interfacing, fabric, and application steps. Even faced treatments vary in complexity and expense, however, according to the type used and to the applicable number of the above-mentioned factors. Facings are categorized as *shaped, bias,* and *extended.* In some cases, more than one type will be found in the same garment. As a general rule, the more narrow the facing and the straighter the pattern shape from which it is cut, the less expense is involved because of reduced fabric requirements.

SHAPED FACING

A shaped facing is cut exactly to fit the garment part to which it will be sewn, with grainline positions identical, or at least very similar, in both garment and facing. It is usually not more than three inches (7.62 cm) deep when finished, but some dresses and women's jackets will have back neck facing that may be six to eight inches (15.24 to 20.32 cm) deep at the garment center back. This is an added expense which may or may not be important to the quality of the garment, depending on fabrication. Supposedly, the extra facing material protects the garment shell from perspiration and body oils. The longer fabric flap is difficult to keep flat and in place when the garment is worn. It frequently can be seen extending above the garment neckline, unknown to the wearer.

Most shaped facings are made of the same fabric as the garment. If the fashion fabric is quite thick and bulky, however, the facing should be cut of a lining-weight fabric in a matching color. On the other hand, if a very sheer fabric is used and the free edge of the facing does not

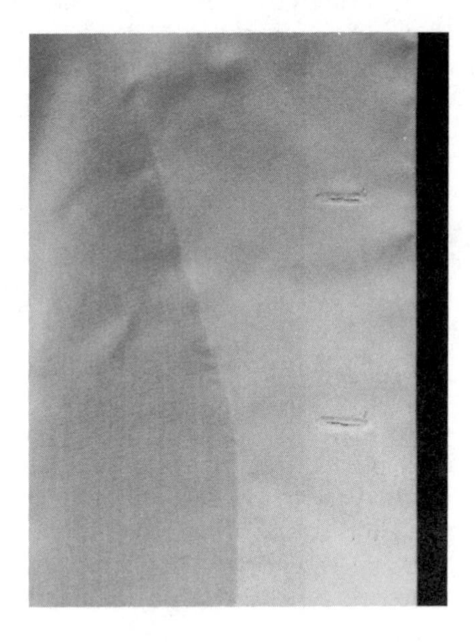

6-5. Shaped facing in sheer fabric.

end at a design line of the garment, then it forms an unintentional and undesirable line which is visible from the outside of the garment. This often occurs when a design is duplicated in a number of colors and fabrics, some of which have more opacity than others. If a more transparent fabric is used for the actual garment than was used in the designer's model, then the result may be quite different from that which the designer intended.

A shaped facing is quite common on dresses and blouses with jewel, pointed, square, sweetheart, and irregularly shaped necklines, as well as strapless and halter styles. It is also used to complete necklines with additional treatments, such as ruffles, collars, or piping.

Most shaped facings require interfacing for body and support. They also require careful handling so that neither facing nor neckline is stretched during construction. In better garments, the facing pieces will be assembled completely before they are attached to the garment. If that order is reversed, that is, if the front neckline facing is attached to the garment front and the back neckline facing to the garment back, and then the shoulder seam made continuously through the garment and facing, the neckline will not be as smooth at the shoulder. Both methods are shown in Figure 6-6.

An exception to the above-mentioned rule is the *combination facing* (Figure 6-7), in which a single unit finishes both neckline and armscye of sleeveless styles (which must be open at either the center back or the

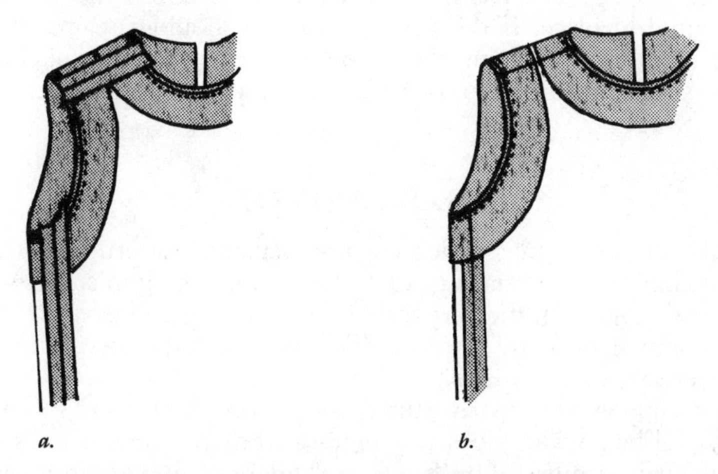

6-6. Facing application: (a) assembled before application; (b) applied to garment section before final assembly and seamed through at shoulders.

6-7. Combination facing in child's jumper.

center front to turn). This construction is found in jumpers, vests, sundresses, and playsuits. If the garment is sewn at the shoulders and sides before the combination facing is applied, then the unit could not be turned right side out. Either the shoulder or the side seams, in addition to the center front or back seam, must be left open. It is easier and less conspicuous to leave open the side seam of both garment and facing, apply the facing, and then close the underarm seams through both garment and facing. The facing is then folded down on the wrong side and secured in place. If the garment has no shoulder seams, then the regular method of applying the facing would be used. Many children's garments that button, snap, or tie at the shoulders utilize open combination facings.

BIAS FACINGS

Unlike shaped facing, which requires separate pattern pieces, grainline matching and interfacing, bias facing is much simpler. It is cut in rectangular strips with the bias of the fabric creating the necessary shaping during construction and pressing. This is a less expensive facing treatment than any of the others.

Bias facing is particularly suited to use on sheer fabrics, since the narrow finished width does not detract from the design lines of the garment. It is also useful on heavy, bulky fabrics. In the latter case, the facing is cut of a lighter weight but color-matched fabric to reduce bulk at the finished neckline. Even with regular weight fabrics, the bias facing usually are cut from fabric different from that used in the garment, since bias stripping can be purchased from notions suppliers in a wide range of colors, precut and rolled on cones or rolls for easy application.

Bias facings are usually cut double the finished width plus two seam allowances. They are then folded, with the fold forming the lower edge of the completed facing. For a curved neckline, the finished width of the bias facing should be no more than one-half inch (1.27 cm), and it may be even slightly less. The wider the finished facing, the greater the size differential between the seamed and the free edge of the facing. If the size differential is too great, the free edge will be too small to lie flat against the garment, and the neckline will pull and pucker.

Since the bias facing depends only on the stretch inherent in the cut of the fabric, and since this is limited, deep and/or intricate curves cannot be handled very effectively with this type of finish. Square and pointed necklines are never finished with a bias facing because of this factor. If they were, the facing itself would have to be seamed, or mitered, at the point, and this would be a costly operation.

Because of its narrow width, the free edge of the bias facing is usually secured with different methods from those used in shaped facings. The bias facing is either topstitched, with one or two stitching rows, or else the free edge must be hand sewn all around. The latter method is seldom used in ready-to-wear. It is found in home sewing, but is considered an unsatisfactory technique.

A very inexpensive variation of the bias facing is the use of a bias-

6-8. Bias facing in sheer fabric.

6-9. Bias cording.

enclosed cording as both trim and finish (Figure 6-9). It is applied, cording edge toward the garment and raw edges aligned, to the closed neckline. After the application seam is made, the raw edges of the garment are trimmed slightly if they are longer than the bias. Then, all three fabric layers are turned toward the wrong side of the garment and topstitched in place. The only point of difficulty is in overlapping the edges of the cording at the point where they meet so that the join is neat and smooth.

EXTENDED FACINGS

Extended facings are cut onto a garment section, then folded rather than seamed to create the finished edge. These occur most frequently at the front openings of jackets, dresses, blouses, and shirts. In most of these applications, the extended facing takes on the contours of a shaped facing as it approaches the neck edge. It may be joined to a shaped back neck facing at the shoulders to complete the facing unit. The fabric requirements are considerable for this type of facing. An extended facing is preferred when the garment neck edge turns back to form a lapel. If the extended facing does not continue into a shaped neckline facing, then the free edge of the facing and/or the wrong side of the garment fabric will be visible.

The extended front facing with no neckline shaping is often used in blouses or dresses that do not turn back. An example is the bias tie

6-10. Extended front facing too narrow for location on garment.

neckline. In this instance, the extended facing serves as a finish for the front edge and a very small overlap portion of the neck edge. The remainder of the neck edge is finished by the application of a bias tie. Binding or a bias facing might serve as an alternate neckline finish in other styles.

Both front and back bateau necklines may have upward-extending facings. These are occasionally folded down in place prior to the joining of the front and back garment sections. This method is bulkier at the shoulder/neckline seam junction, but does automatically secure the free edge of the facing at the shoulders. If the shoulder seam is made and then the facing folded into place, an alternate method of securing the facing edge is required. Surplice garments also may have extended facings in the sections that wrap, usually the front, and a shaped facing for the remainder of the neckline. The same is true of the draped cowl neckline.

One other variation of the extended facing can be seen in garments which have rather shallow shaping, no sharp points, and utilize a very narrow facing. The width of the facing is usually no more than a seam allowance, and serging is a common finish. As shown in Figure 6-12, even a narrow facing in a woven fabric does not shape well around the curves of the neckline, but tends to pull and ripple in places.

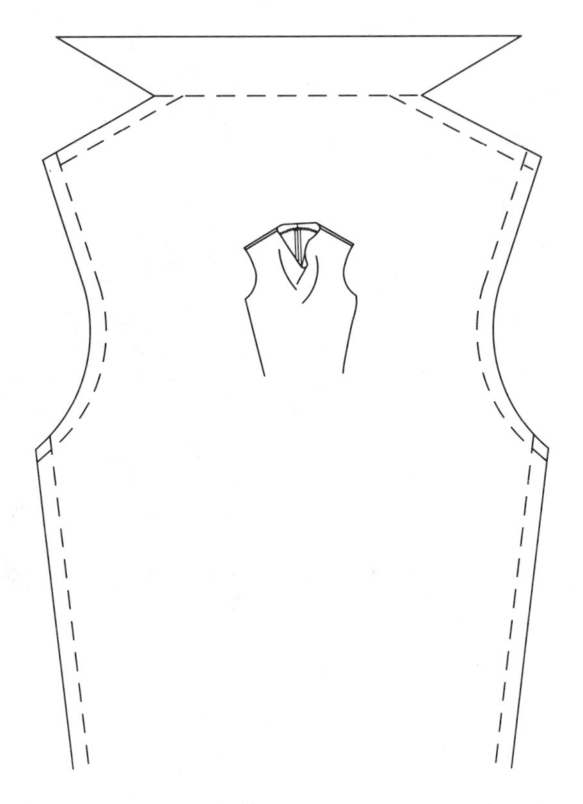

6-11. Cowl neckline with extended facing.

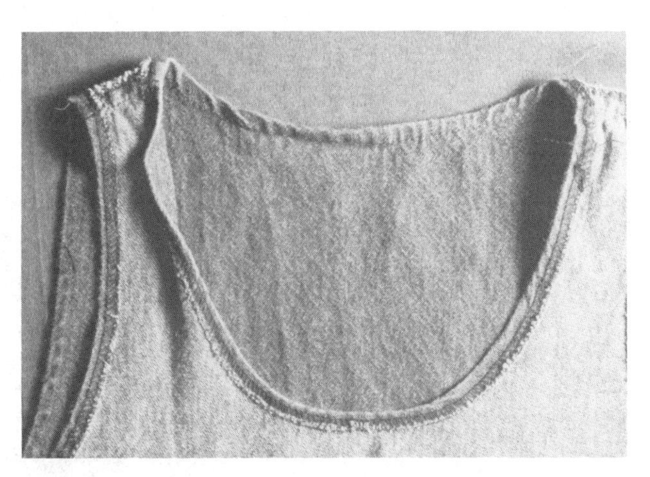

6-12. Narrow extended facing in scooped neckline.

STANDARDS FOR EVALUATING FACINGS

1. Facings lie smoothly with no ripples or puckers.
2. Facings are secured inconspicuously to the garment reverse to prevent their rolling to the outside. Topstitching, when used, serves as a means of securing the facing.
3. The free edge of the facing is finished with an appropriate seam finish to prevent raveling.
4. In garments made of thick, spongy fabric, the facings are cut from a lighter weight but matching fabric.
5. Facings in transparent or translucent fabrics are very narrow or stop at a design line of the garment.
6. The facing is understitched.
7. Most areas that are faced are interfaced as well. Bias facings are the exception and are not interfaced. The extended facing on a cowl neckline is not interfaced, since that portion of the neckline is cut on the bias and intended to drape softly.

INSET BANDS

Although most inset bands are not more than two inches (5.08 cm) deep, there is really no clear line of demarcation at which point an inset band is regarded instead as a yoke. The inset band may even merge into a placket to form a neckline treatment and opening in one unit. It may cut deep into the garment front, back, or shoulder area to form almost the equivalent of a yoke. The choice of fabric determines further distinctions among inset band types.

WOVEN INSET BAND

Considerably more complex, difficult to construct, and expensive than the preceding neckline treatments is the inset band when made from woven fabric. In this technique, a shaped piece, or joined piece, of self- or contrast fabric is set into the garment in order to complete its final size and shape. The addition of the inset band does not, in itself, finish the neckline edge. This is accomplished by additional operations. Most commonly the band is made double; that is, two bands are actually constructed. One is set into the garment and serves as the band proper, while the other is treated as a shaped facing with the free edge attached

a.

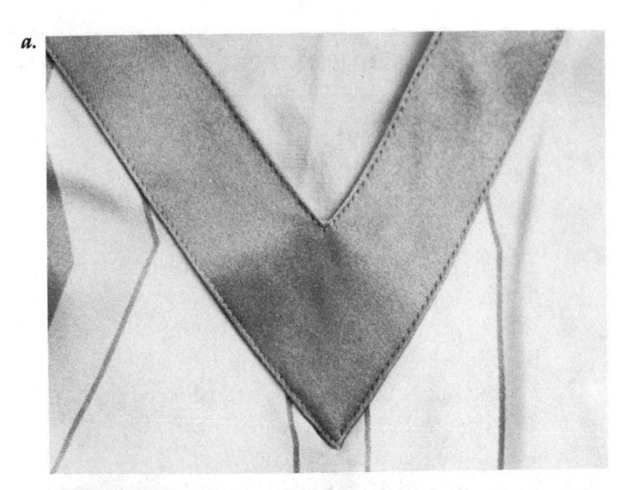

b.

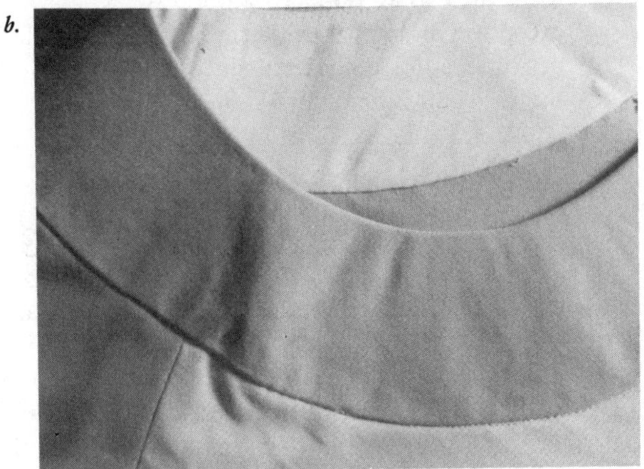

6-13. Inset bands: (a) V-shaped inset band in contrasting fabric; (b) round inset band faced in lighter fabric.

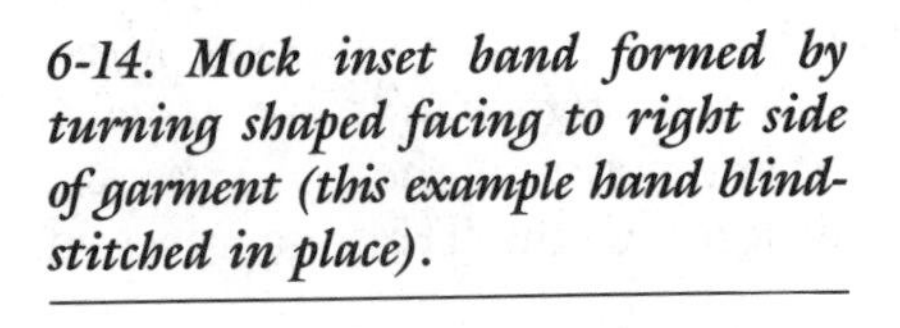

6-14. Mock inset band formed by turning shaped facing to right side of garment (this example hand blind-stitched in place).

all around. The completed band lies flat or nearly flat in the finished garment.

An enormous amount of variety is possible in the design of inset bands. They can be relatively simple as in many kimono-styled garments and sundresses, or they may have very unusual shapes involving deep curves and/or angles which complicate the setting process. Figure 6-13 shows two inset band treatments. The first forms a deep V shape and is made from contrasing fabric. The second, shown in detail, is a curved band faced in a lighter fabric. The band itself is not seamed at the shoulder line, although the garment is.

It is usually impossible to tell from a sketch or photograph when an inset band is present in a garment. In a sketch, a low topstitching line which secures the free edge of a shaped facing may give the appearance of an inset band. If a shaped facing, made of either self- or contrasting fabric, is turned to the outside of the garment and stitched down to form a type of trim, this is very easily mistaken for an inset band. This type of treatment can be seen in Figure 6-14. Only careful inspection of the garment will reveal if either of these methods have been used to simulate the effect of the more expensive inset band.

STANDARDS FOR EVALUATING INSET BANDS

1. The band fits the garment smoothly.
2. All construction points of band and garment are matched.
3. The inside of the band is neatly finished with no raw edges.
4. Interfacing is present in the band.
5. No seam wells are visible at the upper edge of the band.
6. The width of the band is consistent.

RIB-STRETCH BANDS

A variation of the shaped inset band is the rib-stretch neckline. In this treatment, the piece to be set into the garment is cut double the desired width on the crosswise grain of a knitted stretch fabric. It is then folded in half with both raw edges joined to the garment simultaneously. This application is limited to knitted garments with a large amount of stretch, mostly rib knits produced specifically for this use.

In better garments, the band and garment will be seamed before the two are joined. This gives a much neater neckline edge. It is easier and faster, however, to leave one garment shoulder seam open, apply the

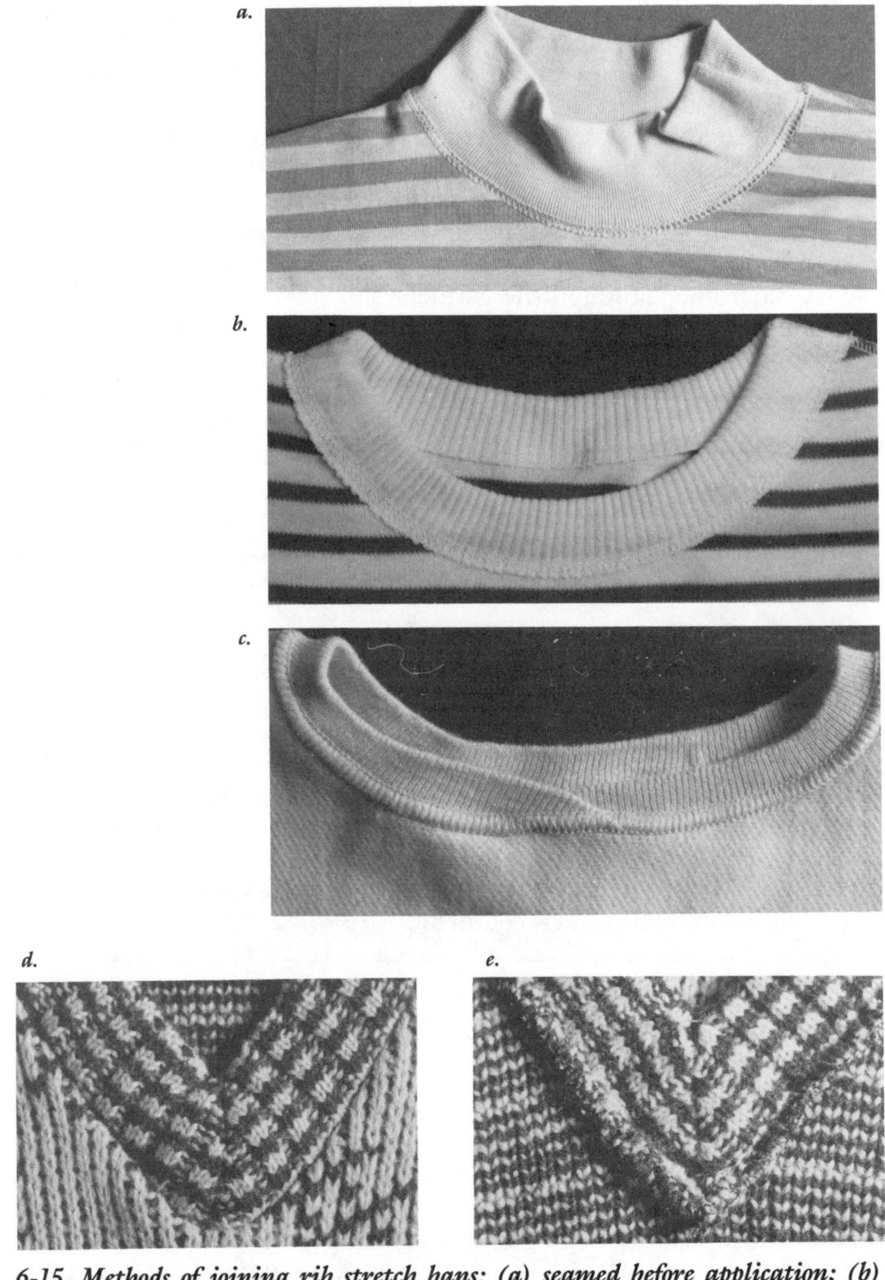

6-15. Methods of joining rib stretch bans: (a) seamed before application; (b) seamed after application; (c) lapped at center front; (d) true miter at point, right side; (e) true miter at point, wrong side.

band, then join the final shoulder seam and band seam in one operation. Alternatively, the ends of the band may be lapped prior to application so that all raw edges are concealed when the application is complete. Figure 6-15 shows several methods of joining the band. The seam joining the band to the garment will usually be serged or double-stitched and trimmed to a very narrow width if it is not enclosed. This application is frequently found in sportswear, men's T-shirts, and children's garments. When it is used on a pointed or square neckline, excess fabric in the angles of the point(s) must be seamed out after the band is applied.

In garments not as casual or sporty as sweat-shirts, a single thickness of ribbed fabric, specially knitted with the upper edge already finished, may be used instead of the cut-and-fold type of ribbing. Sweaters, sweater vests, and dresses that are not knitted to shape, but are cut from sweater-knit fabrics, usually have this type of single-layer ribbed bands.

In all of the bands constructed of stretch knit, the primary point of difficulty is in determining the length of ribbing required to finish the neckline smoothly. Too much ribbing results in a band that will not lie flat, but ripples and crumples. If the ribbing is too short, it will pull the garment and cause it to appear gathered. Figure 6-16 shows both problems.

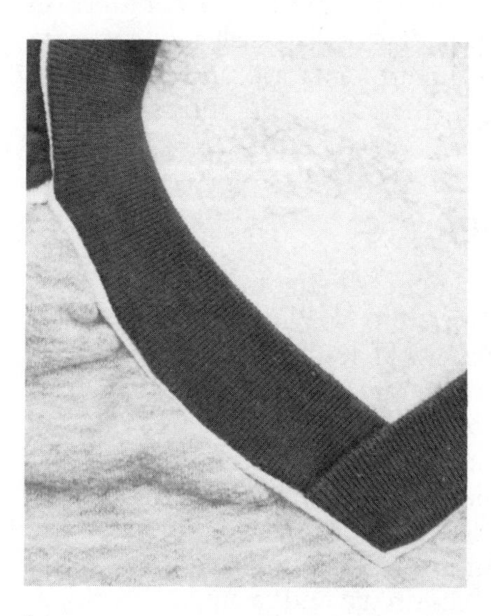

a.

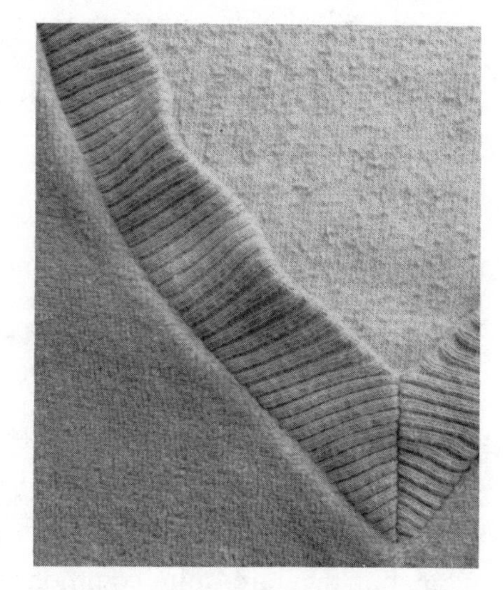

b.

6-16. Rib stretch band problems: (a) band too short for garment; (b) band too large for garment.

STANDARDS FOR EVALUATING RIB-STRETCH BANDS

1. The width of the band is even.
2. The band is joined before it is set into the garment.
3. The band is the correct length for the neckline.
4. The seam joining the band to the garment is neatly finished.

COLLARS

A collar is a single or double-ply fabric extension to the neckline. It may stand, drape over, or both stand and drape over the natural neckline, depending on style variations.

The addition of a collar to a neckline is one of the most important factors in determining the style and price range of a garment. In many cases, the collar design sets the mood for the rest of the garment, and frequently classifies it according to the sex and age of the intended market segment. Only occasionally does the collar itself provide the complete neckline treatment. In most cases, it must be applied in conjunction with one of the other neckline treatments. The collar itself requires extra pattern design time, layout, and cutting time, fabric and interfacing yardage, and construction steps. It can, therefore, add substantially to the cost of the garment.

FLAT COLLARS

Flat collars are cut with a neckline edge nearly identical to that of the garment. They emerge from the neckline seam and lie nearly flat against the garment. If the collar curve is somewhat less shallow than that of the neckline, then the collar will have a slight stand before it folds back against the garment. This common practice prevents the free edge of the collar from rippling and appearing too big. As the difference in curve depth between neckline and collar increases, more and more stand will be evident, and correspondingly less of the collar will lie flat. With the exception of the sailor collar, flat collars are not found on men's wear, but they are quite common in children's and women's clothing. The names of some flat collars include Peter Pan, Bermuda, sailor, Bertha, and Puritan.

A flat collar may be cut in one or two parts, depending on style. A round collar on a dress or on a blouse buttoning in the back is cut in

a.

b.

6-17. Selected flat collar styles: (a) Peter Pan flat collar with ruffle trim; (b) sailor flat collar.

two parts, one for the left side of the garment and one for the right. The upper and under collars are always separate pieces which must be joined at the outer edges after interfacing is applied and before the collar is attached to the garment. Nonwoven interfacing works well in this type of collar, as long as it is not too heavy or stiff for the collar fabric. Single-ply flat collars are attractive alternatives to the traditional two-ply, seamed flat collar. A single-ply flat collar can be made of lace or of any fabric. In the latter case, embroidery or binding can be used to finish the outer edge of the collar before it is attached to the garment. Figure 6-17 shows a variety of flat collars and trimming.

The actual construction of a flat collar is simple unless some trim is to be incorporated in the collar seam. In that case, the trim must be placed accurately. Trim that is applied on top of the outer edge after the collar has been seamed and turned requires less skill in application, but is frequently less attractive. Some difficulty in constructing the collar also arises if the fabric used is very bulky and if the under and upper collars are cut exactly the same size. In this case, the upper collar will not be large enough for the seam to roll to the underside when the collar seam is trimmed and the collar turned right side out. The finished collar will bubble and refuse to lie flat. The alternative is to cut the under collar smaller, then stretch it to fit the upper collar while joining the two. This is rarely done in industrial production, however.

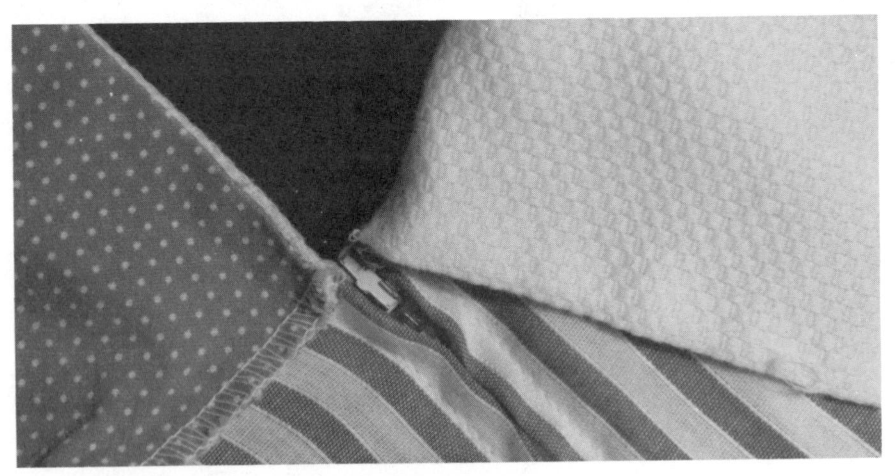

6-18. Collar seamed to right side of garment.

On large collars, understitching is used to prevent seam wells, to help flatten the lower edge of the collar and to keep the under collar from rolling to the right side. When the collar is not large enough to permit understitching, careful pressing can be substituted. Topstitching and/or surface trim should be applied at this stage.

Application of the flat collar often requires a facing, either bias or shaped. The neckline edges of the collar and garment are positioned together with the under collar against the right side of the garment. The facing is then applied just as if there were no collar. Completion of the facing is also done without regard to the collar. An alternative method of attaching the flat collar, used when the collar is not sheer, when the neckline is large enough so that it can be pulled on over the head, or if the opening edge is finished in some way separate from the finish used to secure the collar, is to seam the collar to the garment so that the seam allowances fall between the wrong side of the collar and the right side of the garment. This is a very inexpensive way of attaching the collar, often using an overlock type of seam.

STANDING COLLARS

The standing collar emerges directly upward from the neckline seam with no portion folding back against the garment. Stylistically, standing collars fall into two major classifications—rigid and flexible. Most examples of actual standing collars fall somewhere between these two extremes, however, rather than fitting neatly into these two disparate groups.

RIGID STANDING COLLARS

Standing collars that are more rigid than flexible are best exemplified by the mandarin or band collar. The basic shape is straight or slightly curved, with the upper edge smaller than the neckline seam. The collar opening may have rounded or pointed upper edges. Most rigid standing collars are cut to form a single constructed unit, but for a garment that opens in the back, the collar may be made in two sections, one for the left side of the garment and one for the right.

A rigid standing collar is usually interfaced for support and maintenance of shape. An exception would be a shaped standing collar made of a contrasting fabric such as lace or embroidery. Collars such as these are made to be applied in a single ply and in a one-step operation. Interfacing would be totally inappropriate to the sheerness of the collar fabric.

Additional designs can be incorporated into a rigid standing collar before it is attached to a garment. A common modification is the addition of a pointed shirt collar to the upper edge of the shaped band collar of men's shirts (or to shirts made in the same way as men's). The shirt collar is sandwiched in between the upper and under bands at the upper edge, then the seam is made to join all plies of material, leaving open the neckline edge only. The unit is then ready for application to

a.

b.

c.

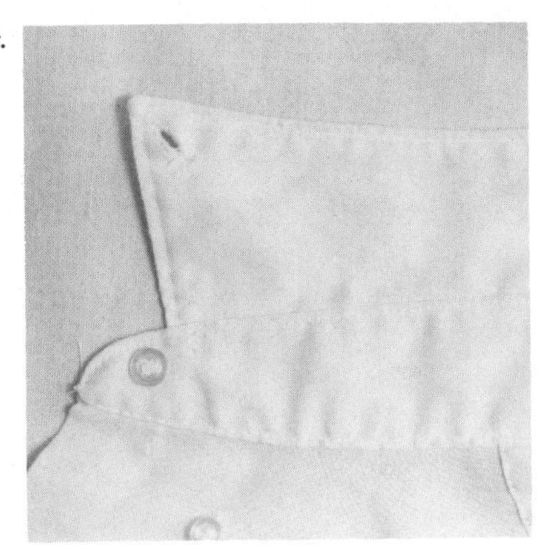

6-19. Rigid standing collars: (a) simple band collar; (b) bias band collar; (c) shirt collar on band.

the shirt. Modern equipment can complete the collar, topstitch it, insert in the band, and apply the entire unit to a shirt in a matter of seconds. Piping or cording, ruffles, lace edging, or other trim may be included in the outer seam edge.

Another style variation of the rigid standing collar is the narrow bias tie. A reference to this was made in the section on bindings, and some bias tie collars are applied as bindings, but others are applied more as rigid standing collars. In the rigid standing collar classification, the bias tie would not have sufficient width to be folded over, but would simply rise directly up from the neckline. The portion of the tie that forms the collar is often interfaced, but the tie portion is not.

Application of the rigid band collar is most commonly done with self-finishes, although facings can also be used. In the former method, most common for shirts, blouses, dresses, and shirt jackets, the neckline edges of the upper and under collars are turned under all-around, slipping over the neckline of the garment, then topstitched close to the fold through all plies. Home sewers more commonly sew just the outer band to the neckline, preferring to hand sew the lower edge of the inner band in place.

Jackets and coats with band collars have them applied more frequently with a complete, shaped facing. The outer band is sewn to the garment proper, and the neckline seam is pressed open. The inner band is sewn to the facing unit at the neckline. The two units are then placed with the right sides together for seaming along the outer edge. After trimming, the facing/inner collar unit is turned to the inside to complete this type of band collar. Garments exhibiting this method of application frequently are lined, and the lining serves to hold the free edges of the facing in place. This method of application produces a neckline seam that is smooth, flat, and non-bulky.

Sandwiching a band collar in between the facing and garment, as is done with a flat collar, is not a very satisfactory method of application, particularly if the collar comes to the foldline of an opening. When this method is used, it is extremely difficult to achieve a smooth edge where the garment and collar join.

FLEXIBLE STANDING COLLARS

The more flexible type of standing collar is exemplified by the tunnel and turtle-neck styles which either wrinkle down or roll over on themselves. They are cut so high above the natural neckline that they cannot remain in a standing position on the body.

The flexible standing collar is frequently made of knitted fabric or soft wovens. When this type of collar is made of knitted fabric, the

6-20. Flexible standing collar.

application will almost always be handled exactly the same way as the application of the rib-stretch band discussed earlier in this chapter. This method may also be used for some woven fabrics, particularly if the garment is to be low to medium in price. In home sewing and couture lines, the raw edges of the inner half of the band will usually be turned under and hand-stitched to the neckline seam to give a smooth, enclosed seam.

Very rarely do flexible standing collars contain interfacing. In fact, in most cases, the addition of interfacing would destroy the desired look of the collar. If the bias tie collar is wide enough to fold or pleat down on itself, then it, too, usually is not interfaced, although the narrow version, covered under rigid standing collars, might be interfaced.

ROLLED COLLARS

The rolled collar is actually a combination of the standing and the flat collars. A portion of the collar, from the center back to a point in front of the shoulder seams, forms a self-stand which extends above the neckline. The entire stand portion of the collar may extend, or it may fold over on itself. The point at which the stand begins to fold back and become the fall depends on the location of the front opening of the garment, if there is one. In garments that close all the way to the neck edge, the stand extends almost to the center front. In styles that turn back to form lapels, the stand is much shorter, and the fall begins further toward the garment back.

Rolled collars can be classified according to the following three techniques: (l) one-piece construction with a fold at the collar outer edge; (2) two-piece upper and under collar cut double and seamed at the collar outer edge; and (3) three-piece construction with under collar cut on the bias, seamed at the center back, then sewn to the upper collar. These three types are shown in Figure 6-21.

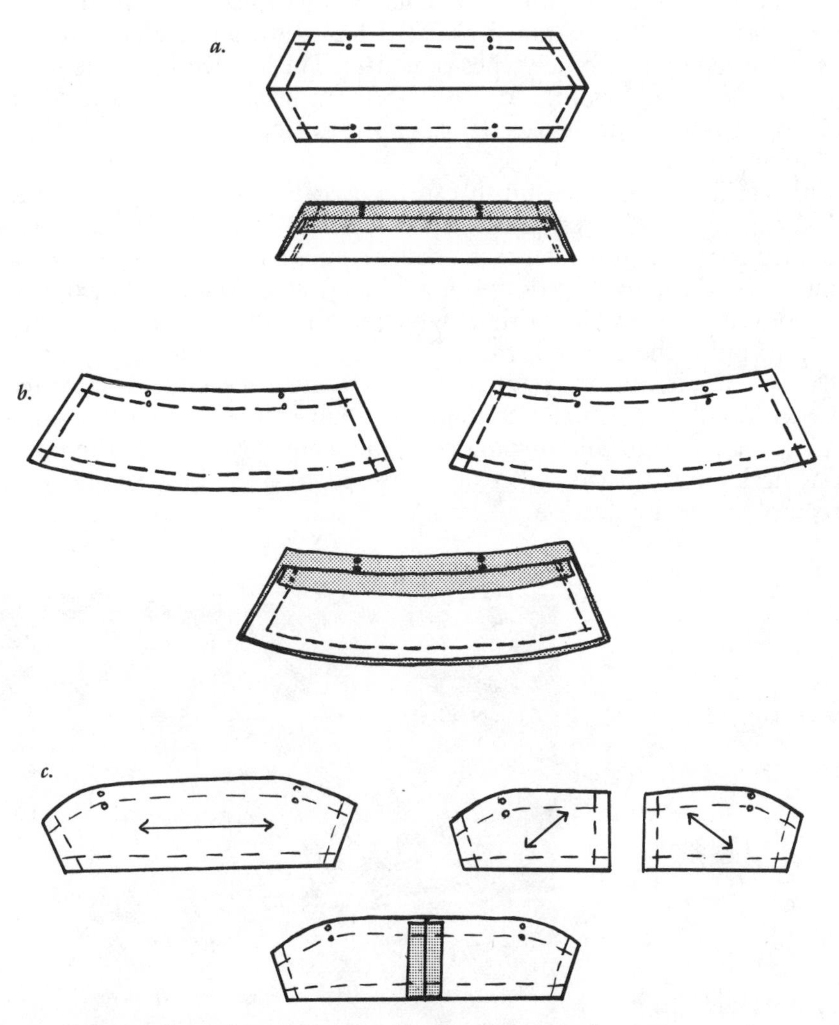

6-21. Rolled collars: (a) one-piece; (b) two-piece; (c) three-piece.

ONE-PIECE CONSTRUCTION

One-piece construction is the simplest and least expensive type of rolled collar to construct. It can be made double or single ply, and only one pattern piece is required. A single cut yields both sides of the double-ply collar, and the outer edge is finished by folding rather than by seaming. Once the collar is interfaced, only the short ends require seaming, trimming, and turning to complete the collar. The one-piece construction is frequently found on children's wear, pajamas, men's sport shirts, and some blouses and jackets. It has a greater tendency to curl at its outer edge than other types of collars. The single ply construction is most often made from a knitted fabric, usually ribbing for stability and stretch. Other, decorative fabrics such as lace may also be used for the single-ply collar.

Either a facing or a self-finish can be used in application. The latter is less expensive. The self-finish can be applied in the same manner as that used for the band collar if the collar comes all the way to the center front of the garment. If it does not, and a notch is to be provided, then two options are possible, both of which involve the use of an extended facing to finish the garment front. For a more finished look, the under collar is sewn to the garment, then the facing neck edge is enclosed. This enclosed seam usually contains one-half inch (1.27 cm) or more of the collar as well. The remainder of the seam allowance of the upper collar neckline is turned under and topstitched over the neckline seam to complete the application.

6-22. Single-ply knitted collar.

It is even easier and quicker to apply the collar and form the enclosed seams of the facing neck edge at the same time, in a single operation using a serged seam. If the facing is not deep enough and if the first button is placed rather low, the serged neckline seam as well as some portion of the unfaced front area of the garment may show.

TWO-PIECE CONSTRUCTION

The two-piece rolled collar is much more adaptable to shape and styling variations and is more common than the one-piece collar. An additional pattern piece is required, as is more time in cutting and seaming, but this usually results in only slight extra expense. In many instances, this extra cost is offset by savings in fabric yardage when the two small pattern pieces can be fit into smaller areas on the marker than would suffice for the one larger.

Two-piece construction is required if any type of trim is to be enclosed at the outer edge of the collar. The trim is applied to a single collar section, then the outer-edge seam is formed, joining the two sections and securing the trim at the same time. Two-piece construction is also required if any variation from an end point is desired—if the collar is to be somewhat rounded rather than pointed, for example. Application is essentially the same as for one-piece construction. Figure 6-23 shows a simple two-piece collar applied to a garment with a serged seam. The extended facing at the front closure does not completely cover the label area when the top button is left open and the collar turned back. The

6-23. Two-piece construction rolled collar simulating shirt collar on band.

shape of the collar simulates the rigid standing collar with shirt collar attached, but with fewer pieces and construction steps.

THREE-PIECE CONSTRUCTION

By far the most complex and expensive rolled collar is constructed of three or more pieces. Styles include the traditional notched collar found on blazers and many women's suits as well as the shawl collar, which has a slightly different method of construction. Figure 6-24 shows several styles of notched collar and lapel treatments.

Notched Collar. In the typical notched collar, the under collar is cut from a separate pattern piece, is cut on the bias, and is usually slightly smaller than the upper collar. The interfacing for the bias under collar should also be cut on the bias, and preferably of a woven fabric, not a fiber web. The bias fold of a woven interfacing is smooth, the fold of a fiber web is not.

Most notched collars have the interfacing attached by pad-stitching in the area of the stand. This is done by machine or by hand and strengthens the stand as well as holds in the interfacing. Hand-done pad stitching is still used in some men's custom-tailored suits and in designer suits for women. The hand-done pad stitching builds in shape as well as support in the collar stand.

In the matter of application, the notched collar also departs radically from the procedures typically used for one- and two-piece collars. The former are completely constructed, trimmed (if applicable), then applied. Application of the three-piece collar is much more complex and slow. The collar is not sewn together until both the upper and the under collar have been individually attached to the facing unit and the garment unit, respectively.

Next, in the case of women's wear, the facing/upper collar unit is applied right sides together with the garment/under-collar unit. (The final application of the three-piece collar on men's suits is treated separately below.) The seam that connects the outer edges is made in three stages: (1) from the bottom of the facing edge to the neckline seam; (2) from the neckline seam upward along the outer edges of the collar; and (3) from the neck edge to the bottom of the facing on the other side. The three steps may be combined if the neckline/collar seams are clipped at the point where the stitching line crosses them. Failure to match the garment sections accurately in any of these areas results in a hole or in ripples at the junction of the lapel and collar.

In men's suits, the three-piece collar is handled differently in final application. (See Figure 6-25.) The under collar is made of a nonraveling, felt-like material and is cut without seam allowances on any side.

6-24. Notched collars.

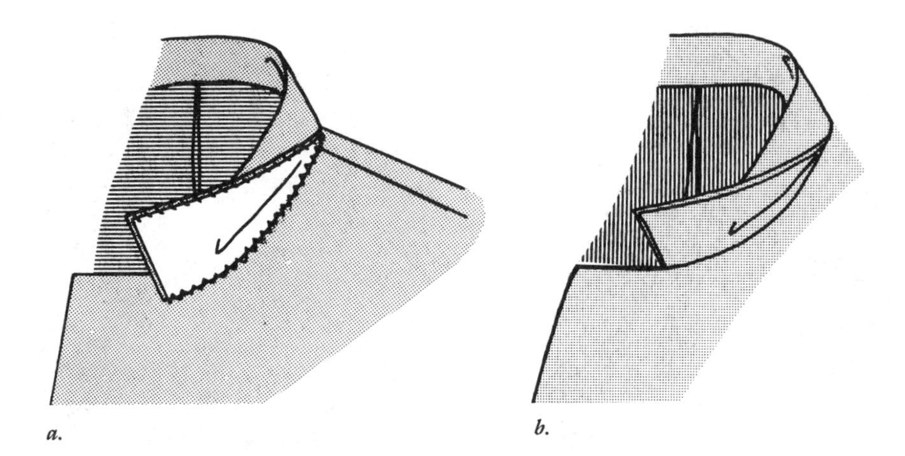

6-25. Application of three-piece rolled collars: (a) on a man's suit; (b) on a woman's suit.

In more expensive garments, French melton may be used for the under collar, but felt is more common. It is joined to the neckline of the garment in a lapped seam, by hand or with a zigzag or felling stitch. The upper collar, with collar points mitered or neatly lapped, is sewn to the facing unit at the neckline. Both sides of the front facing and lapel are joined, right sides together, then trimmed and turned. The outer edges of the under collar and upper collar are joined by hand or by a special felling machine which can duplicate very closely the appearance of hand stitches in a lapped seam to complete the collar section.

In custom tailoring of men's and some women's jackets, the upper collar is completely joined by hand, including the lapel/collar seam. In those cases, the raw edges of both are turned under and abutted, then joined with tiny slip stitches. The method of applying the three-piece collar affects the final cost of the garment considerably, with hand application entailing the higher cost, but also yielding more precise fit and shaping.

Shawl Collar. In the shawl collar, the front closure extends upward to the center back to form a collar which rolls into the first closure. This may occur very high on the neckline or almost at waist level for garments which do not actually close but are worn open or lapped. The collar itself may have a variety of shapes and sizes. One version actually appears at first glance to be a notched collar, but closer inspection shows that the notch is simply an indention in the outer seamline joining the

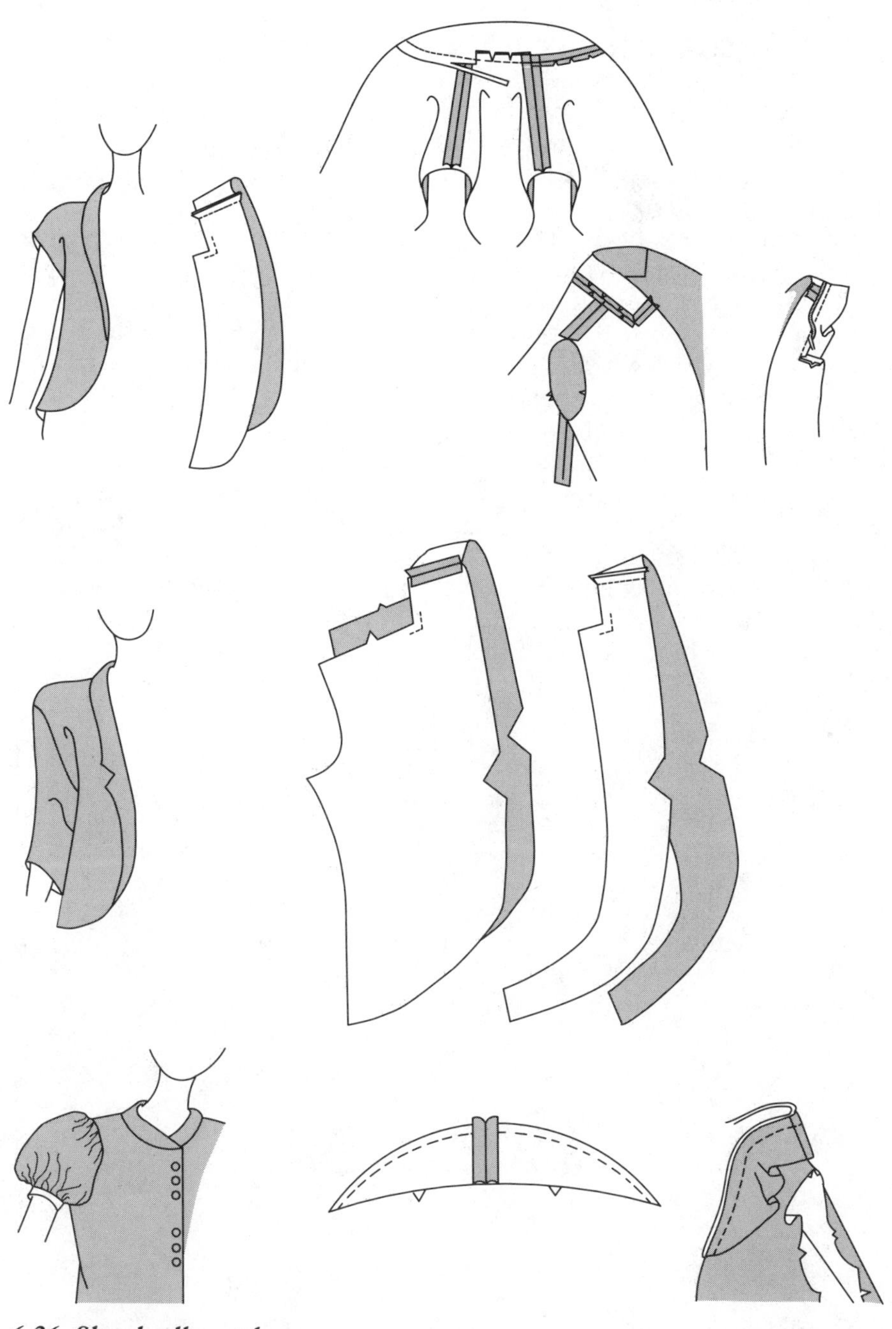

6-26. Shawl collar styles.

collar to the facing. The notch is a potential point of weakness in the garment if the fabric is loosely woven or has a tendency to slip and ravel. The v-clipped area must be sewn with very small stitches for reinforcement to prevent the notch from fraying out during wear. Figure 6-26 shows some typical examples of shawl collars, including the one with a notched edge.

Construction methods differ depending upon exactly which version of the shawl collar is involved, but basically a small under collar, in either one or two pieces and cut on the bias, is stitched to the garment neckline. Along with the portions of the front facing to which it is seamed, this collar forms the undercollar unit of the garment. The facing, cut in two pieces and seamed at the center back, is then applied to the garment unit with a seam which goes from bottom front on one side, up and around the outer edge of the collar, and then down to the bottom front on the other side. When this seam is formed, any piping, unusual shaping, or other trim details would be incorporated. The facing and upper collar must be attached to the garment as the final step. This attachment usually extends only the length of the undercollar, leaving the front facing hanging free except for where it might be secured by topstitching or buttons and buttonholes.

STANDARDS FOR EVALUATING COLLARS

1. The collar is interfaced, when necessary, with appropriate interfacing.
2. The outer edges of the collar are smooth and even with no seam wells or holes.
3. Enclosed seams have been trimmed to reduce bulk.
4. The size and shape of the collar is consistent from one end to the other, except for intentional design variations.
5. The collar fits the neck edge to which it is sewn without stretching or gathering.
6. The collar assumes the proper position on the garment, as intended by the designer. For example, a flat collar lies flat against the garment instead of rolling up.
7. The placement of the collar is symmetrical on the garment. For example, notched collars have the same size of notch on each side of the center front.
8. All raw edges are carefully concealed during collar application so that they are not visible when the garment is worn.

SUMMARY

Since the neckline surrounds and frames the face, it is an important design element in a garment. Also, because it is near the face, it attracts more attention than do other aspects of the garment, such as the hem. This makes quality especially important to neckline treatments. With many standard styles of necklines, like shirt collars on bands and notched rolled collars, automated equipment allows the apparel manufacturer to produce consistent products in a minimum of time. As with other techniques, time requirements relate directly to apparel costs, but not always to quality.

7

SLEEVE TREATMENTS

A backward glance at the development of the basic fashion silhouette will reinforce the importance of sleeves as a strong fashion element down through the centuries. By varying the distinctive shapes, set and fit of sleeves, they have been exaggerated, emphasized, or minimized during different historical periods. Sleeve variations are countless, and terms used to describe them seem just as numerous and occasionally ambiguous. Sleeves may be short or long, full or fitted, cuffed or hemmed, set in or cut in, gathered, ruffled, belled, pleated, darted, tailored, vented, buttoned, tucked, tied, etc. Sleeve design, therefore, can be very important to the success of an apparel item in the marketplace. Good sleeve design, however, must be followed by quality sleeve construction and good fit, or the end product will be disappointing at best.

SLEEVE TYPES

Most sleeve designs fall into one of the following categories: (a) *set-in,* (b) *raglan,* and (c) *kimono*. The term *cap sleeve* refers to sleeve length rather than type, and cap sleeves may be found in each of these three structural categories. Examples of each type are shown in Figure 7-1.

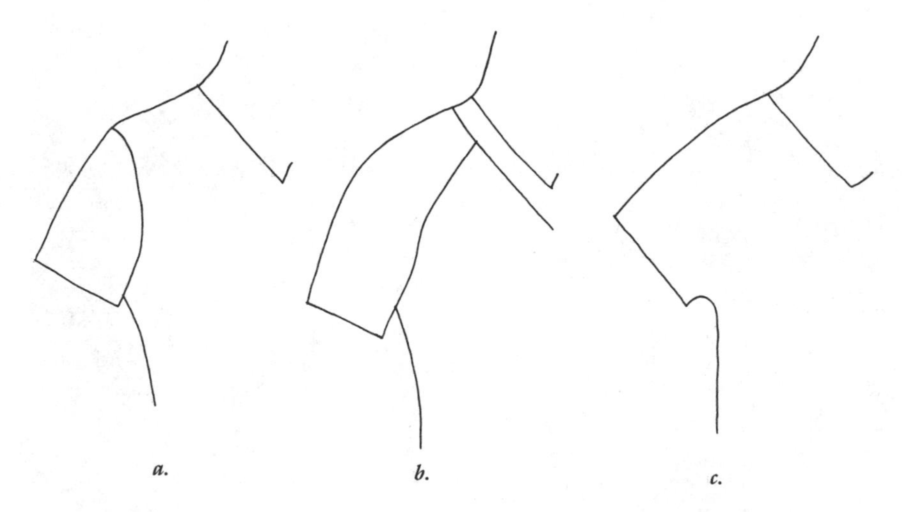

7-1. Sleeve types: (a) set-in; (b) raglan; (c) kimono.

SET-IN SLEEVES

The set-in sleeve is the most common of the three types, and one of the most difficult to construct. It is set into an oval armscye with a seam that passes over the high point of the shoulder and encircles the entire arm. The set-in sleeve is designed with ease to enable the sleeve to fit comfortably and attractively over the rounded portion of the upper arm. The amount of ease needed for these purposes depends on the width and the height of the sleeve cap.

Also, some set-in sleeves are designed so that rather than an eased seam, other means of introducing fullness are used as design features. Pleats, darts, or gathers can all be used to add fullness to the cap of the set-in sleeve and to create a different design effect. Figure 7-2 shows two variations of design features in set-in sleeves.

LOW-CAP SET-IN SLEEVE

The low, wide sleeve cap requires little ease because its design provides the space needed for freedom of movement at the arms and shoulders. The roominess of this sleeve cut is perfect for apparel that is used for active work and play. This loose cut does, however, cause diagonal wrinkles in the front and back of the sleeve when the arm is in a relaxed position (Figure 7-3). Since it is used almost exclusively in casual wear for men and women, and children as well as in men's dress and sport shirts because of its comfort, these diagonal wrinkles are not a problem.

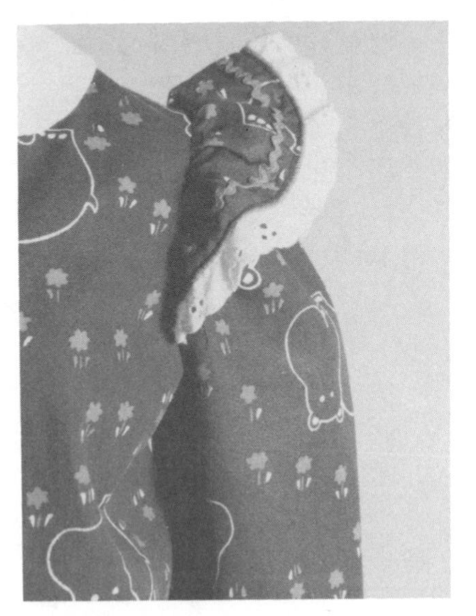

a.

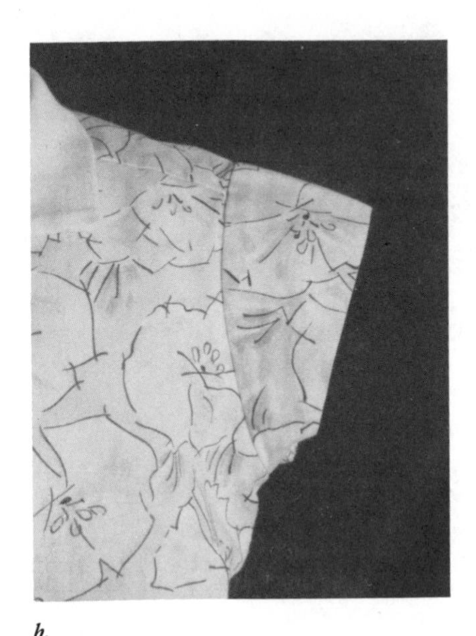

b.

7-2. Variations of set-in sleeves: (a) high cap with ruffle trim; (b) low cap.

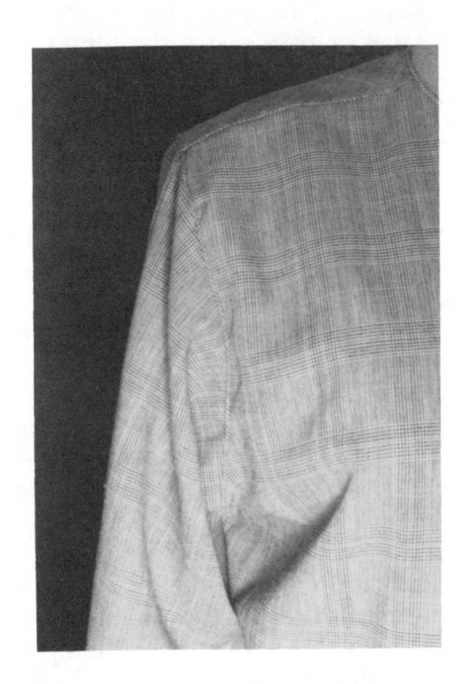

7-3. Low cap set-in sleeve with piped seam and epaulet extension over shoulder.

The ease with which this sleeve can be set makes it very popular among apparel manufacturers. The average machine operator can set this sleeve into the armscye without having to manipulate ease and without having to sew the bodice and sleeve side seams before application. This technique is easier, more accurate, and less costly than closing both seams prior to application.

HIGH-CAP SET-IN SLEEVE

Certain designs, however, require a sleeve that is less roomy and one that has no wrinkles when the arm is in its normal position. Since the low, wide-cap type of set-in sleeve design has wrinkles at both sides when the arm is relaxed, it is not used in designs that require a smooth look. A set-in sleeve without side wrinkles requires a high, narrow cap shape that must be eased several inches over the curved area of the shoulder to attain a good fit as well as the desired look. Sleeves with this type of cap do not allow as much freedom of movement as low, wide-cap sleeves. They are often used in tailored suits for men, women, and children and in other dressy apparel.

These sleeves are harder to set by the home sewer or by the apparel manufacturer because a considerable amount of ease must be inserted

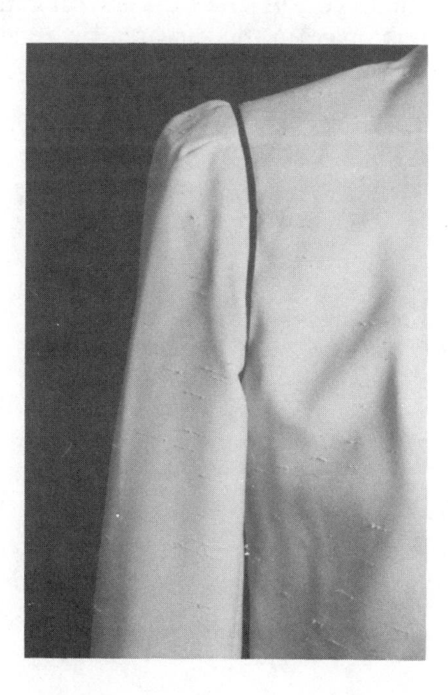

7-4. High cap set-in sleeve fitted to armscye with darts.

into the sleeve cap without creating puckers, pleats, or dimples at the point of attachment. In home sewing, machine basting at the sleeve cap is used to help manipulate the ease. The underarm seams joining the bodice and sleeve are sewn before the sleeve is set into the armscye. These steps make the application much more difficult and time-consuming than the open side seam construction used to apply the low, wide-cap set-in sleeve.

Some manufacturers set the high, narrow sleeve cap by methods similar to those used in home sewing, while others still use an open-seam method, with skilled operators manipulating the ease without the assistance of machine basting. Free-arm sewing machines with a programmable easing function are used by some apparel manufacturers to facilitate the application of high-cap set-in sleeves when the underarm seam on the sleeve and on the garment has been sewn prior to application of the sleeve.

In smooth applications in soft or drapable fabrics, additional reinforcement at the sleeve cap is sometimes used by manufacturers of more expensive apparel lines. This usually takes the form of a folded bias cut of fabric which conforms to the cut of the sleeve cap at the upper edge. The folded edge of the bias extends down two to three inches (5.12–7.68 cm) from the highest point of the sleeve cap. Figure 7-5 shows a child's cotton jersey dress with gathered, high-cap set in sleeves that are reinforced in the cap area by a gathered piece of stiff nonwoven interfacing fabric.

7-5. Sleeve cap reinforcement method.

In sleeves with design fullness such as pleats and gathers, additional reinforcement is often used in better garments to maintain the design line of the sleeve. This feature is often used in bridal wear. The exact form of the reinforcement, as well as the underlying fabric used for the addition, depend upon the design of the sleeve fullness and the fashion fabric used in the garment. In apparel made of stiff fabric such as organza, self fabric may be used to form a pleated or gathered frill which attaches to the top several inches of the sleeve cap seam. Other fabrics such as tulle or net are also used for this purpose. Tiny pads similar to shoulder pads but used instead in the sleeve cap can sometimes be found in sleeves with less fullness than those requiring the frill.

TAILORED SET-IN SLEEVE

The tailored sleeve usually has a high, narrow cap and is often made in two pieces rather than a single unit. If the sleeve is fitted, darts are replaced by ease at the seam nearest the elbow. There is no underarm seam. In the plaid jacket pictured in Figure 7-6, the plaids are so well matched at the outer seamline that the seam is barely discernable, a sign of a well-made garment.

The cap is usually padded with a sleeve head or a sleeve roll and a shoulder pad appropriate in height for the current fashion. In tailored garments, shoulder pads add perceptibly to the appearance of the sleeve

7-6. Tailored set-in sleeve.

STANDARDS FOR EVALUATING SET-IN SLEEVES

1. Plaids, stripes, or directional patterns are matched within the sleeve itself and where the sleeve joins the garment at the sides of the sleeve cap.
2. Bodice shoulder seams are sewn, finished, and pressed before the sleeve is set to avoid conspicuous pulls or puckers at the shoulder area.
3. The sleeve is accurately matched to the bodice armscye at the following points:
   (a) the high point of the sleeve to the shoulder line of the bodice;
   (b) the underarm seam of the sleeve to the underarm of the bodice;
   (c) at the notches at each side of the sleeve.
4. All ease is evenly distributed with no puckers, pleats, or dimples.
5. If darts, pleats, or gathers are used to produce a full sleeve cap, these are neatly made, accurately positioned, and consistent with garment style and fabric used.
6. The stitching that sets the sleeve into the armscye is smooth around the entire seam with no dips or curves present.
7. The underarm area (between notches in home sewing) is reinforced. This can be done with a second row of stitching or with the application of twill tape.
8. The underarm area is trimmed to about one-fourth inch (.64 cm) to reduce bulk.
9. In jackets and tailored garments, the upper portion of the sleeve/armscye seam is left a full five-eighths inch (1.59 cm) wide to help support the sleeve cap. In soft fabrics and less tailored styles, the entire seam is usually trimmed to one-fourth or three-eights inch (.64 or .95 cm) and serged.
10. Shoulder pads and other findings used to support the upper sleeve cap are used only with fabrics that have sufficient weight to conceal their shape and location.
11. Sleeve findings (as noted in #10) are secured inconspicuously without pulling the garment in any way.
12. The sleeve is adequate in size for the designated label size. (Fitting standards and actual sizing vary considerably among manufacturers.)
13. The right sleeve is designed to fit into the right armscye and the left sleeve into the left armscye for correct fit and hang of the sleeve.

cap, not just to the width and height of the shoulder. These are most often sewn to the seam allowance of the sleeve cap/armscye so that they cannot shift out of place. In a lined garment, the shoulder pads are inserted and attached before the lining is applied. By contrast, many casual and dressy garments today have shoulder pads, even t-shirt styles. These are more often attached just to the shoulder seam by thread tacks or nylon hook and loop tape. The latter allows them to be removed for cleaning and pressing. This less expensive type of shoulder pad is also more easily applied, but it must be finished with self fabric or with fabric which matches the garment so that they will be unobtrusive in the finished garment.

Often, the seams are taped, and interfacing may be used at the sleeve hem to retain the sleeve shape. Setting procedures are the same as those described for other high-cap set-in sleeves. The tailored sleeve costs more because of the extra fabric, findings (those materials, other than the garment fabric and pattern, that become a part of the garment, such as thread, seam tape, shoulder pads, buttons, etc.), and number of pattern pieces required, and because more steps are needed to complete the sleeve unit.

RAGLAN SLEEVES

The raglan sleeve is popular for its roominess, comfort, and simple application. The classic raglan can be recognized easily by the softly curved diagonal lines that extend from the underarm upward to the neckline, forming a section of the bodice at the shoulder. Darts, seams, or gathers are used to provide the fullness necessary for the sleeve to curve over the full part of the shoulder, yet tapered to fit the much smaller neckline.

ONE-PIECE RAGLAN SLEEVE

The one-piece raglan requires the use of some technique to introduce shaping at the shoulder/neckline area of the garment. Darts often provide the shaping mechanism on more tailored garments, but it is difficult to construct so that the fitted raglan will appear to its best advantage on many different body types. This is because the point at which fullness is removed and subsequently allowed to return to the upper sleeve area must conform exactly to the shape of the body on which it will be worn, or the discrepancy will be very obvious in bubbles(excess

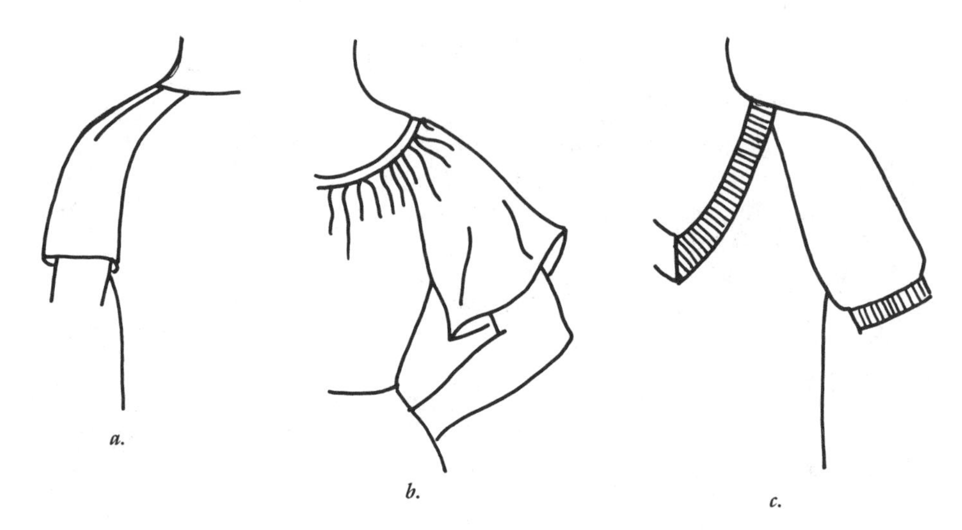

7-7. One-piece raglan sleeves: (a) shaped with a dart; (b) shaped with gathers; (c) knitted fabric expands to provide shaping.

fabric) or wrinkles (insufficient fabric). For this reason, rather thick, spongy fabric which has some molding capability or a loosely fitted garment are better suited to a fitted, darted raglan sleeve.

Another method of introducing shaping into the one-piece raglan is with gathers. The gathered raglan is extremely popular in infants' dresses, peasant-styled blouses and dresses, and nightgowns and robes. In many of these garments, the entire bodice unit, including sleeves, gathers into a curved yoke or inset band. Otherwise, the upper edge may be finished with a casing and drawstring or with elastic to provide the fitting gathers. This is the easiest type of raglan to fit on a variety of figure types, but it is limited stylistically to designs appropriate to a soft, gathered look.

The saddle shoulder variation of the raglan sleeve provides another means of shaping the sleeve/garment unit to the body. In this type, no gathers or easing at the top of the sleeve are used; instead, the shaped seamline which joins the sleeve to the garment provides the necessary fitting. Because of the sharp curve or even angle at the point where the sleeve cap becomes the garment yoke (the saddle), this type of raglan is more difficult to insert than any of the others, and this fact may increase manufacturing costs.

TWO-PIECE RAGLAN SLEEVE

The two-piece raglan has a seam down its center. This seam provides an excellent place for adjusting shoulder slant, should such an alteration be necessary. Since this seam contains a large amount of garment bias, careful stitching is required to avoid puckering or stretching the fabric at the seamline. The two-piece raglan is most often found on coats and men's sports jackets.

Application of the one- or two-piece raglan sleeve is much easier than that of the high-cap set-in sleeve, since the raglan has little or no ease to manipulate as does the set-in style. Furthermore, the raglan may be attached to the bodice sections, allowing the underarm sleeve seam and garment side seam to be sewn in one operation. This application procedure requires less time and is the most common method chosen by industrial apparel producers when raglan sleeves are used.

An alternative method of applying the raglan sleeve requires that the underarm and side seams of the bodice and sleeve be sewn before the sleeve is inserted. This method is more comfortable for the wearer, since the seam conforms to the underarm contour of the body. It is, however, slower and more expensive to construct and, therefore, is found more frequently in expensive apparel lines or in apparel sewn at home.

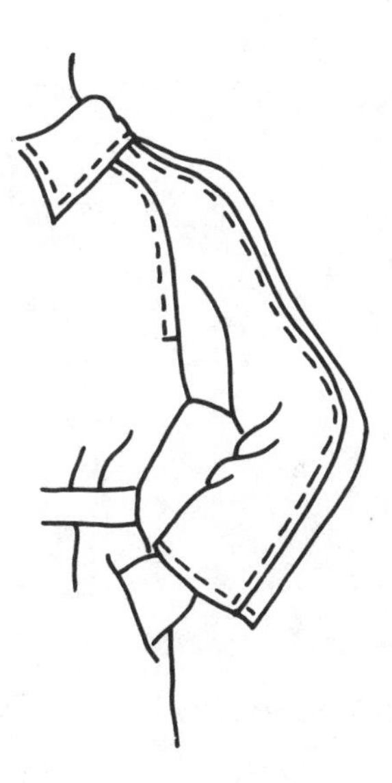

7-8. Two-piece raglan sleeve.

STANDARDS FOR EVALUATING RAGLAN SLEEVES

1. Plaids, stripes, or directional patterns are matched within the sleeve itself and where the sleeve joins the garment across the chest and back.
2. The method of shaping the shoulder and neckline is appropriate to the garment fabric and design.
3. The sleeve-to-bodice seams are smooth and flat with no puckers, pleats, or ripples.
4. The sleeve is inserted into the garment after the underarm and side seams are made, finished, and pressed.

KIMONO SLEEVES

The kimono sleeve is cut as one unit with the bodice front and back. The resulting curved underarm seam may be loose or closely fitted, but in either case must be carefully clipped to prevent pulling and reinforced to prevent the stitches from breaking during wear. Figure 7-9 shows the basic shape of a kimono sleeve.

The looseness of the kimono sleeve is controlled by the point at which the side seam of the garment curves outward to become the underarm seam of the sleeve. On very loose kimono sleeves, this occurs at or slightly above the waistline of the garment. Looseness is also affected

7-9. Kimono sleeve.

by the angle of the upper shoulder/sleeve seam. If it is straight out from the neckline or angled downward slightly, the sleeve will be loose and comfortable.

LOOSE KIMONO SLEEVES

Loose kimono sleeves are the easiest of all to construct. Soft wrinkles on the front and back of the sleeve are formed when the arm is in a relaxed position. They really require no additional reinforcement beyond the serging and trimming which ordinarily finishes the seam.

There is a potential for quite an additional cost factor in the completed garment, however, because of the amount of fabric required to make a garment of this type. Also, if the loose kimono is made to the wrist, and the bodice sections are cut not to have any seams at all, the layout may be extremely difficult to achieve. In narrow widths of fabric, layouts may have to be done crosswise just to get the pattern on the fabric. To economize in terms of fabric use and to take advantage of fabric designs such as stripes or other directional patterns, manufacturers may seam the kimono at any point. As long as the underarm curve is part of the bodice unit, the sleeve is still called a kimono. In most instances, decorative extensions are sewn to the bodice/sleeve units before the underarm seams are sewn.

FITTED KIMONO SLEEVES

When the angle of the shoulder/sleeve seam drops and the sleeve curve moves up closer to the underarm, a closer fitting sleeve with no underarm wrinkles is the result. Also, arm movement is drastically restricted. The strain that occurs at the underarm seam when the arm is raised requires substantial reinforcement. As a consequence, increased labor costs may make the fitted kimono more expensive. This is especially true if a gusset is used to increase freedom of movement and comfort.

A gusset is a bias cut, diamond-shaped inset of fashion fabric. Most gussets are cut in two sections which are sewn together with a curved seam at the underarm to make the gusset fit the body more closely at this point. Sometimes, they are designed as a continuation of a side or underarm bodice and sleeve panel.

Gussets must be set carefully into a reinforced slash on the front and back of the bodice armscye. Either a plain or a lapped seam can be used. Accuracy is critical when setting gussets so that the two sections in the completed garment match. Gussets add extra construction steps and require skilled labor, thereby adding to garment costs.

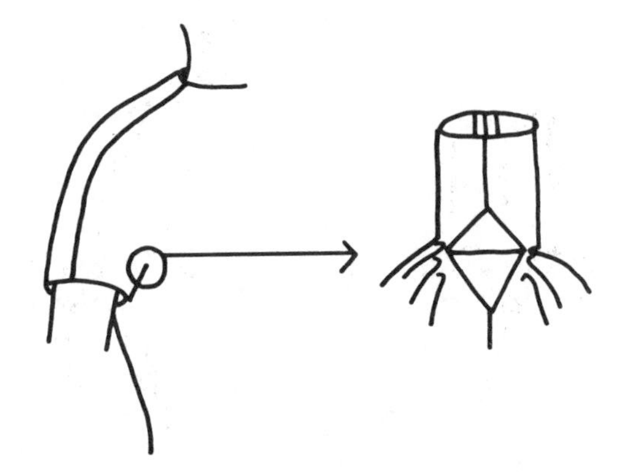

7-10. Fitted kimono sleeve with a gusset.

7-11. Gusset formed by an extension of garment and sleeve sections.

STANDARDS FOR EVALUATING KIMONO SLEEVES

1. Obvious diagonal patterns should not be used in kimono sleeves, except possibly in very short cap sleeves.
2. The shoulder seam is neither stretched nor drawn.
3. Sufficient underarm reinforcement has been used in fitted kimono sleeves to prevent them from ripping out during wear.
4. Sufficient ease was allowed for comfort during wear.

SLEEVE FINISHES

The treatment of the lower sleeve edge is commonly referred to as the sleeve finish, and it should complement the well-set sleeve. The type of finish should be selected to fit the garment and fabric design, the design mood, and the use for which the garment seems appropriate. Design success in the marketplace as well as pleasure derived from wearing the garment is affected by the successful combination of the basic design elements, even one as simple as a sleeve finish.

A well-chosen sleeve finish is a good start, but must be followed by accurate construction methods. Quality sleeve finishes begin with attention to details such as even stitching, matching of fabric patterns, appropriate treatment of enclosed seams, proper use of support fabrics when needed, and adequate pressing. The cost of quality constructed sleeve finishes varies with the amount and cost of the fabric, the use of support fabrics and/or findings, and the amount and expertise of the labor required to execute the technique.

HEMMED SLEEVES

In Chapter 10, "Hem Treatments," all of the basic information applicable to hems in general will be discussed. To avoid unnecessary repetition, the reader is referred to that chapter for information on structure and methods of hemming. Deep hems are generally found on tailored

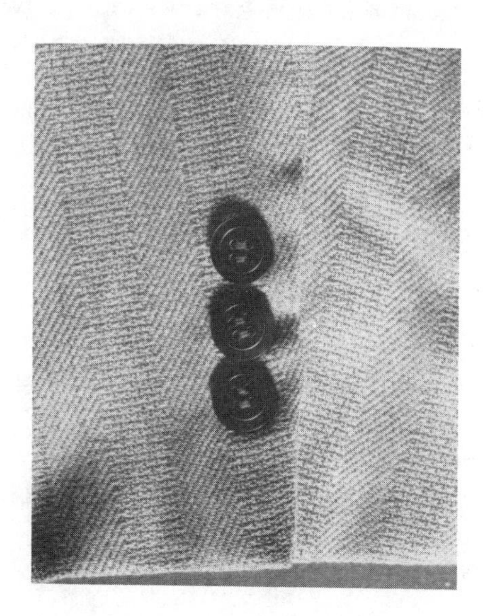

7-12. Vent and hem in man's suit jacket sleeve.

7-13. Lined hem rolled down.

sleeves. If the tailored sleeve is cut in two pieces, then a vent is often included. This is the typical design feature of men's suits and sports coats. The vent is lapped and usually has machine worked buttonholes on the top lap. The buttonholes are not cut, but the buttons are sewn to the ends of the buttonholes through all thicknesses.

Many jackets without vents but with linings have sleeve hems not attached first to the garment. Only the lining hem is attached to the sleeve, with perhaps a stitch or two securing the entire sleeve hem at the underarm seam. This procedure frequently leads to problems as the garment is worn and the lining and sleeve hem tend to roll down, as shown in Figure 7-13. Better quality apparel will have the sleeve hem attached to the garment before the lining hem is attached to the inside of the sleeve hem.

Other types of hems are found on less tailored apparel. Many knit tops have a simple narrow hem secured by topstitching or double needle coverstitch. This type of hem would replace ribbing to secure the sleeve bottom. Short and cap sleeves are usually finished with a narrow hem. A regular blindstitch hem is also found on sleeves. Any narrow hems on single or jersey knits tend to roll to the front, particularly if there is any stress on the fabric.

FACED AND BOUND SLEEVE EDGES

In Chapter 6, "Neckline Treatments," the basic information on facings and bindings has already been provided. Application methods, fabric limitations, and standards for evaluating quality are basically the same, regardless of what section of the garment contains the technique.

Facings are most frequently found on shaped, tapered sleeves where the difference in size between hem edge and hem stitching line is too great to be accommodated by a flange. Facings also serve to conceal the raw edges of decorative cuffs, and allow decorative shapes to be sewn into the sleeve—scallops, for example.

Bindings tend to be preferred when they are used on other portions of the garment as well. They may be applied to a smooth or to a gathered sleeve edge. They may even combine with a placket opening and extend into ties, thereby serving as both sleeve finish and fastener.

CASINGS AND ELASTIC AT SLEEVE EDGES

The softly gathered look at the sleeve edge provided by the use of elastic or drawstring is a favorite for children's, girls', and women's feminine clothing. These finishes vary in cost and complexity, determined by the way the gathers are introduced into the garment. A detailed discussion of casings and applied elastic can be found in Chapter 8, "Waistline Treatments." Methods of application and standards for evaluating these treatments are the same, whether they are used as sleeve finishes or as waistline treatments.

One aspect of using elastic of any sort for a sleeve finish is comfort. Although sewing a single row of narrow elastic onto a hemmed sleeve provides a very simple and economical means of fitting the garment to the arm, it also contains the potential for discomfort. If the elastic fits the wrist of the wearer, then it will not fit the wearer's upper arm should the sleeve be pushed up. With children, sleeves of this sort are pushed up inadvertently. As the child tries to put on a coat or jacket, for example,

7-14. Elasticized ruffle on child's garment.

the ruffled edge left by this type of treatment drags against the inside of the outerwear sleeve, and the sleeve is pushed up.

The elastic then constricts on the arm and often leaves a mark for several hours after the garment has been removed. Parents and caregivers of small children should be very alert to the potential discomfort of elastic used as a sleeve finish. There are many other effective and comfortable ways to achieve a finish which are more appropriate to young children. Ribbing, particularly, is preferred for the style of garment mentioned above. While the ruffle produced by the sewn-on elastic may look feminine, and therefore be preferred for girl's garments, the disadvantages outweigh any possible stylistic use. There are other ways to make a garment design appear feminine, such as using ribbing with a scalloped or decorative edge, or just adding a bow to the neckline. The use of elastic with children's sleeves is rarely justified.

PLACKETS

Plackets are finished openings that are used at the lower edge of the sleeve in order to allow the sleeve to expand over the hand, yet still maintain a tight fit at the wrist. Sometimes, these closures are concealed, and at other times, they are quite visible. They vary greatly in the skill and labor required to construct them, in their styling effects, and in their durability.

HORIZONTAL SELF-FACED PLACKET

This type of placket is a very simple treatment. It is formed by hemming a reinforced, clipped portion of the sleeve seam allowance. In most instances, the little rectangle is trimmed slightly, overcast, and then topstitched in place to make the procedure very quick. Occasionally, a small fabric facing is employed to accomplish similar results. This treatment furnishes an opening to which a cuff or binding can be attached, but it does not provide the length that a vertical placket would. Therefore, the sleeve cannot expand very much in order to fit over a large hand or to be worn pushed up if desired. This placket also has a tendency to stick out on the right side of the sleeve and look unsightly. It is most often found in budget apparel.

VERTICAL FACED PLACKET

This procedure yields a vertical opening, about three inches (7.62 cm) long, which is pointed at the top and which does not overlap at the base. It is rather simple to construct, but takes several more steps to complete than does the horizontal self-faced placket. It is found most often on children's and women's clothing, but rarely on men's, and virtually never in ready-to-wear. It is typically a home sewing method for achieving a placket opening in a sleeve, although it may also be used in boutique and designer sewn garments. It is not suitable for sheers because the facing itself would show through to the right side.

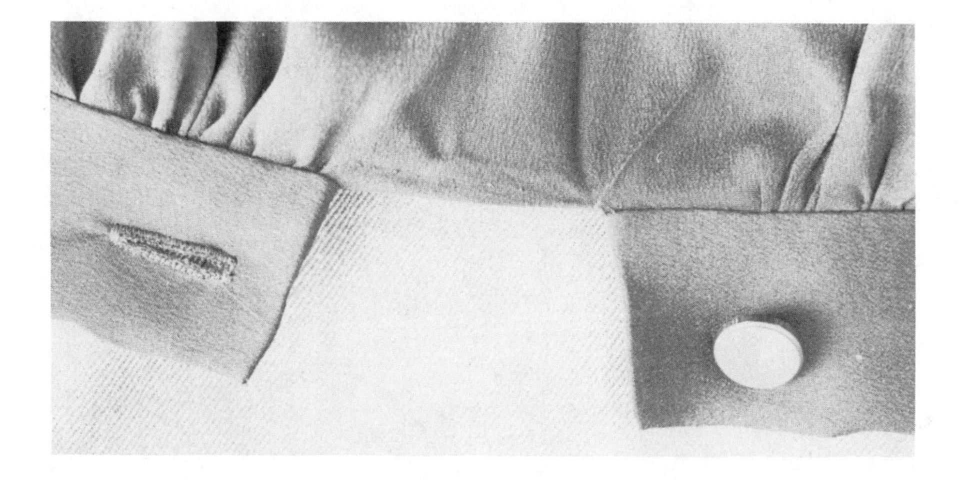

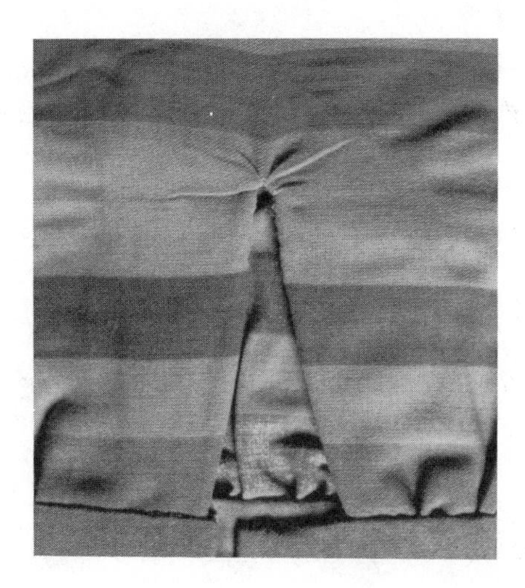

7-15. TOP: Horizontal self-faced placket.

7-16. RIGHT: Vertical faced placket poorly clipped at end causing puckering.

The faced placket must be reinforced at the pointed end to help prevent the end from fraying during wear and laundering. This is usually done by sewing around the point with very small stitches. After the opening is stitched, it must be slashed right up to the stitching at the point so that the facing can be turned to the wrong side without leaving puckers or wrinkles at the point. Understitching, topstitching, and hand-tacking the upper corners of the facing help keep it in place on the wrong side of the sleeve. This type of placket is much more common in home sewing that in ready-to-wear.

CONTINUOUS-BOUND PLACKET

This is one of the most frequently used sleeve plackets found in ready-to-wear. It is strong, neat, and durable. The continuous-bound placket is actually a vertical slash in the sleeve that is concealed within a straight binding. It is often used in combination with cuffs or lower bindings. The durability of the continuous-bound placket depends on adequate reinforcement of the pointed end of the slashed opening and on accurate stitching. These factors also help to avoid holes or puckers at the upper end of the placket.

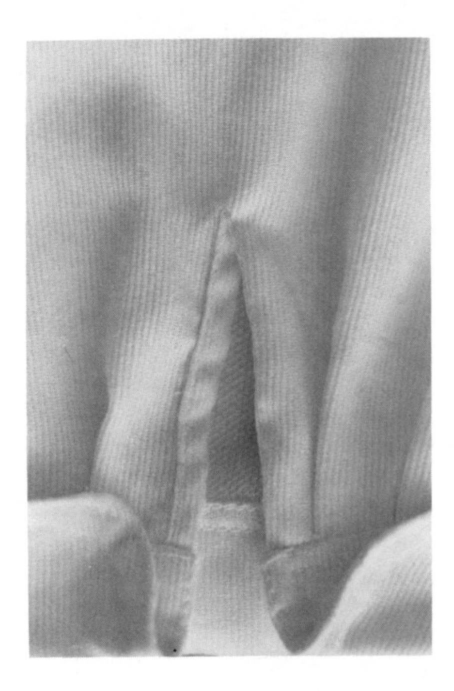

7-17. Continuous-bound placket.

a.

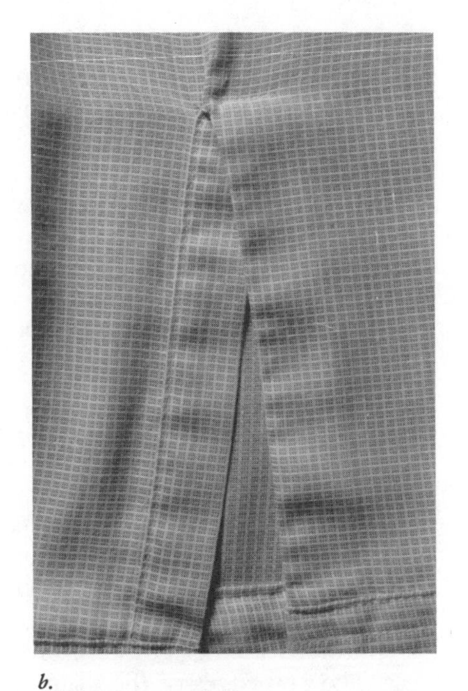

b.

c.

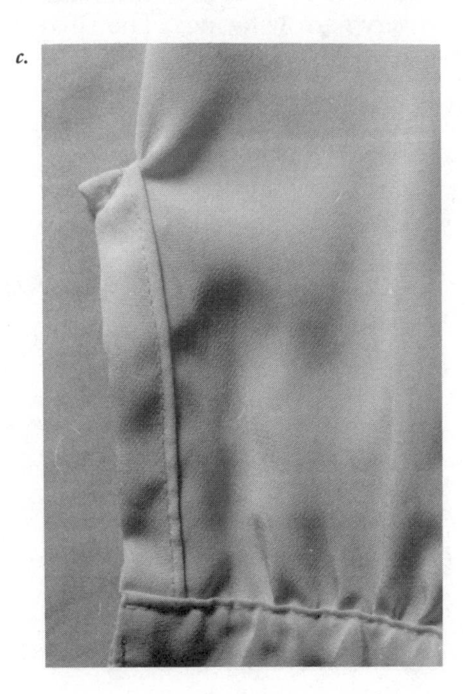

7-18. Selected methods of securing continuous bound plackets: (a) end not secured; placket can flip to right side of sleeve; (b) end topstitched; (c) stitched diagonally across end.

The continuous-bound placket is not appropriate for very thick or spongy fabrics because of the many fabric layers that are superimposed when the sleeve is in a closed position. Some bulk can be eliminated, however, by using the selvage as a finish on the back side of the binding. This eliminates one turned-under edge.

The upper end of the completed placket should be secured to keep the placket in position. This is done by stitching diagonally across the upper edge of the doubled, completed binding on the wrong side of the sleeve. If this step is eliminated, the placket upper edge often rolls outward to the right side of the sleeve. In ready-to-wear, particularly in menswear, a bar tack may be used for the same purpose.

OPEN-SEAM PLACKET

This is not really a placket in the strictest sense of the word, since it is simply a seam left open below a certain point; but it does function as any other vertical placket—to expand the sleeve edge when needed. It is constructed very easily by leaving the seam open above the sleeve edge for about three to four inches (7.62 to 10.16 cm). The seam must be reinforced at this point; it is here that all stress will occur during wear. The raw edges of the seam allowance are then finished and treated as very narrow facings. They may be topstitched in place, or simply left

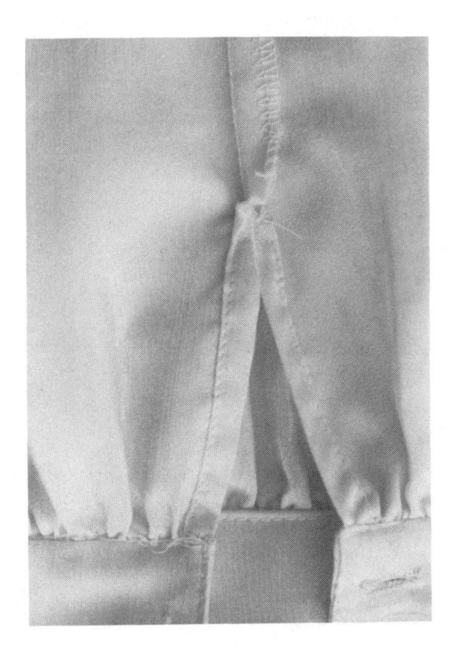

7-19. Open-seam placket.

folded with the cuff application serving to secure them in the correct position.

The low production cost of this type of placket opening makes it ideal for inexpensive apparel lines. The main drawback is that the opening is positioned at the underarm rather than at the side/back location which is more common and more familiar to persons buttoning cuffed sleeves.

OPEN-DART PLACKET

This is made by sewing the pointed end of the dart, as darts are normally sewn, then staystitching the remainder of the dart lines through a single ply of fabric. The dart is then slashed down the center, the raw edges of each side are turned under, and each side is stitched, usually by machine. This placket is difficult to manipulate at the point where the dart becomes an opening. It is more common in home sewing than in ready-to-wear, where the number of steps required for its execution places it at a disadvantage.

PLEATED PLACKET

The pleated placket is made by clipping, hemming, and folding a reinforced rectangle at the side-back of the sleeve. It requires no extra fabric,

7-20. Open-dart placket.

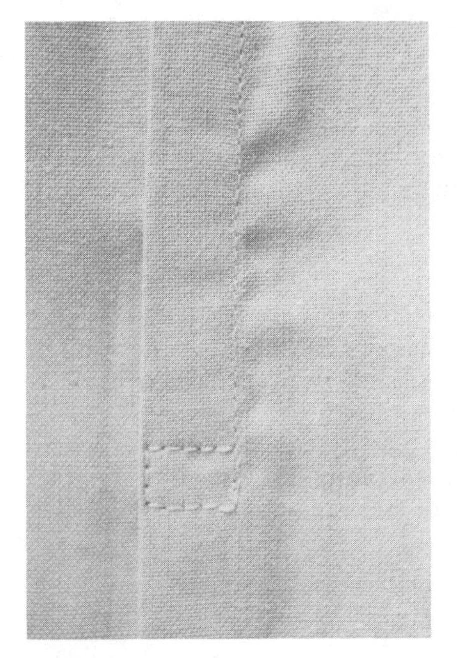

7-21. Pleated placket.

7-22. Tailored placket.

but forms a pleat at the top when it is finished. The overlap side of the placket is finished with a one-half inch (1.27 cm) hem, and the underlap is finished with a one-fourth inch (.64 cm) hem. The wider side is then lapped over the narrow side and held in place with either a bar tack or by a small, machine-stitched rectangle placed at the top of the opening. The pleat at the top of this placket will not allow the sleeve on which it is used to be pressed flat without wrinkling at the pleat. This placket is used primarily on low priced, long sleeve work shirts.

TAILORED SHIRT PLACKET

This placket consists of two sections, a bound underlap not visible in the finished placket and a shaped, usually pointed, wide overlap. The binding is applied over one side of a slashed, reinforced rectangle. The pointed side of the placket is then applied to the other side of the slashed opening and partially topstitched. This portion is then lapped over the binding and the topstitching completed through all thicknesses to hold the overlap in position.

The tailored placket costs more to produce than any of the other types of plackets, but it has a more finished look and is quite strong and durable. It is suited for higher priced ready-to-wear clothing for men, women, and children. It is used almost exclusively in men's better dress and sport shirts. The tailored shirt placket is frequently made several inches long and fastened with a button and buttonhole. Such additional findings and steps will obviously increase the garment cost.

GUSSET-STYLE PLACKET

A relatively new kind of placket to be used in apparel is styled like a gusset, but is not necessarily cut on the bias, although it may be. The wedge-shaped piece of fabric is usually hemmed, then inset into a slash or open seam of the sleeve. A lapped or true inset seam may be used for the application. When the cuff is opened, the wide end of the wedge allows the sleeve to expand the amount of the wedge; when the cuff is closed, the wedge folds back inside like a shaped pleat. An open and closed view of this type of placket is shown in Figure 7-23.

a.

b.

7-23. Wedge-shaped inset placket: (a) open; (b) closed.

STANDARDS FOR EVALUATING SLEEVE PLACKETS

1. Any points or corners should be stitched securely with no fraying or holes.
2. The placket should be completely smooth with no gathers or ripples. The pleats of the pleated placket should be evenly folded and smooth.
3. There should be no extraneous thread or stitching visible on the right side of the placket.
4. The two sides of the placket should be even in length.
5. If the placket laps, the overlap should be on the portion of the sleeve closest to the center, lapping toward the outside of the arm (toward the portion of the sleeve that joins the garment's back armscye).
6. Portions of the placket should not roll outward to the right side of the sleeve.

CUFFS

Cuffs are constructed of fabric bands that finish and/or decorate the lower raw edge of the sleeve. Unlike hems and facings, cuffs are intentionally visible in the completed sleeve. Therefore, they offer considerable design potential. Cuffs can be categorized into two basic types—the *extended cuff,* which adds length to the sleeve, finishes the lower edge, and may also control sleeve fullness; and the *turned-back cuff,* which finishes the sleeve edge and is usually attached for purely decorative purposes.

EXTENDED CUFF

The extended cuff is the most common type of cuff, perhaps because of its usual function of fitting a full sleeve to the smaller wrist or upper arm of the wearer. The extended cuff can be further classified as a *closed band* (but large enough to fit over the hand and arm without an opening) or an *open band* (used in combination with a placket to permit a close fit to the arm). The extended cuff does add length to the sleeve, and can be trimmed for a greater decorative effect.

Open Band Cuffs. One open band style commonly used in apparel today is the *barrel cuff,* a straight, lapped cuff closed with one or two buttons. The majority of men's long sleeve dress and sport shirts have

7-24. Extended cuff: barrel type.

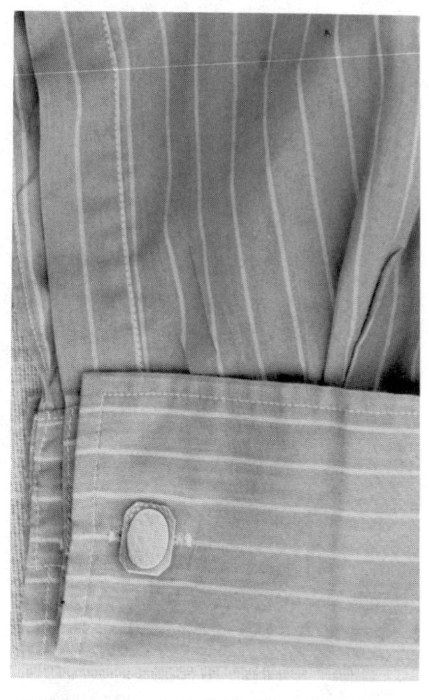

7-25. Extended cuff: French type.

the sleeve finished with a barrel cuff. The French cuff is made similarly to the barrel cuff, but is made twice the desired width. It then folds back on itself and is held closed with cuff links which pass through all four layers of cuff in a protruding, rather than lapped, formation.

Other cuffs without specific style names also fit into the category of open band cuff. They vary in width, method of closing, size and shaping. Victorian style blouses and dresses often have shaped, lapped, buttoned cuffs several inches long, coming almost to the elbow. The open cuff may close with buttons or with a zipper; loops and buttons can be used if a lapped style is not desired. Occasionally, extra length is provided in a regular lapped cuff so that a portion at the bottom turns back to form a "cuff" on the cuff.

Closed Band Cuffs. The closed band cuff may also vary in width, fitting function, and in the addition of decorative details. It is generally simpler to apply to the sleeve than is an open band because the following are not required: a placket opening, a closure for the cuff, and

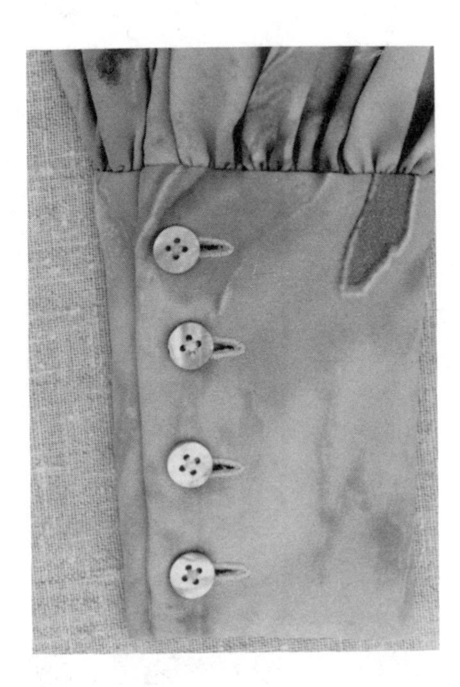

7-26. Extended cuff: Victorian style.

a neat finish on the two ends of the closed cuff, since it is a circle unbroken by any opening.

The closed band must be large enough to be drawn over the hand (or the upper arm if the sleeve is short). A closed band cuff made of rigid material is rarely used because if it is large enough to be drawn comfortably over the hand, it is often too large to appear attractive on the body, and it cannot be adjusted to fit. The exception to this is the closed band made of rib stretch knitted fabric. With this band, the elasticity of the fabric used for the cuff allows it to expand to fit over the hand, then contract to fit closely around the wrist.

The application of the rib stretch cuff is identical to the application of the rib stretch inset band described in Chapter 6, "Neckline Treatments." Like the inset band, the rib stretch cuff should be seamed before it is applied to the sleeve. This is done in better quality garments. When the cuff is applied to the flat sleeve, and the underarm seam of the sleeve is then made through the cuff, an unattractive seam allowance protrudes at the lower end of the cuff. Also, the alignment of the folded and seamed edges of the cuff becomes more difficult. Figures 7-27 and 7-28 show the two methods of applying rib stretch cuffs.

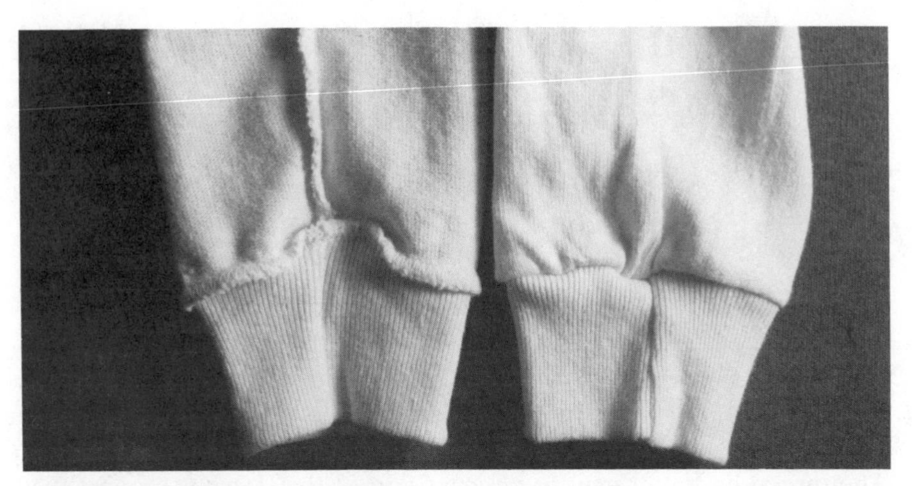

7-27. Extended closed cuff of knitted rib stretch fabric, seamed before application to sleeve.

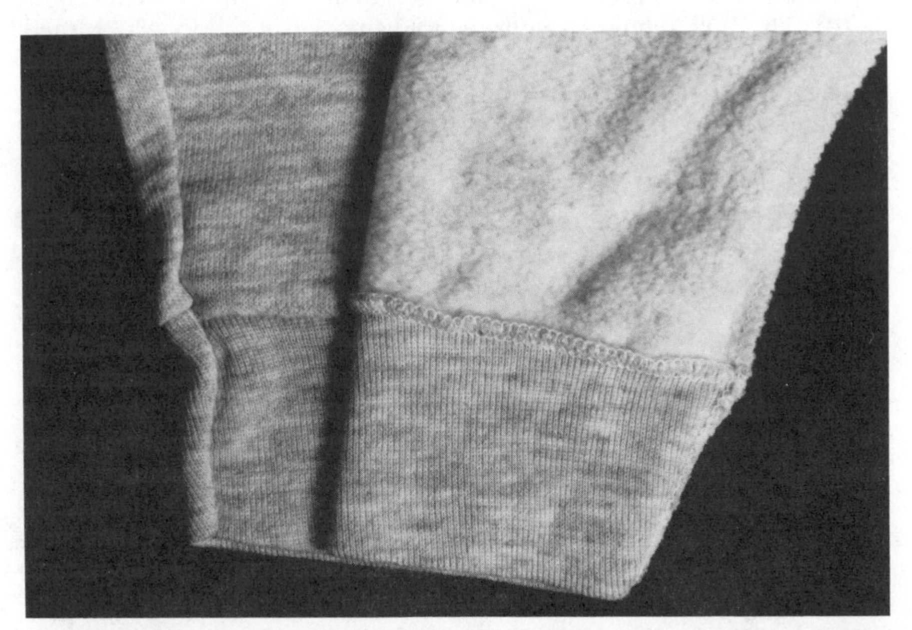

7-28. Extended closed cuff of knitted rib stretch fabric, seamed after application to sleeve.

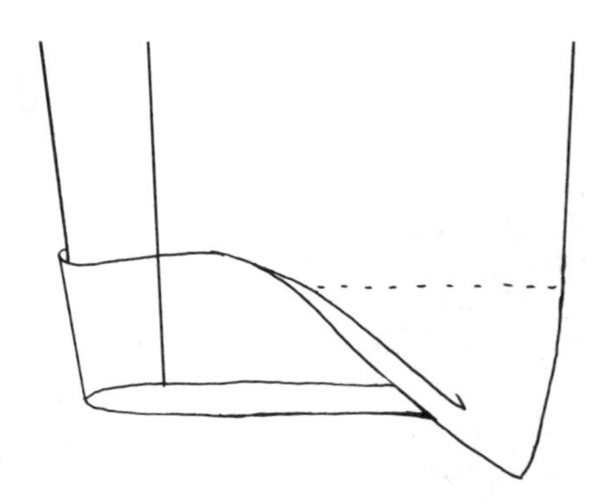

7-29. Hemmed turned-back cuffs.

TURNED-BACK CUFFS

The turned-back cuff may be an extension of the sleeve itself or it may be a separate unit that is constructed and then applied to the sleeve edge. The first type is simplest to construct; it requires only a deep hem, usually machine stitched, to complete actual construction. The hemmed portion of the sleeve must be deep enough so that the turned-back portion covers and extends past the stitching line of the hem (Figure 7-29). This cuff requires a considerable amount of fabric. The turned-back cuff is sometimes referred to as a *rolled-up sleeve*.

The turned-back cuff may also be formed by applying a narrow, machine-stitched hem at the sleeve edge. This hem is concealed with the second role or turn of the sleeve. This simple technique is appropriate only to garments made of reversible fabrics. Also, the sleeve seam should be flat felled or reversed so that the seam allowances are not visible in the rolled-up sleeve.

When the sleeve is shaped or tapered as it approaches the wrist instead of being cut straight, the turned-back cuff must be cut and applied separately rather than being just an extension of the sleeve. This type of cuff is usually applied with a facing to make a neat finish. The applied cuff is prevalent when long, close-fitting sleeves are fashionable.

Turned-back cuffs found on short or cap sleeves are often cut on the bias or lengthwise grain of a directional fabric to give added decorative appeal to the cuff. When used in this way, the extended cuff is usually attached with a serged seam that is located on the outside of the garment and hidden from view when the cuff is folded back. Figure 7-30 shows this method of application in a long, fitted sleeve. If the application seam is on the inside of the garment,it is actually more likely to be visible during wear, especially if the sleeve is quite loose and/or if the cuff fold line is quite close to the application seam.

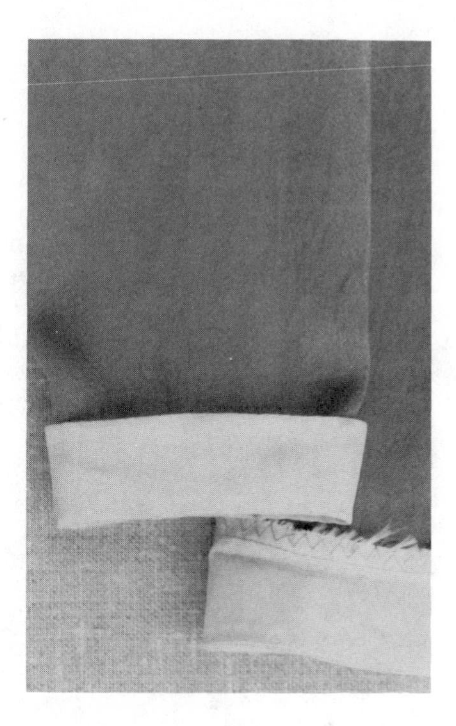

7-30. Applied turned-back cuffs.

STANDARDS FOR EVALUATING CUFFS

1. The cuffs should be interfaced for body and support. (Rib stretch cuffs are excepted.)
2. The ends of open band cuffs should be identical in size and shape and should be finished neatly.
3. The edges of the cuff should be smooth and flat with no seam wells.
4. Any topstitching should be even, straight, and in an appropriate stitch length.
5. Closed cuffs should be seamed before they are attached to the sleeve.
6. The inside of the cuff application seam should be enclosed carefully or (in the case of rib stretch) serged. Woven fabric cuffs applied with extended, serged seam allowances are appropriate only in short or cap sleeves. In long sleeves, they are typical of budget merchandise.

SUMMARY

Both sleeve types and sleeve finishes benefit from the application of technology in terms of production speed and product consistency. Specialized machinery can be programmed to control sleeve cap fullness, to sew in sleeve linings with stitches that resemble hand sewing, to apply and topstitch barrel cuffs in seconds, and even to hem circular sleeves with blind hemming stitches. Apparel manufacturers who have access to this type of equipment are thus at a competitive advantage in the marketplace, and the consumer ultimately benefits. Equivalent or even better products are available at lower prices than would be possible if extensive labor were required to execute the treatments.

8

WAISTLINE TREATMENTS

Most garments have some definition at the waistline position of the body. The garment may end there or slightly above or below the waistline; the garment may be seamed to provide waistline definition; or the garment may have the waistline defined by the fullness that elastic or a drawstring provides. Throughout the history of modern fashion, it has frequently been the waistline position that gave the garment silhouette its distinctive appearance. This has been true especially in the twentieth century. In this chapter, the location of the waistline treatment on the garment will provide the first structural division. Further subdivisions will treat the methods that can be used to provide waistline definition internally or at the edge of the garment.

EDGE TREATMENTS

Edge treatments occur most frequently on bottoms—skirts, slacks, shorts, culottes, half slips, panties, briefs—but they may also be used as a finish for hoods, jacket bottoms, and for other styles of tops. Windbreakers and sweat jackets, for example, are often finished at the lower edge with a drawstring and casing rather than with a traditional hem. Structurally, this finish is more closely identified with waistline treatments than with hem treatments. For this reason, such finishes will be discussed in this chapter. The edge being treated may not always occur at the exact waistline of the body, but may be slightly lower or higher depending on the garment style.

APPLIED ELASTIC

One of the simplest and fastest methods used to finish a waistline edge is to apply elastic directly to the edge. This method not only finishes the edge, but also provides a better fit to a greater number of persons than would a rigid waistline. The major disadvantage in such a treatment is the difficulty of altering the size in case of a drastic fit problem or of replacing the elastic in case it loses its stretch. Elastic that is too tight may be extremely irritating to some persons, especially to children whose skin reacts quickly to compression.

Elastic can be applied more rapidly in a flat garment than in one where all the seams have been sewn and the garment is tubular. When the elastic is applied flat, the seam that closes the garment also closes the elastic. This leaves a stiff ridge on the inside of the garment at the seam line. Such a seamed application is more common to women's lingerie, children's wear, and budget items than to better quality goods. Covering the seam with ribbon or the label makes the join more comfortable.

CONCEALED APPLICATIONS

Elastic applied to the edges of most outer wear is applied on the inside of the garment. Usually the elastic is white and has no decorative value. It is purely functional, causing the completed garment to contract to fit the body. Concealed applications may occur at the very edge of the fabric *(flush application)*, or it may occur lower down in order to provide for a decorative header *(recessed application)*.

In a flush application, the raw edge of the garment is either left as it is cut or it is turned down enough to be concealed between the elastic and the garment; then the elastic is stitched in place. On the outside, the garment appears to be gathered; on the inside, the elastic is visible to the garment edge.

A flush application is used in panties, active-wear, shorts, pajamas, and children's slacks and shorts. The wider the elastic used, the more rows of stitching will be required to hold it flat and smooth. For very wide elastic, a multiple-needle sewing machine is used for the applica-

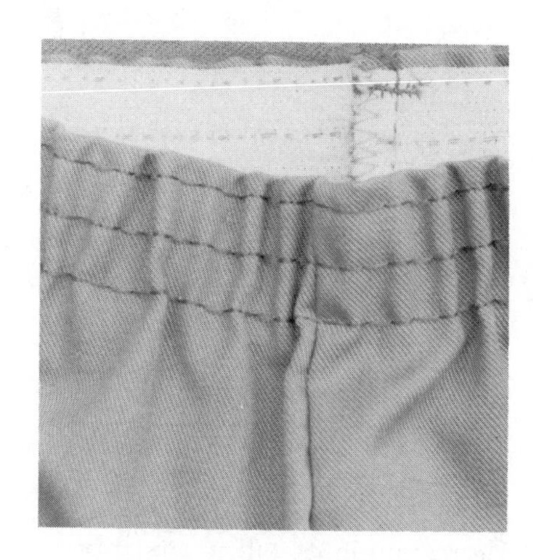

8-1. Applied elastic: concealed application, flush.

tion, so the major additional cost is in the elastic and in the amount of thread used for the stitching.

A more decorative effect is possible with a recessed application. A section of garment fabric extends beyond the elastic to form a ruffle when the waistline elastic contracts. A minimum one inch (2.54 cm) extension is needed to create a noticeable ruffle. Slacks, shorts, and skirts, especially for children and junior sizes, are often treated this way. The construction is identical to the sleeve finish discussed in Chapter 7, but usually it is done with wider elastic than is found in a sleeve. In children's and infants' pants and shorts, the leg edges as well as the waistline may be treated in this manner.

EXPOSED APPLICATIONS

If decorative elastic is used, it usually is applied to the exterior of the garment where its decorative effect can be utilized. Some of the most familiar examples of this type of treatment include the elastic lace found on stylish lingerie and the striped elastic on men's briefs.

Almost all low-cut panties are finished at both the waist and the leg edges with elastic lace. The raw edges of the garment are left raw or are turned down toward the outside of the garment where they will be concealed when the elastic is secured in place with one or more rows of stitching.

If regular elastic is used in an exposed application in lingerie, the elastic is usually lapped rather than joined with a regular seam. In better quality goods, the lapped seam will then be covered with a small square

8-2. Applied elastic: exposed application.

or rectangle of fabric or ribbon to help prevent the raw edges of the elastic from fraying and becoming unsightly.

Exposed applications can also be used on outer wear, especially in garments made from knitted fabric. Special rib-knit elastic made in matching colors, perhaps even striped, is used for some garments. Method of application is the same as for lingerie.

STANDARDS FOR EVALUATING APPLIED ELASTIC

1. The elastic is made with spandex, rather than rubber, for longer flex life.
2. The elastic is an appropriate size (width and length) for its location.
3. The elastic is stretched evenly during application.
4. Application stitches are secured.
5. Sufficient rows of stitching are used to prevent the elastic from folding over on itself.
6. Seams in the elastic, if present, are lapped seams.

EDGE CASINGS

A casing is a fabric tunnel secured by stitching on one or both sides, providing a space for elastic, a drawstring, or a combination of the two in order to adjust the garment fit. The casing may be made of self-fabric or of a different, usually softer and thinner, fabric.

Casings at the edge of garments are usually formed by folding down an extension of the edge itself and stitching it in place to form the tunnel. (Internal casings will be discussed later in the chapter.) A garment finished in this manner must be cut nearly straight or, alternatively, the seams of the extension must be cut in a mirror image of the garment seams against which they will lie when folded down. Otherwise, the casing will not be the same size as the garment, causing pleats and pulls to form in the completed garment.

CLOSED CASINGS

If there is no access to the interior of the fabric tunnel once the garment is completed, the treatment is called a closed casing, and only elastic can be used to control fit. The elastic can come to the edge of the casing, or a header can be created easily by positioning one row of stitching some distance from the garment edge. Both styles are shown in Figure 8-3. The closed casing may circle the entire garment, or it may occur only in certain areas. An example of the latter would be children's overalls with bib front and elasticized back waist.

Most closed casings are made by folding down an extension of the garment edge. When the garment edge is contoured, the casing is cut separately, usually on the bias, and applied. This is a more lengthy operation than simply folding down the edge. Although the applied casing is more typical of neckline treatments, it may occur in waistline areas as well if the garment is very tapered or flared.

If the elastic is inserted into the closed casing after the casing has been stitched (a hole is temporarily left for inserting the elastic, then closed), then the garment can be altered easily if the elastic is too loose

a.

b.

8-3. Elastic in closed casings: (a) flush with top edge; (b) off-set from top edge to create ruffle.

or too tight or if it fails before the garment is worn out. In most instances, however, the elastic is applied and the casing stitched in a single operation. The elastic is firmly attached to both the garment fabric and casing fabric. The advantage is that the elastic cannot twist or roll as it can in a conventional casing. This method is also less costly than drawing elastic through a casing by hand, then having to seam the elastic and close off the casing. The disadvantages of this method are that the elastic is very difficult to remove for alteration or replacement, and the casing and elastic invariably are seamed through after application, resulting in a bulky, stiff garment area.

OPEN CASINGS

If a drawstring is used to control the garment size, then some type of opening must be created to allow the drawstring to leave the casing and come to the right side of the garment for tying. Windbreakers and sweat jackets often have a natural opening where the hem is stitched after the center front is finished. Hoods frequently have this type of opening also. Pull-on garments with no natural openings require that an opening for the drawstring be formed prior to stitching down the casing. Buttonholes worked in the garment, or eyelet holes for a thin cord, will provide such openings. Usually two openings, approximately one inch (2.54 cm) apart, are provided to allow space for the knot or bow in the drawstring to lie flat.

The open casing can come to the very edge of the garment or can

STANDARDS FOR EVALUATING EDGE CASINGS

1. The casing has two rows of stitching—one at the upper edge and one at the lower edge.
2. Stitching lines are parallel to each other and to the garment edge.
3. The casing is the correct width for the elastic or drawstring that it holds.
4. The raw edges of the casing are finished to prevent raveling.
5. The elastic or drawstring is not twisted in the casing.
6. Openings in the casing are neat and durable.
7. Casings for elastic have been stitched closed after insertion of the elastic.
8. Casings are applied and elastic inserted after the garment was seamed into a tube.

occur in conjunction with a header, as with applied elastic. Even if the casing comes to the edge, a row of edge stitching will create a flatter, more attractive casing than if the top edge were left unstitched. Rolling and twisting are also reduced when edge stitching is done. To create a header, the top line of stitching is dropped approximately one inch (2.54 cm) from the top. This extension creates a ruffle when the drawstring is drawn to fit the waist.

WAISTLINE FACINGS

Facings are occasionally used as waistline treatments for women's slacks and skirts and for some costumes. The discussion of shaped facings in Chapter 6, "Neckline Treatments," covers both the technique and quality of traditional shaped facings in considerable detail. There are, however, some additional factors to be considered in the use of such facings at the waistline.

First, the garment will be extremely difficult to alter. The facing will have to be completely removed, altered, and replaced in addition to the alteration of the basic garment. Second, the stress on the garment at the waistline is much greater than at the neckline and may cause stretching if the waistline edge is not reinforced with tape or ribbon or some stable fabric cut on the lengthwise grain. Finally, a straight strip of fabric to use as a waistband is often much more economical to cut than

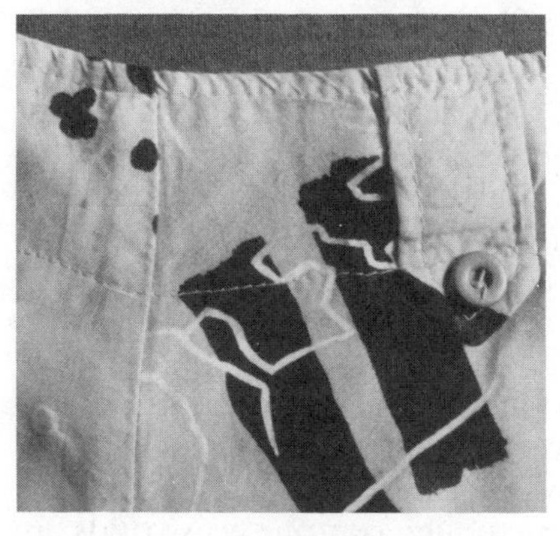

a.

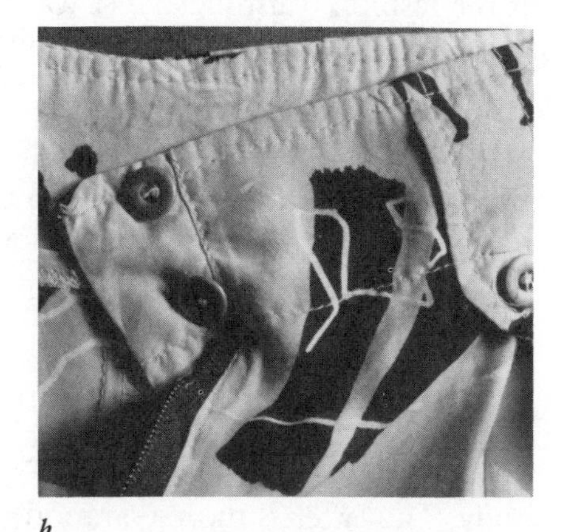

b.

8-4. Faced waistband: (a) (right side) topstitched at upper and lower edge to hold facing in place; (b) (wrong side) facing edge serged to prevent raveling and secured by topstitching.

is a shaped waistline facing. Therefore, this type of treatment is not only less stable, but often more expensive than other alternatives available to provide a waistline finish.

STANDARDS FOR EVALUATING WAISTLINE FACINGS

1. The facing is cut so that its grainlines match garment grainlines.
2. Interfacing is present.
3. The waistline edge is stayed to prevent stretching.
4. The facing lies flat and smooth against the garment.
5. The facing is secured in place on the wrong side of the garment.
6. No seam wells are evident at any point on the facing.
7. The raw edges of the facing are finished appropriately.
8. Belt loops or thread carriers, if present, are sufficient in number, securely attached, evenly spaced, and identical in size and construction.
9. At any opening(s) in the garment, the facing is neat, flat and concealed.

WAISTBANDS

A waistband is an applied piece of fabric that is sewn to the garment at the fashion waistline. Most waistbands do occur at the natural waistline, but the technique is not limited to that position on the garment. Waistbands are by nature very functional, but as with most functional items, they can be made decorative as well. Variations in width, in decorative stitching, in shape, and in the design of the overlap/underlap area can all add distinctiveness to the waistband. Quality construction, regardless of waistband design, is a primary consideration.

CONTOUR WAISTBANDS

A contour waistband is cut to form a slight curve which is intended to conform to the body shape. Such waistbands, shown in Figure 8-5, may be cut to extend above or fall below the natural waistline of the body. The latter is more common. Structurally, contour waistbands are comparable to inset bands already discussed in Chapter 6. Compared to straight waistbands, they are less stable but more costly in terms of fabric requirements and labor. They have a tendency to stretch out of shape because of stress from body flexing which occurs on the bias

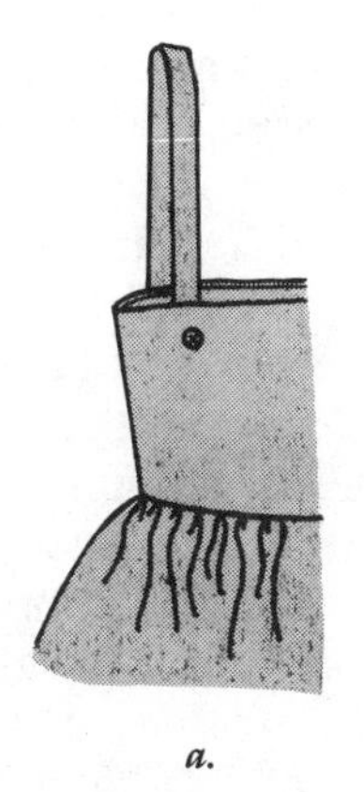

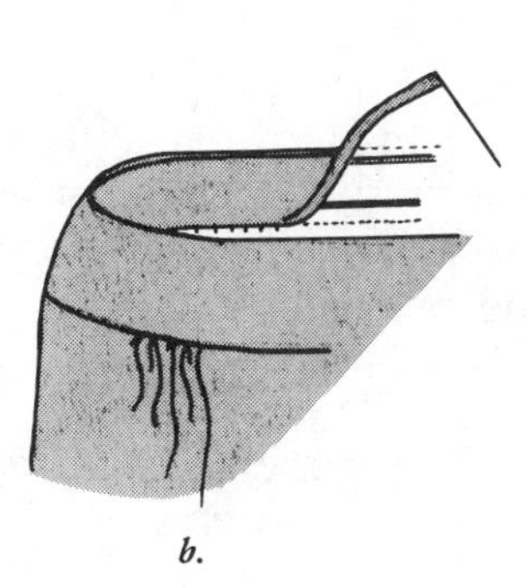

8-5. Contour waistbands: (a) above the waistline; (b) below the waistline.

portions of the band. Contour waistbands require stabilization with non-stretch fabric to prevent this problem. Interfacing alone is not sufficient because it has the same stretch potential as the area being interfaced. Alteration of a garment with a contour waistband is almost impossible if the waistband is cut in one piece. If it is cut with seams corresponding to the garment's seam, alteration is possible, but still a rather lengthy undertaking.

STRAIGHT WAISTBANDS

Straight waistbands are constructed of straight pieces of fabric, usually cut with the lengthwise grain encircling the waist for maximum stability. Since the band itself is straight, it cannot conform to the body shape in any location except at the actual waistline, and there its width is restricted to about one and one-half inches (3.81 cm), occasionally as much as two inches (5.08 cm). If the width exceeds this amount, the lower portion of the wearer's rib cage can be restricted, causing some discomfort.

In its simplest form the straight waistband has no opening—in pull-on slacks, skirts, and shorts, the waistband is elasticized and seamed together into a tube before it is applied to the garment. More commonly, however, the straight waistband has at least one opening. This opening may occur at the center front, center back, or left side. (Back and side openings are not found in men's wear.) Straight waistbands may even have two openings, one on each side of the front. Such double openings may close with D-rings or buckles to allow for some adjustment of the fit, an advantage not usually associated with straight waistbands.

The overlap portion of the straight waistband that does have an opening may exhibit a variety of finishes. It may end flush with the overlap portion of the garment closure (the zipper or button placket) and lap over an extended underlap. On the other hand, the overlap may extend and end with a decorative shape—rounded or pointed. The overlap may even have extensions that wrap, buckle, and/or tie. Such extensions may partially or completely circle the waist, giving the impression of a belt. Such decorative variations add to the cost of the garment, as do the inclusion of belt loops and numerous and/or elaborate enclosures.

Folded Waistbands. The most common type of straight waistband is made of folded garment fabric. The waistband is actually cut to contain its own facing. Both the method of application and the type of garment on which the folded waistband appears vary, however, according to whether the folded waistband is *rigid* or *elasticized*.

One of the easiest folded waistbands to make and one suitable for knit or stretch fabrics is elasticized. It is different from applied elastic or casings in that the waistband is cut separately from the garment, on the lengthwise or crosswise grain, folded over the elastic to enclose it, then applied to the garment in a single operation. The elastic may or may not be caught into the stitching that secures the waistband. Although

a.

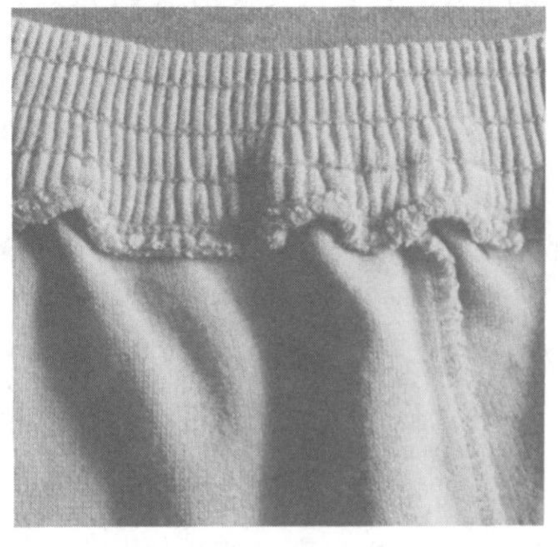

b.

8-6. Folded, elasticized waistband with multiple rows of stitching through single strip of elastic: (a) right side of garment; (b) wrong side of garment.

the waistband is cut smaller than the garment and stretched for application, it is not cut as small as the actual waistline, so that the effect is somewhere between a completely elasticized waist and a rigid waistband. The application seam is usually serged, and it is exposed on the inside of the garment rather than being enclosed within the waistband itself. This type of waistband usually has no opening and is typical of women's sizes, double knit fabrics, and lower price lines. In some cases, an opening is included, or an opening may be simulated by constructing a fake overlap, complete with button, prior to attaching the tubular waistband. Two examples of folded elasticized waistbands are seen in Figure 8-6 and 8-7.

Another variation to the elasticized folded waistband utilizes the elastic characteristics of rib stretch fabric to provide the fitting at the waistline. Many children's garments—slacks, skirts, shorts, leggings, and similar items—have this type of functional and decorative treatment at the waistband. If the ribbing does not have excellent elastic recovery, elastic may be added at the seamline or enclosed in the fold of fabric to improve the flex life of the garment.

By far, the most common type of straight, folded waistband is *rigid;* that is, it does not stretch. In most cases, interfacing is included, but it is rarely firm enough to prevent the waistband from crumpling, especially on persons with large midriffs or abdomens. The easiest application in industry is to take strips of garment fabric folded lengthwise

a.

b.

8-7. Folded, elasticized waistband with two strips of elastic: (a) right side of garment; (b) wrong side of garment.

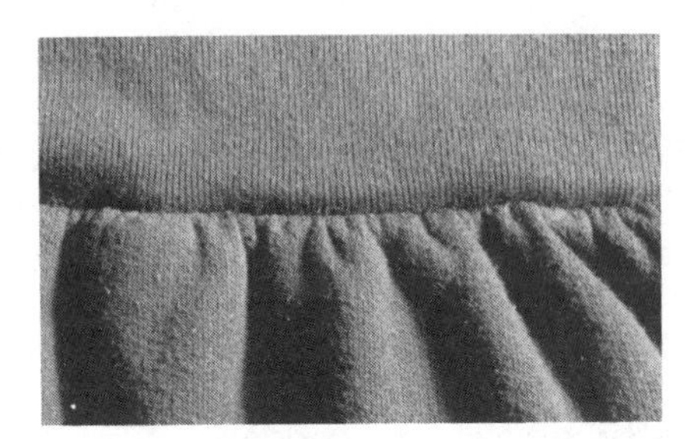

8-8. Rib-stretch folded waistband.

and with the seam allowances along each raw edge folded in and to encase the garment waistline with the strips. The strips are secured by topstitching along the folded edges. Less bulk results when the inside seam allowance is cut on the selvage or is serged and allowed to lie flat, extending slightly below the waistline seam. In Figure 8-9, the wrong side of the waistband is finished with a Hong Kong finish, then secured by stitching in the ditch of the seam which attached the band to the garment at the waistline. The stitching tends to sink down in the "ditch" and be less conspicuous than topstitching.

In better-quality, rigid folded waistbands, both ends are finished with enclosed seams. In many medium to lower priced garments, the underlap will have the end serged instead. This is a less expensive treatment, but it does produce less bulk at the waistband overlap. Occasionally, a very poor-quality garment will have the overlap cut longer than the desired finished length, then folded back on the wrong side and caught by topstitching or just by a buttonhole. This is not an acceptable overlap finish.

Faced Waistbands. A more complicated technique requires that the waistband be faced with a different piece of fabric. The fabric selected for the facing distinguishes the three major types of faced waistbands—the *ribbon backed,* the *elastic backed,* and the *waistband curtain.*

The garment fabric waistband can be faced with a wide *grosgrain ribbon* or with a strip of specially made elastic. The former is more typical in women's wear, although it is not a common technique. The ribbon provides a firm, non-bulky finish and reinforcement. Since the ribbon has selvages on both sides, there are no raw edges to turn under or finish.

The second treatment, use of a wide elastic facing, is found in men's slacks made of double knit or stretch woven fabric. The elastic provides a measure of fitting ease and comfort, but still maintains the firm look

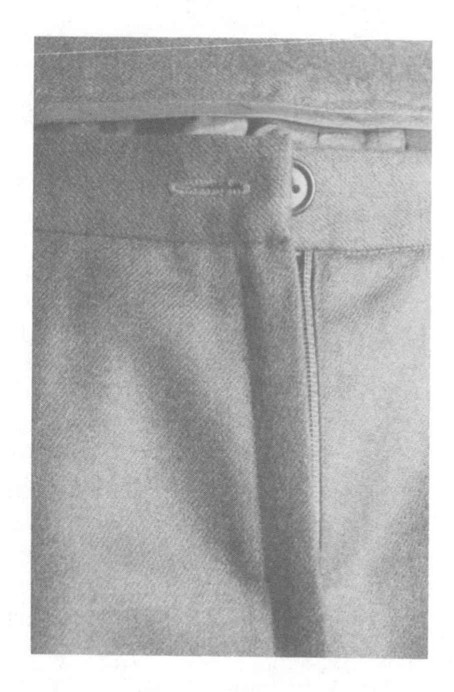

8-9. Rigid folded waistband secured by "ditch stitching."

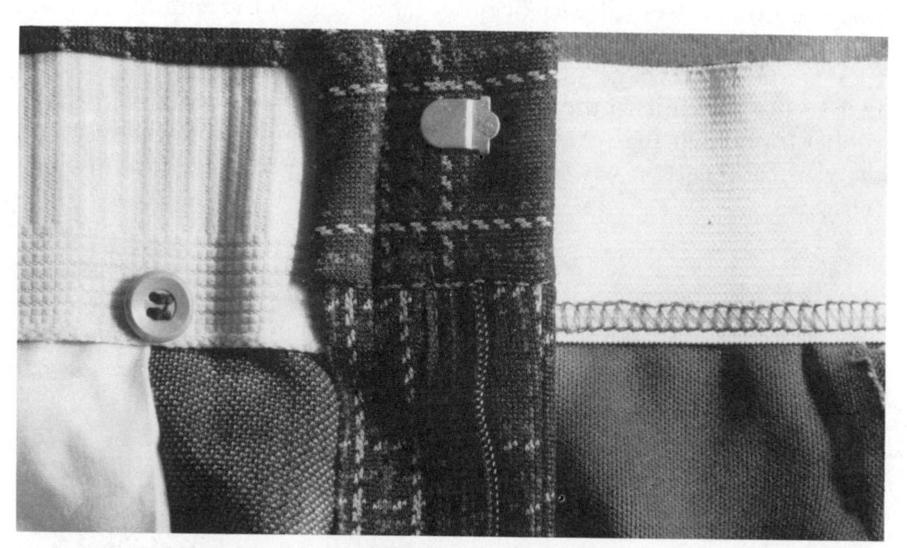

8-10. Two elastic-faced waistbands: in treatment shown on the right, elastic is even with waistband edge; on the left, the elastic facing is recessed slightly.

of a more traditional waistband finish. The elastic is finished at the top and bottom edges and is very firm in order to prevent the completed waistband from rolling. Beltless styles of men's slacks frequently feature this type of waistband facing.

The most elaborate finish for a waistband is the waistband curtain. This facing is composed of a firm woven fabric cut on the bias and at least one piece of stiffener. Better-quality waistband curtains have bias-cut buckram or a similar stiffener, plus a second strip, the width of the finished waistband, of woven monofilament nylon. This special stiffener is very lightweight and flexible, but absolutely prevents the waistband from rolling down. Curtains without this type of stiffener will roll.

The waistband curtain is the most common type of waistband finish found in men's slacks. It is applied separately to the left and right sides of the waistband, then seamed in one continuous seam that joins the pants back at the crotch, then continues up the center back through the waistband and curtain. This method of application makes alteration much easier than if the waistband were applied in one piece. Adjustments to the waist can be made by releasing the curtain at the center back, opening out the entire waistband, and then taking in or letting out the desired amount.

The waistband curtain extends below the waistline on the inside of the slacks, and the bias cut allows this portion to expand slightly to fit body contours. Any stiffener or other fabric cut on the lengthwise grain must terminate at the waistline in order to allow the bias to expand. A tuck at the lower edge of the waistband curtain conceals the stitches that secure the unit to the garment pockets. Strips or patches of foam, rubber, or similar high-friction material may be applied to the inside of the waistband curtain where they function to keep shirt tails from pulling out.

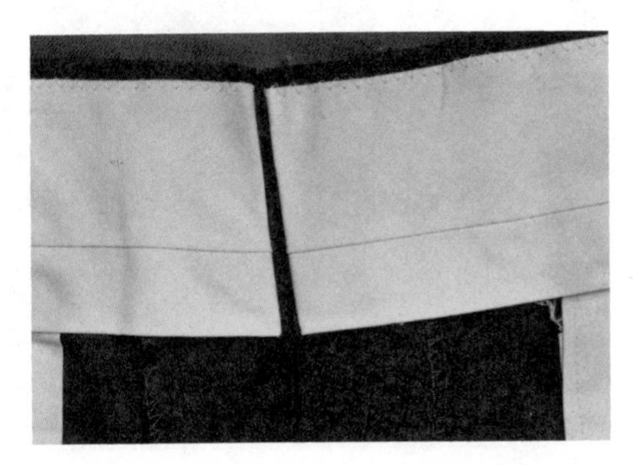

8-11. Waistband curtain.

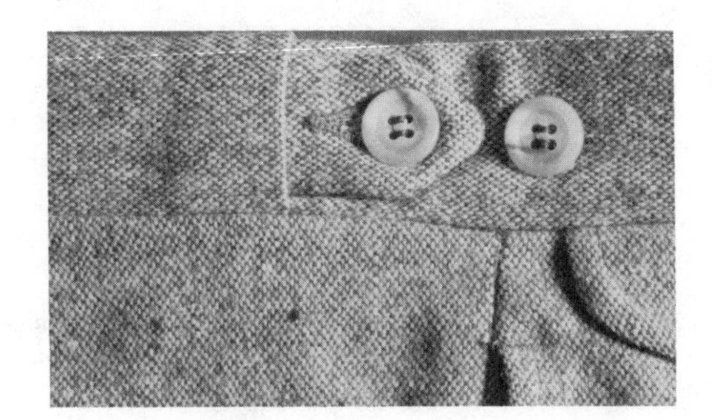

8-12. Button and tab waistline adjustment on man's unbelted, curtained waistband.

An additional point of cost in a waistband treatment is a means of adjusting the waistline size. Figure 8-12 shows a sliding, partially concealed tab with a buttonhole. One of these is positioned on each side of the slacks and can be adjusted via the two buttons provided at each tab end. Such an added construction detail adds considerably to the materials and labor cost of the garment.

STANDARDS FOR EVALUATING WAISTBANDS

1. The garment was not stretched when the waistband was applied.
2. The application seam is smooth and even.
3. The waistband is smooth and flat
4. Sufficient stiffener or interfacing is used to prevent the waistband from stretching or rolling over on itself. (Elasticized waistbands and those with elastic facings are excepted.)
5. Facings of faced waistbands are constructed of good-quality material.
6. Both overlap and underlap are neatly finished.
7. The width of the waistband is even along its entire circumference.
8. Belt loops, if used, are identical in construction and size, evenly spaced, and sufficient in number to keep a belt in place. One at the center back is desirable.
9. The waistband curtain, if present, is inconspicuously attached to the garment.
10. Waistline seams and top edges are matched in waistbands seamed at the center back.
11. Any visible stitching is neatly done in a matching thread color.

INTERNAL TREATMENTS

In the category of internal treatments are garments that do not end at the natural or modified waistline of the body, but utilize some means of waistline treatment to provide definition. Jackets, dresses, bathing suits, blouses, nightgowns, and playsuits are examples of garments that fit within this category.

Internal treatments may occur at a raised waist point (Empire style), at the natural waistline, or at a point below the natural waistline. The treatment may be as simple as stitching a waistline with elastic thread or as complicated as a faced inset band. Whatever the treatment, it can profoundly affect the fit, the silhouette, the alteration potential, the cost and the quality of the total garment.

UNSEAMED WAISTLINES

In this category are garments that have no seams at the fashion waistline. The fit and definition must be provided by the application of some additional material.

ELASTICIZED WAISTLINES

The easiest fitting method for the unseamed, internal waistline treatment is the use of elastic. Fitting is adaptable for a wider variety of body types and sizes, and the application of elastic is usually a relatively simple procedure.

Applied Elastic. One of the fastest and most economical means of producing a waistline in a garment with no waistline seam is to sew elastic horizontally at the desired location. A narrow strip of elastic is usually applied with a single row of stitching, but wide elastic requires more stitching lines. If stitching is not placed close to both edges, there is a tendency for the elastic to roll over in the middle. Some nonrolling elastic is available to prevent this, but it is bulkier and stiffer than regular elastic. Elastic is usually applied to the inside of the garment, but decorative elastic can be used on the outside.

If the garment receiving the applied elastic has a natural opening, the elastic is usually applied over vertical seams, and both free ends are secured by extra stitching or by the application of a fabric patch. Some garments, jackets especially, may have applied elastic just in the area between two vertical seams. The back waist is frequently the location of such a restricted treatment. In these cases, the elastic is usually applied to the back section before the side seams are formed.

Similarly, in a tubular garment such as a dress or a romper suit, the

8-13. Applied elastic, internal treatment, side seam sewn after elastic application.

elastic is usually applied when all but one of the garment's vertical seams have been sewn. In this way, the elastic can be applied to the flat garment, a much easier application than if the garment was sewn into a tube first. The side seam will be bulky in the area where the elastic is joined, but because of its location, it is not readily apparent or uncomfortable unless the elastic is very wide and/or thick. In such cases, a tubular application with elastic ends lapped would be more appropriate.

Smocking and Shirring. Very decorative waistline effects can result from stitching several parallel rows of straight stitches using elastic as the lower thread in the machine. In fact, a very inexpensive garment

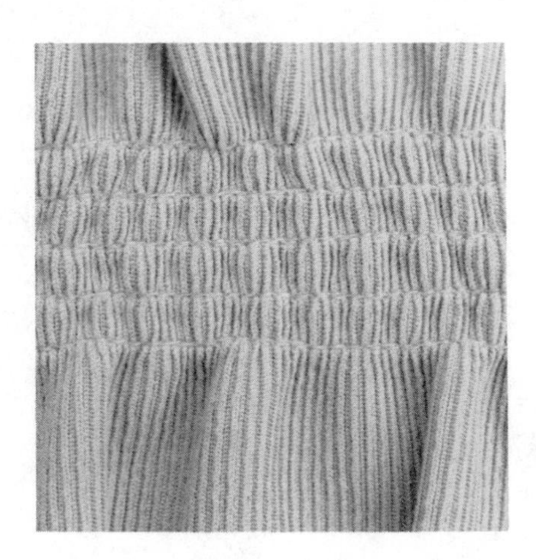

8-14. Shirring used as an internal waistline treatment.

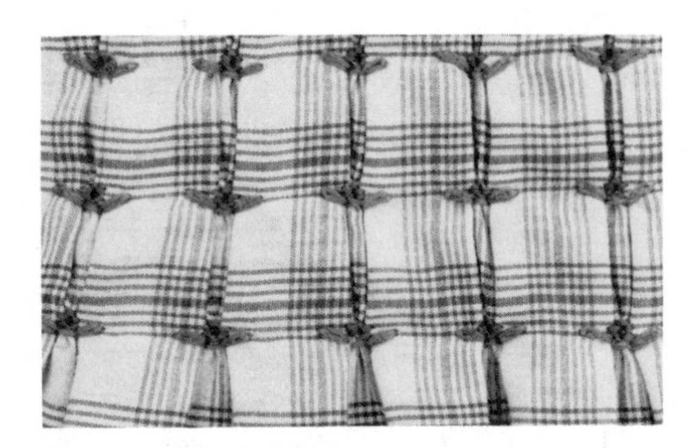

8-15. Smocked waistline.

can result from stitching a wide panel of this elastic shirring, leaving a header at the top finished edge to create a ruffle, then sewing one back seam to make a child's sun dress. Two side seams would probably be required to make such a dress for adult sizes. The elastic shirring expands to fit the bust or chest, then contracts to conform to the waistline.

Smocking gives a similar effect, but does not have the elastic recovery to provide reliable contraction and fit. Only the stitch formation, created by hand, provides for some slight expansion. Smocking is more common today in imported or home-made children's garments than in regular ready-to-wear. Hand-smocking was a popular treatment for the lowered waistlines popular in the late 1920s and 1930s. It enjoyed a revival of interest in the 1980s, but as a craft, not as a wide-scale commercial venture.

STANDARDS FOR EVALUATING ELASTICIZED WAISTLINES

1. The elastic is made with spandex rather than rubber for longer flex life.
2. The elastic is an appropriate size, width, and length for its location. For example, one-eighth inch (.32 cm) elastic is insufficient in width to support a pair of slacks.
3. The elastic is stretched evenly during application.
4. Application stitches are neat and secure.
5. Sufficient rows of stitching are used to prevent the elastic from folding over on itself.
6. Any seams in the elastic are lapped seams rather than regular seams.

INTERNAL CASINGS

Casings used as internal treatments are basically the same as those used at garment edges except that they must be applied—there is no edge to fold down. The casing may be applied to the inside of the garment, in which case the casing fabric should be at least as thin and soft as the garment fabric and preferably cut on the bias for the least bulk. Casings may also be applied to the outside of the garment. In this case, it is more likely that they would be made of garment fabric and cut on the lengthwise or crosswise grain. On the outside of the garment, they have decorative as well as functional impact.

CLOSED CASINGS

A closed casing is used only with elastic since there is no other way to adjust the fitting gathers. An opening must be left in the casing until the elastic is inserted, but then it should be closed.

In partial casings, that is casings that cover only a portion of the garment section, the elastic is inserted before the garment's vertical seams are made. Those seams, when formed, then close the casing and secure the elastic at the same time. If the partial casing does not end at a vertical seam, then the raw edges of the casing ends must be turned under or finished in some way. Stitching is then used to close the casing

a.

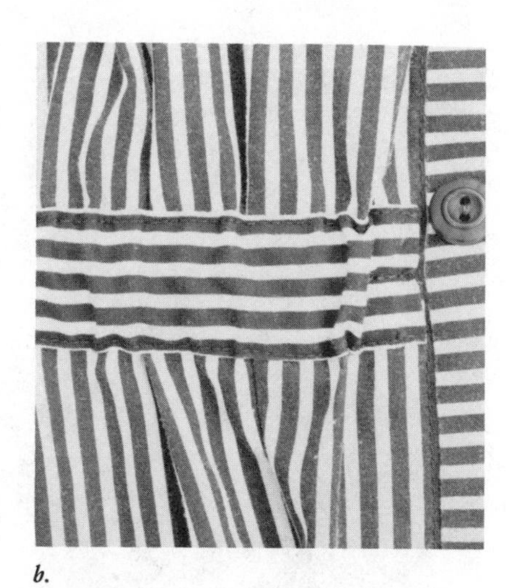

b.

8-16. Closed casings: (a) on inside of garment; (b) on outside of garment.

and secure the elastic. The stitching may be simply back-and-forth or in a decorative pattern.

If the casing encircles the entire garment section, it may be applied and the elastic inserted when one vertical seam remains open, or it may be applied and the elastic joined with a lapped seam after the garment is completely seamed. The latter is the more expensive and less bulky method, but is rarely used in ready-to-wear because of the increased time needed to apply and close it.

OPEN CASINGS

If a drawstring, cord, ribbon, or similar device is used to adjust the waistline fitting gathers, then an opening must be provided, just as in open casings used as edge treatments. Buttonholes, eyelets, or even openings left in seams can serve as outlets for drawstrings. The casing can be positioned on the outside of the garment and both ends finished so that the casing ends form the openings. This is more common when the casing is a partial one than if it completely encircles the waist. A jacket, for example, can have an exposed casing that covers the back waist and perhaps half of each front section. The drawstring would emerge from the casing and the ends function as partial drawstring, partial belt.

8-17. Open casing with drawstring.

STANDARDS FOR EVALUATING INTERNAL CASINGS
1. The stitching lines are parallel. 2. The casing is positioned properly on the garment. 3. The casing is the correct width for the elastic or drawstring that it contains. 4. The raw edges of the casing are finished, if necessary, to prevent raveling. 5. The elastic or drawstring is not twisted in the casing. 6. Openings in the casing, when present, are neat and durable. 7. Casings for elastic have been stitched closed after insertion of the elastic. 8. Thick or bulky elastic in closed casings has been sewn with lapped seams rather than with plain seams. 9. The casing fabric is soft, thin, consistent in grainline, and compatible with the garment fabric.

WAISTLINE SEAMS

More complicated than unseamed waistline treatments are those structures requiring garment sections to be seamed at the waistline. More fabric is usually required in garments with waistline seams, and most of such garments require rather careful matching of major construction points—sides, center front, center back, darts, etc.

A single seam that occurs at or near the natural waistline is most common, but some styles contain an inset band at the waist and thus require two seams to join it to the bodice and lower garment sections. Inset bands in this location are treated much like inset bands at the neckline, except that they are cut straight instead of having to be set into a curve, and they have to have the facing section applied in a separate operation. Inset bands add considerably to the cost of a garment in terms of both fabric/interfacing requirements and labor.

FLAT SEAMS

If no gathers or pleats are provided in either section being joined at the waistline, then the join can be called a flat, or plain seam. When fitted styles are popular, both dresses and jackets for women commonly feature this type of treatment at the natural waistline. The more closely the garment is intended to fit the body, the more care is required in constructing top and bottom sections so that all major construction points will match when the sections are joined at the waistline. A dress might require matching at two front darts, two side seams, the center front, the center back, and two back darts—a total of eight places. Most garments require matching at least at the sides and at the center front and back.

If the garment fabric is stretchy or unstable, the waistline seam will be more durable if stayed. Thread or fabric belt loops may be provided as carriers for belts, but these are not really necessary at the natural waistline since belts tend to stay in place there.

SEAMS WITH FULLNESS

More common to today's styles are waistline seams that incorporate some fullness in one or both plies being joined. The fullness may be in the form of easing, gathers, pleats, and/or tucks. If one ply has no fullness, then this ply frequently is cut straight enough to stabilize the finished seam, especially if the garment does not fit the body tightly. If both garment sections contain fullness, then a stay is required both for stability and as a guide for controlling the fullness of each section. The stay for such a seam would have major construction points indicated on it, or at the very least would be cut the desired finished circumference of the seam.

Some seams with fullness and some flat seams may also be elasticized. Attaching a piece of elastic to a seam made larger than necessary is an effective and inexpensive way of achieving better fit in the garment. It

8-18. Waistline seam with fullness: fitted bodice joined to a gathered skirt.

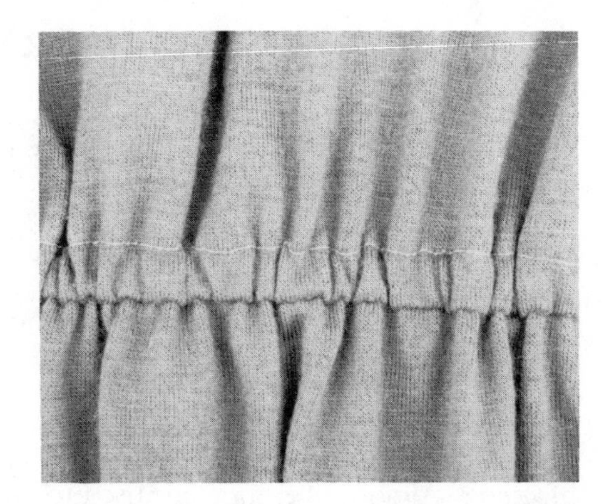

8-19. Elasticized flat seam.

also eliminates the need to cut and mark a stay and to provide for an opening in the garment, both of which would be necessary in a garment that had both bodice and bottom gathered to fit the waistline. In elasticizing the waistline seam, the seam allowances can be stitched together at the upper edges or stitched to the garment to form a type of casing. (The latter is shown in Figure 8-19.) The elastic is then drawn through this casing. The application of the elastic directly to the waistline seam allowances is much more labor efficient. Machinery that will form the waistline seam and apply the elastic at the same time is available, a definite cost advantage to the producer. Such an application is a real disadvantage to the consumer who wishes to remove or replace the elastic for whatever reason.

STANDARDS FOR EVALUATING WAISTLINE SEAMS

1. All major construction points on both garment sections are matched.
2. Fullness, if present, is evenly distributed.
3. The seam is stayed if necessary.
4. Elastic, if present, is attached separately from the waistline seam for ease of removal.
5. Inset bands are interfaced and faced.

SUMMARY

A clear ordering of all waistline treatments according to potential manufacturing costs is not feasible, given the number of variables that can influence the quality of each treatment. In general, simple treatments like applied elastic and closed casings are less costly to produce than elaborately seamed constructions like waistbands. Many of these constructions that appear complicated, however, have been simplified and made more consistent with the application of modern technology. Belt loops, for example, can be produced, fed to an attaching machine, and then attached to the waistband in a matter of seconds and with an identical product time after time. Even the tubular attachment of elastic is simplified with newer equipment now available to the apparel manufacturer. Almost all equipment used to attach elastic to apparel comes equipped with automatic feeds so that the elastic is fed to the garment at a consistent tension on every garment.

Relating cost to waistline complexity is thus a more complicated task than it would at first appear. The garment manufacturer that must rely on older, less automated methods to attach waistbands, for example, will necessarily expend more on labor costs, and will very likely have more inconsistencies in product quality. An analysis of any waistband treatment can, however, lead to a determination of the appropriateness of the technique to the garment design and to a determination on the overall quality, regardless of how the technique was applied.

9

CLOSURES

Garments that fit the body closely require some type of closure, unless elastic or drawstrings are used to provide the fit. Closures can be found at almost any location on the garment. The location and type of closure is frequently a very important design feature of the garment. So important is the aesthetic element of closures that they are frequently simulated on budget lines of apparel. The application of any closure adds to the garment cost, especially if the required closure materials are expensive and if their application requires considerable time and/or precision. Preparing the garment for the closure actually begins at the design stage, for the closure location and type are often major components of the garment design and can even be determined independently of the actual mechanical means of closure selected. For example, the preparation of a placket opening at the front of a pullover shirt could proceed along very similar lines regardless of whether the final garment simply laps, meets flush, buttons, snaps, or fastens with nylon hook and loop tape. The location and type of closure, and the preparation of the apparel parts to complete the selected closure is, then, a major aspect of the garment appearance and cost.

CLOSURE STYLES

The style of closure refers to the preparation of the garment area to receive whatever closure mechanism, if any, is to be used to achieve the closure. The style may be open or closed ended; it may be faced, banded, bound, or some combination. The location of the closure, the degree of fit in the garment, and the intended closure mechanism all influence the closure style to some degree.

OPEN ENDED CLOSURES

Open ended closures are free at both ends, the most common type found at the front of jackets, blouses, shirts, and coats. They may also be found on skirts, jumpers, dresses, robes, smocks, uniforms, vests, and pajamas. The raw edge of the garment may be prepared to accept the closure by being faced, bound, banded, or any other of the methods which can be used to finish the free edge of a garment. A boiled wool jacket may have no finish more complicated than serging or some decorative stitch which covers the raw edge, as the thickness of the wool and its reduced raveling capacity make it behave more like felt than a traditional fabric. By contrast, the front closure of a man's suit may be reinforced with hair canvas, taped at the edges, faced, and fastened with buttons and worked buttonholes.

FACED CLOSURES

Most faced closures will also contain interfacing. For most fabrics some reinforcement is needed to strengthen the area if buttons and buttonholes are to be applied later. In bloused styles made of soft fabrics, a layer of self fabric is often the most appropriate choice of interfacing to preserve the desired fabric drape. An interfacing which is too stiff will buckle outward away from the body and distort the design line.

Facings used at a garment closure should meet the same standards of quality as those appearing at the neckline of the garment, and in most instances the closure facing will be applied in combination with the neckline facing. With wing, shawl, and notched collar applications, only a fold line marks the point at which the neckline treatment becomes the point of closure. Facings should be deep enough to accommodate the desired closure mechanism and to cover the garment interior should the opening be turned back during wear. Figure 9-1 shows a facing which is cut too narrow for its application, and the finished edge of the facing, part of the collar application, and the wrong side of the garment are visible when the garment is worn.

For an edge with shaping, such as a lapel that extends beyond the center front, the facing must be cut separately and seamed in place. Even if the front edge is straight, a cut-on application may be used to introduce contrasting fabric in the facing or even to develop a more efficient marker. For most straight edges, a cut-on facing is usually the most economical as it eliminates an extra pattern piece and seam. A concealed closure can be achieved with the cut-on facing by allowing extra fabric to be formed into a tuck which will lay over the closure. Such an application is shown in Figure 9-2. Such applications usually have one closure mechanism at the top which is visible. The additional fabric and construction of such a closure style adds to the garment expense.

Men's shirts with tab fronts usually have cut-on facings which are folded into place to form the closure style. In many, the tab itself is simply a folded facing. The facing is folded once toward the wrong side, then folded again on the right side so that the second fold encloses the raw edge of the facing. A line of topstitching about three-eighths inch (.96 cm) from that second fold secures the raw edge of the facing and gives the appearance of a sewn-on band. An additional row of topstitching on the outermost edge gives a matched appearance and flattens the edge.

9-1. Extended front facing too narrow for location.

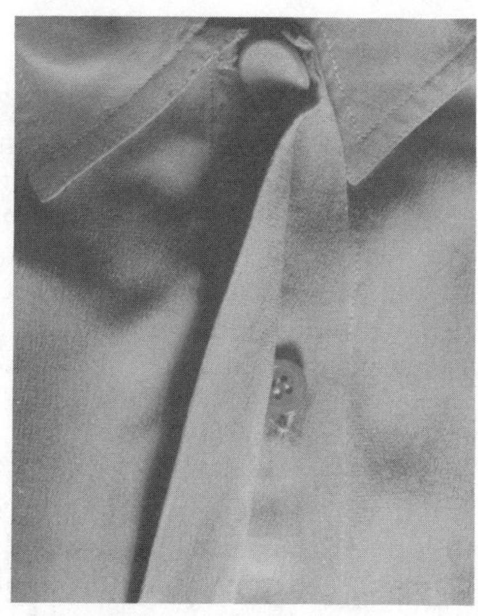

9-2. Concealed buttoned closure in blouse front.

9-3. Faced closure: tab front of man's shirt.

Faced closures, either cut or sewn on, also can be used for zippered application. Figure 9-4 shows two variations of a zippered closure, one concealed with a second, snapped closure and the other the more traditional type used on windbreaker jackets. Much less fabric is required for the latter style; usually only the equivalent of a seam allowance is used. This narrow facing finishes the raw edge as the zipper is applied. Snap tape or nylon hook and loop tape can also be used in such locations.

BOUND CLOSURES

Binding as a finish for a closure follows the same principles of application and quality as those used for neckline treatments, covered in Chapter 6. A binding can be of cut and folded strips of bias cut woven or of knitted fabric with raw edges turned under or of special binding fabrics made of narrow, finished knitted fabric which requires no turning under of raw edges. Braided fabrics such as those shown in Figure 6-3 can also be used to finish the closure location as well as other raw edges of the garment—hem edge, sleeve edge or armscye, and neckline.

BANDED CLOSURES

Either contrasting or self fabric can be applied to the closure location to form a band. The band extends beyond the original cut edge of the garment, and this is the distinguishing feature between the band and the sewn-on facing. Bands can be shaped to the opening edge or cut of straight strips of fabric.

a.

b.

9-4. Faced closures for zipper applications: (a) concealed application; (b) centered application.

Shaped bands follow the grainline placement for the garment piece to which they are sewn. If the band is used to cover a neckline and front or back opening, the amount of shaping may be considerable. This shaping translates directly into fabric costs, for bands are made double—that is each band section must also have a back side to provide the finish. If the band itself is shaped, then the facing section will double the amount of fabric required. The yardage requirement can be further complicated if the garment is made of a plaid or directional fabric which requires matching.

In addition to the increase in fabric yardage required, shaped bands also increase pattern making time and time in creating the layout and marker. Grading is more difficult, as well, for the additional sizing must be placed proportionally along the shaped area, not just added on to the end. Interfacing, if used, must also be cut using the shaped pattern piece with its greater yardage requirements. The advantage of the shaped band is that it conforms to the shape of the garment section(s) to which it is sewn.

Straight bands are usually reserved for locations which have very limited curves. Bands may be applied to front openings following the neckline finish. They may be applied to a skirt opening prior to the application of the waistband, which then finishes off the top of the band. If slight shaping occurs in the garment edge, then the straight band is more successful if executed in the bias cut of fabric, but that cut is not economical of fabric yardage except in very rare circumstances when the layout provides a space on the fabric diagonal. Most of the time the straight band is used on a shaped application for purposes of economy. It tends to stand away from the location to which it is applied.

COMBINATION

In some garments both faced and banded closure styles are used. This is especially true in lapped applications where only one side of the closure will be visible in the finished, closed garment. If specialty fabric, a bias cut, or matched fabric motifs are part of the garment design, then there is even more reason to combine treatment methods.

One of the most common combination treatments occurs in men's shirts with tab fronts. When the tab is a separate, interfaced band, it represents additional construction costs. These can be offset, and a flatter finished closure effected, by facing the underlap side.

CLOSED-ENDED CLOSURE LOCATIONS (PLACKETS)

Plackets, especially neckline plackets, fall into this category. They usually occur in garment sections that have no seamline. In locations such as sheath dresses or tops designed to be pulled on over the head, the placket may be closed at both ends. It opens to allow the fitted waistline location to spread for ease in dressing, then closes with zipper, snaps, or buttons. Styles of garments with such applications were very common in the 1950s and 1960s, but they are much less common now.

The placket which opens at only one end is the most typical style found in contemporary apparel. Men's, women's, and children's sweaters and tops and sweater-styled dresses frequently have this type of opening. Any fabric can be used, and knit goods are frequently favored even though their stretch potential may make achieving a smooth end difficult.

As with open ended closures, the placket treatment may be faced, banded, or a combination of the two methods. A considerable amount of variation in application method, placket location, and end design are possible.

FACED PLACKET

Facings can be used to construct simple or complex plackets. The simplest type of faced placket is the type found at the back, or even front, opening of pull-over garments.

At the back opening of a dress with an elasticized waist or no waistline fitting, the faced placket is usually found in an abutted closure that fastens at the top with a loop and button or hook and eye. This technique is an easy and inexpensive way to provide entry into a garment. If the garment has no center back seamline, then the stitching line for the facing will resemble a dart, tapering to nothing at the placket end. When the placket facing has been cut and turned, the opening will be in the shape of a V. If a closure is used at the top, then the garment back will not lie flat, but will buckle some, relative to the amount of fabric removed at the top seamlines of the facing. During the 1970s, tunics with faced plackets in the garment front were popular, and they were usually left open, occasionally trimmed around with braid or soutache. In that type of application, the width of the upper end can be greater with no problem. In all faced plackets set into a garment with no seamline, the point is an area of potential weakness, as it must be clipped to a thread or two of the stitching so that the facing can be turned to the wrong side. As with the faced sleeve placket, failing to clip close enough results in puckers and wrinkles. Clipping too close to

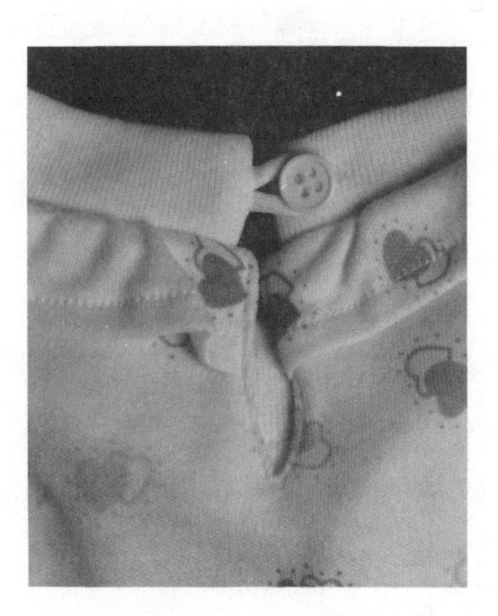

9-5. Faced placket in garment with no seamline.

the end weakens the fabric and can result in the yarns raveling out and a hole developing at the placket end. Also, if the placket is not long enough to provide sufficient opening width to the neckline, the stress of putting the garment over the head during dressing can tear the facing seam at the point.

If the garment has a seamline at the placket location, then the garment can close completely with no distortion along the placket location. This type of faced placket is slightly more difficult to apply accurately, however. The seamline that is left open must be reinforced at the point of the opening, and then the two seams that join the facing pieces to the garment pieces must intersect at exactly the correct point with the garment seamline opening for the entire piece to lie flat and the two sides of the opening to be the same length. This type of faced placket can fasten its entire length with hooks and eyes, loops and buttons, or even decorative details such as frogs that utilize an abutted rather than a lapped location.

One variation of the faced placket uses a self facing that is folded and pleated to create the necessary raw edge finish to the slashed opening. In the section on sleeve treatments, Chapter 7, the pleated placket has

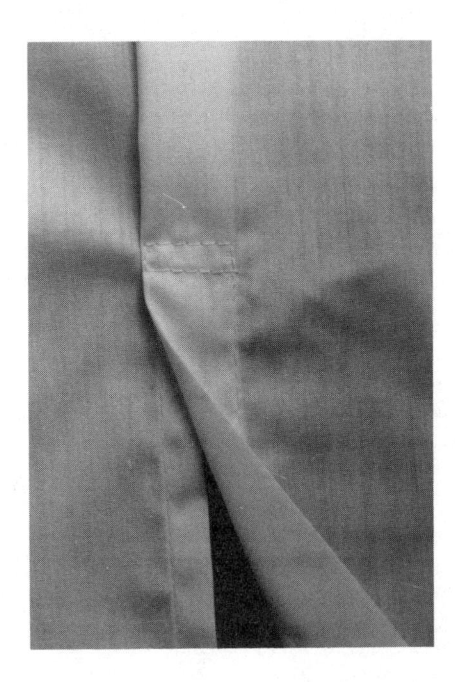

9-6. Pleated, self-faced placket.

a very similar structure. The garment is slashed down the center of the placket location and Y-clipped into the lower corners. In home sewing, this slashing would be preceded by reinforcement stitching outlining the rectangle into which the placket would be set, but this type of detail is rarely used in industrial production. The raw edges are then turned back, secured in a fold, and topstitched in place on each side. The final construction step folds the wedge at the bottom of the clip to the right side and conceals it with folds of the underlap, then the overlap. Final topstitching at the lower end of the placket holds the pleats in shape and secures the opening.

The pleated, self-faced placket requires additional fabric to create the pleats, but requires no additional pattern pieces. The construction itself is not difficult, and the completed technique is very durable. It does, by design, create additional fullness at the bottom of the placket. This design and structural feature make the pleated placket ideal for maternity garments or other garments designed to flare away from the body.

BOUND PLACKET

The same types of binding fabrics used for open-ended treatments can be used in plackets. Application of binding to a placket that is designed to be pointed at its lower end will follow the same type of procedure discussed in Chapter 7, Continuous Bound Placket, page 174. As with that type of placket, pinch mitering or some method of finishing the point is needed to keep the placket on the wrong side of the garment. Little girl's dresses that have a buttoned yoke which has been faced or even made double will often have a bound placket of this type stitched into the upper skirt so that the garment can spread for dressing.

Knitted bindings are also used in placket locations, but the ends are more commonly rounded, creating a kind of "keyhole" opening that closes at the top with a loop and button or hook and eye. Knitted shells or simple tops designed for wearing under suits are often finished this way if the neckline is high and lacks sufficient stretch to be pulled on.

BANDED PLACKET

The banded placket has both underlap and overlap applied as a separate piece of fabric. In most instances, the garment does not have a seamline at the point of application. If there is a seamline present, it may or may not affect the production of the placket itself. If the placket ends in a point, the presence of the seamline may actually complicate the appli-

9-7. Bound placket.

cation, as the point would need to end precisely at the seamline to look symmetrical.

As with the pleated placket, the banded placket begins with a rectangular opening in the garment section. For increased strength in the finished placket, this opening may be stitched around before it is cut open, but in industry this step is most often omitted, and the slash is made directly into the un-reinforced fabric. A folded, usually interfaced band is then applied to the underlap and overlap. The two parts must be kept aligned, even in width and length, and the bottom ends finished off neatly and securely. This last point is the one which creates the most difficulty. In thick, bulky, or stretchy fabrics, the crosswise or diagonal stitching at the end of the placket often stretches the fabric slightly, and the resulting placket application looks somewhat bumpy and/or wrinkled. Because the finished end and the end of the vertical seam must intersect precisely and in a space where the fabric is clipped to only a thread, this presents a potential source of weakness in the garment. Close examination of the right and wrong sides of the placket opening can usually detect if the stitching is too far over and has not caught in sufficient garment yarns to be secure.

The method of shaping and finishing the lower end of the placket is one of the garment's design details. As such, the more complicated shapes and stitching patterns will be found on more expensive garments. Plackets can be pointed, square, rounded, or asymmetrical. Topstitching can be

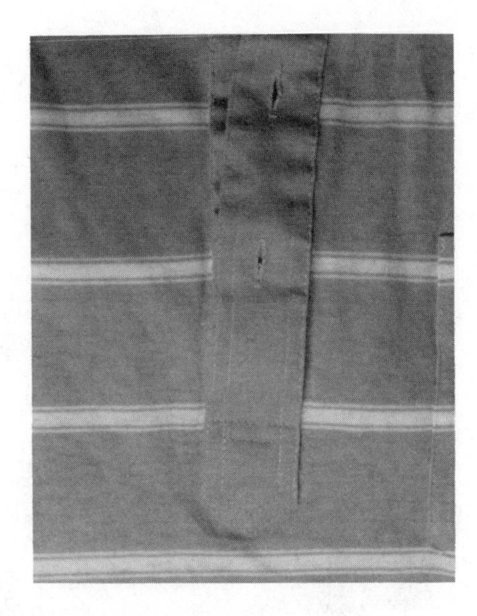

*9-8. **Banded placket.***

done in multiple rows for design effect as well as to secure the placket end.

COMBINATION PLACKETS

Plackets as well as open ended closure locations can be finished with both facings and bands. One of the most common sport shirt styles for men is the pull-over "golfing" shirt, made of a birds-eye pattern double knit. The underlap of this garment is banded, and the overlap is faced. The facing can be self fabric or a contrasting fabric. In rugby shirts, the facing is usually a wide piece of cotton twill tape, and this tape gives reinforcement to the buttonholes which are usually worked through it, and eliminates the need for separate interfacing of the overlap.

If the faced overlap is used on a garment designed to be left open at the neckline, then the upper edge of the facing will need to be shaped at its upper edge. This additional fabric requirement is often omitted in industry, but the result is a garment that shows the inside facing edge and usually some of the wrong side of the garment fabric and neckline finish. A much better appearance is achieved by making the facing wide enough to conceal all of the turned back portion of the upper closure area.

If the free edge of the facing is not secured by topstitching, it may roll. This is especially true if the facing is made of a single knit. Fusible interfacing can help to some degree, but if the interfacing is light in weight, it may not provide sufficient support to keep the facing flat and in place.

STANDARDS FOR EVALUATING CLOSURE STYLES

1. The selection of closure preparation style is coordinated with the remainder of the garment style.
2. Fabrics utilized in the closure preparation are compatible with the fashion fabric in aesthetic and maintenance characteristics.
3. Closure locations designed to be symmetrical are identical on both sides of the garment.
4. Closure locations to have closure mechanisms such as buttons and buttonholes applied are sufficiently reinforced or supported to provide stability to the area.
5. Applied fabrics are aligned properly to the underlying garment location to avoid pulling, puckering, rippling, or wrinkling.
6. Plackets are sufficient in length to permit the garment to be put on easily without pulling.
7. Placket ends are even and smooth, with no holes, puckers, ripples, or wrinkles.
8. Placket ends are secure, with no weak areas or holes detectable.
9. Free edges of applied or self fabric facings are flat and secure on the wrong side of the garment.
10. In garments that will have a portion of the closure location turned back to the front, facings are sufficient in width to conceal the interior of the garment during wear.

CLOSURE MECHANISMS

Even though the title of this chapter is "Closures," a garment can have an opening that is not designed to be closed. Selection of the term "closure" over "opening" is strictly a matter of convenience. Some "openings" are not really functional and are not designed to be actually opened, either. For those locations where a garment can be opened and closed, some mechanism must be used to secure the two or more garment pieces in their closed location. Although something as simple as a belt or ribbon can tie one section of a bathrobe over the underlap portion, in most cases a more complicated system is used. Those are treated below according to their structure.

BUTTONED CLOSURES

One of the most common methods used to join two pieces of a garment is to apply buttons and buttonholes. These are especially effective at sleeve cuffs; center fronts of jackets, coats, blouses, and shirts; skirt or slack waistbands; and center backs of some dresses and blouses. At the center front of garments, the correct position for buttons depends on the sex of the intended wearer: in men's wear, the buttons are placed on the right side (the underlap); in women's clothing, the left side is the underlap, and buttons are placed on the left. On sleeve cuffs, the side of the sleeve that joins the garment back is the underlap and contains the button.

BUTTONS

If buttons are to be used in a visible application, they should coordinate with the garment style and fabric as well as with the location in which they will be used. In applications where the buttons will be concealed by a flap or tab, the main consideration is that the button is flat and durable. In any case, the buttons selected should either complement the garment or be inconspicuous.

The number of buttons used and their spacing should relate to the size of the button. Very large buttons need to be placed further apart than smaller buttons. However, very small buttons may be used in groups of two or three and these groupings then spaced as if each were a single, large button. The weight of the button, both actual and visual, is also an important consideration in coordinating buttons with overall garment appearance. Soft, flexible fabrics can appear to be overpowered by very large, heavy buttons. Also, very elaborate carved, painted, or patterned buttons usually show to best advantage on simple fabrics. Dark colors and/or busy prints tend to camouflage construction details, including buttons.

BUTTON MATERIALS

One of the first considerations in the cost of a button is the material from which it is made. As a rule, natural materials tend to be more expensive than synthetics, but this initial cost can be offset if the natural-material button is small and simple and if the plastic button is very elaborate, large, and/or trimmed. Natural materials include wood, leather, pearl, and horn. Pearl buttons are the most common in this group, and also the most dressy. They may be the natural color of the shell from which the mother-of-pearl was taken, or whiter shells can be given a color treatment which yields a suggestion of the applied color, not complete coverage.

Leather, wood, and horn buttons are much more causal than pearl and are more effective on heavier fabrics, especially wools and suiting weights of other fabrics. Leather buttons are often interwoven strips that are molded in a dome shape before application. They may also be produced in single thicknesses in a flatter shape. Horn buttons are quite expensive, but, like pearl, can usually be laundered. Leather and wood buttons should not be exposed to laundering solutions.

BUTTON STYLES

Buttons come in two basic styles, shank and eyed. Shank buttons have some mechanism for raising the button above the level of the garment section to which it is sewn. In buttons made of synthetic materials, the shank may be molded on as the button itself is molded, yielding a single unit. In other instances, the shank is made of metal with a small plate attached, and this plate is glued to the back of the button. Glued shanks have a tendency to separate if the garment is laundered frequently. Fabric shanks may be used on covered buttons. They cannot be replaced if they tear out during wear and care of the garment. Metal shanks can also rust if exposed to moisture over a long period of time. In such cases, not only is the button ruined, but rust stains may damage the garment as well. If the buttons are carved, the shank will probably be carved too, again resulting in a single unit.

The shank on the button serves as a spacer to keep the button raised far enough from the garment surface to allow the buttonhole or loop to lie under the button smoothly. The presence of a shank is also related to the button's appearance. Certain styles of buttons cannot be produced any other way. Shanked buttons are more difficult to attach to the garment, however, and thus require more construction time in industrial settings.

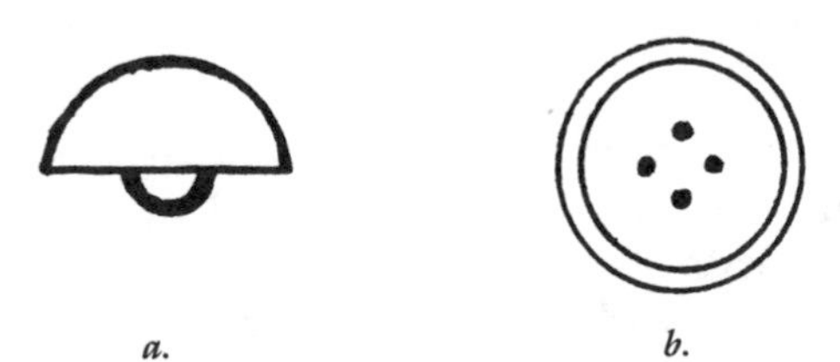

9-9. Button styles: (a) shank; (b) eyed.

Eyed buttons are necessarily flatter than most shank buttons and have either two or four holes (eyes) which permit stitches to be made directly through the button and garment section. This style of button is much easier and faster to apply, because button-sewing machinery can accommodate the flat application much more easily than the angled application necessary for shanks. If a button has only two holes, these should be positioned to follow the same direction as the buttonhole. For example, if the buttonhole is vertical, then the eyes should be placed vertically for stitching to the garment. This allows the button hole to close around the button's stitching more easily. Buttons with four eyes can be attached with parallel or crossed sets of stitches, depending on the desired appearance. Neither is more functional nor durable than the other.

Some button-attaching machinery can also apply thread shanks to eyed buttons. This is a real advantage when the garment fabric is thick. The thread shank reinforces the button's stitching and also raises the button for a flatter, smoother look when the garment is buttoned. Thread shanks are usually reserved for more expensive garments and/or heavy coats and jackets. Even when thread shanks are not economically feasible, allowing some slack in the attachment thread will provide for some buttonhole space under the button.

When a button is sewn to loosely woven fabrics, to leathers or vinyls, or to single layers of fabric, reinforcement of some type helps to prolong the life of the garment. In the first two instances, thin clear plastic buttons may be sewn to the wrong side of the garment. The stitches that join the fashion button also penetrate the reinforcement button. Stress on the button is absorbed by the reinforcement button rather than by the stitches alone, which might otherwise pull a portion of the garment fabric out, leaving a hole. In the final instance, i.e., when a button is sewn to single layers of fabric, found in button-down collars, for example, a small round of interfacing may be used on the wrong side for the same purpose. Similar situations exist when detachable garment parts are buttoned to an area where no other interfacing or fabric layers can add support.

BUTTONHOLES

Once the buttons have been selected for the garment, buttonholes will have to be designed to match them. The size of the buttonholes must be based on exact measurement of the buttons. Even buttons that have the same diameter may require different buttonhole lengths, depending on the style of the button and its thickness. Rough buttons are harder to get through buttonholes and, therefore, require slightly more space than very smooth buttons. Odd shapes and rounded shapes also require more buttonhole length.

The placement of the buttonholes must also be exact in relation to the button placement. In some industrial settings, machinery is positioned to attach buttons and make buttonholes at approximately the same time. Markings on the machinery indicate the distance between buttonholes (and buttons). If there is not an exact match between buttons and buttonhole placements, then the garment sections will ripple and bubble.

Buttonholes are placed on the overlap portion of garments in relation to button placement, previously discussed. Even if abutted rather than lapped closures are to be used, the free-hanging buttonhole is secured to the portion of the garment that occurs in the overlap position.

Wherever they occur, buttonholes will usually require some type of reinforcement for stability through continued wear. Interfacing is the most frequently used type of reinforcement. As a rule, buttoned closures will be interfaced. Exceptions can be found in budget wear and when the buttoned closure is in a softly draped, blouson construction in which interfacing might distort the intended hang of the garment. In that case, rectangles of interfacing should be applied to the facing in the location of each buttonhole (and button). Otherwise, there is a very real possibility that any strain on the garment during wear will cause the button to tear out a hole in the garment and the buttonhole to become stretched and distorted. Distortion is especially problematical with knits.

THREAD-FINISHED BUTTONHOLES

Buttonholes consist of holes in a garment through which the button can be brought to effect a closure. If that hole occurs in a garment location where there is no natural opening, then the garment plies must be cut, and the cut edges finished in some way.

Thread is a very effective finish, especially if applied by machine stitching. The buttonhole is usually stitched with closely-spaced zigzag stitches on both sides and the two ends of the desired opening. A variety of shapes can be effected, depending on the garment type and the machinery used.

An infinite variety of shapes is also possible when the buttonhole is stitched by hand, but hand stitching is rare in ready-to-wear. Some men's suits; entirely hand sewn, imported baby clothes; and designer apparel may contain hand-sewn buttonholes. They are quite durable, but also quite labor intensive.

For applications where durability is essential and where a larger scale is acceptable, there are machine-worked buttonholes that have a purled edge similar to the one formed by hand. These buttonholes are most often found on coats and on men's suits and jackets. They are worked in buttonhole twist, a heavier thread than that normally used for buttonholes.

The *rectangular* buttonhole is one of the most common, especially on shirts, blouses, and some dresses. Buttonhole machinery can stitch these rectangular shapes in four steps, working without pause in between. In the first step, one long side of the buttonhole is stitched; then, the tack at the end is worked; third, the machine stitches backward to form the second long side of the buttonhole; and the final step is to apply the bar tack at the point where the stitching began. The bar tack is made by stitching across the entire width of the buttonhole opening several times. It serves as reinforcement to prevent the cut fabric from fraying or tearing when the garment is worn. A bar tack should always occur at the point where the button shank or stitching rests during normal wear of the garment. Figure 9-10 shows a typically rectangular buttonhole worked with zigzag stitching.

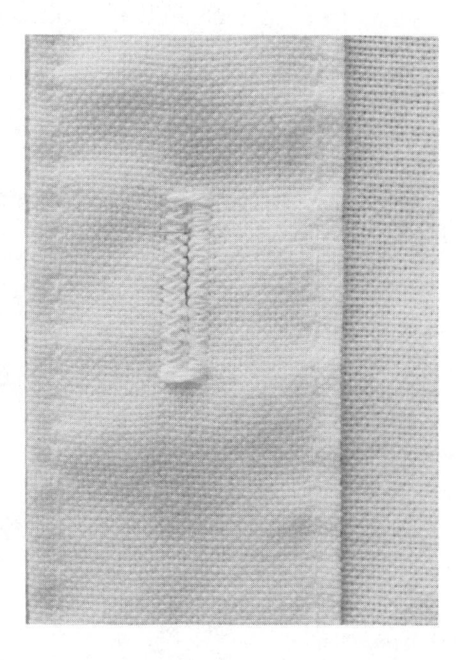

9-10. Rectangular thread-finished buttonhole with bar tacks.

Some machinery, particularly attachments for home sewing machines, can sew a long *oval* buttonhole with no tacks at either end. The narrow zigzag stitches which form the sides begin to angle slightly as they near the buttonhole end, becoming upright at the exact end point. In low stress applications, such buttonholes may be fairly durable, but the absence of stitches perpendicular to the direction of stress introduces a structural weakness.

The oval shape is the one most found when the buttonholes are worked by hand. In hand-worked buttonholes, however, the stitches are usually knotted at the inside edge of the opening. The resulting ridge of thread serves as adequate reinforcement. In heavier weights of fabric, industrial machinery can apply purled, often corded, oval buttonholes which usually have a bar tack at one end. These are similar to the keyhole buttonholes which are discussed below, except for shape. Figure 9-11 shows such a buttonhole.

The *keyhole* buttonhole is rounded at the end where the button will rest during normal use. This buttonhole type is found on coats, rainwear, all men's coats, jackets, and suits. It can be worked by hand, but is much more often made by a special machine which can produce a very close approximation of handmade buttonhole stitches. The thread used is buttonhole twist, and the stitches are knotted at the inner edge. The rounded eye of the buttonhole contains a small round opening, similar to an eyelet, and this opening provides a place for the button shank to rest so that no distortion is placed on the actual buttonhole when the garment is buttoned. Keyhole buttonholes, shown in Figure 9-12, are always placed horizontally on the garment.

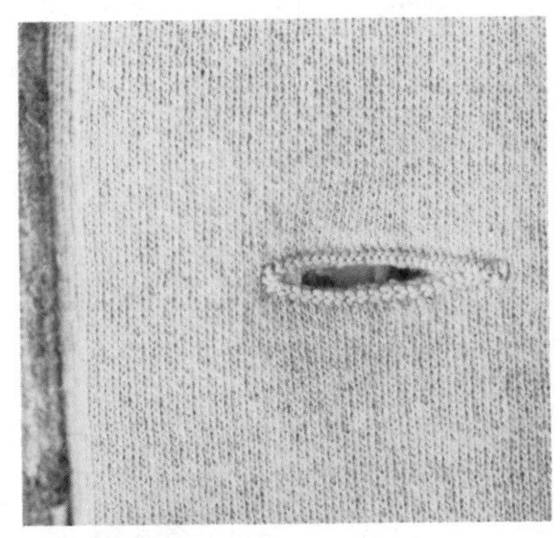

9-11. Oval thread-finished buttonhole.

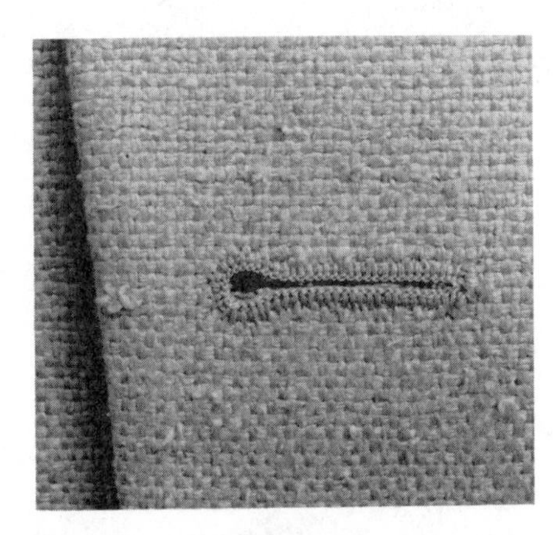

9-12. Keyhole buttonhole.

FABRIC-FINISHED BUTTONHOLES

An alternative to the stitched buttonhole, where thread forms the finish, is the buttonhole finished by fabric, either during the formation of the garment structure or during subsequent application steps. Fabric-finished buttonholes are much less common that those finished by thread, and they are more restricted as to garment types. Fabric-finished buttonholes are typical of women's winter coats and some tailored suits and jackets. They are not found on men's wear.

Structural Buttonhole. If a seam occurs at the desired buttonhole position, then openings can be left in that seam for allowing for buttoning. For example, a narrow tab or extension can be sewn to a jacket, blouse, or dress at the center front. The spaces between buttonhole locations are stitched with backstitching or some other type of reinforcement at the beginning and end. The unstitched areas would then become the buttonholes in the completed garment.

A similar feature may be used when a coat or jacket has a yoke. There, the opening is left in the yoke seam, with the buttonhole space beginning at the center front. There is a single inseam buttonhole in this style of garment, and the remaining buttonholes would probably be bound.

Another, much less common type of structural buttonhole occurs in full-fashioned knitted garments, especially in those knitted by hand. In this case, the buttonholes are actually formed as the fabric structure is formed. This can be done vertically or horizontally. Knitted-in buttonholes are very stretchable and unstable unless they have some additional

9-13. Structural buttonhole.

9-14. Bound buttonhole in leather.

reinforcement. In hand knits, this may be a loosely spaced buttonhole stitch worked by hand, a crochet stitch, or even a simple whip stitch to increase the strength of the opening. In garments crocheted by hand, the buttonholes can also be incorporated at the time the structure is formed, but crochet is somewhat stronger and less stretchable than knit. Therefore, no additional reinforcement is necessary in most instances.

Bound Buttonholes. When the buttonhole must be applied to a structure or garment section that is already formed, a hole can be cut in the fabric and matching or contrasting fabric strips used to finish the slash. This is similar to the application of slashed pockets, but done on a much smaller scale. Precision is even more important in bound buttonhole application; in the small size typical of buttonholes, even a single thread's width of variation can result in a buttonhole that is not symmetrical. Bound buttonholes are found in some tailored and couture women's suits and in most women's better coats. They are not found in men's wear at all. Figure 9-14 shows a bound buttonhole in leather.

In home sewing, bound buttonholes require numerous complicated, difficult steps to complete. They constitute the single most difficult ways to create a closure. Even in commercial production where machinery can be used to combine and simplify some of the steps, they are still much more expensive to apply than a thread-finished buttonhole. The opening must be slashed, finished with strips of fabric (lips) which must be straight or bias, matching or contrasting, corded or flat. Application of the lips, turning them to the wrong side, finishing off the ends, then creating and finishing an opening in the facing portion of the garment are all required to apply a bound buttonhole. The advantages are primarily aesthetic. In a loosely woven fabric, the bound buttonhole may actually be less durable than a thread-finished one. In heavy, thick, and/or spongy fabrics, however the bound buttonhole compresses the fabric less and results in a smoother appearance.

A simple, but often less attractive, alternative to the bound buttonhole is the use of a faced opening. Some European tailored women's suits have narrow, faced slashes for buttonholes. This technique is more attractive in pile or fur garments where the surface fibers cover the opening somewhat.

Fusing the edges of a slashed opening is another method for creating a buttonhole. Ultrasonic machines are used to bring the temperature of thermoplastic fibers to the melting point. Pattern wheels then press a stitch-like pattern into the softened fibers. When cooled, the fibers again become solid, but with the cut edges sealed, and the pattern is a permanent part of the fabric structure. Obviously, this technique can be used only with apparel made of thermoplastic fibers. It is frequently found in rainwear and occasionally in some lower price lines of infants' and boys' suit coats and jackets, particularly those intended for party or semiformal wear. The fused buttonhole is quite distinctive, and many consumers do not find it acceptable in moderate to better apparel lines.

LOOPS

Loops extend from one garment edge to encircle buttons on an opposing garment section. Since they do extend, they are selected when the garment sections to be closed do not lap, but are intended to abut when the garment is closed for wear.

Loops may be constructed of self-filled bias tubing, corded bias tubing, braid or gimp, crocheted chains, or thread chains. Tubing and braids are more commonly included in a seam that attaches a facing to the opening edge. The thinner, more flexible chains can be attached to a completed opening and are especially useful when the opening is finished with an extended rather than a shaped facing. In such a situation, there is no seam at the opening edge, and the loop must be attached to a folded edge. Some braids or gimps are especially created for use in applying to a finished edge. They combine a decorative portion with the looped edge which serves the buttonhole function. These can be used on either seamed or folded edge finishes.

Single loops, especially thread loops, are quite useful in effecting closures in partial openings, such as in a neckline placket. Fabric loops are

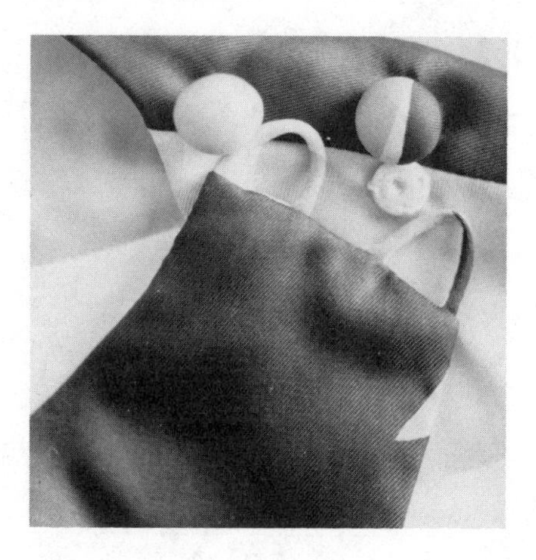

9-15. Fabric loops, covered buttons, and covered snaps.

more often used at sleeve placket openings and at garment center fronts. They may be continuous or widely spaced, depending on the desired style. Figure 9-15 shows a pair of corded bias fabric loops used at the shoulder closure of a dress. Fabric, yarn, or decorative braid can also be elaborately knotted or applied in a design to make what is referred to as "frog" closures. These are often used on garments with Oriental styling details. Frogs are used on both abutted and lapped closures.

All looped closures are limited to areas where there is low stress. Otherwise, the garment areas joined, especially those that are abutted, are likely to gap apart. Loops subjected to great stress are also likely to pull loose from the garment, whether they are incorporated into seams or attached later to a finished edge. Wrapped gimps are especially susceptible to pulling loose from stitching. The thin filaments used to wrap the core are very slippery. They frequently slide free of the stitching and appear on the garment surface even if the core remains secured.

STANDARDS FOR EVALUATING BUTTONED CLOSURES

1. The buttons are of good materials, and well made.
2. The buttons coordinate with the garment design and fabric.
3. The buttons are spaced correctly for their size and for the location of their use.
4. The buttons are located at stress points.
5. The buttons are reinforced according to the dictates of the fabric and location.
6. The buttons are sewn on securely.
7. No loose threads hang from the buttons.
8. The buttons have a shank if the fabric is very thick and spongy. The shank can be part of the button or a thread shank added to an eyed button.
9. The buttonholes are the correct type for the garment design and fabric.
10. The buttons and buttonholes are correctly aligned.
11. The buttonholes are securely stitched with no fraying or loose threads.
12. The buttonholes fit the buttons without gaping open or allowing the buttons to come through too easily.

SNAPPED AND HOOKED CLOSURES

This category contains a wide variety of hardware that can be used to effect closure. Many of these are used in concealed applications, but a few are exposed on the garment surface and, therefore, have the potential for being decorative. When they are exposed, they are usually found on casual, sporty, or work clothing. They are not as versatile in a variety of garment styles as are buttoned closures.

SNAPS

Snaps consist of two units, a ball and a socket. The ball portion is attached to the overlap, and the socket unit is attached to the underlap. The ball snaps into the socket to effect the closure. Snaps vary in size with the smallest suitable only on areas of very limited stress, such as detachable collars or doll clothes. The smaller snaps are more useful to secure garment parts in desired positions than to serve as functional closures. As size increases, the gripping power also increases, and large snaps are capable of sustaining more and more stress. The larger sizes are more often used as functional closures.

Most snaps are made of metal, either silver-colored or black. A colorless plastic is also used and is nearly inconspicuous on most fabrics. Larger snaps used on coats or tailored suits are frequently covered with thread or thin fabric in a color matching the garment shell. Such a snap is shown in Figure 9-15. Covering snaps makes them less conspicuous, but the covering is subjected to considerable abrasion as the snap is used and it may wear away rather rapidly. The fabric used for covering snaps must be selected to minimize raveling and yarn shift.

Concealed Application. If the snaps are to be attached inconspicuously to the garment, they must be either sewn by hand or attached to a fabric strip (snap tape) which is then topstitched into the garment in the closure location. Snap tape is frequently used as the closure in housecoats, housedresses, casual jackets, and the inseam/crotch location of infants' shorts and pants. The snaps are attached mechanically to the tape, which is then sewn into the garment with a row of machine stitching along each edge.

One frequent problem with this type of closure, especially when used in very long applications, is that the tape may shrink disproportionately to the garment to which it is attached. Figure 9-16 shows a dress front in which the snap tape has shrunk during laundering. Usually cotton twill tape is used, and it shrinks more than most apparel fabrics. If this occurs, the only way to correct the problem is to remove the snap tape

9-16. Snap tape which has shrunk during laundering.

from both sides of the garment, then reattach the two strips after smoothing out the length differential in the garment opening.

Snaps sewn by hand are more common to garments made at home or by designers and dressmakers. They may be used to secure the small upper corner of a buttoned front closure, to keep one-button cuffs properly aligned, to close lingerie strap holders on dress shoulder seams, and to attach collars and/or cuffs with different care requirements than the garment.

Visible Application. Visible snap applications are done mechanically and involve four pieces for each snapped closure. The ball portion is placed on the underneath of the overlap in the desired location; then, the teeth of the attaching ring are pushed through the fabric from the garment face to the underside, where they encounter the ball portion. The two are forced together so that the teeth are permanently engaged by opposing rings of the snap. The same steps are repeated for the socket portion. Decorative squares or rounds, which are painted, printed, or filled with other materials such as pearl, plastic, or glass may be substituted for the simple metal rings. Decorative snaps are commonly used on Western-styled shirts and jackets. The less decorative rings are more common as functional closures on pajamas, housedresses, house-coats, and children's playwear.

Firm fabric with good body and fairly high yarn count must be used for mechanically-attached snap closures. Otherwise, stress will cause holes in the fabric where the snap is attached. Rarely do snap portions separate from each other once they have been applied properly; instead, the fabric separates from the snap. Thin knits, such as those used in children's sleepwear, need reinforcing strips or patches of fabric to prevent this from occurring during wear and cleaning.

HOOKS, CLASPS, AND BUCKLES

In this category are hard closures other than the ball-and-socket type. All types included involve the merging of two opposing parts, one of which is attached to one garment section and the other to the adjoining section. In garments that lap, the hook or hook equivalent is attached to the overlap. The eye, loop, or equivalent receptacle is attached to the underlap. As with snaps, these closures can be categorized according to whether they are concealed or visible after application.

Concealed Application. When the closure is purely functional and not intended to form any part of the design of the garment, concealed application is required. Excellent examples of hook-and-eye closures that fit this description are those at the necklines of zippered dresses, those that attach fur collars to winter coats, and the waistband hooks on most men's and many women's slacks. Figure 9-17 shows a commercially applied hook and eye set in a pair of men's slacks.

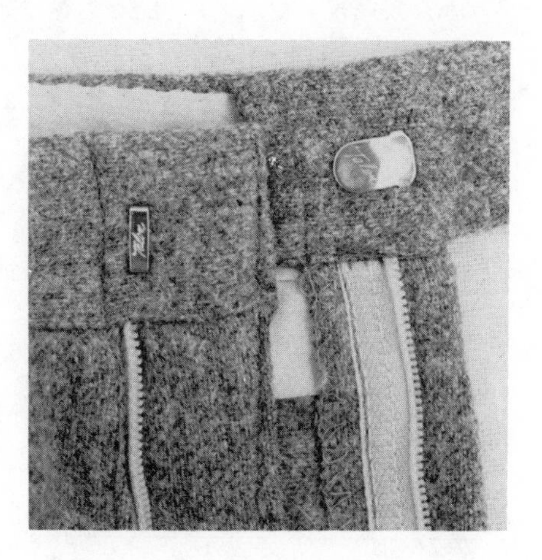

9-17. Concealed hook and eye application at waistband.

As with snaps, hooks and eyes vary considerably in size. The very small ones are made of wire and will not withstand a large amount of stress. As the size increases, so does strength. Very large wire hooks are often thread-covered and used on tailored suits and coats to secure the fabric between buttons and buttonholes or as the only type of closure. The thread covering is applied by hand and is found only in more expensive garments, like the wool and silk faille designer suit pictured in Figure 9-18. The hooks have been covered by hand-worked stitches, and the eyes are make by buttonhole stitches worked over a loop of heavy thread. All of the wire hooks must be attached by hand to the garment so that the stitches do not penetrate to the face of the garment where they would be noticeable. Lingerie and foundation garments are an exception to hand application; machine application is more durable and will be unobjectionable since these garments are later covered by other apparel. When many hook-and-eye closures are necessary, they can be applied first to a tape, then the tape strips applied to the garment with machine stitching, as with snap tapes.

The larger, formed metal hooks are more frequently attached mechanically. To prevent the attachment mechanism from being seen in the finished garment, it must be inserted before the garment section is closed off. In waistbands, it is attached only to the inner portion of the waistband. Because of this, some puffiness or separation of layers

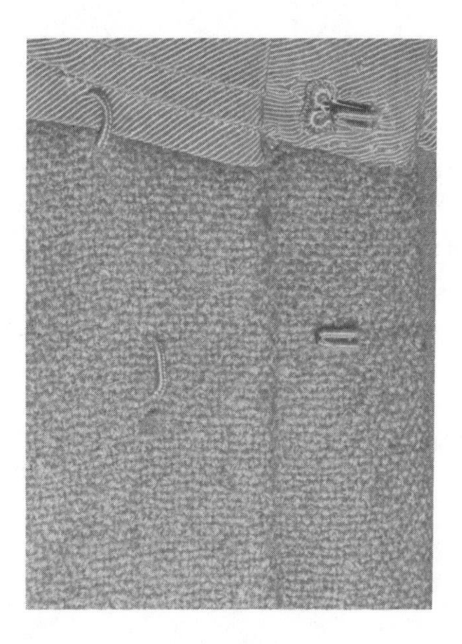

9-18. Thread-covered hooks and eyes.

may occur when this method is used on apparel sections that are not closely joined around the area of application once the garment is complete.

Technically within the definition of hook-and-eye closures is a nylon tape strip with thousands of tiny hooks on one side and thousands of tiny loops on the other. When sewn to the garment, this hook tape allows the two sections to be joined by simply pressing them together. It holds firmly if used in wide and/or long strips, yet releases fairly easily when pulled firmly in opposing directions. Figure 9-19 shows a pair of men's slacks which have that type of closure at the waistband, above a zippered fly.

Although it is supposed to be a concealed application, the thickness of the two strips of tape makes it very obvious. There are some other problems with the use of hook tape. Very small sections do not have enough holding power to be used as closures. Even in doll clothes or toys, tiny scraps of nylon hook tape often stay attached to clothes and other toys more than to the hook strip provided for them. If laundered in an open position, the hooks can cause extensive damage if easily snagged materials are laundered in the same load.

There are many advantages to the use of hook tape, however. It closes and opens easily for the benefit of the ill or handicapped; it is easily manipulated by children who can learn responsibility for dressing at an early age; it is a convenient closure for purse and wallets.

The tape strips are sewn to the apparel sections with regular machine stitches. If stitching is not desired on the garment face, then the attach-

9-19. Nylon hook-and-loop tape closure on men's slacks, underlap portion.

ment can be completed before the underside is folded or turned in place.

Visible Application. Visible applications are restricted to workclothes, playclothes, casual garments, lingerie, and children's apparel. Included in this category are grommets, buckles, hasps, and interlocking plastic or metal hooks for bra and bathing suit closures. The buckles on children's play and adults' work overalls often have buckle-type closures at the strap/bib location. They have a pushbutton type of release. Usually, the strap is inserted in the upper portion of the buckle in such a manner that the strap length can be adjusted. A sliding buckle is usually attached to bra and slip straps for length adjustment, although the buckle does not function as a closure.

D-rings, two metal rings in the shape of the letter "D," also serve as fasteners, although they are more common on belts or coat sleeve tabs than at other locations. Metal, plastic, or even thread eyelets can be used as closures when they provide the means for attachment to a buckle or when they are used for lacing, as in some peasant-styled dress bodices.

STANDARDS FOR EVALUATING SNAPPED AND HOOKED CLOSURES

1. Fasteners are the correct size for the closure requirement.
2. Fasteners are attached securely, whether mechanically or by hand.
3. Concealed applications of fasteners are inconspicuous.
4. Fasteners used in visible applications are suitable for the apparel design and fabric.
5. Durable coverings (thread or fabric) are used when appropriate.

ZIPPERED CLOSURES

Since the 1930s, zippers have been used extensively as closures in skirts, slacks, shorts, casual jackets, and dresses. Zippers are composed of opposing coils or teeth that are interlocked by means of a slide. The slide also disengages them in order to open the zipper. The inherent stiffness of any zippered closure makes it more appropriate to flat applications than to apparel types or areas that are bloused.

ZIPPER TYPES

Zippers themselves can be categorized according to variations in teeth, tape, or opening location. The selection of teeth relates more to fabric type and weight and desired durability. Tape variations are also important to fabric type, weight, and drape, but have less impact on durability. Variations in opening location are important only in terms of where the opening in the garment is.

Teeth Variations. Two types of zippers are typical, those with metal teeth and those with nylon coils. Both serve the same function, but coils may tend to separate more easily under flex stress. However, they can also be repaired rather simply by manipulating the slide up and down once. If a tooth tears lose from the tape in a metal zipper, repair is not possible unless the tear is very close to the zipper bottom. In that case, a new thread-formed stop can be created. Nylon coil zippers are more flexible and are lighter in weight than metal zippers. Metal is more common to heavy-duty applications; nylon coil is found in dressier, lighter weight apparel.

Tape Variations. The tape, or fabric strips to which the teeth or coils are attached, can be either woven or knitted. The former is more common and is also somewhat heavier. Woven tapes are very durable in order to hold the teeth in place during extensive use. They are, however, somewhat heavier and stiffer than the newer knitted tapes. The latter are heat set to avoid any shrinkage, which is often a problem with cotton woven tapes. They are knitted of thermoplastic yarns which can be completely stabilized after the zipper is formed. Nylon coil zippers more frequently have knitted tapes than do metal tooth zippers. The combination is very suitable for "dressy" dresses of polyester interlock, for example.

Opening Variations. The zipper unit can be constructed to open at one, both, or neither end. The single opening is the most common type and is found in slacks, skirts, shorts, and necklines. The opening in the garment is from a finished edge to some point in the garment's interior. The zipper provides a means of enlarging the smaller point of the garment (waistline or neckline, for example) so that it can be pulled over larger body parts (head, shoulders, hips, for example) without tearing or distorting the smaller garment area. Once the garment is on the body, the zipper is closed to effect a smooth fit over the large as well as the small areas of the body.

In jackets that are not designed to be pulled on over the head, a zipper must be open at both ends. This type of zipper is called the separating zipper. It separates completely at the lower end for ease in

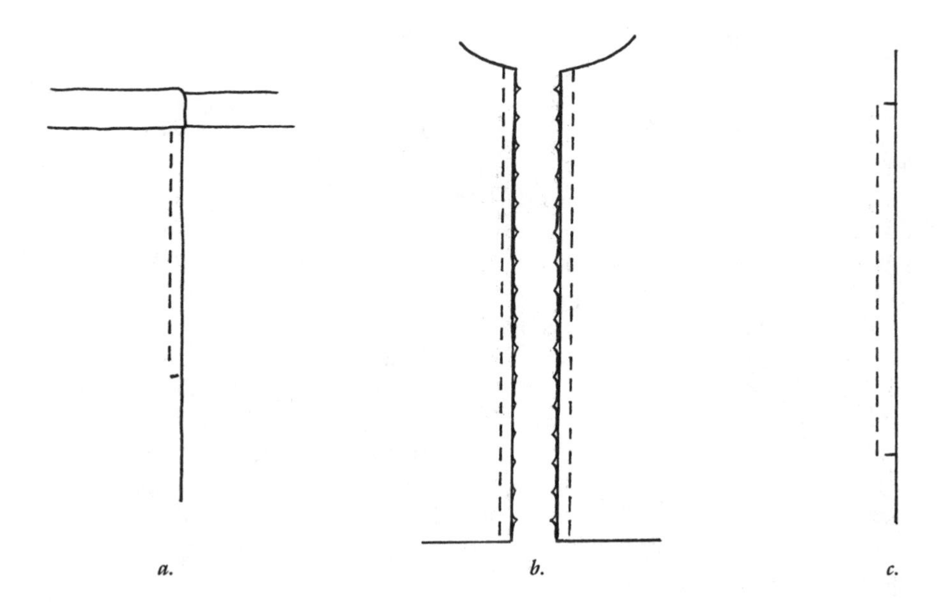

9-20. Zipper opening variations: (a) open at one end; (b) open at both ends; (c) closed at both ends.

removal of the garment. For closing, a tab at the lower end of the zipper is inserted into the slide, and then the slide can be pulled up. Separating zippers are also used to make detachable linings, especially for all-weather coats.

Zippers that are closed at both ends are used in internal garment plackets and in some home furnishing locations. In apparel, a zipper closed at both ends might be found at the side waistline of a fitted dress that has either a wide neckline or some additional type of closure to provide access to the neckline of the garment. The closed zipper would allow the waistline of the garment to spread open during entry, then be zippered closed to effect close fit. Pillow and cushion covers have the same type of zipper.

METHODS OF APPLICATION

In this section, the primary concern is the appearance of the completed zipper application, not the steps used for insertion. Zipper application in industrial settings usually involves stitching each side of the tape into the desired location, cutting it to the appropriate length, then attaching the zipper side. Home sewers do not have the advantage of working with the tape minus the slide, and thus have to manipulate the presser foot of the sewing machine around the rather thick slide. Unless the machine operator is very skilled, this usually results in an uneven stitching line as the presser foot approaches the slide location.

Centered Application. In centered application, the two folds of apparel fabric on each side of the opening are abutted, with the zipper teeth centered under the opening. Topstitching on either side of the opening is equidistant from the folds. This type of application is most often found on separating zippers and in locations where an asymmetrical stitching pattern would be inconsistent with the garment design, for example, in a box-pleated skirt. Figure 9-21 shows a centered zipper application in a designer garment. The application is by hand, using a nearly invisible stitch called a "pick stitch."

The disadvantage of centered application is that the zipper teeth cannot be concealed completely. Since the covering folds of fabric must be abutted, any flexing or movement will cause them to separate slightly and allow the zipper to be seen. If a perfect color match is possible, this may not be too distracting, but if the colors are different, or if the teeth are uncolored metal, then such an application can be visually distracting.

Lapped Application. Much more common than the centered application is the lapped. One advantage is that the zipper teeth can be completely concealed. One side laps over the other approximately one-eighth

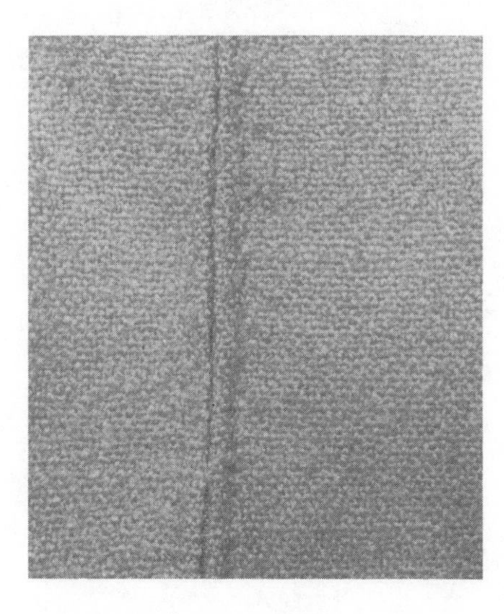

9-21. Centered, hand-picked zipper application.

inch (.32 cm). The stitching on the underlap is usually concealed, and the stitching on the overlap side is approximately three-eights inch (.95 cm) from the folded edge. More seam allowance width is utilized in the lapped application. If seams are not a full width, then a tape or fabric strip extension will be required to make a stable application.

A variation of the lapped application is the *fly front*. This is used only in the fronts of garments, usually slacks, skirts, and shorts. Originally, the fly front was reserved for men's slacks, but this is no longer the case. The topstitching line on the fly front is one to one and one-half inches (2.54 to 3.81 cm) from the folded edge and does not penetrate the zipper tape at all. The zipper tape is secured to a fly facing first, and the facing is topstitched to the garment.

Although an extended facing is the easiest to use and is common to women's and men's clothing, a separate facing is the standard, as is the lined underlay that often extends to a point at the waistline where it buttons to the waistband for a smooth fit. The fly front with facing and with lined underlay is the most complicated and expensive type of zippered closure. Numerous steps are involved in its application, and these steps result in increased costs.

Invisible Zipper. Special zippers and feet for their application are required to create a zipper that cannot be seen at all once it is applied. These are called "invisible" zippers because of the thoroughness with which the teeth are concealed. The stitching that attaches the tape to

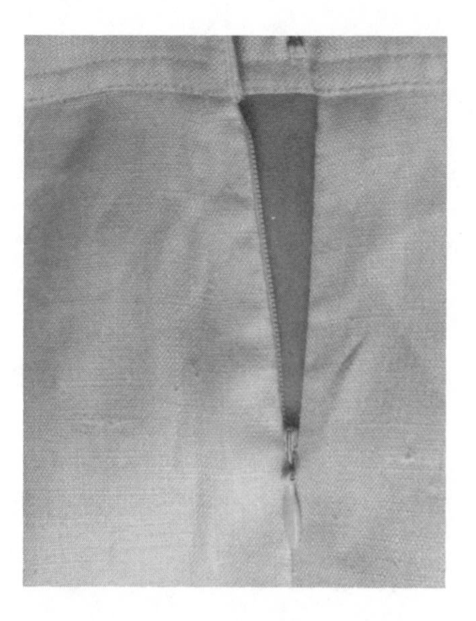

9-22. "Invisible" zipper application.

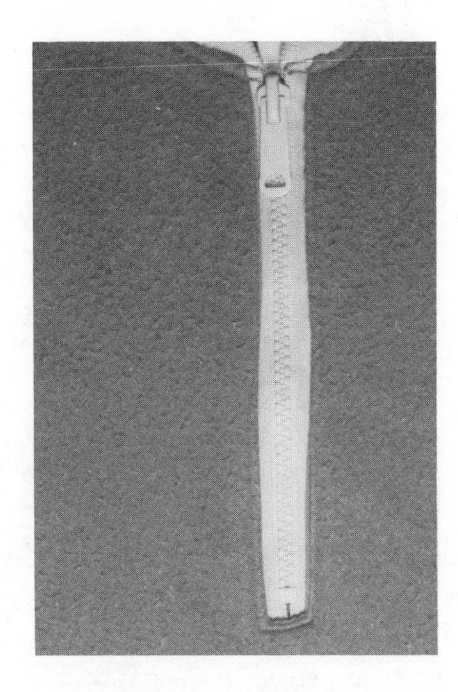

9-23. Exposed zipper application, which has not been successfully applied.

the garment is made almost at the teeth, and it is made while the face of the garment fabric is laid to the face of the zipper tape. The zipper foot is grooved to fit the zipper teeth and guide the two fabric layers together under the needle. Once stitching is completed, the garment seam below the zipper is closed.

This type of application is used when topstitching would detract from the design of the garment. It is more common to dress and to knitted shells worn under suits than to apparel bottoms. The application is very stiff and is not suitable for bloused or draped garment areas.

Exposed Application. If the zipper is to be part of the design of the garment, or if the teeth match in color so as not to detract from the garment design, then an exposed application can be used. In the latter instance, many sweaters and knitted shells or dresses have no natural opening for a zipper at the back neckline. An opening for the zipper has to be created by stitching around the opening location, then slashing it to open or facing a narrow slash at the desired location. In either case, there is no apparel fabric available for either abutting or lapping at the zipper location. The teeth, therefore, must be exposed in the application. Figure 9-23 shows an exposed zipper which has not been successfully applied. The opening itself is crooked, and the zipper buckles slightly in the opening because the garment fabric shrunk during laundering and the zipper did not.

Decorative striped or printed zipper tapes may be used for exposed applications in which the zipper tape is placed on top of the garment for stitching in place. If the zipper tape is not particularly decorative, the exposed application can still be utilized for decorative effect if the teeth of the zipper and perhaps its slide and/or pull tape are decorative. A heavy, metal look results when unpainted metal zippers with large ring pulls are inserted in exposed applications. This styling detail may be used at normal closure locations and as a means of closing slashed or applied pockets.

STANDARDS FOR EVALUATING ZIPPERED CLOSURES

1. The zipper teeth and tape materials are suitable for the apparel design and fabric.
2. The zipper length is adequate for ease in wearing or using the item.
3. The method of attachment is appropriate to the garment design.
4. Any visible stitching is neatly done.
5. The zipper is securely inserted into the garment.
6. Zipper teeth are concealed adequately by lapped application.
7. Lapped applications are evenly formed.

SUMMARY

From the time that apparel evolved from draped squares and rectangles of fabric into complicated seamed and fitted shapes, closures have been important as a means of securing the garment on the body. Today, the variety of closure types is quite large, and many types are quite decorative. In general, buttoned, snapped or hooked, and zippered closures constitute an expensive component of apparel construction. The findings themselves may be quite expensive, but the application also requires substantial investment in machinery and/or labor.

10

HEM TREATMENTS

Historically, the position of the hemline has been one of the most important elements of the fashion silhouette of any period. The importance of the hemline is not limited, however, to its position on the body or to the fact that it finishes the lower raw edge of the garment. Hem depth, weight, and method of application can have important effects on the success or failure of a design, whether the garment is made by a couturier, by an apparel manufacturer, or by an individual at home. A hem that is too deep, improperly finished, puckered, heavy, or uneven can spoil an otherwise effective design. Of importance here, as with other construction elements, is that even when the selection of the hem type, finish, and method of attachment is correct, the selection must still be executed well for complete garment success. This is true whether the hem occurs at the bottom edges of skirts, slacks, shorts, blouses, shirts, jackets, coats, and dresses or at the outer edges of ascots, scarves, and handkerchiefs.

HEM TYPES

Although quite a variety of terms describing hems and hem types exist, these terms can be categorized according to the number of fabric plies present in the complete hem. Further subdivisions based on hem depth provide a more complete structural categorization of some of these popular hemming terms.

SINGLE-PLY HEMS

Single-ply hems are generally economical in terms of fabric utilization. The garment simply is cut at the desired hemline, with a potential savings of several square inches of fabric per garment. However, the savings may not result in a low-priced item if the fabric utilized for a single-ply hemmed garment is relatively expensive or if thread finishing is slow and/or extensive. The single-ply hem may be, but is not necessarily, indicative of a budget item.

UNFINISHED HEM EDGES

Only special nonraveling fabrics such as leather, suede, imitation suede or leather, felt or heavily fulled fabrics, and lace are commonly treated in this manner. Lace is so decorative that typically it is used with its scalloped lower edge, fabricated as an integral part of the lace, serving as the hem. No additional treatment is required or even desirable. Although leather and suede garments usually have deep folded and glued hems, they may also be left as cut. This is more frequently found in less expensive garments. Scallops, points, or other designs may be incorporated in cutting the hem edge, especially if fabric perforations are also used to form a design close to the hem edge. Cutting the lower edge of a suede garment to form a fringe is another example of using just the cut edge in lieu of a more traditional hem.

Trims such as ruffles and flounces on bathing suits and active sports clothing are also sometimes left with a simple cut edge at the lower edge. Three- or four-bar filament tricot with surface heat finishes such as glazing are the fabrics which are typically treated this way in lower price apparel. Although they do present a smooth finish initially, the loose fiber ends will abrade during wear and become unsightly.

THREAD-FINISHED HEM EDGES

If the garment fabric is not stable enough for the cut edge to be treated as a hem, or if particular decorative effects are desired, then thread and

10-1. Machine blanket stitch used to finish and trim hem edge.

stitching can be used to treat the single-ply cut edge. For many knit garments, particularly casual items, sleepwear, or shirts meant to be tucked in, serging over the raw edge is sufficient to produce an acceptable hem. Serging gives a flat finish which stretches and contracts with the garment. In addition, it is very quick and inexpensive to apply. On items such as children's undershirts, it is actually the most effective hem available. This is another example of an instance in which low cost does not imply low quality.

Most decorative effects are produced by embroidery, and many apparel items for women and children are appropriately treated in this manner. A scalloped stitch is favored, but other designs are possible. In some knitwear, an edge-covering stitch resembling a handmade buttonhole or a blanket stitch executed in a large thread is used to cover the cut edge at the bottom of the garment. Such a treatment is shown in Figure 10-1. Any such decorative stitch or embroidery used to complete the hem should be found at other locations on the garment—at sleeve and neckline edges, for example—for design consistency. Figure 10-2 shows such a hem finish used at the collar of a child's dress.

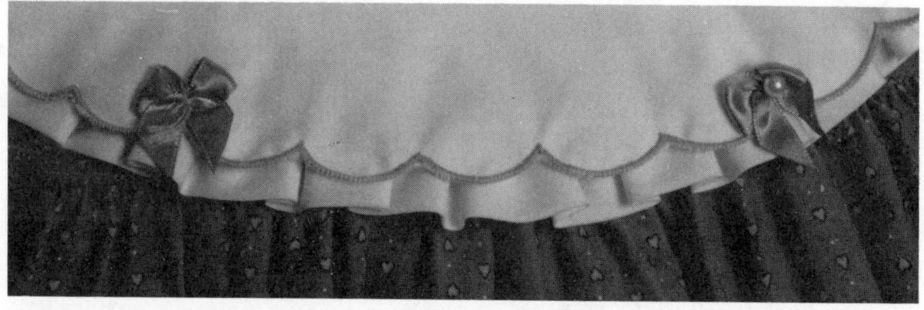

10-2. Thread-covered scallops at lower edge of collar.

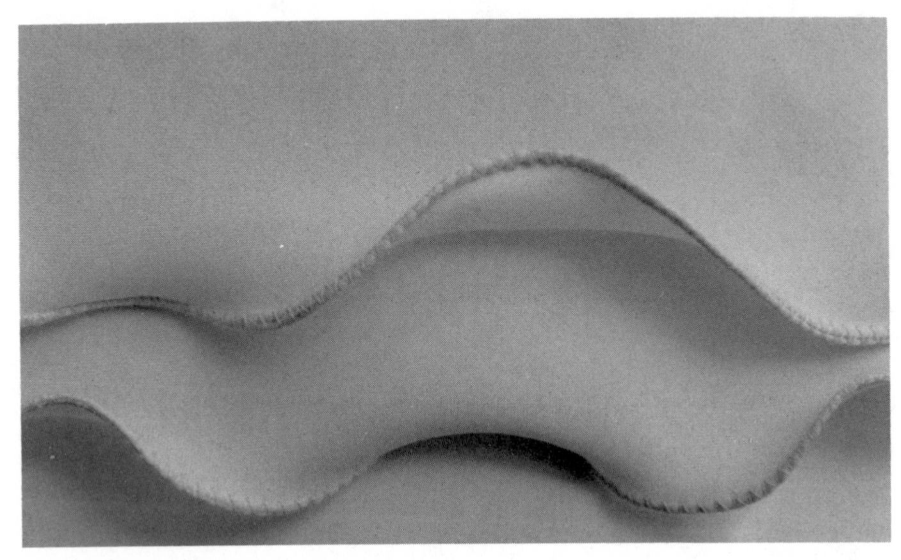

10-3. Lettuce-edge hem.

If the garment fabric already has a thread finish at the hem location, Schiffli-embroidered fabrics with a border design, such as, then no additional treatment is required. The fabric finish serves decoratively as the hem finish. Such fabrics are limited in their application to styles that have straight-cut panels. Flared or A-line styles would result in a hem edge not parallel to the floor.

Another variation of the thread-finished hem is the *lettuce edge* (Figure 10-3). This treatment produces a ruffled effect in fabrics having high stretch—interlock knits, accordion-pleated fabrics, and very crinkled gauze, for example. The ruffled effect is formed when the fabric's cut or folded edge is stretched as far as possible, then held in the stretched position by closely spaced zigzag stitching. The treated edge is then considerably larger in circumference than the remainder of the garment and hangs in small ripples. Ruffles for dress, blouse and lingerie trim are now frequently treated in this manner. The lettuce edge is used on dressy apparel for women and children.

Alteration potential is limited in all thread-finished hems. The only way to preserve the thread finish is to reconstruct the garment, at least partially, so that excess length is removed at horizontal seams rather than at the hem edge. Lengthening is not possible at the hem edge since no fabric is available for letting out.

FOLDED HEMS

The folded hem is the most common hem type in the apparel industry and in home sewing. It is formed by folding and then securing the finished raw edge of the fabric to the wrong side of the garment at the desired length. It is an excellent choice for soft silhouettes and straight cuts with little flare. Hem length can be shortened easily on all folded hems and lengthened on deep folded hems unless the garment has been given a permanent set after construction and pressing. The hem depth and the finish selected affect the cost of using folded hems, with deep hems and elaborate finishes resulting in increased garment cost.

NARROW FOLDED HEMS

If the completed hem is five-eighths inch (1.59 cm) or less in depth, it can be classified as a narrow hem. Such hems are suitable for very flared garments, garments that are to be worn tucked in, trimmings, and accessories such as scarves and handkerchiefs. Narrow hems may be slightly curved or straight, hand or machine stitched, and secured by one or more rows of stitching.

One very familiar type of narrow folded hem is the *shirt-tail hem.* It is machine stitched with a single row of stitching. It can be found on all price lines of blouses and shirts for men, women, and children. It is sometimes used on dress or skirt hems when a sporty look is desired and on flared designs when a wide hem is not possible. Its narrow width minimizes fabric cost while still providing a flat, durable hem and even the possibility of some decorative effect if contrasting thread color is used to secure the hem.

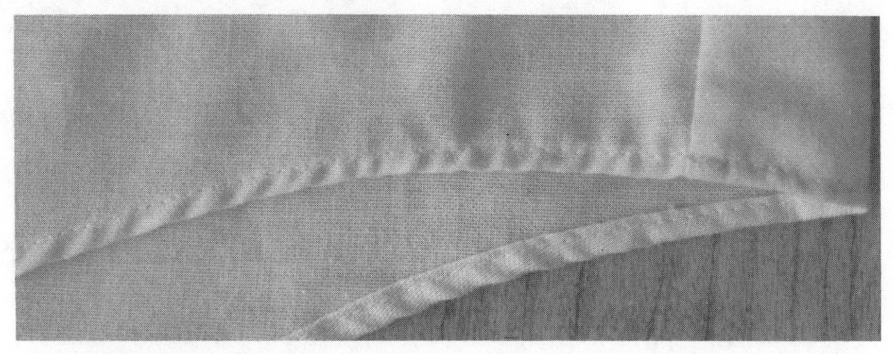

10-4. Narrow folded shirt-tail hem.

Traditionally, the shirt-tail hem is only about one-fourth inch (.64 cm) deep and is seamed by a single row of stitching. On dresses, shirts, or even jackets where the hem will be visible on the outside, a variation is to make the hem about three-eighths to one-half inch (.95 to 1.27 cm) deep and to secure it with two rows of stitching. This has a more finished appearance than the usual shirt-tail hem. Deeper hems can be secured with visible stitching, but anything over three-fourths inch (1.90 cm) in depth is considered a deep folded hem.

The popularity of narrow folded hems in dresses, skirts, ruffles, and tops for children and adults alike has increased in recent years. A serious potential problem with such hems is the tendency of the fabric to roll. In single knits especially, narrow hems may appear flat in the finished, pressed garment as it is shipped, but the first laundering releases the finishing tensions, and the hem rolls to the right side of the garment. The same problem may occur in woven fabrics but usually not to as great an extent. The potential for this type of problem can be estimated by pulling on the hem edge of the garment slightly with hands placed several inches apart. If the hem edge rolls to either side of the garment, then it will probably do so during wear and after laundering. Figure 10-5 shows a single knit (jersey) fabric of all cotton. The garment has been worn and laundered twice. The hem rolls upward several turns and the fabric at the vent portion of the hem rolls inward. Figure 10-6 shows a similar problem in the tiered skirt of a child's dress made of acid-washed denim. The hem edge has rolled upward after only one laundering

11-5. Vent and hem in jersey roll in both vertical and horizontal directions following laundering.

a.

b.

10-6. Narrow hem in denim illustrates rolling: (a) right side of garment following laundering; (b) right side with hem held downward in normal position.

Slightly different from the shirt-tail hem is the *rolled hem*. Traditionally, it was made by hand, but today machinery can closely duplicate the effect of hand-stitching. The rolled hem when finished is scarcely more that one-eighth inch (.32 cm) deep and consists of several plies of fabric that are rolled rather than folded. Whether hand or machine stitched, the stitches are hidden under the rolled edges. The rolled hem is found in scarves and ascots, in more expensive handkerchiefs, and in some designer garments made of sheer fabric in full cuts. If hand stitched, its presence on a garment can add significantly to cost.

The *shell hem* is another type of narrow folded hem. It is frequently found on lingerie and on infants' and children's clothes made of tricot or other soft knits. A special machine stitch, nearly identical to a blind hemming stitch, is responsible for the shell effect. The machine sews several straight stitches, then swings over the folded fabric edge for one stitch. The tension of that swing stitch pulls the folded fabric edge in slightly. When this is repeated along the entire fold, soft scallops results.

DEEP FOLDED HEMS

A hem of more than three-fourths inch (1.90 cm) is considered a deep folded hem and is one of the most common hem types found in apparel. The deeper it is, the more fabric is required for the garment. Although

10-7. Narrow rolled hem, machine blind-stitched.

10-8. Narrow folded shell hem, hand stitched.

the three-inch (7.62 cm) hem is fairly standard for skirts and dresses made at home, in ready-to-wear any hem over two inches (5.08 cm) is the exception. Very deep hems is anything but sheer fabrics signal an unskilled alteration attempt. For a garment that is cut with little taper or flare, the folded hem is on a relatively straight edge.

Straight hems entail less manipulation and can be made deeper than shaped hems. In a typical straight folded hem, the hem edge is finished, then the hem is folded in place and secured to the wrong side of the garment. Finishing the hem edge and securing it to the garment can be accomplished in one step by some industrial machines. Some manipulative skill in hemming is required to avoid pulling the hem out of alignment with the rest of the garment. On straight cuts, the grainline of the hem should match exactly the grainline of the garment section against which it lies. In garments with slight shaping, more care is required to maintain alignment and avoid a hem that ripples when completed.

More complicated methods are required for handling *shaped hems.* These result when a deep folded hem occurs in garments such as flared skirts or tapered sleeves or slacks. The flare or taper produces either an excessive amount of fullness or insufficient fullness at its raw edge when the hem is folded back in place against the garment. Circular and very flared skirts should have hems no wider than one inch (2.54 cm) if they are to be folded. In designs with less severe size differential between hem edge and hemming line, easing can be used to adjust the excess fullness at the hem edge so that it will fit against the garment. Pleating out the fullness at the hem finish is not a professional or desirable solution to handling excess fullness Pressing these pleats results in impressions that are visible on the right side of the garment. A narrower hem

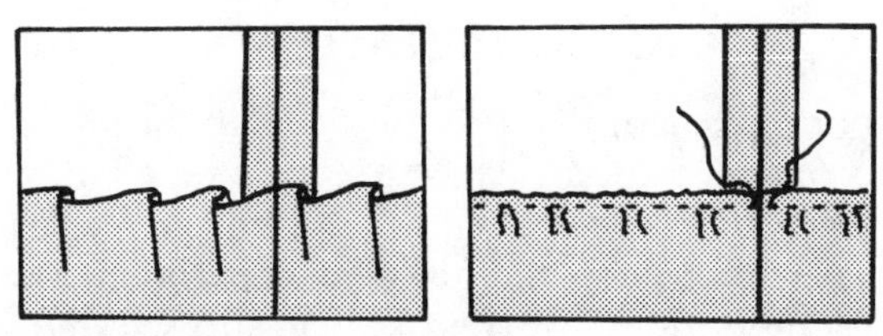

10-9. Deep folded hem with eased upper edge.

depth is a better solution if the garment is in a price line that does not allow for the time required to ease the hem edge properly. A wide eased hem, as shown in Figure 10-9, on a garment with slight flare is found in upper middle to high-price lines.

Special flanges that are cut outward are necessary to provide a smooth fit when folded hems are to be used on sleeve or slack legs that are tapered toward the bottom. The flange, shown in Figure 10-10, provides the extra width necessary for the hem to fit smoothly when it is folded into position. Without the flange, the seam would have to be left open, up to the point where the hem folds, in order for the hem to fit the garment without causing a pucker at the hem line. Hems on better quality garments will have an adequate flange at hem edges. Narrow hems or bias facings or bindings are more typical of the way tapered garments are hemmed in lower price lines.

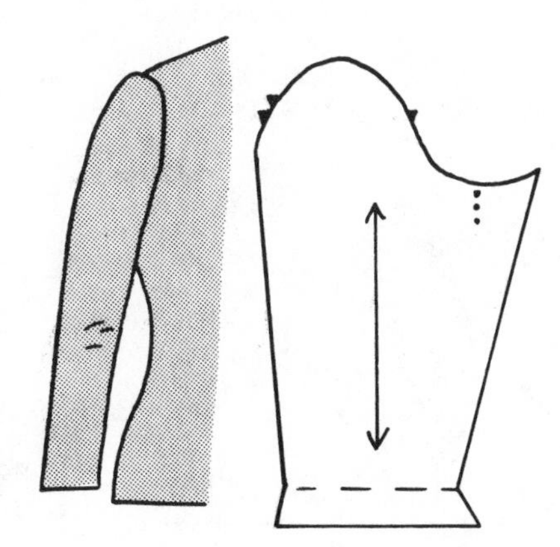

10-10. Deep folded hem with flanges to accommodate sleeve taper.

ENCLOSED HEMS

In this category are hems that require the application of some additional fabric to produce an enclosure for the free edge of the garment. A minimum of four fabric plies will be present at the seamed edge, so the weight and bulk of both the garment and the enclosure fabric are important considerations. The type of enclosure selected is also important in controlling bulk, since some type of enclosures introduce more layers of fabric into the completed construction.

FACED HEMS

Faced hems are often used when hemlines have an unusual shape (scallop, for example), when the fabric is too thick for a folded hem, when the garment is extremely flared or tapered, or when the facing itself adds some function to the garment, as in the case of elastic facings. Hem facings can be very narrow and cut on the bias, or they can be cut like the area to be faced (shaped facing). The shaped facing is handled in the same manner as shaped neckline facings (see Chapter 6, pages 122–155). The facing is stitched to the garment at the lower edge, then the seam is trimmed and clipped as necessary before the facing is turned back to the wrong side of the garment and pressed. The upper edge, finished as necessary, is then attached to the garment.

The extra pieces required for the shaped hem facing and the extra steps involved in the construction process make this hem more costly to apparel producers than many other types of hems. Production costs are even higher if trims such as lace, ruffles, piping or cord are added at the facing seam. Also, faced hems may tend to stiffen the silhouette, a factor than can limit its application. Length adjustments of faced hems are much more difficult to make than with folded hems. The narrow

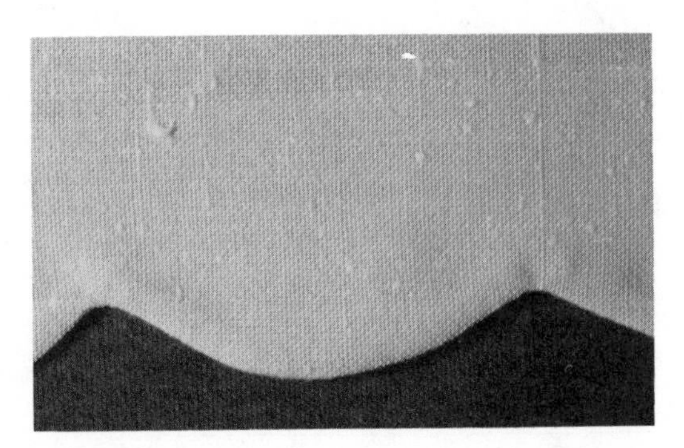

10-11. Faced scalloped hem.

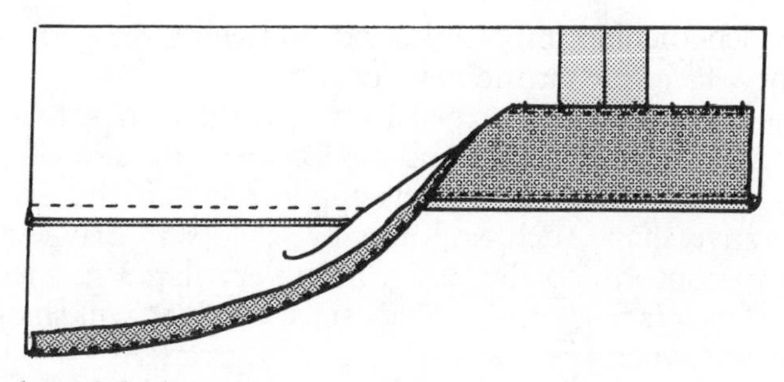

10-12. Faced straight hem.

10-13. Elastic faced hem on biking pants (wrong side of garment in upper right).

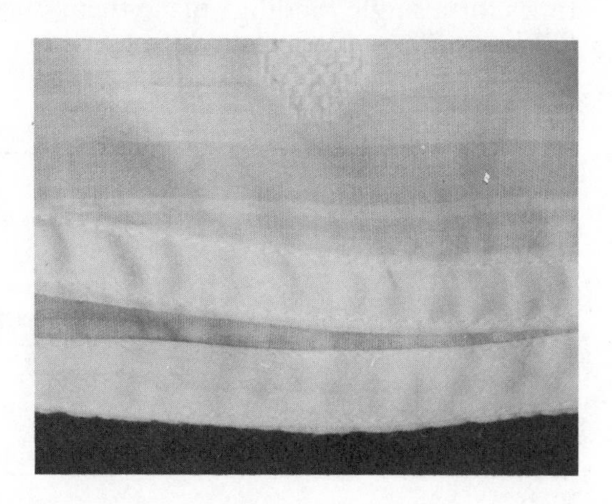

10-14. Narrow bias faced hem (wrong side of garment illustrated in lower portion of photograph).

seam makes lengthening impossible, and shortening the garment requires cutting a new facing to fit the new location.

Bias facings are much less expensive to use than shaped facings, especially in terms of fabric costs and replacement in case of alterations. They are also more limited in their applicability. If the garment edge has a decorative shape such as points or scallops, a bias facing cannot be shaped to conform to the design. On very flared garments, only a very narrow bias facing can be used, since the bias will shape to some extent, but not when the size differential is great. As with the shaped facing, the bias facing does not allow the hem to be lengthened, only shortened, and shortening requires the application of a new bias facing.

BOUND HEMS

Bound hems are often used on reversible garments where they serve the dual purpose of encasing the raw edge and accenting the hem edge. Bound hems use bindings to encase the cut edge of the garment. The bindings are made from woven, braided, or knitted strips of fabric cut in various widths. Many are specially made so that both sides have a natural finish. If the binding fabric has no such natural finish, then at least one of the edges must be turned under for application. Once applied, the binding is visible on both the right and wrong sides of the garment. Braided, knitted, and bias-cut woven bindings give the best results on curved edges. Crosswise cuts of single or double knits can be employed successfully, but they do not hug curves as smoothly.

Bindings may be cut double or single to perform particular jobs on varying weights of fabric. The extra thickness formed by using a double binding (six times the desired binding finished width compared to four times for a single binding) make them excellent choices for lightweight fabrics, such as batiste or chiffon, where bulk is not a problem. The

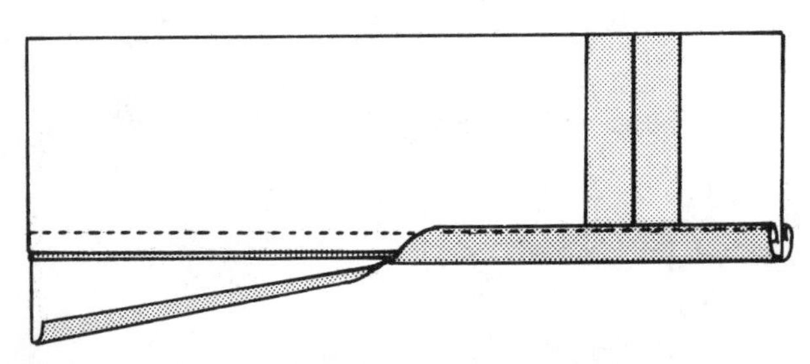

10-15. Bound hem.

double binding adds body which prevents the bias cut from rippling, as bindings sometimes do, yet provides an edge that is easier to secure by hand or machine in home sewing. In the apparel industry, bindings are usually applied with specialized machinery which can topstitch the bindings close to its edge on both sides in one operation. In home sewing, accurate application often requires two steps. Double bindings add slightly to the cost of the garment—a factor that prompts most apparel producers to use single bindings.

Two construction problems are unique to the bound hem edge. First, the binding can pull away from the edge because of inaccurate placement of the fashion fabric at the fold of the binding, either before or during the construction. Second, machine stitches may not have caught the binding to the fashion fabric at all points or on both sides when it was applied. Problems of this type can often be detected by careful examination of all parts of the bound hem.

BANDED HEMS

A banded hem encases the raw edge of the hem while extending some distance below the application seam, resulting in added length to the garment. The band can be of self-fabric or of a contrasting color and/or texture for additional emphasis. Figure 10-16 illustrates the structure of a bound hem edge.

To be classified as a banded hem, the band portion must be two ply with either a seam or a fold at the lower edge. A single-ply fabric that is attached to the lower edge of a garment still has to be hemmed and, therefore, is just a garment extension, not a hem type. The band can be

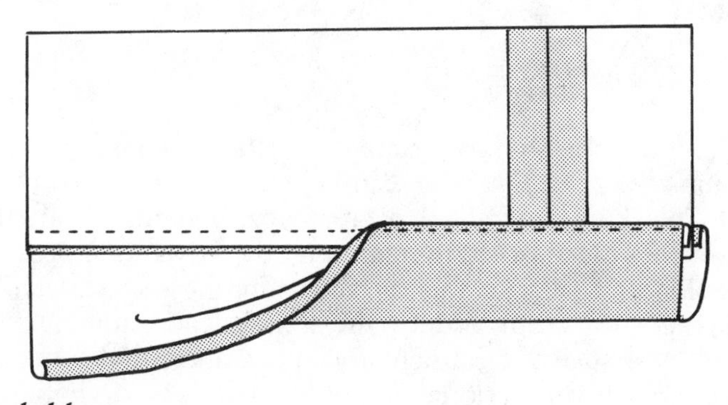

10-16. Banded hem.

cut on the bias or crosswise grain of the banding fabric, or the banding can be cut with the same grainlines as the garment itself.

If the garment has any shaping at all, even a slight flare, a shaped band is more effective. Even narrow bands that are cut without shaping mar the design line of the flared garment. Shaped bands often require more fabric and are more exacting to apply, resulting in increased garment costs. As with bound hems, alterations can be difficult or impossible depending on the fitting problem.

HEM FINISHES

A hem finish is the treatment used to control raveling, rolling, or stretching of the cut edge of the hem. Hem finishes can be applied before, after, and sometimes during the actual hemming process. Finishing can be as simple and inexpensive as leaving the edge raw, exactly as it was cut, or as complicated and expensive as applying trim or special hand details. The type of finish selected should be appropriate for the fabric, the hem location, and the garment design. In home sewing, personal preference is also an important factor.

SINGLE-PLY FINISHES

If the fabric is amenable to these types of treatments, single-ply finishes can be among the simplest and most economical to produce. The garment fabric dictates whether the edge can be left as cut or requires some sort of stitching for completion. Obviously, a single-ply finish does not introduce any bulk at the hemming line, and this is another advantage.

RAW EDGE TREATMENT

If the garment fabric is very stable—resistant to raveling, stretching, and rolling—then the raw edge can be left as is, with no further treatment. Double knits, many warp knits, real and imitation suedes and leathers, real and fake furs, and many tightly woven, napped, or heavily fulled wool fabrics fall into this category. Cutting the edge with pinking or scalloping shears can add to the finished appearance. Many producers will add such a treatment for appearance alone, but such cuts are not particularly functional. In unlined jackets or light coats, the decorative cuts to the raw edges are more common, since the hem finish is frequently exposed during wear.

THREAD TREATMENTS

If the garment fabric ravels, stretches, or rolls too much to be left as cut, thread treatments can provide some of the quickest and most effective finishes to the hem edges. Depending on fabric requirements, the hem edge may be straight stitched to prevent stretching, stitched and pinked to prevent stretching and to reduce raveling, or serged (zigzagged in home production) to provide some give and to eliminate raveling. The edges can also be hand overcast to provide the same benefits as serging, but at such high labor costs that the finish is simply not used in ready-to-wear.

Some variation of the thread treatment is used almost entirely on budget to moderately priced apparel lines and, more often than ever before, on higher priced lines because of its durability and its flat, smooth appearance. In some instances, the edge receives its finish at the same time the hem is secured. Combining the two processes saves the producers money in construction costs, but such an application is a real disadvantage when the hem must be altered. In such cases, the thread finish must be reapplied before the new hem is inserted. Thread treatments can be used successfully on most fabrics, but they may be objectionable on sheers where the finish could show through to the right side of the garment.

FOLDED HEM FINISHES

In medium- to lightweight fabrics, the raw edge of the hem can be turned under one-fourth inch (.64 cm) and stitched. This technique, known as a clean finish, is much more common to garments made at home than to ready-to-wear, but it can be found in the latter as well. The fold at the edge is an effective place to hide hand hemming stitches, but beyond that advantage, it offers no other over serging as an effective finish, and it has the possibility of adding considerable bulk at the hemline.

APPLIED FABRIC FINISHES

Applying a separate ply (or plies) of fabric to the hem edge is the most expensive of the three types of hem finishes. There is, of course, the cost of the applied fabric—lace, narrow woven tape, bias bindings, for example—but equally important are application costs. Because of the expense involved in applied fabric finishes, they are used primarily when the fabric cannot be finished acceptably by other methods, in home sewing, and in more expensive garments.

Fabric, such as twill tape, hem tape, hem lace, and bias tape, are lapped over the raw edge with approximately one-fourth inch (.64 cm) extending above the cut edge of the hem and stitched in place with a lapped seam. Single-ply finishes are ideal for thick, spongy fabrics which are too loosely woven to hold a thread finish. Bias bindings can add considerable bulk to the hem edge, but a Hong Kong finish (see page 81) is a very attractive and durable hem finish which is usually made of a very thin or soft lining fabric so that the three plies introduced at the hemline do not create a problem. The Hong Kong finish is especially useful for partially lined garments in which strips of the lining fabric are used for this finish.

Less attractive than the regular bound or Hong Kong finished hems are those finished with such specialty fabrics as nylon net or tulle, sheer tricot, and fiber webs. Folded strips of these fabrics are slipped over the hem edge and stitched in place. As the fabrics do not ravel, no raw edges have to be turned under. These fabrics can be used to create very functional hem finishes as long as they are compatible with the hand and drape of the garment itself.

ATTACHMENT METHODS

Once the hem type has been selected and the finish applied, the hem must then be attached to the garment. As with type and finish, the garment fabric, design, and desired durability dictate the most acceptable method for hemming the garment. The attachment of the hem to

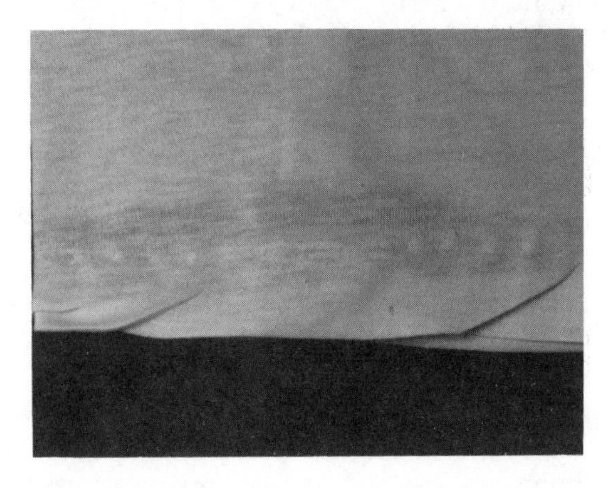

10-17. Hem and garment not aligned properly, resulting in puckering.

10-18. Hem stitches too large, visible on right side of garment.

the garment should be either decorative and compatible with other decorative details on the garment, or it should be completely inconspicuous.

Many of the problems that occur with hems in both ready-to-wear and in home sewing relate to appearance rather than to durability. Appearance problems are frequently introduced at the attachment stage and include such errors as pulling the hem out of alignment from the garment during the attachment process; taking too large a bite from the garment fabric during hemming so that supposedly "blind" stitches show through as floats on the right side; and pulling the stitches too tightly so that the hem tends to gather and pucker at the hemline. Regardless of the attachment method selected, machine or hand, these problems can occur and detract from the quality of the finished hem.

MACHINE-STITCHED HEMS

As a result of the extensive labor costs involved in applying any construction techniques by hand, hems are most commonly attached by machine. A variety of automated equipment exists to simplify the hemming tasks in industrial settings. Special devices can apply the double-turned hem characteristically found on jeans in a matter of seconds. Other machines are available for other equally specialized hemming operations. They are usually programmed to handle specific fabrics, hem types and sizes, finishes, and locations.

10-19. Deep topstitched hem.

TOPSTITCHED HEMS

Machine topstitching is a very common hemming method used in the apparel industry. Single or multiple rows of straight or decorative stitches can be applied in matching or contrasting thread on a narrow or deep hem. Such hems are more difficult to remove for alteration than the chain stitches frequently used for blind-stitched hems, and embroidery stitches worked closely may be impossible to remove. They do, however, add a decorative effect to a very functional element in a garment.

Machine topstitched hems should occur in conjunction with the same type of stitching used elsewhere on the garment. On a tailored suit of wool tweed with no topstitching anywhere on the garment, for example, a topstitched hem would look very incongruous. On the other hand, a knit shirt with corded, double-needle topstitched hems on the sleeves and at the garment bottom looks appropriately finished. Such a treatment is shown in Figure 10-19.

BLIND-STITCHED HEMS

One of the most common types of machine-made hems used in the apparel industry is the blind-stitched hem. Specialized machines allow the hem to be applied blind with great speed and accuracy. Even alteration departments use machine-made hems rather than hand hems when the garment length has to be altered. Chain-stitching hemming machines are used extensively in the apparel industry. This hem stitch can be

10-20. Blind-stitched hem.

readily removed if mistakes are made in hem application or if alteration has to be done for the consumer.

A blind hem can be applied using most newer home sewing machines, but these stitches, although durable, are frequently more obvious than those made on industrial machines or those made by hand. They are also quite difficult to remove. Their use is more appropriate in situations where durability is very important and where the hem will not need to be adjusted in the future, in workclothes and children's playclothes, for example.

HAND-STITCHED HEMS

Hand-stitched hems are reserved for special items in couture fashions and for apparel made or altered at home. The stitch and the thread used should be appropriate for the fabric, for the hem finish, and for the location of the hem. A stretch fabric requires a stitch that will give readily without breaking; sheers require a stitch and finish combination that will allow the thread floats to be hidden between stitches; and heavy fabrics may benefit from a double-stitched hem to support the weight of a fairly deep hem. A great variety of hand stitches can be used, depending on personal preference, fabric, and hem finish.

Hand stitches should be barely visible on the right side of the garment, with each stitch catching only one or two yarns of the garment fabric. They should be left somewhat slack to avoid puckering and should be spaced approximately one-half inch (1.27 cm) apart. Hand stitches are much more expensive to apply than machine hems because of labor costs, and they can be less conspicuous on the right side of the garment. However, the durability of hand-stitched hems is usually less than that of machine hems, so no great advantage is gained unless the fabric is so tightly woven and smooth that a machine blind stitch cannot be applied without showing.

NON-STITCHED HEMS

The final method available for attaching hems involves not using any stitching at all. Either a thermal or a traditional physical adhesive is used to secure the hem in place. The choice of adhesive is determined by the garment fabric. Non-stitched hems have long been favored for disposable apparel items and low-budget productions. Continued research and improvement of adhesives and application systems has led to greater acceptance of these nontraditional methods for a greater range of apparel items.

GLUED HEMS

Glued hems are found most frequently in fabrics made of leather, suede, fur, and imitations of these products. If topstitching is not desirable on such garments because of overall design, then the glued hem is the only alternative, aside from leaving the garment with the cut edge as the hem edge. The deep folded hem cannot be secured with blind stitching because of the nature of the animal skin. There are no yarns to pick up during the stitching as there is with typical fabric, and the action of the blind stitching might actually sever small pieces of the skin, resulting in a hole or in a series of holes at the hemline. If a durable adhesive is

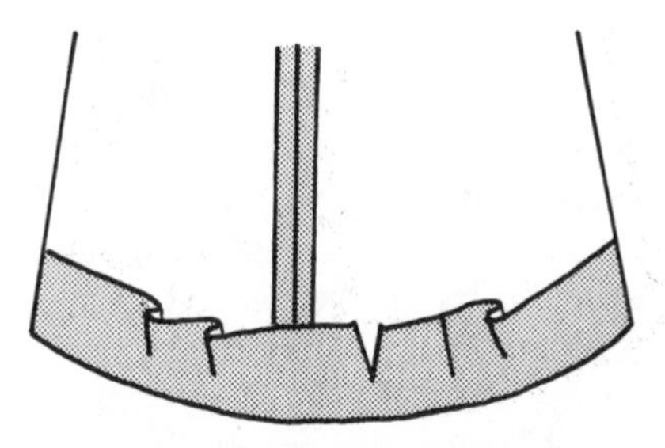

10-21. Wedged hem in leather or leather-like fabric.

selected, then the glued hem is a desirable solution. It is inconspicuous and durable, but alteration is difficult.

Glued hems present special problems when the hem is in a flared garment. Easing, used on more traditional fabrics to control hem fullness, is not possible on leather and leather-like fabrics. Wedging, the removal of sections of fabric where fullness occurs, is a very effective method of fullness removal at hems in nonraveling fabrics. The technique is shown in Figure 10-21. Wedged hems will lie flat against the garment from the upper edge to the fold without bulk; gluing holds the wedged edges together. In wedging, small pieces of the hem are removed from the cut edge to a point short of the hem fold. The exact depth, size, and spacing of the wedges cut are determined by folding the hem back in place and wedging out just enough to achieve a flat, smooth appearance.

FUSED HEMS

Fusing utilizes a very heat-sensitive fiber web which is cut in strips, placed between the hem and the garment, then pressed until the web melts and secures the two plies together. Hems of this type are inconspicuous and are options for fabrics that show conventional hem stitches badly. They may be used either with or without some supporting machine stitches. Their holding power depends on durable fusing materials, secure application, and a relatively flat fabric surface. They can reduce or eliminate rolling in single-knit garments where even the hemmed edge is frequently flipped upward during wear by the inherent pull of the knit fabric.

Fused hems are used by the home sewer occasionally to provide a fast, inconspicuous hem when time is at a premium and durability is not a high priority. Party clothes, costumes, stage clothing, and disposable garments are examples of good applications of the fused hem. Alterations are possible, but difficult, and the change in hand at the fused location may be objectionable in many fabrics and styles. When fusing is an appropriate attachment method, the fused hem should be smooth, without air pockets, pleats, or puckers, and without the fusing material bleeding through to the right side on thinner materials.

SPECIAL HEM TREATMENTS

There are several types of fabric and/or constructions that require additional treatment beyond finishing and attaching to create an attractive, durable hem. Thick or stiff fabrics may require special treatments for reducing bulk at seams or pleats; soft fabrics may require support or weighting to produce the desired effect; linings and garment openings also present special handling requirements. These treatments are in addition to the techniques covered in the preceding sections of this chapter.

REDUCING BULK

When the garment fabric is thick or spongy or hard to manipulate or when several layers intersect at the hemline, trimming and pressing open the vertical seams that are enclosed by the hem is a simple procedure for reducing bulk. It is found on better quality garments with standard seam allowances. For garments with seams trimmed to three-eighths inch (.95 cm) or less and finished with both allowances together, this procedure is not possible.

Long pile fabrics, such as fake furs, need to have the pile removed at the hem edge at least. Removing the pile from the seam allowances enclosed within the finished hem is also advisable. This can be done by clipping or shaving, and it allows the hem to lie much flatter in the garment. Finally, the entire folded portion of the hem itself can be clipped in the same way if the pile is very long.

STABILIZING PLEATS

Another special hem treatment is required when pleats are present at hems. The results of poor handling can produce a hem where the underfold of the pleat pushes to the outside rather than staying out of sight. There are, of course, some styles of pleats that have shallow folds and are intended to give the effect of a sunburst, but most pleats have deep folds to help ensure that they maintain their proper position when the wearer is motionless, and remain open during movement. Pressing plays an important part in maintaining pleats at hems when no seams are present, but when seams extend into the hem at a pleat location, special handling is required to stabilize the pleat at the hem.

One of the most effective means of stabilizing pleats at seam/hem locations is to hem the garment before the seams are sewn. (See Figure 10-22.) The resulting seam is then trimmed and serged, or regular seam allowances will be mitered at the hem edge to prevent the seam allowances from being visible on the right side of the garment. This method is durable for the life of the garment and is very effective in holding the pleats in position. The disadvantages are that there is no margin for error in determining garment length and evenness, and any alteration

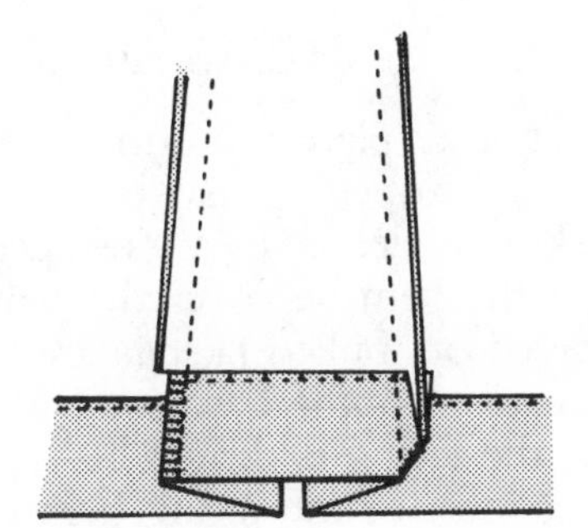

10-22. Pleat stabilized by seaming through hem.

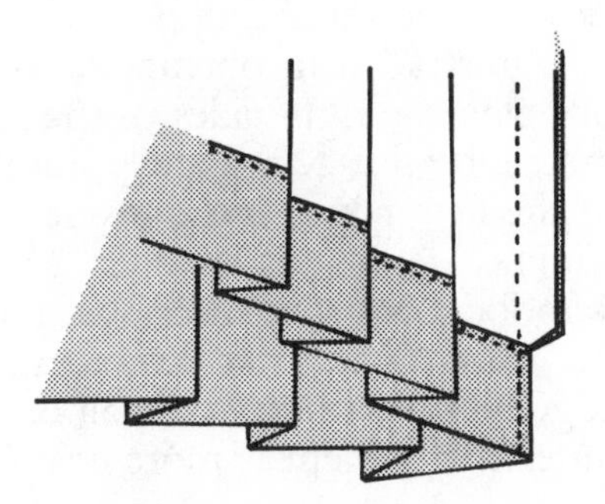

10-23. Pleat stabilized by clipping and turning seam at hem.

attempts require that the vertical seams as well as the hem itself be opened.

Another stabilization method requires that the seam covered by the hem be pressed open and trimmed while the seam directly above the hem is then clipped, turned, and pressed in the direction that allows the pleat to fold flat (Figure 10-23). After careful pressing, a row of machine stitching can be placed through the inside pleat fold, holding it permanently in place. An alternative to this row of stitching is possible when thermoplastic fibers and/or a permanent press finish are to be used to set the garment in its pressed shape. If stitching is used, and it is more effective than pressing alone in thick fabrics, it may extend the entire length of the pleat or stop at the top edge of the hem. This type of pleat stabilization may be found in garments with pleats all around, or just in one location—a kickpleat in the back or side of a skirt, for example.

HEMS AT GARMENT OPENINGS

Another place requiring special hem treatments is at garment openings. The opening may be the buttoned front of a jacket or the vent on a skirt or sleeve. In all instances, however, good construction requires that the hem be covered when the garment opens during movement. Folded or applied facings are typically used to accomplish this, and are secured after the garment has been hemmed. As shown in Figure 10-24, the facing is turned back over the hem and sewn on the hem fold after most of the facing hem depth has been trimmed away to reduce bulk. Topstitching, machine blind stitches, or tacking by hand can be used to hold the lower folded edge of the facing hem in place against the garment hem. If a more finished look is desired, mitering can be used to join the facing hem and garment hem.

A mitered hem opening, shown in Figure 10-25, is constructed by bringing the right sides of the facing and hem together and sewing an exact forty-five degree angle seam from the corner or fold of the opening to the hem edge on the inside of the facing. The seam is then clipped, trimmed, and pressed open to provide accurate, flat coverage at the hem location. The success of the technique hinges on the accuracy of the seam angle. If it is not exactly forty-five degrees, the hem/facing edge will be either too small or too large to fit against the garment. A mitered treatment is more costly to the apparel manufacturer than is a

10-24. Faced, folded hem at garment opening, bulk reduced by trimming.

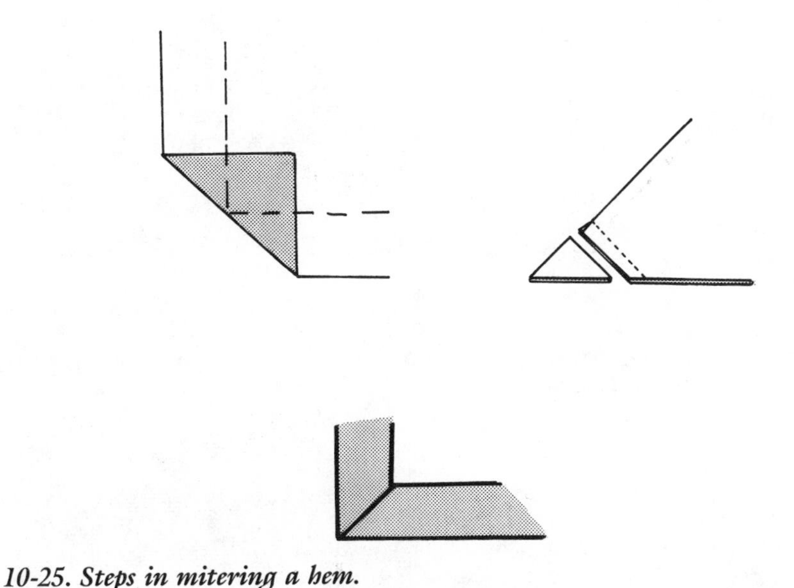

10-25. Steps in mitering a hem.

folded treatment. Hem adjustments are not possible when a true miter is used. Mitered hem openings are limited almost entirely to higher priced apparel.

HEMS IN LININGS

Special techniques are used to apply the hemmed lining to the finished hem of the garment. Linings may be free-hanging, as in most long coats, skirts, and long jackets; or attached, as is common in shorter jackets and in sleeve hems. Free-hanging linings are hemmed separately and applied to the garment with French tacks at seam locations. These tacks keep the lining from shifting too far out of position during wear and cleaning. A free-hanging lining is shown in Figure 10-26. Figure 10-27 shows the lining attached.

Attached linings are secured to the fashion fabric hem at all points with a blind stitch or a plain seam. The point at which the lining is attached to the hem is recessed one-half inch (1.27 cm) from the lining hem fold to allow vertical ease for movement. Vertical ease may not be provided on inexpensive jackets at sleeves or hems, but it is expected in garments purchased in moderate to better priced lines. Both lining types carry a hem depth similar to that of the garment, but their folded edges are one-half to one inch (1.27 to 2.54 cm) shorter than the garment to

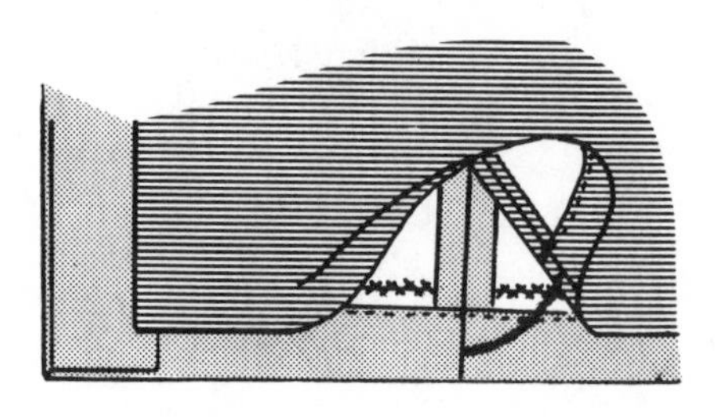

10-26. Free-hanging hem in a lined garment with swing tack securing lining to garment at seamline.

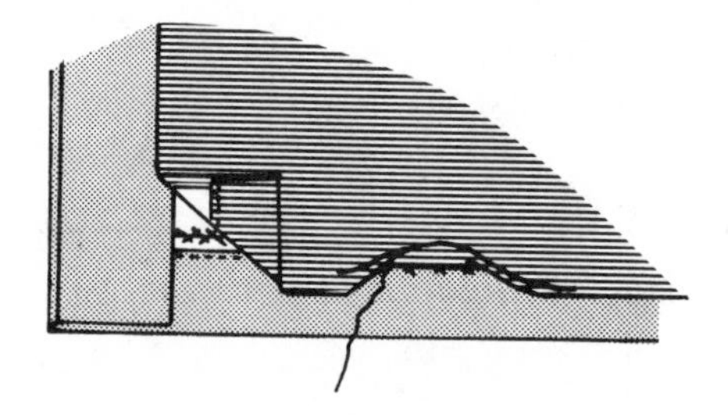

10-27. Attached hem in a lined garment.

prevent the possibility of the lining hanging below the finished hem after wear and cleaning.

SUPPORTED HEMS

When the style demands a silhouette with more body, as in tailored garments, interfacing can be applied to either the straight or the shaped hem to achieve and hold the desired shape. Interfaced hems are used in most tailored jackets and coats and occasionally in skirt and dress hems when style and fabric require extra body.

The type of interfacing used and the application method employed determine whether the hem is flat or rolled at its folded edge. For a flat fold, the interfacing is cut just to the fold line, and the hem fold is pressed. For a rolled look, the interfacing is cut to extend approximately one-fourth inch (.64 cm) beyond the fold, and the hem is not pressed flat at the fold.

Interfacings used at the hem should be cut on the bias to prevent raveling and to enable them to conform easily to the hem shape. In more expensive apparel lines, interfacing is cut to extend one-fourth inch (.64 cm) above the fashion fabric hem to lessen bulk at the fabric edge. This extension is concealed when the garment lining is applied, and most garments that have interfaced hems are lined. The addition of interfacing at the hem increases construction costs, but it can add considerably to the appearance of a quality garment.

Horse-hair braid is another type of supporting fabric that can be used to give extra body to the hems of formal and bridal wear. Its braided construction of large monofilament yarns allows it to conform to the hem shape in the same manner as a bias-cut interfacing would, but no raw edges are present. It is applied to the lower raw edge of the hem with a one-fourth inch (.64 cm) seam, and its width becomes the garment's hem depth. It acts both as a facing and as a stiffener. It can be treated in the same way as any other faced or folded hem as far as method of attachment is concerned.

WEIGHTED HEMS

Hem weighting is seldom done in the apparel industry, but apparel produced by couturiers and by individuals sewing at home may occasionally contain weights to help hold the hem edge in position or to give a particular effect. Suits, jackets, and coats constructed from heavy fabric are examples of apparel items that may contain weights at their hem edges.

Single weights are used to control certain points of the garment such as seams that have a tendency to hike up during wear. These weights are usually about the size of a nickel and are enclosed in fabric bags before attachment. Each bagged weight is positioned just above the hem fold and hand-sewn into place before the hem is turned into position. The weights remain in place during laundering or dry cleaning; therefore, hard pressing at weighted points should be avoided. In most instances, the seam acts as a buffer to minimize pressing problems. Single weights may also be used to control the cowl drape at neckline hems or elsewhere on the garment as needed.

Chain weights produce a more even effect by weighting the entire hem rather than just individual points. They are usually applied to the hem by hand directly underneath the lining ease pleat, and they extend the entire circumference of the hem. The chain should be removed before laundering to prevent corrosion and impressions that would occur during pressing. Reapplication must take place after each cleaning. Chain weights are useful for keeping hems properly aligned, especially when the hem would not otherwise fall back into place easily after body movement, or if the fabric has a high degree of stiffness in relation to its weight. Such a ratio causes the hemmed edge to stand away from the body. The chain weights reverse that ratio and create a more flattering line.

STANDARDS FOR EVALUATING HEMS AND HEM FINISHES

1. The hemline of the garment is parallel to the floor during wear, unless the garment design dictates an uneven hemline.
2. The hem is even in depth.
3. The hem is flat and smooth, with no pulling, ripples, puckers, or pleats.
4. The hem type is appropriate for the garment fabric and style.
5. The hem finish is appropriate for the garment fabric and the hem type.
6. The attachment method is appropriate for the garment fabric and style.
7. Excess bulk has been eliminated from the hem area.
8. Topstitched hems should be evenly stitched with appropriate thread and stitch length.
9. Blind stitching, fusing, and gluing should be inconspicuous on the right side of the garment.
10. Thread-covered edges should be smooth, well-covered, and free from frayed or hanging threads.
11. Hems at garment openings should be covered by the facing.
12. Hems in linings should allow for ease in wearing.
13. Hems in pleats should be handled to reinforce the pleat crease.

SUMMARY

One of the main aspects of evaluating any hem treatment is that the overall design of the garment has been either preserved or enhanced. The selections of hem type, hem finish, method of attachment, and treatment of hems at special locations must complement each other and the garment fabric and design. In general, garment cost is increased if hems are very deep or shaped, if additional materials are included during hem formation, and if automated equipment is not available to handle the entire hemming operation.

11

DECORATIVE DETAIL

Since decorative detail is one of the three basic factors in costing a garment, along with fabric and workmanship, it is especially important to recognize quality as it relates to this aspect of apparel. In less expensive ready-to-wear, trim is often the first place where cost can be cut. In other cases, trim may be used to update a basic garment for which patterns and markers already exist.

In evaluating decorative detail in general, several points should be considered. Trim should always be integral to the garment design. The trim should enhance the garment or make it unusual in some way, but without overpowering the garment design. In short, the garment's potential for sale should be increased by the trim.

The cost of the trim itself, as well as the extent of work involved in applying the trim or incorporating it into the structure of the garment, greatly affects the quality of the garment. The creativity of the designer must also be figured into the final cost in some manner. The more creative and unique the garment becomes through the use of trim, the greater is the potential cost of the garment. As a general rule, elaborate trims should be coordinated with simple garments, and simple trims with elaborate garments. The trim should relate structurally to the basic garment design.

In selecting trim for a garment, the manufacturer has two options. Which of these he selects may affect the final cost of the garment. The manufacturer may select a ready-made trim, just as he would select a fabric, or he may create a trim design and then search for a contractor to produce the trim. The manufacturer who creates an in-house design may be able to save some money and may also have an advantage in producing a more creative garment. On the other hand, working with contractors may produce unwanted delays or timing problems.

The extent to which decorative trim is used in apparel differs from one fashion period to another. At times, the use of trim will be widespread and very decorative. At other times, trim may be limited in use and more functional than purely decorative. Three apparel categories that use trim frequently and consistently, however, are children's wear, lingerie, and bridal wear.

In garments that are imported, trim may increase the duty charge and, consequently, the garment cost. Low or standard duty is applied to simple garments. Garments with nonfunctional trims, however, are charged a higher duty.

There are countless styles and types of trim made for different uses and methods of application. For simplicity, these will be discussed under four major headings; *soft trim, hard trim, fabric and stitchery,* and *structural trim.* These four types generally involve only two procedures for application: they are either incorporated during garment construction, or they are applied after the garment is completed. It should be understood that some of the trims in the first three categories could possibly be either structural or applied, depending on the method of application. No attempt will be made to present an exhaustive coverage of all trims currently available. The most important and most frequently used trims under each of the designated categories will be discussed.

SOFT TRIM

Soft trims include such items as lace, braid, and ribbon. Depending on the type and width of the trim, soft trim can be used almost anywhere—around necklines and collars, at yokes, sleeves, cuffs, front openings, and around hems. These trims may range from very inexpensive to very expensive, depending on the width, on the amount used, and on the complexity of the trim itself.

Most often, soft trims are applied by machine stitching after the garment or garment section is completed. This is a rapid means of application which produces a casual look and a sturdy finish. For areas demanding increased control or for a more finished appearance, hand

11-1. Inset application of soft trim.

application with tiny, invisible slip stitches may be used. Because of the expense, this is rarely done on any other than couture clothing and/or imported infant wear.

A second method of application used with soft trim is inset application. In this method, one or both raw edges of the trim are enclosed between two layers of fabric. This method of application is done during construction. A variation of the inset method involves lapping, rather than enclosing, the raw edge or edges of the trim with the garment fabric. This is essentially a piecing technique and can add considerably to labor costs if many seams are involved. Figure 11-1 shows the inset application of soft trim.

LACE AND LACE-LIKE FABRICS

Only a very few of the most expensive designer garments today are trimmed with real lace, the type made slowly and painstakingly by hand. From time to time, imported garments will feature hand-crocheted lace, and an occasional boutique item will be trimmed with antique lace. By far the most important types of lace, from a commercial standpoint, are those made by machine.

Among the most expensive machine laces are those done on the Leavers machine. The pattern is controlled by a Jacquard mechanism and can be very elaborate. Most of the lace imported from Europe is Leavers lace. Increasing width and pattern complexity add to the cost. With the exception of Alençon with its heavy cordonnet (shown in Figure 11-2), most of the Leavers laces are rather soft, sheer, and easily gathered, making them suitable for ruffled applications. A Chantilly type Leavers lace is shown in Figure 11-3.

Actually, Venice lace is merely very heavy machine embroidery. No ground fabric remains in the final product. The layering of the stitches is quite thick to give the lace durability and the three-dimensional look associated with seventeenth-century needlepoint laces. A comparison of needle-made lace and its embroidered counterpart are shown in Figures 11-4 and 11-5 respectively.

A considerable amount of handmade lace can be found on contemporary apparel and home furnishings fabrics such as bedding and napery at the present time. Most of the handmade lace and lace-like fabrics currently marketed are being imported from China. The cost of these fabrics is relatively low, and they represent excellent value in terms of the amount of labor required in their production.

Raschel knitting machines are used today to make lace much faster than is possible on the Leavers machines. Raschel lace often has less softness and complexity than its counterpart, however, and is much less expensive. All of the stretch laces used on lingerie are made on Raschel knitting machines. Raschel lace is the type found on most lingerie and lower-priced party wear for women and children.

Schiffli embroidery on net, organza, or some other sheer ground fabric is frequently used as a substitute for lace. The embroidery itself is done in a shiny, filament thread. Collars and cuffs are made by this method, as well regular lace yardage.

Embroidery plus some cutwork yields another popular lace substitute—eyelet. More casual than the preceding laces, eyelet is favored for children's wear, Victorian or Edwardian styled dresses and blouses, and even for decorating bed linens, towels, and other home furnishings. The ground fabric is usually a cotton or polyester/cotton batiste. The size and complexity of the design and the closeness with which the stitches are set vary among different price levels of embroidery.

The soft laces are more frequently gathered before they are applied to the garment. The firmer laces are more commonly applied flat. Some types have openwork slots, or beading, through which ribbon is threaded for an even more decorative effect. If the lace has one straight edge and one scalloped or shaped, it is called edging. Lace with both edges straight is usually called insertion or *entredeux*. Galloon has both edges in a curved decorative shape and is always applied flat.

RIBBONS AND OTHER STRAIGHT TRIMS

Straight trims such as grosgrain ribbon, satin ribbon, and novelty woven ribbon and bands must be sewn to the garment in a straight

11-2. Alençon-style Leavers lace.

11-3. Chantilly-style Leavers lace.

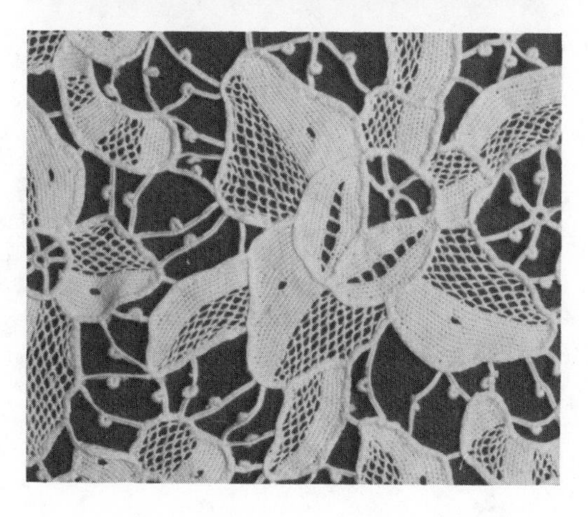

11-4. Needle-made lace.

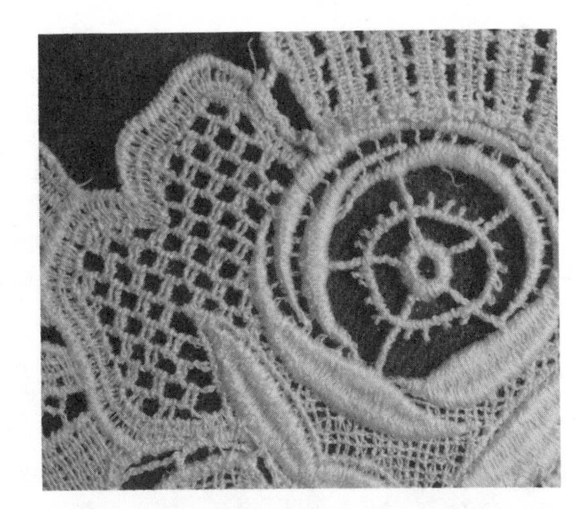

11-5. Machine-embroidered Venice-type lace.

11-6. Schiffli embroidery on net.

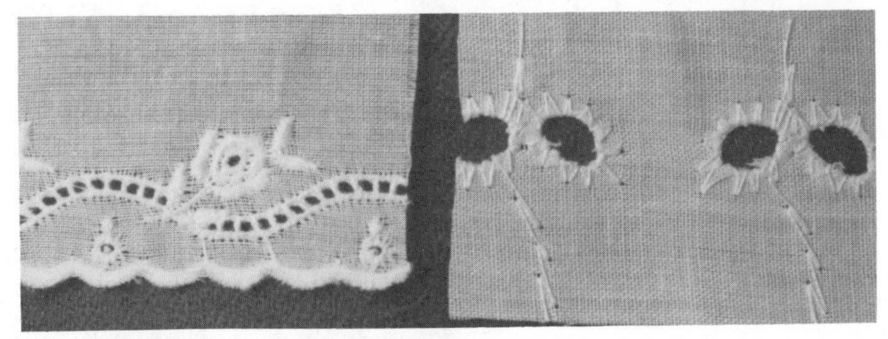

11-7. Two qualities of eyelet embroidery.

line. They may be used on corners if the corners are mitered.

Ribbons can be yarn dyed, piece dyed, or printed. Since yarn dyeing is more expensive than piece dyeing, this technique is usually reserved for ribbons or bands having a woven-in design. This design is controlled by Jacquard looms which interlace the different colors of yarn to create the pattern. If the ribbon is to be a solid color, it is much less expensive to dye the ribbon after it is woven, usually to match the apparel manufacturer's color specifications. Pattern can also be applied by printing, a much less costly method than Jacquard weaving with dyed yarns. Printed ribbons, however, are not very popular. The more complex, and often most expensive, trims of this type are usually imported from Europe.

Throw-away ribbon is the least expensive type. It is woven on a very broad loom and then cut into strips of the desired width. The resulting cut edges must be finished with a heat or adhesive finish to prevent raveling. This type of ribbon is primarily used for gift wrap and floral ties, but it may be used on budget apparel and accessories. It has low durability, however, and withstands very little wear or cleaning. In the garment pictured in Figure 11-8, flocked ribbon with cut edges was used under the eyelet beading of the collar edge and to tie a small bow

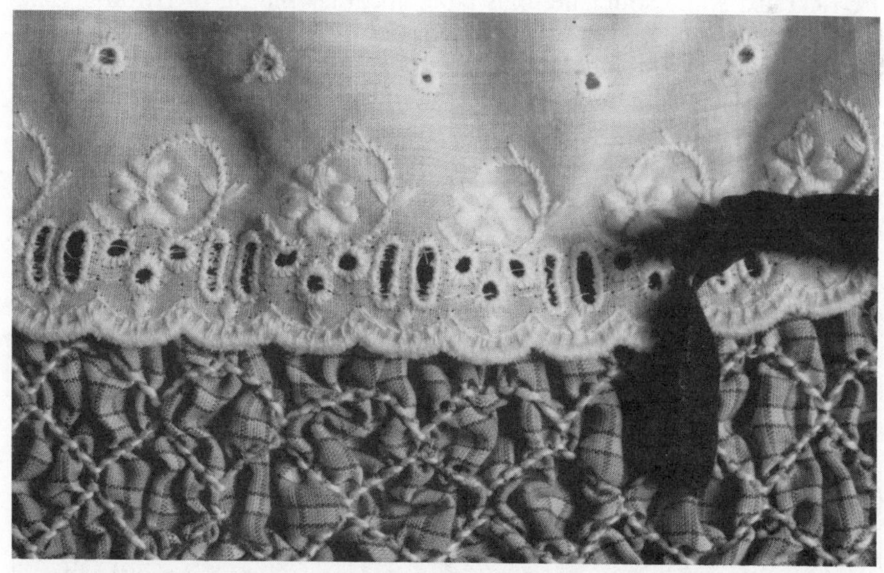

11-8. Flocked ribbon with cut edge used under eyelet beading of edge and to tie small bow.

for additional trim. Both the quality of the ribbon itself, as well as the poor quality of its use (topstitched below the beading rather than woven through the openings), indicate budget techniques, even though the smocking is hand done.

Some so-called braids are actually no more than wrapped cords. They are not flexible, but must be applied in straight or nearly straight lines. Soutache braid, the type used on sailor collars, may fall into this category, or may be flexible, depending on the method used to fabricate the braid. It must be examined carefully if intended for use on curved areas.

BRAIDS AND FLEXIBLE TRIMS

Trims in this category are braided, knitted, or cut on the bias of woven fabric. The important factor is that they can be shaped to fit curved areas. Flexible trims can be sewn in a straight line, of course, but the fact that they can be fitted to curved areas allows much more freedom of design in their application.

In addition to functional braids which cover the raw edges of a garment (see, for example, Figure 6-3, page 126), there are braids intended to be applied flat to accentuate a certain design line. Other flexible trims are rickrack, some soutache, bias tape, and bias piping or cording. The last two must be used as structural trim in order to conceal their raw edges. Bias tape and bias piping are enclosed in seams, with just the narrow, folded or corded edge protruding to give the decorative effect. The other types can be much more freely applied. The matador bolero jackets are almost always trimmed with the application of scrolling, a narrow braid.

STANDARDS FOR EVALUATING SOFT TRIM

1. The trim is compatible with the garment fabric in terms of weight, design, and care requirements.
2. Flexible trim is used on curved areas and applied without stretching or gathering of the trim.
3. Trim is securely attached to the garment.
4. Trim is attached in an inconspicuous manner, unless the method of attachment constitutes part of the decorative effect.
5. Trims used at corners are mitered.

HARD TRIM

Hard trims include such decorative items as buckles, buttons, zippers, snaps, studs, beads, and sequins. Most are made of wood, metal, or plastic. Many of the hard trims are particularly effective when used on sportswear. Beads and sequins, on the contrary, are more appropriate for formal wear.

FASTENERS

Buttons are used both for function and decorative effect. Only occasionally are buttons added without some provision for actually using them, and then it is usually on lower-priced apparel. Buttons can be made of synthetic materials or in the more expensive naturals, such as wood, bone, pearl, and leather. Structurally, buttons are either of two types, shank or eyed. Shank buttons, with a loop on the back through which they are sewn to the garment, are dressier and more costly to apply. The eyed buttons, whether with two or four holes, are easily and quickly attached by machine.

When used for decorative value, zippers always add a sporty or casual look to a garment. They may also add versatility: a lower skirt or slack panel may be zipped off for a new look; zippers at the hems of tight-fitting slacks can be opened for a looser look.

Snaps and brads may also serve a decorative purpose. The pockets and front tab of Western-style shirts most commonly are fastened with decorative snaps. Frequently, these are styled to look like buttons. These are attached quickly and easily, give a casual look to the garment, and require less labor than buttons and buttonholes.

BELTS AND BUCKLES

Belts may be categorized as soft trim, fabric, or hard trim depending on the type of material of which they are made. Because buckles are most often made of metal, belts will be discussed under hard trims. Most garment belts are made of inexpensive materials such as vinyl and ribbon. The material for the belt may be glued or sewn onto a stiff backing. Stitched belts tend to hold up longer and cost slightly more than the glued ones. The stitching is one of the crucial construction elements in a quality belt. It should be tight, uniform machine stitching. Widely spaced stitching is sometimes used in sportier belts. Even though, from the point of fashion, it may look better, it is still a poorer value in terms of belt construction and life. This element of construction is probably more important in leather belts than in fabric ones.

Another quality checkpoint of leather belts is the method of lining. On a less expensive belt, the manufacturer will simply finish the suede side of the leather instead of putting another piece of leather on the belt's underside. Any leather belt sold with a garment will increase the garment cost considerably.

Novelty belts may be made from a wide variety of materials, such as braid, rope, or chain. Garment fabrics may also be used to make belts. In this case, the manufacturer orders buckles from the button supplier and then constructs the belt along with the garment. These usually inexpensive belts are made by stitching fabric to a staff backing and then attaching this unit to a buckle. This is most often used for clothing with a more tailored look.

In any of the above situations, the buckle should be of a durable, solid material. Metal tends to hold up better than other materials. Often, metal buckles are hollow and break easily. The buckle should be attached very firmly to the belt, since this is the point of greatest stress. A fine-quality leather belt will have an added piece of leather behind the buckle base. The holes on a belt should be cleanly punched with no frayed material visible. They should not be too small or too large for the belt tongue.

Another type of belt made from the garment fabric consists of cloth with no backing or buckle. This type of belt requires more fabric and is often used with children's clothing or to achieve a feminine look in women's clothing. It may be made of contrasting or garment fabric or of ribbon or braid. It is always made in-house. Such belts require tight, even stitching for durability.

BEADS AND SEQUINS

Beads, sequins, rhinestones, pearls, and other gem-like materials traditionally have been used to add glamour, excitement, and fantasy. Queen Elizabeth I of England, for example, used pounds of real gems to ornament her clothing, but since the nineteenth century such ornaments have been manufactured rather than natural.

These items may be incorporated into the garment design by the use of one of several methods. The most painstaking and consequently the costliest method is to attach them by hand, whether individually, in groups, or in a long strand. This method is used in the bridal industry quite frequently as well as in costume houses and in very expensive couture clothing.

Bands or strips with the trim already attached may also be purchased, then attached to the garment. This is most often done with invisible slipstitches through the backing. Because this method is quicker than the one discussed above, it may be less expensive. Of course, the cost always depends on the amount of trim used as well as on the labor involved. If an entire garment or large garment area is to be trimmed in this manner, it may be more economical to purchase beaded or sequined fabric for the garment area.

STANDARDS FOR EVALUATING HARD TRIMS

1. Hard trim is compatible with the garment fabric in terms of weight, style, and care requirements.
2. Hard trim is securely attached.
3. Hard trim is smooth so as not to constitute a snagging hazard for the remainder of the garment.
4. When two or more fasteners (such as buttons or snaps) are used to join garment sections, the two sections are perfectly aligned when closed.
5. Eyed buttons should have a thread shank.
6. Belts meant to be firm have a stiff backing securely attached.
7. Belts should not crock or bleed color onto garments with which they are worn. (This is often a problem with suede belts.)
8. Belt buckles are securely attached to the belt.
9. Belt buckles hold the free end of the belt securely when closed.

FABRIC AND STITCHERY TRIM

The use of stitchery and fabric trims allows the apparel designer and manufacturer to develop very unique decorative effects. Since this type of trim is usually done in-house, there is also a greater potential for saving time and money.

FABRIC TRIMS

These trims offer the manufacturer the opportunity of eliminating the extra steps of ordering trims separately from fabric. Fabric trims may range from ruffles to bows to such decorative effects as appliqué and patchwork. Because ruffles are usually stitched into seamlines as a garment is put together, they will be considered as structural trim. Only rarely are strips of fabric gathered and stitched on top of a garment for decorative detail alone.

11-9. Bows cut on the bias and on the straight grain.

BOWS

Bows are common fabric trims. They may serve functional purposes as fastenings, or simply act as adornment. Bows can be made from the garment fabric or from contrasting fabric including flexible or straight ribbons and braids. The type and amount of fabric used are the most important factors affecting the cost of this type of trim. Bows on more expensive garments are usually full rather than skimpy.

Fabric bows may be formed in several ways. A width of fabric may be folded in half, then stitched and turned, or two strips of fabric may be stitched along the long edges and turned. The fabric may also be attached to the neckline as a structural technique. Fabric bows should be cut on the bias for a soft, draped effect. If the cut is not on the true bias, the knot will not lie smooth.

APPLIQUÉ

Appliqué is a fabric trim that consists of a separate piece of fabric applied to a larger background for the purpose of decoration. The appliqué may be purchased or made in-house by cutting out a motif from a piece of fabric. Many purchased appliqués are made almost entirely with embroidery of different colors. Contrasting solids, prints, and fabrics with definite texture lend themselves to appliqué. Fabrics that ravel easily are not satisfactory. It is important that the care requirements of the appliqué are compatible with that of the background.

The appliqué may be attached either by hand or by machine. Of

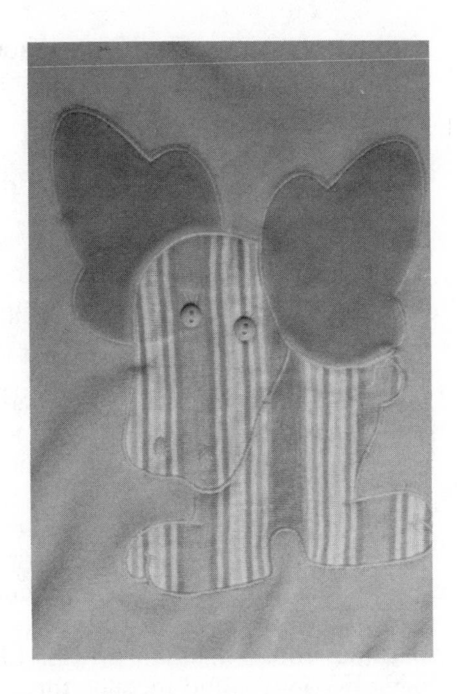

11-10. Appliqué of contrasting fabrics on child's dress.

course, any handwork is costly for the manufacturer. In some instances, however, it is necessary to use the hand method. Such is the case where the care requirements of the appliqué are not compatible with the background. The hand-attached appliqué can be more easily removed for separate cleaning, etc. A great deal of imported infants' wear has intricate hand-done appliqué and embroidery.

With the current popularity of designer names and logos, appliqués have become common items of apparel decoration, while at the same time, serving to promote the manufacturer or designer. Fabric appliqués are less expensive than embroidered insignias. Children's wear and sportswear also make wide use of appliqués. Knits and other soft fabrics or appliqué fabrics cut on the true or partial bias will need some stabilization to keep the parts of the motif flat during stitching. When fusible interfacing or fusing web is used for this purpose, the resulting appliqué is often extremely stiff, even scratchy. Appliqués on infants clothing should be checked carefully for this characteristic, for some are stiff enough to scratch delicate skin. Also, stiff appliqués over large areas of a garment can change the hang and drape of the fabric enough to create a distorted effect in the completed garment.

Often, a completely contrasting fabric, such as fur or leather, may be used for a design effect. These fabrics may be quite expensive, so this type of trim will add considerably to the cost of the garment, and may decrease serviceability.

STITCHERY

The sewing machine may play a decorative as well as a functional role in apparel construction. It offers a variety of trim possibilities through the use of straight or decorative stitches. As mentioned in the previous section, embroidered insignias are widely used today by major manufacturers.

Figure 11-11 shows two variations of embroidered insignias, one embroidered directly on the garment and the other embroidered on a nonwoven fabric and then appliquéd to the garment. The latter method may utilize fusing material rather than stitching in the final application to the garment. Such insignias are generally ordered from companies that specialize in embroidered trims. The apparel manufacturer may, however, elect to invest in a machine designed exclusively for decorative stitching. Some apparel categories, such as children's wear, use these machines more than do others. Elaborate embroidery, especially utilizing decorative and metallic threads, can add considerably to garment cost, whether embroidered directly or in appliqué form.

Perhaps the most common form of fashion stitchery is topstitching, which is used to emphasize the structural lines of the garment. This is a quick and inexpensive method of trim. It may be a construction procedure used regularly on such areas as pockets or garment edges. Topstitching may also serve to keep seams and edges flat and smooth. It is

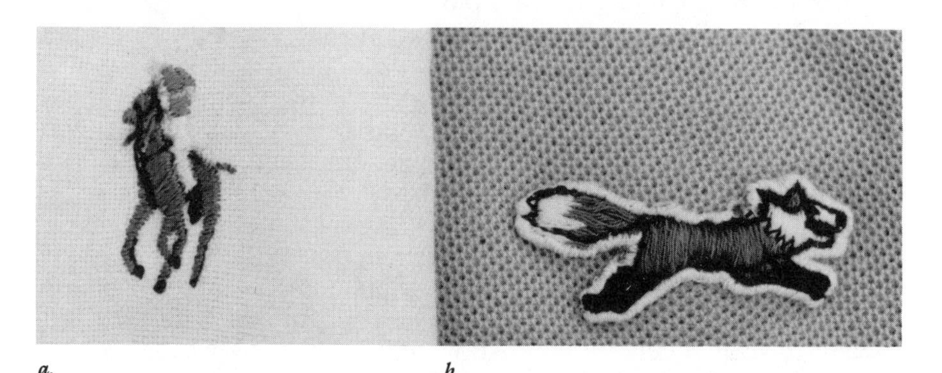

a. *b.*

11-11. Stitchery trim: (a) embroidered insignia directly on garment; (b) appliquéd to garment.

important that the topstitching be straight and at an equal distance from the edge.

Embroidered fabric or embroidered motifs applied to the garment sections or finished garment can also be used as trim on a design. The latter, especially, constitutes an expensive method of trimming, for the individualized application slows the production process. In addition to the time of applying the embroidery, the cost of the design process and of the thread adds to garment cost. If the design is hand embroidered, as is sometimes the case with garments imported from countries with low wage rates, the value for price is often considerable. Hand embroidery can be detected by examining the back of the fabric carefully, looking for knots in the thread, irregular floats from similar design parts, and

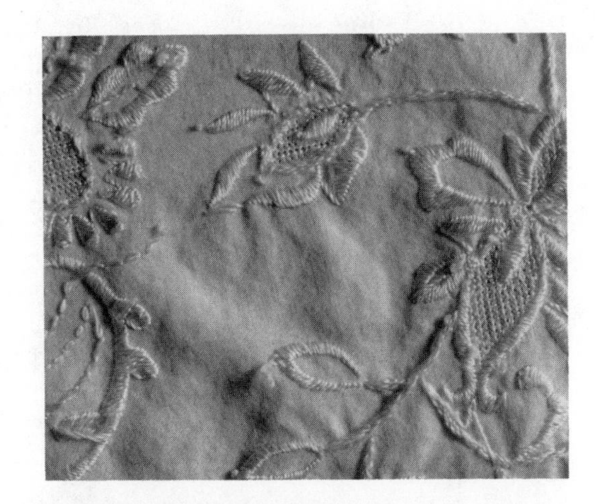

11-12. Wrong side of fabric showing hand embroidery.

11-13. Wrong side of fabric showing machine embroidery.

inconsistencies in stitch coverage. Machine embroidery, with the very rare exception of Swiss handloom embroidery, will show both bobbin and top thread, and the tension on the lower thread will usually be tight enough to pull part of the top thread to the fabric reverse. Figure 11-12 shows the wrong side of a cotton blouse which was hand embroidered in silk thread. Figure 11-13 shows the wrong side of a filament sheer curtain fabric machine embroidered.

STANDARDS FOR EVALUATING FABRIC AND STITCHERY TRIM

1. Fabric bows are cut on the true bias.
2. Turned edges of fabric bows are neatly turned, with no seam wells and with symmetrical ends.
3. Appliqués are securely attached to the base fabric, with no raveling or fraying apparent.
4. Care requirements of appliqués are compatible with the garment fabric.
5. Appliqués, whether fabric or stitchery, do not alter the intended hang and drape of the garment fabric.
6. Appliqués are not unduly stiff and scratchy on the outside or inside of the garment.
7. Stitchery is done in an appropriate stitch length.
8. Thread used in stitchery is colorfast.
9. Topstitching is even.

STRUCTURAL TRIM

Structural trims are those ornamentations or decorative touches that are created during the actual construction of the garment, as opposed to being applied to a completed garment or garment section. This type of decorative detail is more appropriately evaluated as a construction procedure. Examples of structural trims include *pleats, ruffles,* and *tucks.*

PLEATS

Pleats are folds of fabric providing controlled fullness. Whether they are sharp, crisp pleats or soft, rolled pleats, they should be made with precision. Fabric is very important in achieving this precision. Pleats generally look best when executed in firm, resilient fabrics such as synthetics, blends, heavy silks, and wools. Soft, rolled pleats, however, are attractive in any soft fabric. If a sharp finish is desired on fabrics that have a pre-cure durable press finish, edge stitching may be necessary.

A special contractor is used for most pleating. Skirts are seamed and hemmed before being sent to the contractor. The majority of pleated skirts are constructed from straight pieces of fabric, but they may also be made from circular-shaped patterns. In order to save fabric, pleats on inexpensive garments have a small underfold. This shallow pleat will more easily show wear than the full pleat, and generally looks skimpy.

There are four basic kinds of pleats: *knife, box, inverted,* and *accordion.* Each of these offers a different look to a garment.

The knife pleat is constructed by making folds of fabric all facing in one direction. This pleat offers a crisp and tailored look to a garment when it is pressed sharply all the way to the bottom edge. On the other hand, the same type of pleat, if left unpressed, can be a slimming alter-

11-14.
Knife pleats.

11-15.
Box pleats.

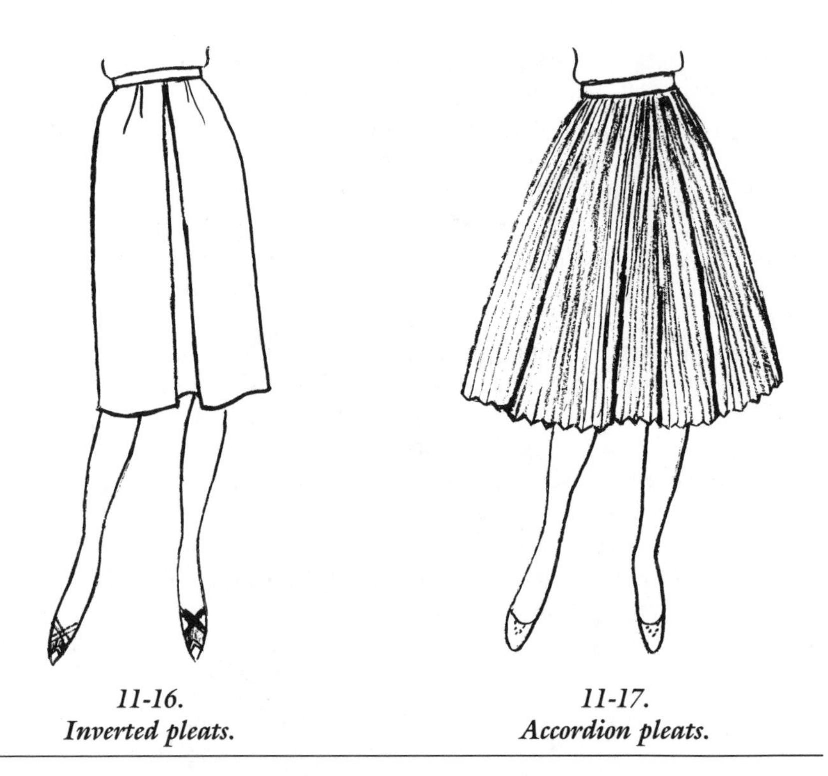

11-16.
Inverted pleats.

11-17.
Accordion pleats.

native to a gathered skirt, while still providing considerable fullness. If the depth of the pleat, that is the amount of fabric concealed inside the fold of the pleat, is shallow, then the garment will look skimpy and may buckle rather than drape with body movement.

The box pleat places two folds of fabric in opposite directions. This pleat is particularly appropriate for plaids because one pleat can emphasize one color while the underfold can emphasize another. This type of pleat is difficult to graduate at the waistline unless the blocks of color in the plaid are large enough to allow some manipulation while still maintaining the design effect.

The inverted pleat is the box pleat in reverse. The folds are turned toward each other and meet. As is true with the box pleat, the inverted pleat is very useful as a design effect when used with plaids or stripes.

The accordion pleat looks very much like the bellows of an accordion. There is no underfold of fabric, and the pleats must taper to nothing at the waist. It is sometimes called a sunburst pleat, referring to the radiating lines. This type of pleat is used in many dressy garments made of crepe or chiffon. In fabrics that have a lot of body, accordion pleats tend to be stiff and add considerable size to the body.

An engineered pleat is one that is designed for an individual garment. It must be built into the pattern and pressed in by hand after or during garment construction. Usually this type of pleat is used in a restricted area; for example, three knife pleats at the center front of a straight skirt.

RUFFLES

Ruffles are strips of self or contrasting fabric which have greater fullness than the garment areas to which they are applied. Although some ruffles can be gathered and applied directly to a flat garment surface, the majority of ruffles are structural. Even ruffles applied to a hem edge function as a means of lengthening the garment and are therfore more appropriately treated as structural components of the garment.

A major point in evaluating ruffles is the amount of fullness that is incorporated into them. For a minimum of fullness, the fabric strip should be at least twice the length of the area to which it is to be attached. A fabric strip three times the length of the area will provide a very full ruffle. The wider the ruffle the more sheer or soft the fabric from which it is made, the fuller it should be. Figure 11-18 shows an eyelet ruffle used at the hem edge of a child's dress. Only a very small amount of fullness is incorporated into this ruffle.

Ruffles should be cut either on the lengthwise grain or on the true bias for the best effect. Both cuts may be made double for a self-facing, or they may have a narrow hemmed edge. They may even have additional decorative detail, such as narrow lace edging or embellishing

11-18. Eyelet ruffle with minimum of fullness used as finish for hem edge of child's dress.

11-19. Shaped ruffle.

machine-stitching, at the outer edge. The self-faced ruffle is rather expensive in terms of fabric requirements, but there is some saving in labor. If elaborate decorative detail is added to the outer edge of the ruffle, then the labor costs may be considerable. Some ruffles in children's garments may become quite elaborate with the addition of lace, beading, and ribbon.

Ruffles are gathered by a shirring attachment on the sewing machine. This makes for quick and easy construction and for smooth, even gathers. Some ruffles are made from pleated fabric, in which case no additional gathering is required. There is another type of ruffle that does not require gathering—the shaped ruffle, which is cut from circles that are then joined in narrow seams. After hemming or self-facing, the small inner circles are clipped so they will open out flat, and they are then joined to the garment. Thus, the seam itself is flat, but the ruffle flares from the seam to the lower edge to provide a soft, wavy ruffle. Figure 11-19 shows this type of ruffle in its final form. This is the slowest and most difficult type of ruffle to construct, and fabric requirements are great, especially if the ruffle contains a self-facing.

TUCKS

Tucks may be strictly structural, or they may serve a very decorative purpose as well. They are small folds of fabric which are usually most effective when they follow the straight grain of the fabric. When used for decoration, the folds are generally formed on the outside of the

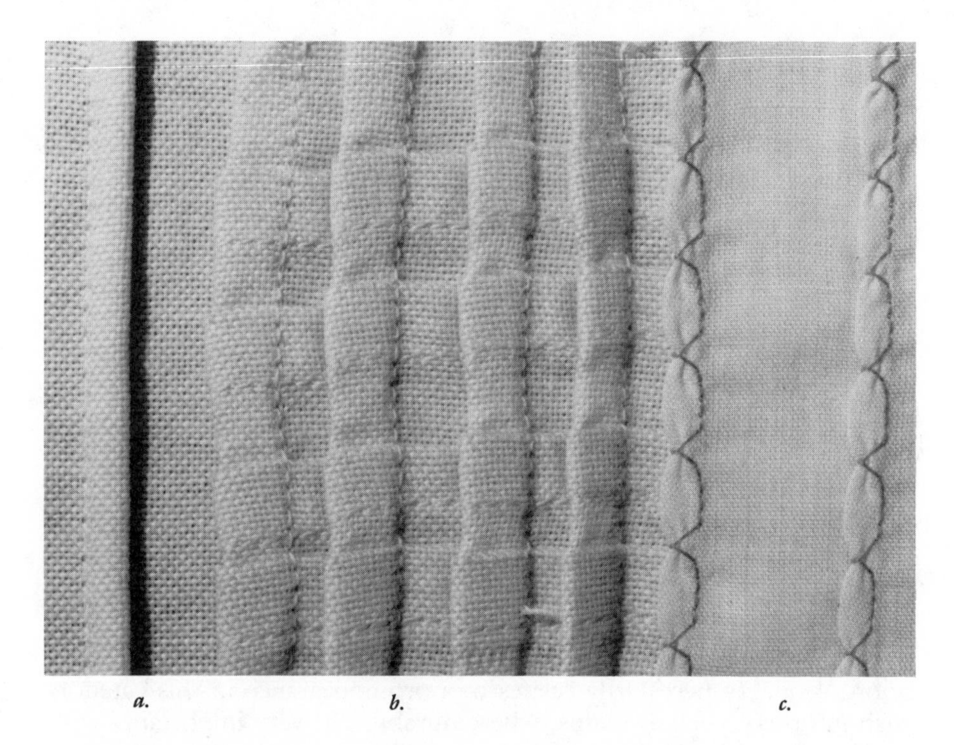

11-21. Decorative tucks: (a) corded; (b) crossed; (c) shell.

fabric. A great amount of variety is possible depending on the size of the tuck, the spacing between tucks, and the direction in which the tucks are pressed. The wider the tuck, the more fabric will be required to complete the garment. In garments with many deep tucks, the fabric requirement will be substantial.

Crossed tucks, corded tucks, and *shell tucks* offer still other decorative variations. (See Figure 11-20.) Crossed tucks are done before the fabric is cut. They are made by first making small lengthwise tucks at regular intervals, then sewing new tucks at right angles to the first group.

Corded tucks are made by adding a piece of cording in the fold of the fabric prior to sewing the tuck, which is usually very narrow. The cording adds depth to the tuck.

Shell tucks are made by sewing over each tuck at precise intervals. This may be done by hand or by a special machine that sews a straight stitch to form the tuck proper, yet throws out a horizontal stitch to cover and pull in the folded tuck edge at regular intervals.

STANDARDS FOR EVALUATING STRUCTURAL TRIM

1. Tucks and pleats are composed of straight, even folds of fabrics.
2. Fabric is compatible to the desired design effect.
3. Adequate fabric depth is provided to ensure the proper look for the pleat.
4. Ruffles have ample fullness to be attractive.
5. Ruffles have smooth, even gathers, with no puckers or pleats.
6. Free edges of ruffles are neatly finished.

SUMMARY

The nature of decorative detail is to attract the attention of the viewer, so precision is particularly important in executing many of the operations described in this chapter. Irregularities in seaming or topstitching, mismatched lines, frayed edges, and poor matching of decorative detail to garment design and/or fabric are glaringly apparent. Thus, an evaluation of quality necessarily relates more to appearance in this category than in others, such as seams, where durability is very important.

Cost is obviously affected by the use of decorative detail, sometimes substantially. The cost of any applied trim is a consideration, as is the cost of application. However, some of the most expensive trims are structural, requiring pattern manipulation and additional fabric yardage. This is one aspect of cost that automation cannot address.

12

FIT AND ALTERATION

Well-fitted garments can be defined as those that are comfortable to wear, that allow sufficient ease for freedom of movement, that are consistent with the current fashion, and that are free of undesirable wrinkles, sags, or bulges. Individuals do not rate fit in the same way, and standards of good fit do not remain constant.

Fitting standards developed by individuals or by groups are affected by a variety of factors. Fashion is a major influence among these factors. The yearly fluctuation of the various apparel components—skirt length, silhouette, waistline position, sleeve style and length, and neckline—is important to the fitting standards established for any given period. The hemline for one season may be considered appropriate or well-fitted at mid-calf, the next season at mid-knee, and the following season at mid-thigh. In each instance, fashion influences the perceived appropriateness of hem length for that season.

Another example of fashion's influence on fit is in the degree of ease allowed for free movement. Ease is commonly associated with comfort and good fit in apparel. Styles such as the tent and the smock top are fitted much larger than the body demands, but they are nevertheless accepted as well-fitted garments when in fashion. The shrink and tube tops are examples of the opposite extreme. Similar examples of the influence of fashion on fit can be found throughout history. Fashion, therefore, is an important influence on the standards of fit applicable during any given period.

Fabric is another factor that has a great impact on fit. All aspects of fabric development—fiber content, yarn structure, fabrication method, and finish—affect apparel fit. For fabric to provide the fit desired by the apparel manufacturer, it must be selected carefully. Accurate cutting and sewing are important, but they cannot make a poor fabric choice hold the shape of a particular fashion silhouette. Sagging hemlines and skirts or pants that stretch out of shape at the seat and/or the knee are obvious fitting problems that are a direct result of a poor fabric choice. Stretch fabrics and knits, on the other hand, provide for greater variety in body size and contour within each garment size than do nonextensible fabrics.

Other concerns in fitting apparel are associated with body imperfections such as posture. Poor posture is often the only reason why ready-to-wear or standard patterns do not fit some individuals properly.

Body asymmetry can also affect fit. Few bodies are perfectly symmetrical, but most are close enough to present no fitting problems in purchasing ready-made apparel. When differences vary more than small fractions, however, fitting problems may result. In ready-to-wear, for example, padding may be used to realign shoulders or to camouflage a small hip in order to secure a better fit and maintain body symmetry. Home-sewn garments can be cut differently on the right and left sides to compensate for differences, but alterations should not call attention to the problem.

Body deformation may present special fitting problems. In these cases, the aim is to conceal the problem through the use of style selection rather than to fit apparel items closely to the problem area. The same principles hold true for the problems associated with obesity and with protruding bone structures at the hip and shoulder blades of individuals who are very thin.

Other factors that play a role in apparel fit include accuracy in size selection by the consumer, accuracy in altering the garment after purchase or accuracy in the pattern placement on the fabric and cutting in the manufacturing process or at home, and accuracy in garment construction and pressing on an assembly line or at home. If there is an error in size selection, in quality production, or in alteration after the apparel item has been purchased, a poor fit can result.

The impact of social variables, such as socioeconomic status, religion, race, sex, occupation, and age, can affect the personal opinions of individuals concerning the appropriate fit of the apparel they wear. The impact these variables have on fit will not be the same from one individual to another and cannot be readily defined, but their presence does affect personal opinions of appropriate fit.

ELEMENTS OF FIT

In addition to the personal and social factors that affect fitting standards there are five other very well-defined conditions present in every garment that can be used to describe good fit: *grain, ease, line, set,* and *balance*. These elements work together, not as separate entities, to provide guidelines for evaluating apparel fit. A thorough understanding of these five factors and their interrelationship plays a vital role in one's ability to understand fit, to analyze fitting problems, and to recommend solutions to problems when they occur.

FABRIC GRAIN

Grain is the first of the five factors that affect apparel fit. It interacts and affects the others to such a degree that it is referred to by some as the key factor in recognizing good fit and in defining fitting problems. Grain is formed when woven fabrics are constructed of yarns that are interlaced at right angles to each other. The lengthwise yarns of the fabric are stronger and form the lengthwise grain. Since they hold their shape better in wearing and laundering than the crosswise yarns, they are aligned with the center front and the center back of most apparel items. If this alignment in apparel is not perpendicular to the floor, whether due to a mistake, because of a figure fault, or because of a special design effect, the hemline will ripple and often sag after several wearings and washings. The seat, elbow, or knee of the garment may also show signs of distortion, especially if the garment is fitted tightly at these points. Furthermore, the garment may pull or twist over some body bulges, creating undesirable wrinkles and distorting line, balance, and set as well.

The position of the crosswise fabric grain is affected by its lengthwise reciprocal. In most garment designs, it should be at right angles to the lengthwise grain, which places it parallel to the floor at the basic body bulges. If the alignment of the crosswise grain is distorted by body bulges that are larger than those intended by the design of the apparel item, the grainline will curve upward instead of resting parallel to the floor. This causes diagonal wrinkles below the bulge and, depending on its size, often above the bulge. Also, the circumference seam will hike at the waist in the case of a large bust and round shoulders, and the hemline will hike in the case of a protruding abdomen or hips.

If the alignment of the crosswise grain sags downward due to bulges that are smaller than those intended for the design, diagonal wrinkles will result. In case of flat hips, for example, the hemline will sag at the center back of a skirt, and pants will bag in the seat. Sagging will also occur at the front waist of the bodice front if the bust is small.

Grain in fabric can be compared to the support beams of a building. Although these beams are not always visible when the structure is complete, their presence is evident. Grain, too, is not easily seen, but disregard of proper grain position in apparel made at home or purchased ready-made will result in garments that hang and fit poorly.

EASE

Ease is the second of the five factors affecting apparel fit. It can be defined as the difference between the body measurements at any given point and the apparel item or the pattern at the same point. Ease is built into ready-made garments and patterns to allow for comfort when moving. A garment constructed or purchased to conform exactly to personal body measurements would be uncomfortable to wear since it allows the person no room for reaching, sitting, or even breathing, unless, of course, the garment is made of an extensible fabric.

The amount of ease built into a garment varies, depending on the style and the use of the garment. The amount of ease provided may not always be acceptable to the wearer. If not, adjustments (decreases primarily) may be made after a garment is purchased or before it is cut from fabric. Keep in mind, however, many fabrics cannot withstand the strain at the hip and back when they are tightly fitted. Furthermore, closely fitted garments display figure faults, especially bulges at the midriff, upper arm, and thighs in women; the undefined waist of the small child; and the "bay window" on the stout male. Ease allotments are also affected by fashion. At times, the ease allotment may be very full, and at others, very skimpy. Whatever the case, the ease allotment used in an apparel item should be becoming to the wearer and not selected only for fashion's sake.

LINE

Line is the third factor, working with grain and ease, to affect apparel fit. Line is composed of the structural and/or decorative seams, fabric folds, and darts that define the shape of the silhouette and control the shaping of flat fabric to conform to the body contours. In most instances, basic garment seams should follow the natural silhouette of the body. Seams are normally perpendicular to the floor at the center front, the center back and the side. Shoulder seams should be atop the shoulder, and darts should point toward the bulges they are intended to accommodate.

When larger or smaller bulges are present than those intended for the design, seam alignment is distorted. This causes side seams that are normally perpendicular to the floor to swing toward the front or the back, producing diagonal wrinkles which distort balance, set, and grain.

Curved lines, which include the circumference seams at the waist, neckline, and armhole, should be smooth and lie flat against the body. Ripples or pulls at these points indicate poor fit. The hemline, also a curved line, should be parallel to the floor and be balanced an equal distance from the legs and other body parts at all points. The alignment of any of the curved seams can be distorted by posture problems, large bulges, poor size selection, body hollows, and grain violations as well as poor construction.

Apparel lines intended to provide extra fullness or that are strictly decorative should also appear smooth and, in most instances, symmetrical. Fabric folds made by pleats, gathers, and tucks are usually perpendicular to the floor. Draped fabric folds usually form smooth curved lines at the neck, hip, or shoulder. Line, like its counterparts grain and ease, is a very important consideration in evaluating apparel fit.

SET

Set is the fourth factor that aids in the recognition of good fit. For the purposes of this chapter, set is defined as the absence of undesirable crosswise, lengthwise, or diagonal wrinkles when the garment is on the body. Wrinkles that are a part of the design should not be confused with wrinkles caused when the fabric strains over a bulge or sags due to a hollow (such as a sway back).

Wrinkle direction provides clues to analyzing fitting problems. Horizontal wrinkles occur when the garment is too tightly fitted above or below the bulge. A very common example is the skirt that cups under the seat and wrinkles horizontally above the hips to the waist. Wrinkles in the vertical direction are indicative of a garment that is too large. These wrinkles are common at the back of jackets and dresses, but do occur in skirts, pants and sleeves as well. The third wrinkle direction, diagonal, indicates that the bulge at the shoulder or hip, for example, is too large or too small for the garment design. In these instances, diagonal wrinkles usually point to the problem bulge or hollow. Set is greatly affected by the other fit factors of grain, balance, line, and ease.

BALANCE

The last of the five fit factors is balance. Defined in this context, it is the symmetrical relationship of the garment to the body, and its affect on fit. Balance, as it relates to apparel fit, demands that the garment stand away from and/or hug the body in the same way on both sides of symmetrical designs. Balance problems are seen most often in jackets and skirts that do not extend evenly from the body at the hemline. Poor posture, bulges, or body imperfections, such as one hip higher than the other, can cause balance problems that affect fit. Balance is interrelated to the other fit factors; a change in one or more of the others affects balance as well.

READY-TO-WEAR SIZING

The Standards Division of the United States Department of Commerce and the apparel industry have coordinated their efforts over the years to establish apparel sizing standards for the various figure types, sexes, and age groupings. Unfortunately for the apparel consumer, these standards are voluntary. Although many manufacturers use them, many do not. This lack of conformity to standards is why a female consumer may wear a size 8 in one brand and a size 12 in another, or a twelve-month-old child may wear an 18 months size in one brand and a 12-months size in another. As a rule, more expensive apparel lines are cut larger than their less expensive counterparts, but it is advisable to try on apparel before purchase rather than relying on marked size alone.

WOMEN'S SIZES

Women's clothing comes in four major size classifications: *misses, women's, half size,* and *junior*. Each classification provides for different relationships of one body part to another, allowing for better fit.

Misses sizes are designed for the women who have average proportions and height. Sizes range from 6 to 20. Two subdivisions of the misses category have been established for the shorter and taller figure: *petite misses* and *tall misses*.

Women's sizes range from size 32 to 52 and are designed for the fuller, more mature figure of average height. These sizes are cut with longer sleeves and a longer torso.

Half sizes are designed to accommodate the shorter woman with a full, mature figure. These sizes are cut with a lower full bust and a larger but shorter torso and shorter sleeves. Sizes range from 12 1/2 to 26 1/2.

Junior sizes are designed for the more youthful, short, and slim figure. The torso is cut shorter and the bustline higher than in misses. Sizes range from 3 to 15. A subdivision of the junior size is the *petite junior*. This size category is designed for the shorter junior figure. The torso, sleeves, and the skirt are shorter than their junior counterpart.

OUTERWEAR

This category includes all women's wear intended to be seen when worn—coats, suits, dresses, blouses, shorts, tops and sweaters, for example. The size ranges already discussed provide for considerable variety in sizing, but in addition there are specialized sizing arrangements that apply to specific categories of apparel. Fitting standards are frequently not consistent from one apparel category to another. There is, however, more similarity in sizing of outerwear in general than there is between outerwear and underwear.

Women's dresses are available in the size ranges previously discussed, but with considerable variation in sizing by different manufacturers. Pants and skirts are sometimes sold by waist measurement rather than by dress size. Even if hip dimensions are provided, most pants should be tried on by the consumer. Crotch depth and waistline can vary tremendously, even if the hip dimensions are adequate. Some pants manufacturers size pants by waist measurement, hip shape (slim, average, or full), and by leg length or height (short, regular, or tall).

Women's blouses and sweaters may be sold by bust measurement rather than by dress size. Lettered sizing is more common in sweaters. These sizes are typically, S, M, L, or XS, M, L, XL. The frequency with which the lettered sizing systems are found today relates to the number of imports. Sizing is often a problem with foreign manufactured garments. Consolidated sizing, such as that provided by the lettering system, is easier to follow.

Women's coats, jackets, suits, rainwear, and maternity wear are usually sold by dress size. Even though these garments are designed to be worn over other apparel (or a temporarily larger body in the case of maternity wear), the consumer should still purchase these garments in her regular dress size. They are cut with sufficient ease to fit over other apparel. Even though a great deal of expansion occurs during pregnancy, maternity wear is cut with sufficient ease to allow for the growth which will occur during this time.

SLEEPWEAR AND LINGERIE

Considerable diversity in sizing exists in the category of sleepwear and lingerie. Sleepwear is usually sized in less restricted ranges, since the cut is full enough in most styles to allow for more comfort, and a very precise fit is not desirable. In lingerie, however, more precision is necessary because of the close fit of items such as bras and slips.

Gowns, robes, and pajamas designed for women are usually sized by figure height and dress size. The lettered size symbols, S, M, L or XL, may also be used by some manufacturers. These symbols are based on bust size. Common height choices are *short, regular,* and *tall,* but some manufacturers extend their offerings to include extra tall and petite lengths. Bras are sized by chest measurements expressed in two-inch (5.08 cm) increments from 32 to 52, and by cup size ranging rom AAA through F. Most sizes have numerous styles with varying degrees of support from which to choose. Good fit and comfort in a bra is as dependent on style, support features, and fabrics as it is on size. All of these factors must interplay to obtain a good fit.

Support garments, such as girdles and corsets, are usually sized by waist measurement or S, M, L, XL, XXL, which are lettered symbols for specific waist dimensions. Many support garments are proportioned to fit the crotch comfortably on the short, average, and long figure.

Full-length slips are sized by bust measurement, and half-slips by waist measurement or S, M, L, XL, XXL, which correspond to waist measurements. Proportioned lengths are available in most brands. Many brands offer a full or regular hip choice for a smoother fit at the hips. The regular hip size should be chosen if the hips are up to ten inches (25.40 cm) larger than the waist, and the full hip chosen when the waist and hip difference exceeds eleven inches (27.94 cm). Hip measurements along with waist measurements may be specified on some brands, especially when the design of the slip fits the body closely.

Panties come in three basic lengths: *bikini, hip hugger,* and the *regular brief.* They are sized by numbers or letters which correspond to hip measurements. The cut, length, fabric, trim, and type of elastic affect comfort and fit and should be considered along with size.

Thermal and long underwear are produced in sleeveless and sleeved, short- and long-legged varieties, measured by bust size for the upper portion and by height and hip size for the lower portion of the garment. Either lettered or numbered sizes may be used, depending on the manufacturer.

Hosiery manufacturers must provide a number of sizes to accommodate a variety of leg shapes and lengths. Pantyhose and leotards are purchased according to height and weight, and some manufacturers provide specific leg types: *petite* (short lengths), *shapely* (average length and slender), *classic* (average length and full), *tall* (long and/or full), and *statuesque* (extra long, extra full). Manufacturers may also correlate height and weight to lettered sizes.

There are a great variety of sizing systems used by different manufacturers. This variety makes it very important to read package sizing carefully. Items labeled "One Size Fits All" cannot really be expected to provide an exact fit to persons on either end of the height/weight scale. Full-fashion stockings designed to be worn with girdles or garter belts are sized in the same manner as described for women's socks.

Casual or sport socks are knitted from thicker, heavier yarns than those used for dress hose. They are produced in a variety of styles and lengths (footlets, ankle, midcalf, and knee). They are purchased by numbered sizes that relate to shoe sizes. The introduction of stretch yarns has led to the more common practice of manufacturing only two sock sizes for women. These are intended to fit all size categories. One of these sizes, referred to as regular, fits traditional sizes 9 through 11, while the longer/fuller size is designed to fit traditional sizes 10 through 12.

MEN'S SIZES

The sizing of men's apparel is not as abstract as that of women's apparel. Instead, sizes are related more directly to actual body measurements, except for some sweaters, casual items, some sleepwear, and underwear, which may be sized with the symbols XS, S, M, L, XL, and XXL. In men's wear, the size is frequently taken as the body measurement that the garment is expected to fit. This practice is changing, however, since more style variation is occurring in men's clothing. For example, men's sport shirts are now frequently sized with the lettered symbols rather than by measurements.

OUTERWEAR

This category includes all men's wear intended to be seen when worn—coats, suits, jackets, slacks, shirts, and sweaters, for example. Comfort is important in this category, of course, but appearance assumes more importance than with underwear. For that reason, fitting elements that camouflage figure faults to enhance appearance plays a larger role in evaluating accuracy of fit.

The sizing system used for suits is proportioned by chest and waist sizes as they relate to body build. Classic body types include *average, stout, portly,* and *athletic.* In each of these body types there are height and width variations that determine the length of the jacket, sleeve, crotch and pants. The classic body types are coordinated with the various heights to produce sixteen different suit sizes. Even though this example shows a wide range of size possibilities, individual manufacturers lack uniformity in their sizing practices and have their own specific designations for body types. Some offer more sizes than those mentioned, and some offer less.

Men's jackets, coats, and rainwear are sized, like suits, by chest measurement, body type, and height. Lettered symbols that correlate to chest measurements may also be used, especially in casual jackets. The consumer should purchase a coat or a jacket in the same size as his suits. The ease allotment needed in these garments is designed into the coat to provide good coverage and a comfortable fit.

Men's sport and dress slacks are sized by waist measurement and by inseam. In some instances, varying crotch lengths are provided to give a smoother, more comfortable fit at the seat. The fuller crotch is designed for the huskier physique which needs a fuller seat and a larger upper leg. The regular fit is designed for the average physique which needs an average fit at the seat and upper leg. The tall fit is designed to be longer in the crotch, but average in size at the seat and upper leg. The big and the big-and-tall fit is designed for the very husky physique which needs a full seat and extra room at the upper leg and thigh. Sweat and jogging pants may be sized by height and by lettered symbols which correlate to waist measurements.

Jumpsuits are sized by chest and height. If they are to be worn over apparel other than underwear a size larger than normal worn should be selected, except in the case of insulated coveralls. These garments are designed to be worn over other apparel and should be selected by chest measurement and height.

Bib overalls are sized by waist and inseam as are pants. The upper torso lengths can be adjusted by the straps. These straps are not, however, designed to adjust leg length. Since these garments are designed for workers, adequate ease allotment is necessary.

Shirts are sized by neck measurements and sleeve lengths. Some manufacturers specify body build; in these cases, the body of the shirt is sized *slim, regular,* or *full* to fit the physique more accurately. Tall men cuts are available with longer tails and sleeves as are fuller cuts for the large man. Work shirts are sized like dress shirts, but are cut fuller with a longer tail and more ease allotment in the back shoulder area for more freedom of movement in physically active jobs.

Sport shirts, knit shirts, and sweaters of many varieties are sometimes proportioned to body length, but most often they are simply sized by the lettered symbol. Chest measurements may also be used by some manufacturers. With the wide variety of fabrics, knitting techniques, and size standards in use, it is wise to try on sweaters and knit shirts to check fit at the shoulders, sleeve length, neck circumference, and for overall comfort before the garment is purchased.

UNDERWEAR AND SLEEPWEAR

Considerable diversity in sizing exists in this category. Sleepwear is usually cut full enough to allow for comfort, and a very precise fit is not desirable. Loose fit is usually the rule in most undershorts and undershirts. There are some underwear styles that are cut to conform closely to the body, but these styles are produced in stretch fabrics which allow the combination of close fit and comfort. These close-fitting styles allow a smooth appearance to outer garments that are designed to hug the body closely.

Pajamas, robes, and long underwear (two-piece or union suits) are sized by height and lettered sizes, S, M, L, and XL. Some manufacturers use the letters A, B, C, D, and E to size pajamas. Outsizes, for physiques too large to wear traditional sizes, are also available from some manufacturers.

Lower torso undergarments, including undershorts and briefs, are usually sized by height (average or tall) and by waist measurement, but some manufacturers use lettered sizes that correlate to a range of waist measurements. Boxer, brief, and bikini styles have varying degrees of ease in each of the size ranges. Boxer styles have the most ease, and bikini styles have the least. Style is an important consideration in evaluating fit. The fit must be not only comfortable, but also appropriate for the outer apparel with which the undergarment is to be worn. A good fit provides a smooth look, free of bulges or lumps.

Upper torso undergarments, including T-shirts and undershirts, are sized by height (average and tall) and by chest circumference. Lettered sizes S, M, L, and XL are used in place of numbered chest dimensions by some manufacturers. These undergarments are expected to hug the body closely, yet not bind or restrict free movement. The soft single and rib knit fabrics from which these garments are constructed makes this type of fit possible.

Men's knitted socks range in size from 10 to 16 with size variations at one-half inch (1.27 cm) intervals. The stretch characteristic made possible by the yarn and the weave used in the production of socks today allows them to fit a range of sizes rather than individual foot sizes. The first of the two ranges is referred to as *regular* and fits sizes 10 to 13, while the second range, referred to as *extra large,* fits sizes 14 to 16.

The length of the upper portion of the sock, which fits the leg above the ankle, can be varied by the manufacturer. The more common lengths are: *executive length,* which fits over the calf; *mid-calf length,* which stops at mid-calf; *slack* or *crew length,* which ends about 4 to 6 inches above the ankle; and *anklet,* which stops at the ankle. Some manufacturers vary the length in each category mentioned to accommodate the extra length needed for tall men. Tube socks, knitted without a heel, fit any foot size, but they are bulkier at the top of the foot than are heeled socks. The fiber content, degree of absorbency, knit variety (terry, rib, etc.), length on the leg, amount of stretch, and finish all interact to affect fit and comfort.

INFANT'S AND CHILDREN'S SIZES

Proper size selection and subsequent fit for infants' and children's apparel is as much a problem as that of selecting appropriate sizes for adults. Even though the U.S. Department of Commerce has developed standard measurements for infants and children, the use of these standard body dimensions by apparel manufacturers is totally voluntary. It is extremely important, therefore, that infants' and children's apparel be purchased by height, weight, chest circumference, and waist circumference rather than by numbered or lettered sizes. Most manufacturers provide this data on packages, on sewn-in labels, or on charts available in children's departments. An accurate knowledge of the child's body dimensions is necessary to select the best size that will secure the most accurate fit of ready-to-wear apparel in this category.

OUTERWEAR

Children's sizes range from 0 to 36 months for infants, sizes 1 to 6X for toddlers and juveniles, and sizes 7 to 18 for girls and boys. In the infants' segment of the children's category, apparel is sized by age increments: 0 to 36 months as well as the NB, S, M, L, and XL size denotations. These increments relate to specific height and weight averages. Size selection must be based on height and weight rather than age due to the variations in growth patterns of infants who are the same age, but who are far from the same size. Dress, casual, play, underwear (except diapers), and even sleepwear are purchased using these sizing methods.

In the toddler and juvenile segment of the children's category, some items are sized S, M, and L as well as the traditional 1T to 4T, 1 to 6 and 6X. Some manufacturers offer slim and regular cuts in sizes 3T to 4T and sizes 1 to 6 as well as 6X. On most sizing charts, garments sized 1 and those sized 1T can vary from no significant difference up to two and one-half inches (6.35 cm), even though toddler sizes are supposedly cut larger to accommodate diapers. It is always advisable to base size selection on height, weight, and body build, since they can be compared to manufacturer sizing charts, rather than using a particular number or letter size.

In the girls' and boys' category, sizes for girls range from 7 to 18, which are correlated to height, chest, hips, and waist circumference as well as body build *(slim, regular,* and *pretty plus)* by some manufacturers. Boys' sizes range in numbered sizes from 7 to 24 and are correlated to height, weight, chest, waist, neck, sleeve length, and inseam. Some manufacturers provide as many as four body builds from which to choose: *slim, regular, husky,* and *husky-plus.* Special cuts designed to fit the slim and full builds for both girls and boys have filled a gap in children's sizing which has existed for many years. Names assigned to the various body types and body dimensions will vary to some degree among manufacturers, emphasizing the importance of referring to charts provided in children's departments which will help consumers select the best possible size. Some items may also be sized using letters, usually S, M, L, and XL. This type of sizing is common in sweaters, crew-neck shirts, and some jackets, usually in less expensive apparel lines.

Those styling features that provide a longer life and fit for apparel items purchased in these groups include ample ease provided by full cuts and stretch fabrics, undefined waist, raglan sleeves, deep hems, and jumper styles. Legged garments should have a crotch seam that allows ample width and length for comfort, especially in infant and toddler sizes where the depth must accommodate a diaper and still remain fastened during play. Decorative details and design features that include lace, sashes, elastic, collars, cuffs, dress or pants length or width, etc., should not irritate the skin, bind body parts, or interfere with free movement. Closings should produce a smooth, flat line that does not ripple, bulge, or pop open during wear. Chest and shoulder ease should be adequate for active play.

UNDERWEAR AND SLEEPWEAR

Children's sleepwear is often sized by letters that correspond to height and weight. Sleepwear should be cut full enough to allow for comfort, especially when woven fabrics are used. Closer cuts are appropriate when soft, stretchy knit fabrics are used. Even in knitted sleepwear, however, it is important to make sure that adequate length allowance is provided to prevent strain at the toes on sleepwear garments that enclose the feet. For the very young child, sleepwear must also have openings of sufficient length in order to allow easy diaper changing.

Underwear for children is sized by numbers or letters that correspond to body measurements. Panties for girls and undershorts for boys come in a variety of styles and fabrics. Knitted underwear will provide a closer fit than its woven fabric counterpart. Cut, fabric, length, trim, and elastic type will affect comfort and fit. They should be considered along with size when making choices.

Socks for infants, toddlers, and children are usually sized by shoe size or by lettered sizes that correlate directly to shoe size. The stretch characteristics of the knit and yarn make it possible for manufacturers to produce socks in ranges of sizes rather than individual sizes. With the rapid, overall growth of children, socks can be worn longer because of this stretch characteristic. Tube socks knitted without heels can also be worn longer, but they do not fit as smoothly across the top of the foot as heeled socks. Hosiery, tights, leotards, thermal underwear, and other body-wear are sized by letters and/or numbers that correlate to height and weight dimensions of the body for each of the children's groups.

ALTERATION POTENTIAL

After the garment is constructed, alteration potential is diminished considerably, especially when increased width or length is desired. More potential for adjustment is possible if a decrease in size or length is needed. This is true because most manufacturers minimize fabric costs by cutting narrow seams ranging from one-fourth inch to three-eighths inch (.64 to .95 cm) and by finishing them together with a one-fourth inch (.64 cm) serging stitch. Width adjustments, therefore, are impossible with seam allowances that are this small. Exceptions to this use of narrow seams are occasionally found in some of the more expensive women's apparel lines. There, one-half inch (1.27 cm) seams are more common. Also, in men's wear and some tailored women's wear, the centerback seam of better trousers usually carries a one-inch (2.54 cm) seam for adjustment purposes. Some children's lines will feature deep hems, tucks, or straps that make length and/or width adjustments possible.

Length adjustments can be made on apparel items that contain a tuck, a strap, or a seam that can be let out. Another alternative would be an insert of fabric or the addition of a lower edge trim. If these alternatives are not desired, extra length cannot be obtained.

Alterations to increase width at the hip, waist, bust, or shoulder present problems similar to those of length. Unless there are gathers, tucks, or seam allowances that can be let out to provide the extra width needed, the garment cannot be altered effectively.

Decreasing size is usually less of a problem. Length decreases can be made easily by trimming away excess length at the lower edge of a pair of trousers, a sleeve, or a skirt, for example, and replacing the hem evenly at the desired location. Doubling a hem is not desirable because of the weight and extra bulk it creates at the hemline. Trimming excess length from the lower edge can distort designs that are flared at their edges. An alternative adjustment in cases of this type is to remove excess length at the waistline instead of the hem, if this procedure is feasible.

STANDARDS FOR EVALUATING FIT

1. Styles have sufficient ease for comfort in moving and sitting.
2. Neckline, collar, sleeves, and pockets rest smoothly in their appointed position without gaping or binding.
3. Long-sleeved styles have sufficient ease at the elbow to allow the arm to bend comfortably; they extend to the wristbone when the arm is relaxed.
4. Closings lie flat and smooth, close evenly at their ends, have sufficient overlap, and close the closing neatly without pulling or gaping at the chest, bust, waist, and/or hip.
5. The garment is free of diagonal, vertical, or horizontal wrinkles that are not part of the design.
6. Vertical seams are perpendicular to the floor, and hems are parallel to the floor.
7. Free hanging or attached linings do not hang below the outer hem fold at the sleeve or lower edge.
8. Zip-out linings do not make the outer garment ripple, pull, or appear lumpy.
9. Bands and/or ribbing at the neck, waist, and lower edge of the sleeve hug the body without appearing stretched or loose and without binding.
10. Drawstrings, elastic, bands, and trims do not bind or irritate the skin.
11. Support garments give adequate, comfortable support during motion and are proportioned to the size of the wearer.
12. Underwear comfortably hugs the body at the waist, hips, and legs, complementing the outer garment by producing a smooth silhouette free of undesirable ridges or bulges.
13. Hosiery fits smoothly with sufficient ease and elasticity to stay in place without binding.

Waistlines that are banded, contain belt carriers, and have several rows of topstitching make waistline alterations very time-consuming. Simple elasticized bands or those attached with one or two rows of stitching are easier to adjust. Another instance in which length can be decreased at the waistline instead of the hemline is when the seat of a pair of pants sag due to flat hips, or when the crotch is too long and sags uncomfortably between the legs.

Decreasing the bust and hips on garments with an undefined waist can be successfully handled by increasing the side seams. Decreasing the waistline when a band or a waistline seam is present requires more time, but the alteration can be accomplished. Care must be taken not to distort the design line by removing too much width at any one point.

Removing excess width in the neckline and shoulder area is more difficult, but in many cases it can be done successfully. Decreasing size at these locations will require that comparable adjustments be made on facings, collars, sleeves, or any other garment part that is affected.

Although altering ready-to-wear is a common practice for those individuals who are unable to find a size that fits their body dimensions, the cost of the alteration in addition to the original cost of the garment must always be considered in order to be sure that the item is worth the price. Furthermore, difficult alterations should not be undertaken without the skill necessary to produce good results. The successfully altered garment is the one that fits the figure without diagonal, vertical, or horizontal wrinkles, and where the alterations do not "scream" their presence because poor alteration techniques were used.

SUMMARY

Some aspects of apparel fit have always been in a state of flux, being adapted to suit the dictates of fashion and society as well as physical changes in the human body which have occurred over time. Understanding the interrelationship, however, of the five factors of fit—grain, ease, line, set, and balance—provides a basis for recognizing good fit and analyzing fitting problems when they occur.

Because of the considerable lack of conformity in sizing standards among producers of men's, women's, and children's apparel, good fit cannot be guaranteed by selecting a particular numbered or lettered size. If the best possible fit is to be obtained, garments should be tried on before purchase, or they should be purchased after following the measurement charts provided by various manufacturers at the point of purchase.

The attainment of good fit by the alteration of a ready-to-wear garment is limited by seam width, hem depth, fashion fabric, and garment design as well as by the skill of the person performing the adjustment. Adjustments that require a decrease in width or length are usually less of a problem than those requiring an increase. In any case, the successfully altered garment is one free of undesirable wrinkles and any sign that would indicate the garment had been adjusted.

Although good fit in an item of apparel is considered by some as illusive, changing, and susceptible to personal opinion, garments that are fitted well have the following characteristics: they are comfortable to wear; allow sufficient ease for freedom of movement; are consistent with current fashion; and are free of undesirable wrinkles, sags, and bulges.

CONCLUSION: THE CONCEPT OF QUALITY

What is quality? How does technology and research affect this vague concept called quality? How should the information presented in this text be put together when evaluating an item of apparel? Although these are difficult questions to answer, they are very important to consider.

WHAT IS QUALITY?

A dictionary definition of quality is "degree of excellence; grade." In the production of apparel, each manufacturing firm must decide on the degree of excellence that will be the mark of its product. This sounds relatively easy, but in fact it is a difficult task. "Degree of excellence" can be defined accurately only in regard to each consumer's values, needs, and perceptions. There is no mechanical device in the clothing industry that can measure, in very precise terms, the quality of the industry's products. At what point on the list of quality standards offered in this text does the garment become a "quality" garment? There is no easy answer.

Each manufacturer and, in turn, each buyer and consumer defines quality within a particular cost framework. Each level of production and/or purchase should be the best possible product for the money paid, recognizing, for example, that the same degree of excellence should not be expected from a $19.99 shirt as from a $75 shirt. Still, the $19.99 shirt may be a good quality purchase. To the consumer who has high expectations of aesthetics and comfort in apparel, the hand and sheen of a long staple cotton fiber and the styling details on the more expensive shirt might represent minimum standards of quality, although the shirt has no greater durability than the less expensive selection. For a person in a lower economic bracket or whose values are oriented toward durability and practicality, the less expensive shirt might represent the higher quality. The key is the degree of match between consumer expectations and product characteristics.

One of the demands made of today's successful retail professionals is to identify the values of the market to which their firms are oriented and then to look for the product characteristics which will come closest to meeting those expectations. "Market niche" is as much related to varying concepts of quality as variation in fashion statements and economic strata.

Just as quality may differ from one consumer to another and among retail firms, it may change from one time period to another. Structures requiring elaborate boning and hand stitching were considered high quality in 1880. Today, such techniques are obsolete. With today's proliferation of consumer protection and testing agencies, there seems to be a greater consumer concern for quality than ever before, but there does not seem to have been a corresponding increase in consumers' ability to define and judge quality or more general agreement on what constitutes quality. While many people tend to link the term quality with the durability of a product, the majority of published standards of quality deal more with appearance and fit. Even an article in *Consumer Reports* on "The Good Gray Suit" was weighted heavily on factors affecting appearance and fit. Of the twenty-three points which the authors used to evaluate a suit, only four contained statements that could be construed to relate to durability.[1]

Expectations of quality and the ability to distinguish various quality characteristics also vary from one group of consumers to another. Generally, the more educated and sophisticated the consumer, the more

[1] "The Good Gray Suit," *Consumer Reports* (August, 1986), p. 502–10.

specific are the expectations of quality and the more precise the ability of the consumer to express those expectations.

Increased competition in the apparel industry has also affected the concern for product quality. The evidence dealing with the relationship of quality to costs, sales, competition, and profitability shows that "product quality is increasingly essential to success in an extremely competitive global market."[2] If this statement is true, then more and more emphasis must be afforded this sometimes illusive characteristic called "quality."

TECHNOLOGY/RESEARCH

Due to the nature of the product, the fashion industry has been rather slow in incorporating technology into its production process. The manufacture of clothing is perhaps one of the most difficult of all factory operations. The limp fabric parts which must be manipulated make automation difficult. The lack of compatibility with robotics and other such machinery is one of the major reasons that almost half of the $125 billion of garments purchased in this country are made largely by hand in countries where wages are low.[3]

Technology is expensive. Until very recently the majority of apparel manufacturers operated on a small scale, and few had the volume or financing to invest in specialized, high-technology equipment. It is only since 1960 that any appreciable amount of technological advances have been applied to apparel manufacturing. Even into the early 1980s, the technology was available, but used to a limited degree. It has been only in the middle and late 1980s that some major changes have occurred in the apparel industry, and this was born out of necessity. The fierce and increasing competition from foreign countries mandated that something be done; given the current wage advantage enjoyed by many of our foreign competitors, the advantages of technology seem to present the only alternative to the demise of the American sewn products industry.

More and more large companies are moving to computer-aided design systems and new automated sewing assembly lines. The conventional method for developing a new item of apparel required a designer to sketch styles, select fabric swatches and color samples, and then wait

[2] Y. K. Shelty, "Product Quality and Competitive Strategy." *Business Horizons* (May/June, 1987), Vol. 30, p. 52. Vol. 30.

[3] Ralph King, ed., "Made in the USA." *Forbes* (May 16, 1988), p. 108.

while a mill worked up some samples. The resulting samples might not be exactly what the designer had envisioned. It was a painstaking creative process that took weeks. With computer-aided techniques, a designer can electronically "sketch" design, color, and texture right on the computer screen. Millions of combinations can be produced from the computer's almost infinite bank of colors and designs. The designer can experiment with the styles on the monitor until the right mix is developed. Once accepted and approved for production, computers can turn the designs into patterns for all sizes and configure layouts on fabric for minimum waste. This data can then be sent to the factory floor where mechanical or laser cutters cut thick plies of fabric into parts for assembly. If the computerized marker also drives the laser cutter, then it can be economical to make small runs of garments for reorders, an advantage not afforded by more labor-intensive methods.

It is the actual assembly process of the garment that has too long defied automation. But technology is finally making a breakthrough even in that area. Some of this has come as a result of the Textile Clothing Technology Corporation which was established in 1981 to explore technological innovations for the apparel production process.[4] Their study resulted in an automated sewing line marketed by Singer Company at a cost of $100,000 to $400,000 each. This machine, which uses vacuum power to flatten the fabric and computer-guided robotic arms to pick it up, can cut the time in making a sleeve for a man's suit from two minutes to seventeen seconds.[5]

The state of the art sewing line is located in Allentown, Pennsylvania (owned by Greif Co.). The line, which is used to join suit coat backs, consists of a 30-foot-long machine and includes conveyors and hydraulic "arms" to move pieces of fabric through the assembly process. Cameras visually check the fabric's position before a machine stitches the individual pieces together. The machine automatically sews one suit back every fourteen seconds. This is three times faster than when done manually.[6] Much experimentation has been done and must continue to be done before complete automation will rule the production lines of apparel factories. But certainly great strides have been made in the past decade.

One of the biggest technological breakthroughs in the business aspect of the clothing industry has been electronic data interchange (EDI) and bar coding. Industry spokespersons have predicted that within the next

---

[4] Ralph King, ed., "Made in the USA." *Forbes* (May 16, 1988), p. 110.

[5] *Time Magazine* (September 15, 1986), special advertising insert.

[6] Ralph King, ed., "Made in the USA." *Forbes* (May 16, 1988), p. 110.

two years this aspect of technological adaptation known as "Quick Response" will no longer be an option but will be a part of regular operations for virtually every major retailer and supplier in the fashion industry. The year 1989 has been labeled as the year of Quick Response.[7] (See also Chapter 1.)

Many view this concept as the breakthrough to a more cost-effective and higher quality product which will offer United States producers a competitive edge over foreign producers. Certainly this technology, which greatly decreases the length of the production cycle, brings the consumer and supplier closer together. Studies have shown that the process from weaving the fabric to displaying the merchandise in the store can be cut from months to three weeks through Quick Response.[8]

Technology may well be the tool which can best keep the manufacturer in tune with exactly what the consumer wants and demands. John Naisbitt, author of *Megatrends,* predicted that our society would continue to move at a rapid pace from an industrial to an informational society and that factories would be operated with information rather than laborers.[9] His prediction has been slow in coming to the apparel industry, but indications are that they are viable. Now that the technology is finally falling into place, it only follows that the use of automation will continue to grow.

SUMMARY

Most of the factors which have been examined in trying to arrive at statements about apparel quality are rather precise, and they provide a mechanism for apparel quality evaluation as a rational process. Much of the difficulty in attempting to examine the apparel products in such isolation, however, is that fashion consumption is often an irrational process. Fashion behavior is extremely complex; values, beliefs, identity, are all caught up in and expressed by fashion behavior. A structural approach to apparel evaluation is important and can be very helpful to consumers, retailers, and manufacturers. That approach must be used in conjunction with a fuller understanding of the many reasons people buy, wear, and discard fashion apparel.

---

[7] *Connections: Textiles, Apparel, Merchandising.* Supplement to the March 1989 issues of *America's Textiles International, Apparel Industry Magazine,* and *Apparel Merchandising.* (Atlanta, Georgia: Billian Publishing Company, 1989).

[8] Jean Dimeo, "Computers Speed Retailer's Reaction Time," *Dallas Times Herald,* (Wednesday, March 15, 1989), C-1 and C-8.

[9] John Naisbitt, *Megatrends.* (New York: Warner Books, 1984), p. 446–7.

BIBLIOGRAPHY

APPAREL INDUSTRY

BOOKS

Arpan, Jeffrey S., et al. *The U.S. Apparel Industry: International Challenge, Domestic Response*. Atlanta: Georgia State University Press, 1982.

Fringe, Gini Stephens. *Fashion from Concept to Consumer*. Second Edition. Englewood Cliffs, New Jersey: Prentice-Hall, Inc., 1987.

Hudson, Peyton. *Guide to Apparel Manufacturing*. Greensboro, North Carolina: MEDIApparel, Inc., 1988.

Jarnow, Jeannette, et al. *Inside the Fashion Business*. New York: John Wiley & Sons, Inc., 1981.

Naisbitt, John. *Megatrends*. New York: Warner Books, Inc., 1984.

Packard, Sidney. *The Fashion Business*. New York: Holt, Rinehart and Winston, 1983.

Stamper, Anita, ed. *Mississippi Homespun: Nineteenth-Century Textiles and the Women Who Made Them*. Jackson, Mississippi: State Historical Museum, Mississippi Department of Archives and History, 1989.

Tate, Sharon Lee. *Inside Fashion Design,* Third Edition. New York: Harper and Row, Publishers, 1988.

DOCUMENTS

Apparel Manufacturing in the 90s. Atlanta: American Apparel Research Conference, 1982.

Connections: Textiles, Apparel, Merchandising. Supplement to the March 1989 issues of *America's Textiles International, Apparel Industry Magazine,* and *Apparel Merchandising.* Atlanta, Georgia: Billian Publishing Company, 1989.

Federal Standard 751A. Washington, DC: U.S. Government Printing Office, January 25, 1965.

Statistical Abstracts of U.S. Washington, DC: U.S. Department of Commerce, 1984.

PERIODICALS

Barrier, Michael. "Walton's Mountain," *Nation's Business Reprint,* April, 1988.

"The First Hundred Years: 1776–1876," *American Fabrics and Fashion,* Vol. 106 (Winter, 1976), p. 61–68.

Federal Register, Vol. 50, No. 74 (Wednesday, April 17, 1985), p. 15100–107.

Fusaro, Dino G. "Quality Is Not a Precise Art, But a Scientific Concept," *Apparel World,* Vol. IV (September, 1983), p. 50.

"The Good Gray Suit," *Consumer Reports* (August, 1986), p. 502–10.

Heisey, Francesann. "The Future of Apparel Production and Construction," *Journal of Home Economics,* LXXVI (Fall, 1984), p. 8–13.

Hinerfeld, Norman. "Demographics, Technology to Affect Apparel Marketing," *Apparel World,* Vol. III (December, 1982), p. 20–25.

King, Ralph. "Made in the USA.," *Forbes* (May 16, 1988), p. 108, 110, 112.

McLendon, D. Steven, and Walter T. Wilhelm. "High Tech: Where the Sewing Room is Headed," *Apparel World,* Vol. V (August, 1984), p. 51–57.

Shelty, Y.K. "Product Quality and Competitive Strategy," *Business Horizons,* Vol 30 (May/June, 1987), p. 52.

Swift, Robert E. "Sales Power of 'Made in USA.' " *The FIT Review,* Vol. 5, No. 2 (Spring, 1989), p. 14–17.

Textile Hi-Lights. (September, 1989), p. iii.

CONSTRUCTION

Gioello, Debbie Ann, and Beverly Berke. *Fashion Production Terms*. New York: Fairchild Publications, 1979.

Musheno, Elizabeth A., editor. *The Vogue Sewing Book*. New York: Vogue Patterns, 1975.

Reader's Digest Complete Guide to Sewing. Pleasantville, New York: Reader's Digest Association, Inc., 1976.

FIT AND ALTERATION

Brinkley, Jeanne, and Ann Aletti. *Altering Ready-to-Wear Fashions*. Peoria, Illinois: Charles A. Bennett Company, Inc., 1976.

Chambers, Helen G., and Verna Moulton. *Clothing Selection*. New York: J.B. Lippincott Company, 1969.

Erwin, Mabel, and Lila Kinchen. *Clothing for Moderns*. New York: The Macmillan Company, 1964.

Farmer, Bonnita, and Lois Gotwals. *Concepts of Fit*. New York: Macmillan Publishing Company, Inc., 1982.

Gioello, Debbie Ann, and Beverly Berke. *Figure Types and Size Ranges*. New York: Fairchild Publications, 1979.

Liechty, Elizabeth G., Pottberg, Della N., and Judith A. Rasband. *Fitting & Pattern Alteration: A Multi-Method Approach*. New York: Fairchild Publications, 1986.

Perry, Patricia, editor. *The Vogue Sewing Book of Fitting, Adjustments and Alterations*. New York: Butterick Fashion Marketing Company, 1972.

Tate, Mildred, and Oris Glisson. *Family Clothing*. New York: John Wiley and Sons, Inc., 1961.

Tolman, Ruth. *Guide to Fashion Merchandise*. New York: Milady Publishing Company, 1973.

Wingate, Isabel B., and others. *Know Your Merchandise*. New York: McGraw-Hill Book Company, 1964.

Wingate, Isabel B. *Textile Fabrics and Their Selection*. Seventh Edition. Englewood Cliffs, New Jersey: Prentice-Hall, Inc., 1976.

TEXTILES

Gioello, Debbie Ann. *Profiling Fabrics: Properties, Performance and Construction Techniques*. New York: Fairchild Publications, 1981.

Gioello, Debbie Ann. *Understanding Fabrics: From Fiber to Finished Cloth.* New York: Fairchild Publications, 1982.

Hollen, Norma, and others. *Textiles.* Sixth edition. New York: Macmillan Publishing Company, Inc., 1988.

Joseph, Marjory L. *Textile Science.* Third edition. New York: Holt, Rinehart and Winston, 1977.

Lyle, Dorothy Siegert. *Modern Textiles.* New York: John Wiley and Sons, Inc., 1976.

Pizzuto, Joseph J., and others. *Fabric Science.* Fifth edition. New York: Fairchild Publications, 1987.

Tortora, Phyllis G. *Understanding Textiles.* Third edition. New York: Macmillan Publishing Company, Inc., 1987.

Wingate, Isabel. *Fairchild's Dictionary of Textiles.* Sixth edition. New York: Fairchild Publications, 1979.

Wingate, Isabel. *Textile Fabrics and Their Selection.* Seventh edition. Englewood Cliffs, New Jersey: Prentice-Hall, Inc., 1976.

INDEX

A

Abutted seam, 57
Accordion pleat, 289-290
Acrylic/modacrylic, characteristics of, 24-25
Alteration, elements of, 297
Amalgamated Clothing Workers Union, 3
Apparel industry
  history of, 2-4
  imports, 9-12
  inside shops, 7-8
  manufacturing process, 4-6
  outside shops, 8
  technology/research, 314-316
Applied pockets, 112-116
  application methods, 115-116
  decoration, 114
  linings, 112-113
  pocket press, 113-114
Applique, as decorative element, 284-286

B

Balance of garment, fit and, 300
Banded closures, closure style, 214-216
Banded hems, 257-258
Beads and gem-like materials, as decorative element, 282-283
Belts, as decorative element, 281-282
Bias binding, neckline, 123-124
Bias direction, 39-40
Bias facing, neckline, 130-132
Bias seam, 64-65
Bindings
  necklines, 122-127
  sleeves, 170-171

Blind-stitched hems, 262-263
Body, of fabric, 33
Book finish, 78
Bound buttonhole, 230-231
Bound closures, closure style, 214
Bound hems, 256-257
Bound seam finish, 78-79
Bows, as decorative element, 284
Box pleat, 290
Braid, as decorative element, 280
Braided binding, neckline, 125-126
Buckles, 238
Bulky fabrics, 44
Buttonholes, 225-232
  bound buttonhole, 230-231
  fabric-finished buttonholes, 229-231
  keyhole buttonhole, 228
  loops, 231-232
  oval buttonhole, 228
  placement of, 226
  rectangular buttonhole, 227
  structural buttonhole, 229-230
  thread-finished buttonholes, 226-228
Buttons, 223-225
  eyed buttons, 225
  materials for, 223-224
  shank buttons, 224

C

Casings, waistlines, 190-193, 205-207
Clean-finished seam, 79-80
Closed application, inseam pockets, 105-108
Closure mechanisms
  buckles, 238
  buttonholes, 225-232
  buttons, 223-225
  D-rings, 238
  hook-and-eye, 236-237
  snaps, 233-235
  velcro, 237
  zippers, 238-244
Closure styles
  banded closures, 214-216
  banded plackets, 219-221
  bound closures, 214
  bound plackets, 219
  combination closures, 216
  combination plackets, 221-224
  faced closures, 212-214
  faced plackets, 217-219
Collars
  flat collars, 140-143
  importance of, 140
  rolled collars, 146-154
  standing collars, 143-146
Collection, 4
Combination closures, closure style, 216
Concealed applications, elastic in waistline, 188-189
Continuous-bound placket, 174-176
Contour waistbands, 194-195
Corded seam, 65-66
Corded tucks, 293
Costing of garment, 6-7
Cotton, characteristics of, 18-19
Count, fabric, 35
Crafted with Pride in the USA Council, Inc., 9
Crossed seam, 66
Crossed tucks, 293
Crosswise grainline, 38-39
Cuffs, 180
  closed band cuffs, 181
  open band cuffs, 180-181

D

Darts
  dart equivalents, 53-55
  double-pointed dart, 52
  French dart, 51-52
  single-pointed dart, 50-51
Decoration, applied pockets as, 114
Decorative trim
  applique, 284-286
  beads and gem-like materials, 282-283
  belts, 281-282
  bows, 284
  braid, 280
  embroidery, 286-288
  fasteners, 281
  lace and lace-like fabrics, 275-276
  pleats, 288-291
  ribbons, 276-280
  ruffles, 291-292
  tucks, 292-293
Deep folded hems, 251-253
Directional fabric, 42-43

Double-pointed dart, 52
Double-stitched seam finish, 80-81
D-rings, 238

E

Eased seam, 66-67
Ease of garment, fit and, 298
Elastic at edges, sleeves, 171-172
Elastic waistline treatments
  concealed applications, 188-189
  exposed applications, 189-190
  shirring, 203-204
  smocking, 203-204
Embroidery, as decorative element, 286-288
Enclosed seam, 58
Exposed applications, elastic in waistline, 189-190
Exposed seam, 58
Extended facing, neckline, 132-133
Eyed buttons, 225

F

Fabric
  acetate, 20-21
  acrylic/modacrylic, 24-25
  body, 33
  bulky fabrics, 44
  cotton, 18-19
  count, 35
  directional fabric, 42-43
  finishes, 37-38
  flaws, 36
  gauge, 35
  grainline, 38-41
  hair fibers, 15-17
  large designs, 44
  linen, 19-20
  nylon, 24
  olefin, 26-27
  opacity, 34-35
  polyester, 22-24
  ramie, 25-26
  rayon, 21-22
  silk, 17
  spandex, 25
  stability, 35-36
  triacetate, 21
  weight, 33
  wool fabrics, 15-17
  yarn structure, 27-28
Fabrication method
  knitted fabrics, 29
  knit variants, 29-30
  leather and suede, 31-32
  multicomponent fabrics, 32-33
  nonwoven fabrics, 31
  woven fabrics, 29
Fabric-finished buttonholes, 229-231
Faced hems, 254-256
Faced plackets, closure style, 217-219
Facings
  necklines, 127-134
  sleeves, 170-171
  waistlines, 193-194
False French seam, 59
Fasteners, as decorative element, 281
Federal Standard 751a, 56
Fiberweb interfacings, 90-91
Filament yarns, 27-28
Finishes
  fabric, 37-38
  hems, 258-260
Fit
  affecting factors, 297
  balance of garment and, 300
  ease of garment and, 298
  grain of fabric and, 297-298
  line of garment and, 298-299
  set of garment and, 299
Flat collars, 140-143
Flat-filled seam, 59-60
Flat seams, waistlines, 207-208
Flaws, fabric, 36
Flexible standing collars, 145-146
Flush application, elastic in waistline, 188
Free-hanging linings, 100-101
French dart, 51-52
French seam, 60
Full linings, 98-101
Fused hems, 265
Fused seam, 60-61
Fused seam finish, 77
Fusible interfacings, 93-94

G

Garment district, 3
Gauge, fabric, 35

Glued hems, 264-265
Glued seam, 61
Glued seam finish, 77
Grain of fabric, fit and, 297-298
Grainline, 38-41
  bias direction, 39
  crosswise grainline, 38
  lengthwise grainline, 38
  off-grain fabrics, 40-41
Gusset-style placket, 179

H

Hair fibers, characteristics of, 15-17
Hairline seam, 62
Hand application, interfacing, 94
Hand-stitched hems, 263-264
Hem finishes
  applied fabric finishes, 259-260
  folded hem finishes, 259
  raw edge treatment, 258
  thread treatments, 259
Hemmed sleeves, 169-170
Hems
  banded hems, 257-258
  blind-stitched hems, 262-263
  bound hems, 256-257
  bulk reduction for thick fabric, 266
  deep folded hems, 251-253
  faced hems, 254-256
  fused hems, 265
  at garment openings, 268-269
  glued hems, 264-265
  hand-stitched hems, 263-264
  lettuce edge hems, 248
  in linings, 269-270
  machine-stitched hems, 261-263
  narrow folded hems, 249-251
  rolled hems, 251
  shaped hems, 252
  shell hems, 251
  shirt-tail hems, 249-250
  stabilization of pleats, 266-267
  straight hems, 252
  supported hems, 270-271
  thread-finished hem edges, 246-248
  topstitched hems, 262
  unfinished hem edges, 246
  weighted hems, 271
High-cap set-in sleeve, 159-161
Hong Kong seam finish, 81
Hook-and-eye, 236-237
  application of, 236-237
Horizontal self-faced placket, 172

I

Imports
  indicators of country of origin, 9
  quality control and, 10-11
  Quick Response and, 11-12
Infants/children's sizes, 306-308
  outerwear, 306-307
  sleepwear, 307-308
  underwear, 307-308
In seam application, interfacing, 94
Inseam pockets, 104-110
  closed application, 105-108
  open application, 108-110
Inside shops, 8
Interfacing
  fiberweb interfacings, 90-91
  fusible interfacings, 93-94
  hand application, 94
  knitted interfacings, 92
  purpose of, 89
  in seam application, 94
  strip-sewn interfacings, 94
  weights, 89
  woven interfacings, 90
Interlining, purpose of, 96
Inverted pleat, 290

K

Kimono sleeves, 166-168
  fitted, 167
  loose, 167
Knife pleat, 289-290
Knits, seams in, 74
Knitted binding, neckline, 124
Knitted fabrics, fabrication method, 29
Knitted interfacings, 92
Knit variants, fabrication method, 29-30

L

Labeling, origin of garment, 9
Lace
  as decorative element, 275-276
  seams in, 74-75

Ladies Garment Workers Union, 3
Lapped seam, 67-68
Lapped seam with raw edges, 62
Large designs, 44
Leather
  fabrication method, 31-32
  seams in, 75
Lengthwise grainline, 38
Lettuce edge hems, 248
Line of garment, fit and, 298-299
Linen, characteristics of, 19-20
Lingerie, women's sizes, 302-303
Linings
  applied pockets, 112-113
  attachment methods, 101-102
  fabric for, 97-98
  free-hanging linings, 100-101
  full linings, 98-101
  hems, 258
  partial linings, 98
  purpose of, 97
Loops, for closure, 231-232
Low-cap set-in sleeve, 157-159

M

Machine-stitched hems, 261-263
Manufacturing process, 4-6
Men's sizes, 303-306
  classification of, 303
  outerwear, 303-305
  sleepwear, 305-306
  underwear, 305-306
Modacrylic, characteristics of, 24-25
Multicomponent fabrics, fabrication method, 32-33

N

Narrow folded hems, 249-251
Neckline
  bias binding, 123-124
  bias facing, 130-132
  braided binding, 125-126
  extended facing, 132-133
  knitted binding, 124
  rib-stretch bands, 137-139
  shaped facing, 128-130
  woven inset band, 135-137
Net-bound seam finish, 82
Nonwoven fabrics, fabrication method, 31
Notched collar, 150-152
Nylon, characteristics of, 24

O

Off-grain fabric, 40-41
Olefin, characteristics of, 26-27
Opacity, fabrics, 34-35
Open application, inseam pockets, 108-110
Open-dart placket, 177
Open-seam placket, 176-177
Outerwear
  infants/children's sizes, 306-307
  men's sizes, 303-305
  women's sizes, 301
Outside shops, 8
Overcast seam finish, 82-83
Overedged seam, 63
Overedge seam finish, 83

P

Partial linings, 98
Patch pockets. *See* Applied pockets
Pile fabrics, seams in, 75-76
Pinked seam finish, 77
Piped seam, 65-66
Plackets, 172-180
  closure styles, 212-216
  continuous-bound placket, 174-176
  gusset-style placket, 179
  horizontal self-faced placket, 172
  open-dart placket, 177
  open-seam placket, 176-177
  pleated placket, 177-178
  tailored shirt placket, 178-179
  vertical faced placket, 172-174
Plain seam, 68
Plain seam finish, 77-78
Pleated placket, 177-178
Pleats
  accordion pleat, 289-290
  box pleat, 290
  as decorative element, 288-291
  inverted pleat, 290
  knife pleat, 289-290
  stabilization of, 266-267

Pocket press, 113-114
Pockets
  applied pockets, 112-117
  inseam pockets, 104-110
  slashed pockets, 117-120
Polyester, characteristics of, 22-24
Pre-shrunk garments, 18
Princess seam, 68

Q

Quality, elements, 312-314
Quality control, imports and, 10-11
Quick Response, 11-12

R

Raglan sleeves, 163-166
  one-piece raglan sleeve, 163-164
  two-piece raglan sleeve, 165
Ramie, characteristics of, 25-26
Rayon, characteristics of, 21-22
Recessed application, elastic in waistline, 189
Ribbons, as decorative element, 276-280
Rib-stretch bands, neckline, 137-139
Rigid standing collars, 143-145
Rolled collars, 146-154
  notched collar, 150-152
  one-piece construction, 148-149
  shawl collar, 152-154
  three-piece construction, 150-154
  two-piece construction, 149-150
Rolled hems, 251
Ruffles, as decorative element, 291-292

S

Seam finishes
  book seam finish, 78
  bound seam finish, 78-79
  clean-finished seam, 79-80
  double-stitched seam finish, 80-81
  fused seam finish, 77
  glued seam finish, 77
  Hong Kong seam finish, 81
  net-bound seam finish, 82
  overcast seam finish, 82-83
  overedge seam finish, 83
  pinked seam finish, 77
  plain seam finish, 77-78
  self-bound seam finish, 83
  serged seam finish, 83-84
  stitched and pinked seam finish, 84
  zigzagged seam finish, 84-85
Seams
  abutted seam, 57
  bias seam, 64-65
  corded seam, 65-66
  crossed seam, 66
  eased seam, 66-67
  enclosed seam, 58
  exposed seam, 58
  false French seam, 59
  flat-felled seam, 59-60
  French seam, 60
  fused seam, 60-61
  glued seam, 61
  hairline seam, 62
  in knits, 74
  in lace, 74-75
  lapped seam, 67-68
  lapped seam with raw edges, 62
  in leather, 75
  overedged seam, 63
  in pile fabrics, 75-76
  piped seam, 65-66
  plain seam, 68
  princess seam, 68
  slot seam, 68-70
  square-set seam, 70
  stayed seam, 70
  strapped seam, 70-72
  taped seam, 72
  topstitched seam, 72
  tucked seam, 73
  unfinished seams, 63-74
  waistlines, 207-209
  welt seam, 73-74
Self-bound seam finish, 83
Serged seam finish, 83-84
Set of garment, fit and, 299
Set-in sleeves, 157-162
  high cap set-in sleeve, 159-161
  low-cap set-in sleeve, 157-159
  tailored set-in sleeve, 161
Shank buttons, 224
Shaped facing, neckline, 128-130
Shawl collar, 152-154
Shell hems, 251
Shell tucks, 293
Shirring, elastic in waistline, 203-204

Shirt-tail hems, 249-250
Silk, characteristics of, 17
Single-pointed dart, 50-51
Sizing
  alteration and, 308-309
  infant's/children's sizes, 306-308
  men's sizes, 303-306
  women's sizes, 300-303
Slashed pockets, 117-120
  application methods, 117-120
Sleepwear
  infants/children's sizes, 307-308
  men's sizes, 305-306
  women's sizes, 302-303
Sleeves
  bindings, 170-171
  cuffs, 180-185
  elastic at edges, 171-172
  facings, 170-171
  hemmed sleeves, 169-170
  kimono sleeves, 166-168
  plackets, 172-180
  raglan sleeves, 163-166
  set-in sleeves, 157-162
Slot seam, 68-70
Smocking, elastic in waistline, 203-204
Snaps, 233-235
  concealed, 233-234
  materials for, 235
  visible, 234-235
Spandex, characteristics of, 25
Spun yarns, 27-28
Square-set seam, 70
Stability, fabric, 35-36
Standards
  for buttons/buttonholes, 232
  for closure styles, 222
  for collars, 154
  for cuffs, 185
  for darts, 55
  for fit, 309
  for hems, 272
  for interfacings, 96
  for interlinings, 97
  for linings, 102
  for neckline bindings, 127
  for neckline facings, 135
  neckline inset bands, 137
  for pockets, 110, 116, 120
  for rib-stretch bands, 140
  for seam finishes, 85
  for seam types, 76
  for sleeves, 162, 166, 168, 180
  for snaps/hook closure, 238
  for trim, 280, 283, 288, 294
  for underlinings, 88
  for waistlines, 190, 192, 194, 201, 204, 207, 209
  for zippers, 244
Standing collars, 143-146
  flexible standing collars, 145-146
  rigid standing collars, 143-145
Stayed seam, 70
Stitched and pinked seam finish, 84
Stitches
  decision-making in use of, 47-50
  length of, 50
Straight hems, 252
Straight waistbands, 195-201
Strapped seam, 70-72
Strip-sewn interfacings, 94
Structural buttonhole, 229-230
Suede, fabrication method, 31-32
Supported hems, 270-271

T

Tailored set-in sleeve, 161
Tailored shirt placket, 178-179
Taped seam, 70
Technology/research, in apparel industry, 314-316
Textile Fiber Products Identification Act, 9
Thread, decision-making in use of, 46-47
Thread-finished buttonholes, 226-228
Thread-finished hem edges, 246-248
Topstitched hems, 262
Topstitched seam, 72
Triacetate, characteristics of, 21
Tucked seam, 73
Tucks
  corded tucks, 293
  crossed tucks, 293
  as decorative element, 290-293
  shell tucks, 293

U

Underlinings
  fabrics for, 88

Underlings (*continued*)
  procedure for underlining garment, 88
  purpose of, 87
Underwear
  infants/children's sizes, 307-308
  men's sizes, 305-306
Unfinished hem edges, 246
Unfinished seams, 63-74
Unions, origin of, 3

V

Velcro, 237
Vertical faced placket, 172-174

W

Waistline treatments
  applied elastic, 188-190
  contour waistbands, 194-195
  edge casings, 190-193
  elasticized waistlines, 202-204
  faced waistbands, 198-201
  facings, 193-194
  flat seams, 207-208
  folded waistbands, 196-198
  internal casings, 205-206
  seams with fullness, 208-209
  straight waistbands, 195-201
Weight, fabric, 33
Weighted hems, 271
Weights, interfacing, 89
Welt pockets. *See* Slashed pockets
Welt seam, 73-74
Women's sizes, 300-303
  classification of, 300-301
  lingerie, 302-303
  outerwear, 301
  sleepwear, 302-303
Wool fabrics, characteristics of, 15-17
Wool Products Labeling Act, 9
Woven fabrics, fabrication method, 29
Woven inset band, neckline, 135-137
Woven interfacings, 90

Y

Yarn
  filament yarns, 27-28
  spun yarns, 27-28

Z

Zigzagged seam finish, 84-85
Zippers, 238-244
  centered application, 241
  exposed application, 243-244
  invisible zipper, 242-243
  lapped application, 241-242
  opening variations, 239-240
  tape variations, 239
  teeth variations, 239